Cuba Was Different

Studies in Critical Social Sciences Book Series

Haymarket Books is proud to be working with Brill Academic Publishers (www.brill.nl) to republish the *Studies in Critical Social Sciences* book series in paperback editions. This peer-reviewed book series offers insights into our current reality by exploring the content and consequences of power relationships under capitalism, and by considering the spaces of opposition and resistance to these changes that have been defining our new age. Our full catalog of *SCSS* volumes can be viewed at https://www.haymarketbooks.org/series_collections/4-studies-in-critical-social-sciences.

Series Editor
David Fasenfest (Wayne State University)

Editorial Board
Eduardo Bonilla-Silva (Duke University)
Chris Chase-Dunn (University of California–Riverside)
William Carroll (University of Victoria)
Raewyn Connell (University of Sydney)
Kimberlé W. Crenshaw (University of California–LA and Columbia University)
Heidi Gottfried (Wayne State University)
Karin Gottschall (University of Bremen)
Alfredo Saad Filho (King's College London)
Chizuko Ueno (University of Tokyo)
Sylvia Walby (Lancaster University)
Raju Das (York University)

Cuba Was Different

Views of the Cuban Communist Party
on the Collapse of Soviet
and Eastern European Socialism

Even Sandvik Underlid

Haymarket Books
Chicago, IL

First published in 2021 by Brill Academic Publishers, The Netherlands
© 2021 Koninklijke Brill NV, Leiden, The Netherlands

Published in paperback in 2022 by
Haymarket Books
P.O. Box 180165
Chicago, IL 60618
773-583-7884
www.haymarketbooks.org

ISBN: 978-1-64259-619-9

Distributed to the trade in the US through Consortium Book Sales and Distribution (www.cbsd.com) and internationally through Ingram Publisher Services International (www.ingramcontent.com).

This book was published with the generous support of Lannan Foundation and Wallace Action Fund.

Special discounts are available for bulk purchases by organizations and institutions. Please call 773-583-7884 or email info@haymarketbooks.org for more information.

Cover design by Jamie Kerry and Ragina Johnson.

Printed in the United States.

10 9 8 7 6 5 4 3 2 1

Library of Congress Cataloging-in-Publication data is available.

Contents

Acknowledgments   VII
List of Figures   VIII
List of Abbreviations   IX

Introduction   1

PART 1
The Collapse According to Granma (1989–1992)

1   Written Sources on the Collapse   43

2   *Granma* and the Written News as a Method   58

3   Analyzing the News Accounts   67

4   Reflections on the Written News   168

PART 2
The Collapse as Viewed by Cuban Party Members

5   Contextualizing the Testimonies   175

6   Oral Source Methodologies   195

7   Analysis of the Interviews   205

8   Insights from the Oral Testimonies   320

Conclusion: Viewing the Collapse through PCC Lenses   325

Afterword   335

Appendix 1: Information for the Interviewees   336

Appendix 2: Interview Guide   338

Appendix 3: Core Sources 342

Appendix 4: Example Table for Data Visualization 349

Bibliography 353
Index 364

Acknowledgments

I am deeply grateful to all who contributed to this book.

First and foremost, I must mention my father Kjell Underlid (1950–2016)—with whom I discussed the original idea at length—you are greatly missed.

I am indebted to my Ph.D. tutor María Álvarez-Solar and co-tutor José Bell Lara, and my assistant on the project, Raynier Hernández Arencibia.

I am also highly grateful to the people at the Institute of Foreign Languages at the University of Bergen: Åse Johnsen, Synnøve Ones Rosales, Hans Jacob Ohldieck, Kari Soriano Salkjelsvik, Jon Askeland, Roxana Sobrino, Håkon Tveit, Andrea Rinaldi, and many others. Furthermore, I would like to thank the staff at FLACSO in Havana that offered great moral and practical support, especially my professors Delia Luisa López and María del Carmen Zabala.

I would like to acknowledge Ann Cathrin Corrales-Øverlid and Veronica Øverlid, both of whom offered first-class help with the translation. Series editor Ricardo Alan Dello Buono has guided me through the publication process in the best possible way.

Clearly, this book would not have been possible without the participation of my informants in Cuba, but also the staff workers of the archives, and so many other Cubans that I have met over the years, in Cienfuegos, Havana and other places. I am very much thankful to Tania (she will be forever missed), Euclides, Marta and Luis.

The warmest of thanks also to my relatives and friends in Norway, both in the beautiful city of Bergen and the beautiful island of Karmøy. Thanks to Tone, Heidi, Vigdis and family, and to Inger and Ragnar. To Marcos, Alex Z., Katrine, Anders, Fredrik, Jonas, Baste, Adilson, Marco Antonio, Margrethe, and all others for friendship, food, assistance and rewarding discussions. I know that I have been a most distracted and asocial person at times.

Finally, a most sincere expression of gratitude goes to my wife Karen who helped make this possible through her love and support. I dedicate this book to her, and to our young son Kjell Ragnar, whom I hope to introduce to Cuba sometime after the *annus horribilis* of 2020.

Figures

1 *Granma*, Sept. 25, 1990; the upper part of the international page, with its "Soviet Box" in the middle and "Direct Link" (*Hilo Directo*) on the left 66
2 *Granma*, August 25, 1989; "Tadeusz Mazowiecki, elected first minister of Poland" 74
3 *Granma*, November 10, 1989; the day after the Fall of the Berlin Wall, "The GDR announces the opening of its borders" 99
4 *Granma*, November 11, 1989; back cover, "Support for the SED [ruling party] at rally in the GDR where Egon Krenz gave a speech" 102
5 *Granma*, August 20, 1991; "Yanayev affirms that the most energetic measures will be taken to get the USSR out of the crisis" 151
6 *Granma*, August 22, 1991; "Gorbachev resumes presidential functions. Returned to Moscow from Crimea" 152
7 *Granma*, March 20, 1992; drawing published on the front page 164

Abbreviations

Note: When naming Cuban organizations, we have used their Spanish abbreviations, since this is common in the literature. With regard to entities from other countries, we have used abbreviations and names when such exist in common English language. When using the original language name, we have included either an explanation or a translated name to make things clear.

ADN	Allgemeiner Deutscher Nachrichtendienst (the state news agency in East Germany)
AFP	Agence France-Presse (an international news agency with HQ in France)
ANAP	Asociación Nacional de Agricultores Pequeños (National Association of Small Farmers)
ANSA	Agenzia Nazionale Stampa Associata (the leading Italian news agency)
AP	Associated Press
CEE	Centro de Estudios Europeos (Center for European Studies)
COMECON	Council for Mutual Economic Aid (also known as Comecon, CAME)
CDR	Comités de Defensa de la Revolución (Committees for the Defense of the Revolution)
CPSU	Communist Party of the Soviet Union
CTC	Central de Trabajadores de Cuba (Workers' Central Union of Cuba)
DEU	Directorio Estudiantil Universitario (University Student Directorate, existed between 1927 and 1933)
DOR	Departamento de Orientación Revolucionaria (Department of Revolutionary Orientation)
DRE	Directorio Revolucionario Estudiantil (Revolutionary Student Directorate, Catholic student group founded in 1954)
EFE	Agencia EFE (Spanish news agency)
FAR	Fuerzas Armadas Revolucionarias (Cuban Revolutionary Armed Forces)
FMC	Federación de Mujeres Cubanas (Federation of Cuban Women)
FRG	Federal Republic of Germany (West Germany, also known as BRD)
GDR	German Democratic Republic (East Germany)

HSWP	Hungarian Socialist Workers' Party
ICRT	Instituto Cubano de Radio y Televisión (Cuban Institute of Radio and Television)
IPS	Inter Press Service
OPP	Órganos de Poder Popular (Organs of People's Power)
ORI	Organizaciones Revolucionarias Integradas (Integrated Revolutionary Organizations, a predecessor to the current Party)
PL	Prensa Latina (Latin Press, Cuban news agency)
PCC	Partido Comunista de Cuba (the current Communist Party of Cuba)
PUWP	Polish Unified Workers' Party
PRC	Partido Revolucionario Cubano (Cuban Revolutionary Party, founded by José Martí in 1892)
PSP	Partido Socialista Popular (the first Communist Party of Cuba)
PURSC	Partido Unido de la Revolución Socialista de Cuba (United Party of the Cuban Socialist Revolution, predecessor to the PCC)
SDPE	Sistema de Dirección y Planificación de la Economía (System for Management and Planning of the Economy, Cuba)
SED	Socialist Unity Party of Germany
TASS	Telegraph Agency of the Soviet Union (Telegrafnoye agentstvo Sovetskogo Soyuza – Soviet news agency)
UJC	Unión de Jóvenes Comunistas (Young Communist League; the youth wing of the Communist Party of Cuba)
UNITA	National Union for the Total Independence of Angola (pro-US/ South Africa)
UPEC	Unión de Periodistas de Cuba (Union of Journalists of Cuba)
USSR	Union of Soviet Socialist Republics

Introduction

> No one ever imagined that something that
> seemed as unshakeable and certain
> as the sun would disappear in a few days,
> like the disappearance of the Soviet Union.
> FIDEL CASTRO, 1993

∴

The above words by the historic leader of the Cuban Revolution were uttered in the context of his speech on the celebration of the Cuban National Rebellion Day, July 26.[1] That was almost four years after the fall of the Berlin Wall and less than two years after the formal dissolution of the country that had been the center of the socialist community—the Union of Soviet Socialist Republics (USSR)—with which Cuba had enjoyed a close and privileged alliance for three decades. Castro spoke these words even though he had already warned, in his commemoration speech on July 26, 1989, that "If tomorrow or on any day we were to wake up with the news that a major civil strife has been created in the USSR, or, even, if we were to wake up to the news that the USSR had disintegrated—something we hope will never occur—even in those circumstances, Cuba and the Cuban Revolution would continue to fight and to resist!"[2]

The phenomenon often referred to as the End of Communism, or what might more precisely be referred to as the collapse of Soviet and Eastern European socialism (in this study I will often refer to these events as simply "the Collapse"), is globally remembered as one of the most important events in

---

[1] Fidel Castro, "Discurso pronunciado por el Comandante en Jefe Fidel Castro Ruz, Primer Secretario del Comité Central del Partido Comunista de Cuba y Presidente de los Consejos de Estado y de Ministros, en la clausura del acto central por el XL Aniversario del asalto a los cuarteles Moncada y 'Carlos Manuel de Céspedes,' efectuado en el teatro 'Heredia,' Santiago de Cuba, el 26 de julio de 1993, 'Año 35 de la Revolución,'" http://www.cuba.cu /gobierno/ discursos/1993/esp/f260793e.html.

[2] "Discurso pronunciado por Fidel Castro Ruz [...] En el acto conmemorativo por el XXXVI Aniversario del asalto al Cuartel Moncada, celebrado en la Plaza Mayor General 'Ignacio Agramonte,' Camagüey, el dia 26 de Julio de 1989, 'Año 31 de la Revolución,'" http://www.cuba.cu/ gobierno/discursos/1989/esp/f260789e.html.

contemporary history. For a brief period, between 1989 and 1991,[3] capitalism and liberal democracy were introduced in country after country in Eastern Europe, as well as in what had been the cradle of twentieth-century state socialism, the USSR itself. Characterizing the changes, political scientists have described the sweeping changes as a *double* or even *triple transition* that not only included the liberalization of the economy and the introduction of multiparty liberal democracy, but also, in Eastern Europe and the former Soviet republics, the transit toward national independence.[4] Francis Fukuyama famously referred to the changes as the "End of History,"[5] while historian Eric Hobsbawm considered them as the end point of what he called "the short twentieth century."[6]

At the time, many predicted that similar changes would also take place in Cuba, which had a system strongly inspired by the Soviet model. This is reflected in popular books with titles such as *La Hora Final de Castro*[7] and *Fin de siècle à La Havane*,[8] while similar predictions were also made in the academic world. However, there was no immediate transition, nor has this happened as I write these lines decades later. This is despite the fact that Cuba had been strongly economically dependent on the USSR and the countries of the Council of Mutual Economic Assistance (Comecon) and that the weakening and later disappearance of this trade provoked a severe crisis in Cuba,

---

3   Robert Bideleux and Ian Jeffries speak of "the Eastern European Revolutions from 1989 to 1991." See: *A History of Eastern Europe: Crisis and Change* (London: Routledge, 1998). Rachel Walker, in a book that deals with the USSR specifically, considers that in that country, there was a process of change that began in 1986 and ended in 1991; however, she also points out that after 1989, changes accelerated when a "revolution from below" started taking place in that country. For further information. See: *Six Years that Shook the World: Perestroika: The Impossible Project* (Manchester: University Press, 1993). Martin K. Dimitrov argues that what he calls the "collapse" of "communist regimes" takes place between 1989 and 1991. He considers that in Hungary and Poland that collapse began in 1988. See: *Why Communism Did Not Collapse: Understanding Authoritarian Regime Resilience in Asia and Europe* (Cambridge University Press, 2013), 14. For practical reasons, in our study we had our main focus on the 1989–1991 period. We would also argue that it is from 1989 that the most intense changes, the most emblematic events are seen, and it is from 1989 that the perception that a crisis of European state socialism is taking place and extends to a large part of the world. That said, events and processes that precede these years will also be touched upon, when relevant for analysis.

4   Claus Offe, "Capitalism by democratic design? Democratic theory facing the triple transition in East Central Europe," *Social Research 58*, No. 4 (1991).

5   Francis Fukuyama, "The End of History?," *The National Interest*, No. 16 (1989); *The End of History and the Last Man* (New York: Free Press, 1992).

6   Eric Hobsbawm, *Age of Extremes: The Short Twentieth Century 1914—1991* (London: Michael Joseph, 1994).

7   Andrés Oppenheimer, *La hora final de Castro* (Buenos Aires: Javier Vergara, 1992).

8   Jean-François Fogel and Bertrand Rosenthal, *End of siècle à La Havane: Les secrets du pouvoir cubain* (Editions du Seuil, 1993).

INTRODUCTION 3

christened by Fidel Castro in January 1990 as the Special Period in Time of Peace.[9] In total, foreign trade fell 75%,[10] and the real gross domestic product (GDP) fell by 35%.[11]

When the Cuban system did not collapse, a quite extensive academic debate about the "non-transition" was spawned in response.[12] In this book, I will address Cuban perceptions and views of the collapse of Soviet and East European socialism, in particular how this phenomenon was viewed by the Communist Party of Cuba (PCC). The book is based on my PhD thesis, which was written between 2013 and 2017, and which gathered and analyzed the memories and views of Cuban communists on the Collapse. My hope was that this data and its critical analysis could help us understand why there was a considerable degree of cohesion in the Communist Party of Cuba in regard to the defense of the Cuban system. This was all quite contrary to what happened in Eastern Europe and the USSR, where apparently similar parties suffered strong divisions, lost their leading role, and in some cases, completely disintegrated.

In conducting this research, I used both written and oral sources. In the case of written sources, I relied extensively on materials from the *Granma* newspaper from 1989 to late March 1992.[13] Copies of this newspaper are available at Biblioteca Nacional José Martí (José Martí National Library) and at the archives of *Granma*, both located at or close by Havana's Plaza de la Revolución (Revolution Square). To make it possible to identify and analyze these materials, it was necessary to photograph all editions of the newspaper that came out during those specific years. In charge of digitalization was our fellow researcher and assistant on the PhD project, Raynier Hernández Arencibia.

My oral sources consist of 17 interviews, all of which were with individuals who had been members of the Communist Party of Cuba (PCC)—these are

---

9   "Discurso pronunciado por Fidel Castro Ruz, presidente de la república de Cuba, en la clausura del XVI Congreso de la CTC, celebrado en el Teatro 'Carlos Marx,' el 28 de enero de 1990, 'Año 32 de la Revolución,'" http://www.cuba.cu/gobierno/discursos/1990/esp/f280190e.html.
10 Carmelo Mesa-Lago, *Cuba en la era de Raúl Castro. Reformas económico-sociales y sus efectos* (Madrid: Colibrí, 2012), 36.
11 Ibid., 38.
12 This debate was still going on at the end of the first decade of the 2000s, and to some extent still is. An example from the first decade of the new century is the essay collection, *Debating Cuban Exceptionalism*, Studies of the Americas (New York: Palgrave Macmillan, 2007).
13 We have also used as sources, although to a lesser degree, some of Fidel Castro's speeches. Moreover, we have sifted through issues of the Communist Party magazines *El Militante Comunista* and *Cuba Socialista* from the period, and we analyzed selected materials that were of special relevance to our study.

often referred to as *militantes* in Cuba—at the time of the Collapse. The interviews were conducted by myself in Havana in 2013 and later transcribed by Hernández Arencibia, resulting in almost 400 pages of text. For the analysis of these sources, I formulated the following central questions: A) What were and later remained the impressions of Cuban communists about the Collapse, as reflected in the *Granma* newspaper (1989–1992) and interviews with members of the PCC (2013)? B) How can these impressions help us understand the way the Party and its militancy responded to the extraordinary circumstances that arose in the late 1980s and the early 1990s?

In so doing, my study makes an original contribution to the existing historiography on contemporary Cuban politics and society.

As Historian Antoni Kapcia has pointed out, academic studies on Cuba done during the 1990s often tended to focus on the material and spiritual problems of the country.[14] The interest in Cubans' views and interpretations of the dramatic international events that affected Cuba so strongly—yet did not produce the regime change expected by many—has been remarkably less. Therefore, there was considerable room left for additional study on Cuban perceptions of the Collapse.

It is also important to note that the Communist Party of Cuba is little studied in general. This may seem surprising since it is the only party in Cuba. It is described by the Cuban Constitution of 1976 as the "organized Marxist–Leninist vanguard of the working class, the superior force of society and the State," which should guide society toward socialism and later communism (§ 5).[15] It is also remarkable that, at the time when Cuba felt the shock of the Collapse, the Cuban party did not severely fracture nor did it lose its monopoly on power, a situation that contrasts sharply with that of similar institutions in Eastern

---

14 Antoni Kapcia, "Does Cuba Fit Yet or Is It Still 'Exceptional?,'" *Journal of Latin American Studies* 40, No. 4 (2008): 640.

15 There have been notable changes to the Constitution's paragraph number 5 since 1976, reflecting a turn toward more nationalist positions. In 1992, the Party was described as "(...) *martiano* (following the ideas of Cuba's national hero José Martí) and Marxist–Leninist, organized vanguard of the Cuban nation." In other words, the mention of the "working class" was actually substituted by "the Cuban nation," and a reference to the ideas of José Martí was added alongside Marxism–Leninism. In the new Constitution of 2019, the Party is described as "the only (permitted) one, *martiano, fidelista*, Marxist and Leninist, organized vanguard of the Cuban nation, supported by its democratic character and the permanent link with the people." The ideas of Fidel Castro are thus explicitly mentioned, and the reference to "Marxism–Leninism" has been replaced by "Marxist" and "Leninist," as a way of distancing citizens from "Marxism–Leninism," which was a dogmatic approach to the ideas of Marx and Lenin that were often associated with the USSR The party's organic relation with the masses was also underlined.

Europe and the USSR.[16] While the particularities in Cuba that favored the continuity of its Communist Party and its political order might largely be external to the Party itself, there is clearly a dialectical relation between the Party and many of its surrounding circumstances. Consequently, I believe more knowledge on how the Collapse was seen and responded to by its members, as well as some characteristics of the Party and its collective response to the Collapse, might help us toward a better understanding of both the PCC's "survival" and Cuba's status today.

Many reasons have been cited for the "Cuban non-transition," some of which I will touch upon later in this study. Still, in regard to the "internal factors," Cuba's charismatic leader during half a century, Fidel Castro, had often been seen as a major guarantor of stability and continuity. Kapcia considers that the "Fidel factor" was widely highlighted in academic work especially in the early years of the Revolution and then again in the 1990s.[17] Yet he warns against a one-sided emphasis on the leader: "[W]hile it is always erroneous to ignore 'the Fidel factor,' the greater the focus on Fidel, the less analytical and perceptive the study."[18] Kapcia views the Party as "one critical element of continuity," yet suggests it "has never really been given the attention which it merits."[19] If the Revolution survives Fidel Castro, Kapcia claims in the same article, which was written in 2008, this will be tied to the "underlying system,'" which is again tied to a "five-decade long political culture."[20]

More than a decade has passed since Fidel Castro withdrew from his role as Cuba's head of state (in 2006, temporarily for health reasons; and in 2008 in a permanent manner). In 2011, he left the role of the leader of the Communist Party of Cuba, and in 2016, he passed away. It remains to be seen which path

---

16 Valerie Bunce links the collapse of a regime to the disorganization of political power and the "multiplication of sovereignty," drawing on a concept that Charles Tilly uses in his book on European revolutions. It is theorized that in the context of European state socialism, this occurs when the Communist Party loses political hegemony. See: Valerie Bunce, *Subversive Institutions: The Design and the Destruction of Socialism and the State*, Cambridge studies in comparative politics (Cambridge: Cambridge University Press, 1999), 11. Bunce argues that the hegemony of the Communist Party was *the* defining characteristic of European state socialism and, "as a result, *the* necessary condition for its existence" (ibid.). Although this statement might be of a polemic nature, there is no doubt that the functioning of the system depended heavily on the monopoly of power of the Communist Party. Bunce highlights growing divisions within the ruling party as *one* of the main factors in understanding the collapse of European socialist regimes (ibid.).
17 Kapcia, 644.
18 Ibid.
19 Ibid., 647.
20 Ibid.

the country will take over the long run, but as I write these words, the Cuban system is still in place, and this of course seems to confirm the validity of Kapcia's argument.

An additional particularity of this study is that it is based in part on oral history, and few oral history studies have been conducted in Cuba.[21] To our knowledge, no such study has been done centered primarily on the Party, and no oral history study has as its central theme the Collapse of Soviet and East European socialism. This in itself amounts to a necessity so as to complement the written sources on the subject. Indeed, Cuban documents published during this period are relatively scarce considering the magnitude of the events and their importance for Cuba. During the so-called Special Period, there was strict rationing of paper within the country, and publishing activity was very much limited. Furthermore, there has always been strict control over the media in Revolutionary Cuba, and this was strengthened beginning in 1991 when the Cuban monopoly press left behind a period of relative openness and began developing a sort of "war-time journalism" (further discussed in Chapter 1). This of course further underlines the importance of interviewing individuals who were politically active at the time. But even before this period, *Granma* tended to reflect the views and perceptions of some groups within the Party (notably, its leadership, and perhaps the journalists amongst its members) and not necessarily those of all its members.

Finally, it is worth keeping in mind that not only in this specific situation, but in all sorts of situations, what people express orally often differs from what they express in writing. I will elaborate more on this at the beginning of Part 2 of this book.

A central objective of this work is not only to demonstrate how the Collapse was seen from the viewpoint of the PCC but also to help explain how the Cuban Communist Party and its militancy responded to the events and changes.[22]

The manner in which the Collapse was seen by the PCC and its members is especially important due to the central role of this institution in society.

---

21   Perhaps the absence of such research should not surprise us much, as according to Paul Thompson, founder of the Oral History Society, "In the Communist world in general there was very little tape-recorded oral history," although it mentions as one of three exceptions the literature of testimonies in Cuba, together with oral history work in Hungary and popular autobiographical competitions in Poland. Paul Thompson, *Voice of the Past: Oral History*, 3rd ed. (Oxford; New York: Oxford University Press, 2000), 67.

22   The intention of the study is *not* to give a comprehensive answer to the question "Why did the Cuban system 'survive?'"; this would require a wider analysis. Rather, we have chosen to focus on the role of the Party.

A common perception is that Cubans have grown up in an information bubble and therefore have acted on the basis of erroneous information. This is a perception that will be touched upon and will be partly refuted in this study. In any event, one's understanding of a situation conditions how one reacts, as the *Thomas theorem* suggests: "If men define situations as real, they are real in their consequences." On the basis of this, I would like to propose a hypothesis: "The party members in Cuba had worldviews that favored the continuity of the country's hegemonic political project."

I will begin with a brief presentation of the historical context in which Cuba was affected by the Soviet collapse, where I will briefly reprise some key events and changes in Eastern Europe and the USSR at the time. After this contextualization, a short review of the existing literature will be given, along with explanations of important terminology used in the study.

1 Historical and Institutional Context

The close Cuban–Soviet relationship arose after Fidel Castro and his guerrilla forces seized power on January 1, 1959.[23] These links were consolidated, though not without setbacks, in the context of a hard confrontation between Cuba and the US. Though US policies are not the only elements to keep in mind for understanding Cuba's alignment with the Soviets, they were important. The literature refers to a triangular relationship between Cuba, the USA, and the USSR,[24] which lasted for more than 30 years.

The insurrection against Fulgencio Batista's regime—one propped up by US support—was led by Cubans, and Fidel Castro's guerilla forces had a nationalist and democratic program, largely in consonance with popular national demands and a political tradition with roots in the late nineteenth-century's Wars of Independence against Spain, where a nationalism had developed that not only strived for formal independence but a profound decolonization of society and social justice. According to Kapcia, it had "a much greater social dimension than any contemporary nationalism in Latin America."[25] Poet and

---

[23] There had also been contact between Cuba and the USSR before Fidel Castro seized power in 1959, but it was "(...) very limited due to the hegemonic power of the United States in the region." See: Mervyn J. Bain, *Soviet-Cuban relations 1985 to 1991: Changing Perceptions in Moscow and Havana* (Lanham: Lexington Books, 2007), 21.

[24] Cole Blasier, "The End of the Soviet-Cuban Partnership," in *Cuba After the Cold War*, ed. Carmelo Mesa-Lago (Pittsburgh: University of Pittsburgh Press, 1993), 90.

[25] Antoni Kapcia, *Cuba in Revolution: A History since the Fifties* (London: Reaktion Books, 2010), 13.

philosopher José Martí was an organizer of this independence movement, yet died at the start of the Second War of Independence (1895–1898), a war that ended in national humiliation as Cuba became occupied and then was turned into a protectorate of the US. Yet Martí became a national symbol, and many political movements were to promise to fulfil his ideals, amongst them Fidel Castro's.[26]

Yet after taking political power in 1959, the Revolution underwent a process of radicalization, geopolitical reorientation, and major ideological changes. In 1961, Fidel Castro declared the Revolution as socialist and Marxist–Leninist. Although the ties with the USSR were consolidated, and Cuba became increasingly dependent on economic terms, there were also notable contradictions between the two countries throughout the 1960s. Important moments of tensions arose during the Missile Crisis (1962), when the Soviets opted for direct negotiations with the US without involving Cuba in the process and later with regard to Cuba's active support of guerilla movements in Latin America. There were also considerable differences on issues regarding the development and character of socialism, internally in Cuba and between the two countries. Cuba undertook some largely endogenous experiments with socialism, eventually opting for a radical model in contrast to the "orthodox" model of the Soviet Union. According to Jorge Domínguez, between 1962 and 1968, "the relations between Cuba and the Soviet Union oscillated between collaboration and confrontation,"[27] while Mervyn Bain describes the entire period between 1962 and 1972 as a "very traumatic" one in the countries' relationships.[28]

In the late 1960s, tensions were reduced, and in 1972 Cuba entered COMECON, an economic mechanism of collaboration led by the USSR. During the 1970s, one could speak not only of a growing integration but also of a partial "Sovietization" of Cuba.[29] Open tensions on foreign policy were largely avoided, and Cuba embarked on a *process of institutionalization* that introduced an

---

26 Fidel Castro would eventually, as we know, be very successful in inscribing himself into a narrative of "a hundred years of struggle," promising to fulfil the promises of the independence movements of the nineteenth Century. Yet Martí was already a national hero and source of inspiration, and by the 1950s he was "an inexhaustible supply of truths, for all occasions, on all subjects" for Cubans, according to Louis Pérez Jr., *Structure of Cuban History: Meanings and Purpose of the Past* (Chapel Hill: University of North Carolina Press, 2013), 189.

27 Jorge I. Domínguez, *La política exterior de Cuba (1962–2009)* (Madrid: Editorial Colibrí, 2009), 244.

28 Bain, 27.

29 Mervyn Bain in a heading puts "Sovietization" between quotations marks, denoting perhaps that the term should not be taken too literally, that Cuba's process was ambiguous. Ibid.

economic model and a political system that were similar to the Soviet model—though the new model was not in all aspects identical to the Soviet one.[30] Cuban ideology was overshadowed to a large degree by Soviet-style Marxism–Leninism, and even Cuban history was largely adapted to fit into a Marxist–Leninist framework.[31]

By the mid-1980s,[32] Cuban–Soviet relations were "very healthy" and of an "extremely expansive" and "all-encompassing nature," according to Bain.[33] There was a "huge level of Soviet aid" to Cuba[34] during the years that the relationship existed. From the 1980s, certain differences began to emerge, but Cuba retained a privileged relationship with the USSR until the latter's August 1991 coup—though trade had been falling throughout that year—and relations were still intact in December 1991, when the USSR was dissolved. Still, the Revolution was always nationalist, and although Soviet ideology was broadly introduced by the State from the 1970s, nationalist currents never disappeared. Cubans were already "previously formed within a historically determined value system of sovereign nationhood."[35] Moreover, as Bert Hoffmann has asserted, Cuba maintained a double identity during the three decades that Cuban–Soviet relations existed: It identified not only with the USSR but with both the Second (socialist) and the Third Worlds.[36]

The Collapse of the Soviet Union is a complicated topic, and one that is a matter of controversy amongst researchers and others. It is uncontroversial to say, however, that the roots of some problems that contributed to this process go far back in time. This being said, the process of disintegration of the political order that had first been implemented after the 1917 Revolution in Russia is often identified with the changes in policies during the leadership of Mikhail Gorbachev, who rose to General Secretary of the Communist Party of the Soviet Union (CPSU) on March 11, 1985, and a month later launched the process of *Perestroika* (restructuring). This process marks the beginning of a new stage

---

30 The radical tendency in the late 1960s, represented by Fidel Castro at the time, had often clashed with the advice of Soviet advisers and Cuban technocrats in the government. By this point, the Soviet Union had already implemented modest market reforms. Later, in 1970, as part of Cuba's institutionalization process, there were new economic policies, "emphasizing more extensive use of material incentives, wage differentials, and piece rates to stimulate productivity," according to Jonathan Rosenberg, "Cuba's Free-Market Experiment: Los Mercados Libres Campesinos, 1980–1986," *Latin American Research Review* 27, No. 3 (1992): 51.
31 Pérez Jr., 258.
32 Bain, 31.
33 Ibid.
34 Ibid., 33.
35 Pérez Jr., 263.
36 Bert Hoffmann, "Transformation and continuity in Cuba," *Review of Radical Political Economics* 33, No. 1 (2001): 2.

in the Soviet and East European socialist community, where old problems came to the surface and new tensions arose. One could say that this moment marked the beginning of the more or less immediate historical context of the Collapse. According to Rachel Walker, the Soviet reforms had four phases:

1) The first, from 1985 to the end of 1986, was not characterized by reform but the "rationalization of the 'administrative command system.'"[37] Economic reforms and reforms for more transparency (*Glasnost*) were so far very limited.

2) In 1987–89 there was a "revolution from above" in the USSR, which implied a democratization of the political system (limits on the executive power, the allowance of greater public participation, a democratization of the ruling party, etc.) that was implemented in parallel with economic reforms (transfer of some control over the economy of the CPSU to other entities, decentralization of decision-making) and a deepening of the Glasnost policy (however, despite the promise of increased transparency, the authorities still intended that the debate should stay within certain limits defined by the Party). Conflicts became more pronounced in 1987, and tensions within the Party became visible in June 1988 (between the so-called conservatives who opposed reforms, followers of Gorbachev, as well as more radical reformists).[38] In 1988, pro-independence movements also emerged in the Baltic republics, new political parties appeared (to establish a political party remained illegal at this point), and conflicts arose between Azerbaijan and Armenia.[39] The economic situation worsened.[40]

3) From 1989 to February 1990, "a revolution from below" began, and the CPSU started to lose control over the reform process.[41] In March 1989, national elections to the new Congress of People's Deputies took place, which were not totally competitive but gave rise to a belief among people that it was possible to keep many Party candidates out of power.[42] The debates in parliament in May and June 1989 were characterized by conflict. These marginalized the Party, and they were broadcast on television.[43] At this point, a transfer of power to the republics took place,

---

37 Walker, 77.
38 Ibid., 78–85.
39 Ibid., 84–85.
40 Ibid.
41 Ibid., 85.
42 Ibid., 85–86.
43 Ibid., 86.

especially in the Baltic countries. Also, according to Walker, there was an "effective abolition of democratic centralism" at this point—referring to a principle according to which discussions are done internally, and decisions are binding on all Party members—and different platforms emerged within the Communist Party.[44] As the political system began to disintegrate, the economic system also began falling apart.[45]

4) In Walker's view, the period between March 1990 to August 1991 was characterized by "crisis management," with "hasty policy reversals and several radical shifts in political direction."[46] Gorbachev established a new executive presidency with "extraordinary powers" to prevent the collapse of the country,[47] while remaining as general secretary of the CPSU. However, the authority of this new presidency was undermined by various factors (lack of a new constitution; strong conflicts with the republics that were gaining autonomy, independence, or sovereignty). Gorbachev did not stand for elections, and his retention of the post of secretary general of the Party was very much questioned. He tried to maneuver between conservative forces and radical reformists but failed at this, and there was a high level of polarization.[48] The central power continued to crumble.[49]

By mid-1991, the institutions "no longer had any power or authority."[50] Since the end of the Second World War, Eastern Europe had been an area of influence of the USSR, governed by a series of "formally independent People's Democracies,"[51] where, however, there had been an "indirect imposition" of political and economic models[52] from the Soviet Union. Since the early years of these popular republics, there was a growing resentment over Soviet tutelage.[53] It would have been impractical to analyze the processes of change of each particular country in Eastern Europe here, so instead, a general overview will be given.

In the interviews with members of the Communist Party of Cuba, most of my initial questions also regarded the USSR, since this was Cuba's main ally, and furthermore, the hegemonic force of Comecon and the Warsaw Pact.

---

44   Ibid., 87–88.
45   Ibid., 89.
46   Ibid.
47   Ibid., 89–90.
48   Ibid., 92–93.
49   Ibid., 94.
50   Ibid., 95.
51   Bideleux and Jeffries, 523.
52   Ibid.
53   Ibid.

I look into the views and perceptions regarding certain key events and processes of change in Eastern Europe, especially in Part 1 of this book, as reflected by the newspaper *Granma's* coverage. To facilitate reading for people not closely familiar with these events, relevant historical contexts will be integrated into the analysis itself.

It should be mentioned that particularly important changes took place in the relationship between Eastern European socialist countries and the USSR from 1985, when the Soviet authorities decided that Eastern European countries were allowed to establish trade agreements with the European Community (now EU). In July 1989, Gorbachev declared what was later dubbed the Sinatra Doctrine, which constituted a break with the former *Brezhnev Doctrine* and guaranteed those countries the right to self-determination.[54] But even before this, Eastern Europe was affected—in different ways and to varying degrees—by the reform process in the USSR, and changes in Eastern Europe in return had a strong effect on the Soviet Union. Mark Kramer describes a process where there was a unidirectional influence from the USSR from 1986 to 1988 that was promoting reforms in Eastern Europe.

From the first half of 1989, however, the reforms of Hungary and Poland began to resonate in the USSR and later changes in Hungary, Poland, and the USSR influenced events in four other countries in Eastern Europe (East Germany, Bulgaria, Czechoslovakia, and Romania). Thus, one could speak about a multidirectional influence.[55] As revolts spread in Eastern Europe, pressure on the USSR grew and "[t]he ensuing recriminations in Moscow [...] helped to fuel a hardline domestic backlash in late 1990 and 1991, culminating in the failed coup in Moscow in August 1991."[56]

According to Bideleux and Jeffries, all Eastern European regimes collapsed during 1989, except Yugoslavia (1990) and Albania (1991),[57] countries that were not part of the Soviet-led Comecon alliance. For Martin K. Dimitrov, the process of regime change did not conclude until 1990 or 1991, except in the cases of Poland and Hungary, where regime change ended in 1989.[58] It should not be forgotten, though, that even if the former regimes ceased to exist, transitions in a broader sense might take a long time (referring to aspects of the economy,

---

54   Ibid., 581.
55   Mark Kramer, "The Dynamics of Diffusion in the Soviet Bloc," in *Why Communism Did Not Collapse: Understanding Authoritarian Regime Resilience in Asia and Europe*, ed. Martin K. Dimitrov (New York: Cambridge University Press, 2013), 151.
56   Ibid.
57   Bideleux and Jeffries, 582.
58   Dimitrov, 14.

law, culture, etc.). But in a short period, not only did the former socialist countries change profoundly, so did the world. The collapse of Soviet and East European socialism meant the end of the bipolar order between East and West,[59] as well as the end of Soviet dominance over Eastern Europe.[60]

From an early moment, Fidel Castro had concerns that Gorbachev's Perestroika "could get out of control and wreck the very system that it was intended to improve."[61] In the mid-1980s, Cuba proposed introducing changes into its own model—through what was called the *Process of Rectification of Errors and Negative Tendencies* (from now on this will be referred to as "Rectification" or "Rectification process"). José Bell Lara summarizes Rectification as a "practical critique" of the model of *real socialism*,[62] that is, Soviet and East European socialism, which had also been a central paradigm for Cuba, especially during the 1970s and early 1980s. Rectification contains contradictions and its implementation perhaps even more so, but with regard to the economy, it could be said to move in the opposite direction of Gorbachev's reforms. Rather than opening up spaces to market logic, it restricted or closed existing ones. Rectification was presented as a criticism of the model existing in Cuba, one that had many similarities to the pre-Gorbachev model in the USSR. However, it was often seen as a response to, and an alternative to, Perestroika.

Rectification was first announced in the context of the Third Congress of the Communist Party of Cuba, which took place in 1986 and was divided into two separate sessions. During the first part, which took place between February 3 and 6, there was a large renovation in the Central Committee that resulted in about 40% of its members being replaced.[63] However, no significant political changes were announced. According to Lutjens, the first indication of the beginning of the Rectification process was the creation of a committee with the task of doing an "emergency revision" of the national plan for 1985.[64] Pérez-Stable considers that Rectification was introduced between the first session of the Third Congress of the PCC, in February, and the second, in

---

59 Bideleux and Jeffries, 599.
60 Ibid., 607.
61 Although Castro's assessment of Perestroika was in general negative, some specific measures appealed to him, such as a campaign against alcoholism and actions against incomes that did not come from work. This is according to Yuri Pavlov, Soviet–Cuban Alliance 1959–1991 (Miami: North-South Center Press, 1996), 111–114.
62 José Bell Lara, *Globalization and the Cuban Revolution* (Havana: Editorial José Martí, 2002), 44.
63 Janette Habel, *Cuba: The Revolution in Peril* (London: Verso, 1991), 69.
64 Sheryl L. Lutjens, "Democracy and socialist Cuba," in *Cuba in Transition*, eds. Sandor Halebsky et al. (Boulder, Colorado, USA: Westview Press, 1992), 61.

December 1986,[65] although scholars disagree on the exact date. For Mesa-Lago, it was already "in place" when the first session of the Congress took place, that is, in February 1986.[66] Habel argues that the process began in April 1986,[67] while Domínguez avers that it was publicly announced that month,[68] apparently referring to the speech given by Fidel Castro on April 19, on the 25th anniversary of the military victory at The Bay of Pigs, where CIA-backed rebels had tried to invade Cuba and overthrow Fidel Castro and his government.

The ideas behind Rectification might be better understood by looking at some characteristics of the early Cuban revolution. In the 1960s, the authorities had been much concerned about fomenting a revolutionary *conciencia* or *consciousness*,[69] through mobilization, voluntary work, and so on, and before institutionalization, there were strongly personalized politics based around a charismatic leader who somehow mobilized and involved the masses in politics or played a political role as a "teacher." These policies culminated in ultra-radical, idealistic experiments in the late 1960s; in this utopist phase, almost all the few remaining small private companies were nationalized, and anything deemed to be "capitalist methods" (such as material incentives) were virtually eliminated. One purpose of this was to create socialist consciousness, as opposed to the "capitalist" consciousness that competition and market logic might foment.

As this ultra-radical experiment failed, in the 1970s, the country embarked on the aforementioned Process of Institutionalization, during which improvised institutions built around Fidel Castro's former guerrilla army were replaced by more permanent ones, such as the Communist Party and the political system known as *Poder Popular* or People's Power, with a national parliament. The Party, though created in the early 1960s, had been growing for years—perhaps gaining influence at the expense of Fidel Castro's leadership—and the authorities introduced a more pragmatic model of economic management

---

65 Marifeli Pérez-Stable, *The Cuban Revolution: Origins, Course and Legacy*, 3rd ed. (New York: Oxford University Press, 2012), 127.
66 Carmelo Mesa-Lago, "Cuba's economic counter-reform (rectificación): Causes, policies and effects," *Journal of Communist Studies* 5, n.º 4 (1989), cited in Rosenberg, 81.
67 Habel, 91.
68 Domínguez, 276.
69 According to Joseph A. Kahl, in Cuba, the word *conciencia* "conveys an amalgam of consciousness, conscience, conscientiousness and commitment and is one of the most repeated words in the Cuban language of revolution." See: "The moral economy of a revolutionary society," *Trans-action*, Volume 6 (1969). In this book I have mostly used "consciousness," which in most case would be the closest option in English.

similar to the USSR, known as the System of Management and Planning of the Economy (*Sistema de Dirección y Planificación de la Economía*, SDPE).

As he launched Rectification, Fidel Castro recognized a series of advances over the years of 1970–1986, such as improvements in living standards, the creation of *Poder Popular*, which was not identical to the Soviet political system, and Cuba's *internationalism* in Africa. But he also accounted for the problems of the model that had been implemented, such as bureaucratization and the consolidation of a "technocratic" administration of the economy, as well as the tendency to uncritically imitate and assimilate practices of European "real socialism."[70] Yet it was also Castro's view that during the previous phase, economic growth had been prioritized above the development of socialist consciousness.[71]

The Rectification Process coincided with the closing of the so-called Free Peasant Markets (*Mercado Libre Campesino*, MLC), where the authorities had allowed the sale of agricultural products under the principle of supply and demand.[72] The mid- to late 1980s saw a greater emphasis on moral incentives and volunteer work. During Rectification, Fidel Castro emphasized the socialist state enterprise, but the government also launched so-called Construction Brigades, and a food program was developed. While Rectification did not imply a return to the 1960s, it echoed some priorities of the early years of the Revolution.

According to Marifeli Perez-Stable, the Rectification Process had two phases. During the first (1986–1989), the importance of the Party was emphasized, as something "that the SDPE had supposedly sidelined."[73] The use of what was deemed to be capitalist methods for the direction of the economy was being criticized. At the same time, political work, a socialist conscience, and collective needs were emphasized.[74] In 1987, 400,000 Cubans participated in volunteer labor, and PCC cadres were called upon to visit "enterprises, schools, and neighborhoods" to "feel the popular pulse."[75] During the second session of the

---

70   Bell Lara, 44–45.
71   Ibid., 46–47.
72   Let us not forget a period when a more radical development model was being promoted in Cuba; in the 1970s the country accepted a model largely similar to the "orthodox" or pragmatic model of socialist development in the Soviet Union. Notably, beginning in 1972, Soviet and Bulgarian advisors within the Ministry of Agriculture actively promoted the development of agricultural markets based on supply and demand. These were opened in 1980 under the name of Free Farmers Markets, until their disappearance in 1986.
73   Pérez-Stable, 127.
74   Ibid.
75   Ibid.

Third Congress of the PCC in December 1986, a call was made to strengthen the Communist Party, although Fidel Castro himself had "single-handedly initiated Rectification."[76] In general during Rectification, rather than strengthening institutions, moral principles were invoked as a way to "safeguard the exercise of power."[77]

The second phase of Rectification began in 1989, asserts Pérez-Stable. That summer, the Division General and Hero of the Republic Arnaldo Ochoa, Colonel of the Interior Ministry Antonio de la Guardia, and 12 other military and security officers were arrested. Ochoa, de la Guardia, and two assistants were accused of drug trafficking and of endangering national security and executed after a lengthy, televised trial.[78] For Pérez-Stable, these events highlight "the pitfalls of charismatic authority and the weakness of the Cuban institutions," and they could have had a political script.[79] Yet they were presented as justice being made against corrupt officials.

In the 1990s, the authorities clearly put much of Rectification on hold or even went in another direction, although without reporting this explicitly. For instance, the crisis made it necessary for Cuba to make considerable concessions that went against the spirit of a "purer" socialism than Rectification had pretended.

Yet there might also have been some continuity. Different authors have described how there was a reorientation toward the Revolution's national and even Latin American roots in the 1990s.[80] I would argue that this is the continuation of a process that started in the mid-1980s: Rectification was to a large degree about marking distance from Soviet influence and sending a message that Cuba would follow its own route. In 1987, a book about Che Guevara's ideas was published in Cuba.[81] This is noteworthy because Guevara, originally from Argentina, was a symbol of the Cuban Revolution who had strong differences with the USSR, and he had virtually disappeared from official discourse and thinking since the late 1960s, until the mentioned book was published.

Neither Perestroika nor Rectification brought about an immediate or radical rupture in Cuban–Soviet relations. For a long time, ties between the

---

76 Ibid.
77 Ibid., 128.
78 Ibid.
79 Ibid.
80 See for example: Louis Pérez Jr., *Structure of Cuban History: Meanings and Purpose of the Past* (Chapel Hill: University of North Carolina Press, 2013), 264; Maria Gropas, "The Repatriotization of Revolutionary Ideology and Mnemonic Landscape in Present-Day Havana," *Current Anthropology* 48, No. 4 (2007).
81 Carlos Tablada Pérez, *Ernesto "Che" Guevara: hombre y sociedad* (Buenos Aires: Editorial Antarca, 1987).

countries were not fundamentally changed. According to Mervyn Bain, the Cuban government largely adopted a policy of "wait and see" when Gorbachev introduced Perestroika.[82] The Cuban authorities expressed, for the first time, a "veiled criticism" toward the USSR in the speech given by Fidel Castro to the 27th Congress of the CPSU, in February 1986, referring to the importance of the liberation movements of the South, an issue of controversy between the two countries that was especially visible in the 1960s.[83]

According to Bain, 1989—which he calls the "the critical year"—marked a new stage in Cuban perception of the Soviet reforms, as Cuba stated that it would not deviate from its course no matter what happened in the USSR and definitely closed doors toward reform socialism. Also, events in Eastern Europe and Central America affected the relation adversely. Gorbachev visited Cuba in April 1989, and official media portrayed the visit as a success, but it is possible that there were considerable tensions behind the scenes.[84] On July 26 that year, Fidel Castro made his famous warning to the Cuban public that the Soviet Union definitely might disappear.[85]

By 1991, Cuban criticisms of the USSR had increased and become increasingly direct.[86] In the official Soviet policy toward Cuba there were also "big changes" between 1985 and 1991.[87] However, for Bain, it took "some time" before these changes became apparent,[88] and Bain describes it as surprising that these changes did not occur faster, considering the profound transformations that were taking place internally in the USSR. Among the factors that favored the relation were Gorbachev's continued loyalty to Cuba until the end of the USSR, US hostility against Cuba, and "conservative" politicians in the USSR who pressed for continued relations. Also important for the Soviet government was the symbolic value of maintaining an ally in the Caribbean after the loss of Eastern Europe[89] and the role of the important Cuban lobby in Moscow.

Despite Fidel Castro's attitude toward reform socialism, not all Cubans were against reforming socialism. In August 1989, only a few months after Gorbachev's visit, the Cuban authorities announced that they would cease distribution of the Soviet publications *Novedades de Moscú* (*Moscow News*) and

---

82 Bain, 119.
83 Ibid., 101.
84 Ibid., 104.
85 Ibid., 103–107.
86 Ibid.
87 Ibid., 67.
88 Ibid.
89 Ibid., 67–68.

Sputnik in Cuba. These were Spanish-language editions of Soviet publications that—taking advantage of freedom of expression in the USSR—criticized Cuba and its non-reformed model of socialism.[90]

While this highlights the limits of what the Cuban authorities were willing to tolerate and that by 1989 they went as far as stopping the circulation of these magazines, it should also serve as a reminder that these publications were indeed permitted to circulate for years before that, and thus Cubans were not totally cut off from the changes in the Soviet Union. Even in the Cuban media, there was some space for the reformist ideas inspired by Gorbachev's Perestroika, with some difference in the degree of receptiveness between each media outlet. In Jorge Domínguez's words, Cuba allowed a "certain freedom of expression with regard to thinking about changes in communist Europe," although there were also warnings from Cuban authorities against the dissemination of such ideas.[91] The moment of the strongest reformist influence was between 1987 and 1989.[92] As for the "[u]nguarded public endorsement" of reformist ideas in Cuba, it reached its highest expression in 1987, but there were cases of support throughout 1989.[93]

According to Domínguez, "intellectuals, including academic economists, were the most receptive to some features of Gorbachev's early reforms."[94] Also, according to Domínguez, "Those who had long been sympathetic to ideas from the Soviet Union, no matter what their content, were also more receptive to reform communism," referring likely in part to former members of the Popular Socialist Party, a pro-Soviet party that existed before the Revolution (more information on this party will soon be presented).

Certain sectors of the youth could be said to constitute a third group. Kapcia asserts that in the second half of the 1980s, members of the *Unión de Jóvenes Comunistas* (UJC), the youth wing of the PCC, "began to gravitate enthusiastically towards Gorbachev's model of reformism," also pointing out that there were some existing tensions with the mother Party: "Evidence of careerism [in

---

90 According to Max Azicri, they were not actually removed from the shelves until March 1990. See: "The Rectification Process Revisited: Cuba's Defense of Traditional Marxism–Leninism," in *Cuba in Transition*, eds. Sandor Halebsky et al. (Colorado; Oxford: Westview Press, 1992), 40.

91 Jorge I. Domínguez, "The Political Impact on Cuba of the Reform and Collapse of Communist Regimes," in *Cuba: After the Cold War*, ed. Carmelo Mesa-Lago (Pittsburgh: University of Pittsburgh Press, 1993), 99.

92 Ibid., 111–112.

93 Ibid.

94 Ibid., 117.

INTRODUCTION 19

the UJC] made it a prime target for the Rectification drive after 1986."[95] Habel notes that the authorities withdrew an edition of the UJC magazine *Somos Jóvenes* (which had published an article on prostitution in Cuba) and also refers to a meeting between leaders of the UJC where participants expressed criticism of "The cult of Fidel Castro in the media and the slavishness of the press [...]."[96]

In contrast, Domínguez notes that people who had identified with Che Guevara's radical positions in the 1960s were often more skeptical of Soviet reforms.[97] Enrique A. Baloyra and James A. Morris describe the last half of 1980 as "a period characterized by conflict, according to any standard"[98] and mention how high-level leaders were removed from their positions, such as Humberto Pérez, head of the Central Planning Youth, Roberto Veiga, head of the Workers' Central Union of Cuba (CTC), and José Ramírez Cruz, general secretary of the National Association of Small Farmers (ANAP). A member of the Central Committee of the PCC was arrested in 1987, and there were, of course, the aforementioned trials in 1989. The two scholars consider that there was a "prolonged rivalry" between the Ministry of the Interior (MININT) and the Revolutionary Armed Forces (FAR), which ended when the first of these two institutions was reorganized under the control of the latter one.[99] Pérez-Stable argues that while the CTC and the Federation of Cuban Women (FMC) had been criticized by the Party since 1986 for holding practices "contrary to national interests, socialist objectives and correct *conciencia*," at the end of the decade, the FMC even saw its existence questioned,[100] and criticisms of the organization were made from within the Communist Party as late as 1990.[101] According to Baloyra and Morris, during the late 1980s, more young people began to protest the authorities or were "engaging in disorderly and unruly conduct,"[102] while Alfred Padula claims that in 1992 there were "perhaps fifty

---

95   Kapcia, 77.
96   According to Habel, Carlos Aldana, the ideological secretary of the Party that was associated with pro-Gorbachevista ideas, was present at the meeting. Fidel Castro himself also "appeared," without saying anything. See: Habel, 70.
97   Domínguez, 113.
98   Enrique A. Baloyra and James A. Morris, *Conflict and Change in Cuba* (Albuquerque: University of New Mexico Press, 1993), 6.
99   Ibid., 8.
100 Pérez-Stable, 130.
101 According to our informant Esteban, in 1994, during the so-called Workers' parliaments that were occasions for public debate, "many people said the FMC should disappear." This indicates that the FMC was still controversial several years later.
102 Baloyra and Morris, 9.

human-rights groups with over one thousand members."[103] These faced public "acts of repudiation" (*actos de repudio*), according to Baloyra and Morris.[104]

I cannot completely agree with the two authors when they say that the second half of the 1980s was "a period characterized by conflict, according to any standard," which seems a somewhat exaggerated and slightly sensationalist way of describing conditions. There is no denying that there were serious tensions and certainly more than were easily observable: Jonathan Rosenberg has argued that "[g]iven Fidel Castro's predominance in most aspects of policy-making and the centrality of socialist principles to his long-term developmental project, conflict within the Cuban state tends to be attenuated and muted when compared with that occurring in pluralist societies. Yet the conflicts are real and decisive."[105] Still, if one takes into account the social and political instability in neighboring countries—the Venezuelan *caracazo* left more than 2,000 dead in 1989, and there were guerilla wars in Central America—then Cuba could hardly be characterized as a society "characterized by conflict."

A general characterization of the period should not downplay the conflicts that existed, but it should also take into account that they were mostly intra-elite and did not really involve broad segments of the population. Furthermore, many of these tensions were not new, though they became somewhat strengthened at the time. Baloyra and Morris's characterization could lead the reader to perceive a correlation of forces different from what was really the case. To my knowledge, there are no data or arguments that suggest that a *large* part of the elite was clearly opposed to the leadership of Fidel Castro, though many actors would have preferred he had opted for a somewhat different line. The fact remains that he was also largely respected, not least because of his role during the early years of the Revolution. The unauthorized opposition, on the other hand, did not have much influence within the country.

The Cubans who I interviewed for this study, as well as hundreds of other Cubans representing all sorts of political beliefs that I have talked to informally over the years, mostly tend to describe that decade—at least after the end of 1980, when the Mariel exodus took place—as one of relative

---

103 Alfred Padula, "Cuban Socialism: Thirty Years of Controversy," in *Conflict and Change in Cuba*, eds. Enrique A. Baloyra and James A. Morris (Albuquerque: University of New Mexico Press, 1993), 35.
104 Baloyra and Morris, 9.
105 Rosenberg, 85. The author's article is not about the situation in the late 1980s, but rather on the debate on the role of the market and centralization/decentralization of the economy in the 1970s and early 1980s. He considers that "intense infighting" took place between different branches of government and the Party (p. 57).

stability and material well-being. They sometimes have contrasted the 1980s with much more tense moments in the history of the Revolution, such as most of the 1960s and the first five years or so of the Special Period (1990s). Despite increasing tensions in the economy from approximately 1985 and certain limitations of the model becoming clearer to many after they had lived more than two decades with state socialism, Cuba's degree of social development was, in 1989, in many areas, comparable to industrialized capitalist countries.[106] There was a life expectancy as high as those countries, and in some cases it exceeded them: infant mortality was lower, the number of doctors per inhabitant slightly higher, and there was a higher level of primary schooling.[107] Although there was discontent and sectors in favor of change, this did not in most cases imply that they would have wanted a complete change of system, and the Party press could celebrate the "achievements" of the Revolution without this seeming strange to most.

Yet conditions worsened dramatically from 1990 and onwards. That year, the deterioration of trade relations with Eastern Europe and the USSR began to be felt strongly. On January 28, 1990, Fidel Castro declared that the country was approaching a moment of crisis. He named both this approaching crisis and the plan to address it, the *Special Period in Time of Peace*. The first part of the name refers to a plan that was originally developed in case of a war situation; by adding "in Time of Peace," it was suggested that the situation and the measures to be taken could be similar to those originally projected for a war scenario. The Cuban economy "collapsed" between 1990 and 1993[108] because Cuba had become dependent on "a world that was fading."[109] During 1990 and 1991, according to Domínguez, "Cuba's government seemed as it was on the verge of ruin."[110]

Despite the great changes in Eastern Europe and the USSR and in Cuba's situation in general, during 1989 and 1990 no Party Congress was held, nor did the Cuban government announce radical changes in its political, economic, and social models, although saving measures were announced: in May 1990, others in September of the same year, and then a third round in 1991 and 1992.[111] The expected Fourth Congress of the Communist Party was postponed twice

---

106   Bell Lara, 39.
107   Ibid.
108   Domínguez, *La política exterior de Cuba (1962–2009)*, 370.
109   Ibid.
110   Ibid., 380.
111   Carmelo Mesa-Lago, "Cuba and the Downfall of Soviet and East European Socialism," in *Cuba: After the Cold War*, ed. Carmelo Mesa-Lago (Pittsburgh: University of Pittsburgh Press, 1993).

until it was finally announced for October 1991.[112] In March 1990, Raúl Castro presented the convocation for the congress, better known as the *llamamiento*,[113] which could be translated as the call or the calling. This lengthy document formed the basis of a wide national debate on the future of the country, but shortly after the debates started, the authorities stopped them for several months. When later signaled that the debate could continue again, the Party newspaper made it clear that the one-party system, the socialist economy, and the leadership of Fidel Castro were non-negotiable.[114]

Since the early years of the Revolution, there has been a "siege mentality" in Cuba, a product partly of the US pressures upon the country.[115] This siege mentality was reinforced during the late 1980s due to changes in the country's geopolitical context. At the time, Cuba was located between a US that continued to exert pressure to obtain regime change and a Latin America that, with few exceptions, had pro-American governments. Latin America, including Cuba, was also economically affected by the debt crisis during that time.

The situation in the Americas was very unfavorable for Cuba. Rapprochement with the US did not seem to be a realistic option, as the super power's policies toward Cuba remained inflexible. The transfer of the American presidency from Ronald Reagan to George Bush (now known as George Bush Sr.) in January 1989 did not significantly alter policies toward Cuba. In contrast to the "carrot policy" and dialogue they adopted to a Soviet Union in crisis, there was no such approach or change of strategy for dealing with Cuba. The economic blockade was maintained. Taking into account that Cuba had experienced little growth during the second half of the 1980s, the country was vulnerable to any decline in its trade with Comecon, and it should be recalled that these trade relations had almost vanished completely by 1992.

In the early 1990s, Cuba's situation was adverse in almost every way. While Domínguez argues that there was "international insertion of Cuba in the Americas since 1990,"[116] this was mainly an insertion at the diplomatic level and was also related to Cuba's decision to stop supporting armed movements

---

112   Pérez-Stable, 129.
113   Ibid., 130.
114   Ibid.
115   Kapcia refers to a "siege" of Cuba since the early 1960s that he considers partly real and partly imagined. It was real since Cuba was a victim of subversion and sabotage, but also imagined "to the extent that it came to represent a frame of mind about Cuba's place in the world." He notes that "It suited the Cuban leadership to talk of an ongoing 'state of war,'" but that it was also "never difficult to persuade Cubans that the Revolution's success was being prevented by US policy [...]." See: Kapcia, 133.
116   Domínguez, *La política exterior de Cuba (1962–2009)*, 375.

and to pursue a more defensive foreign policy, so it cannot necessarily be understood as a strengthened Cuba within Latin America and certainly not a strengthened Cuba in general.

Earlier, it was pointed out that Latin America was affected by the debt crisis,[117] and it could be added that the Cuban government was the only one in the region that completely rejected neoliberal reforms.[118] The Latin American left, a traditional ally, was very weak at this time,[119] due to factors such as the severe repression it faced from military regimes during the 1970s and 1980s, as well as the crisis of the USSR.[120] In the Caribbean, Cuba had lost its only close ally, Granada, following a US invasion in 1983. In Jamaica, a former ally, Michael Manley, returned to power in 1989, but with a less radical program than during his previous term.

It is possible that Cuban leaders had some hopes with regard to Central America. But in El Salvador, an offensive toward the end of 1989 by the socialist guerilla group Farabundo Martí National Liberation Front (FMLN) did not bring the expected results, and in 1990, Daniel Ortega lost his bid for reelection in Nicaragua. Both meant a setback of the forces allied with Cuba in Central America. Also, there was the invasion of Panama where the US overthrew dictator Manuel Noriega, who was originally a US ally but had by 1989 pursued more independent positions. Already in August 1989, the *Granma* newspaper warned that an invasion of Panama could be imminent, and when this finally occurred at the end of the year, this increased tensions in the region and gave rise to a pro-American government in that country. In addition, many Cubans, including the country's leadership, probably feared that something similar could happen to them. In an entirely different part of the world, the invasion of Iraq in 1990 could have reinforced this fear.

Politically and ideologically, there was one important event that favored Cuba. By winning the war in Angola in the early 1990s, Cuba helped Namibia gain its independence from South Africa. Previously there had been tensions with a number of "developing countries" due to Cuba's policy in Africa and for its support of the Soviet invasion in Afghanistan.[121] According to Erisman, by

---

117   John Ward, *Latin America: Development and Conflict Since 1945* (London; New York: Routledge, 1997), 60.
118   Ibid.
119   Silvia Borzutzky and Aldo Vacs, "The Impact of the Collapse of Communism and the Cuban Crisis on the South American Left," in *Cuba After the Cold War*, ed. Carmelo Mesa-Lago (Pittsburg: University of Pittsburg Press, 1993), 291.
120   Ibid.
121   H. Michael Erisman, *Cuba's Foreign Relations in a Post-Soviet World* (Gainesville: University press of Florida, 2000), 116.

winning the war in Angola, Cuba once again reinforced its image in the Third World and internationally.[122] But these events did not contribute to any notable degree to solving the material problems of Cuba, which were rather to become much more acute.

The most significant progress with regard to the commercial and political ties of Cuba was the approach to China that began at the end of the 1980s, probably partly motivated by the crisis in the Soviet Union. A rupture had previously taken place in Cuba–China relations. Though Cuba received considerable help, notably one million Chinese bicycles at a time when Cuba suffered severe oil shortages, the trade and the benefits that could be obtained from that relationship were in no way comparable with those lost with the disappearance of the USSR.

Finally, it should also be noted that although the disappearance of the Soviet Union brought "enormous challenges" to Cuba at the time[123] and strongly affected the Latin American left, it also gave Cuba an opportunity to project a new, more independent image, as a defender of revolutionary socialism and as a firm critic of US hegemony.[124] This may have allowed the country to earn points with domestic and Latin American opinion.

Before moving on to the analysis, we should briefly introduce the Communist Party of Cuba (PCC). First, let us recall that this is the leading force in Cuban politics and is the only political party allowed, and it does not present itself for elections; its monopoly on power was enshrined in the 1976 constitution. Unlike the so-called mass organizations (the CTC union, the Federation of Cuban Women, and others), membership is selective; not just anyone can simply say that he or she wants to join.

There are many similarities with the ruling parties in the Soviet Union and Eastern Europe, but also notable differences. The PCC was founded after 1959. This makes it a unique case, as Leninist parties see themselves as at the forefront of the revolutionary struggle and should thus win their vanguard status by organizing the power takeover.[125]

The decision to create a single party was justified and not only inspired by the Soviet Union, but by referring to the foundation of the Cuban Revolutionary Party in 1892 by the national hero José Martí.[126] At the same time, the new

---

122 Ibid.
123 Ibid., 316.
124 Ibid., 316–317.
125 Hans Magnus Enzensberger, "Portrait of a Party: Background, Structure and Ideology of the PCC," 1970, 2.
126 Pérez Jr., 253.

party positioned itself as the heir of the old pro-Soviet Communist Party by taking its first name.[127]

In Cuba, according to Pérez-Stable, the PCC "did not legitimize the Revolution," but Fidel Castro and the Revolution gave legitimacy to the PCC.[128] The Party emerged as a merger of three different movements. In July 1961, the following three forces joined together forming the Integrated Revolutionary Organizations (ORI): the 26 of July Movement, the Revolutionary Directory, and the Popular Socialist Party.[129] These ideological divisions were still present during 1989–1992, and probably some remnants could be found also in 2013.

Of the three groups mentioned, the 26 of July Movement (M-26) was at the forefront. This was a political and military organization founded by Fidel Castro in June 1955 that led the Revolution in its insurrectional phase. During the clandestine struggle, M-26 was dominated by a nationalist-democratic ideology, not communist, although it brought together people of different ideologies and creeds.[130]

---

127 Enzensberger, 2. The author also suggests that this signaled that Fidel Castro had total control, as he could lay claim to the old name. Although the name of the Party could suggest an even closer identity with the Soviet Union than in the case of Eastern European ruling parties during the Cold War—the latter avoided calling themselves Communist Parties like the one of the Soviet Union but rather referred to themselves as Workers' Parties or similar (except Romania). But it is possible that the intention was the opposite. The Communist Party of the Soviet Union saw itself as the vanguard of the global revolutionary movement, and its name implies so, according to the Leninist theory that a communist party should lead the (international) working class. One interpretation of the decision to take the PCC name might be that it was meant to suggest that Cuba would make its own decisions and play a proactive and even leading role in international affairs.

128 See: Pérez-Stable, 87. This point is also reflected by a popular phrase from the 1960s: "If Fidel is a communist, include me on the list" (*Si Fidel es comunista, que me pongan en la lista*).

129 All of the three organizations joined the ORI, but the first two are of most relevance to this study, as the DRE was the weakest organization before 1959. It had lost its leader José Antonio Echeverría Bianchi on the day of an attack on the presidential palace during the Batista dictatorship, and was split in 1959 as many of its adherents went into opposition under Eloy Guitérrez Menoyo. The part that remained pro-Fidel Castro, under Fauré Chomón, left a much more limited mark on the Revolutionary process from the 1960s and onwards, as compared to the M-26 or even the PSP. The PSP also disappeared in the 1960s, but had an organization counting 6,000 members as Fidel Castro gained power, and some of its members became influential political actors and were so even in the late 1980s.

130 There were tensions between *la sierra* ("the mountains") and *el llano* ("the plains"), with the guerrilla members active in the Sierra Maestra mountains known to be forming the most radical wing of the organization. But the guerilla force itself was quite plural in ideological terms, and not free of tensions. Raúl Castro and Ernesto "Che" Guevara were declared Marxists, and Raúl Castro had been a member of the youth wing of the PSP. Fidel

The second organization, the Popular Socialist Party (PSP), was a "typical *Comintern* party," according to Enzensberger,[131] referring to the international communist organization that formally existed between 1919 and 1943 and that had relations with the Soviet Union. There were, however, at some point differences with the Communist Party of the Soviet Union because of the PSP's nationalism and its proximity to the leader of the Communist Party of the USA, Earl Browder,[132] whose ideas were considered a rightist deviation from true Marxism–Leninism. In this sense, perhaps one could say that the Party "had one leg" in Soviet official ideology, but also one in a more moderate, Western communist current. The party was "deeply rooted in the Cuban working class,"[133] unlike M-26, in which the middle class predominated.

The old Party had emerged in 1925 under its first name, the Communist Party of Cuba and was shortly thereafter banned by the elected president and then dictator Gerardo Machado (1925–1933). It was legalized in 1939, when Fulgencio Batista was the country's ruler.[134] That year, it ran in the elections, forming a pact with Batista, who advocated social reforms. The party participated later in the drafting of the Constitution of 1940, and Batista gave a green light to the PSP to establish a labor movement under the leadership of the party, the CTC.[135] The communists exerted some influence, and in return they had to make concessions, even to the US, despite considering it an imperialist power.[136] One could thus say that the Party had some experience in taking part in liberal representative politics.

After Fulgencio Batista's coup in 1952, the PSP was banned again. At the same time, insurrectional groups, such as M-26, began to emerge. The PSP

Castro came from the youth branch of the Party of the Cuban People—Orthodox, better known as just the *Partido Ortodoxo* ("Orthodox Party"), a name that referred to its identification with the national project of José Martí, that had been betrayed by other politicians. The leader of that organization, Eduardo Chibás, was a nationalist politician who emphasized the fight against corruption and social justice. He committed suicide with a gun during a radio broadcast in 1951. Other prominent members of the July 26 movement (M-26) were Frank País, known as an actively religious evangelical, who at the age of 22 had already been Chief of Action and Sabotage for M-26 at a national level. Armando Hart, who became an important politician and ideologist of the Revolution, could be described as a radical democrat when he joined M-26.

131   Enzensberger, 2.
132   Bain, 17.
133   Richard Gott, *Cuba: A New History* (New Haven: Yale University Press, 2005), 158.
134   Enzensberger, 3.
135   Pérez-Stable, 40.
136   Enzensberger, 3.

described the actions of Fidel Castro as "adventurist,"[137] although Guerra and Maldonado claim that in the final fight against Batista, the Party "allied in practice" with the guerrillas.[138] Nevertheless, the fact that the PSP had established a distance from the guerrillas became an awkward topic after 1959.

As for the other Cuban parties, these had disappeared after Batista's coup or had collaborated with the de facto government and thus had little legitimacy. With the Revolution of 1959, the parties that had collaborated with Batista "were dissolved" and, at the same time, the revolutionary government legalized the PSP.[139] Initially, the old communists were not included in the new leadership of the country,[140] where more centrist forces predominated. But there was a radicalization in the country as well as in the circles of power during 1959. By the beginning of 1960, "the predominance of the left wing [of M-26], discretely allied to the PSP, was practically a fact."[141] Even so, since 1962, shortly after the PSP entered the new unified party, previous members of the former communist party were marginalized, according to Kapcia, until they were "rehabilitated" in 1975.[142]

During the 1970s, more pro-Soviet elements within the PSP reached the highest ranks of government, "including" important figures of this party, such as Carlos Rafael Rodríguez and Blas Roca.[143] The PCC also grew much in strength at this time, and it should be mentioned that in its early years, the Cuban party was organizationally weak and thus in this sense quite different from the ruling parties of the USSR and Eastern Europe. LeoGrande asserts that in the 1960s, the new unified party had a weak organization,[144] and Kapcia claims that during its first ten years, the PCC tended "to be little more than a

---

137 Sergio Guerra and Alejo Maldonado, *Historia de la Revolución Cubana* (Navarra: Txalaparta, 2009), 60.
138 Ibid., 61. In the historiography produced in Cuba it is sometimes emphasized that the PSPs historical leader, Blas Roca, found himself in exile during the years of insurrectionary struggle in Cuba, and that the Party had been in charge of Aníbal Escalante (who later, in 1962, was criticized by Fidel Castro for "sectarianism" and then accused of conspiracy and imprisoned in 1968). It is considered that much of the grassroots of the PSP had, in differing degree, sympathies with Fidel Castro. A prominent member of the PSP, Carlos Rafael Rodríguez went to the Sierra Maestra mountains to join Fidel Castro's guerilla—in July 1958. Many PSP party militants joined the Rebel Army at their own initiative.
139 Ibid., 72.
140 Cited in Guerra and Maldonaldo, 71.
141 Ibid., 89.
142 Kapcia, 75.
143 Bain, 27.
144 LeoGrande, "The Communist Party of Cuba since the First Congress," 399.

mechanism to exercise political hegemony over [its] members."[145] For Leo-Grande, it was "[o]nly in the 1970s [that] the PCC became an organization that was strong enough to impose a real direction on the Cuban political system."[146] As part of *institutionalization*, a new constitution that was "very similar to the Soviet one" was established in December 1975,[147] which, like the Soviet constitution, grants a leading role for the Party. However, the PCC was still the smallest communist party in power in the world (per capita).[148] Political power was divided between the PCC and the new Organs of Popular Power (OPP),[149] in a representative governmental system, with three levels: Local Assemblies, Provincial Assemblies, and the National Assembly.[150] Thus, the position of the PCC was similar to that of the communist and workers' parties in the USSR and Eastern Europe, which had a double monopoly over politics and the economy and thus an extraordinary power.[151] In neither case was any opposition permitted and other institutions generally responded to Party policies.

Still, historian Fernando Martínez Heredia claims that in the Cuban case there was actually "a very strong pretension to differentiate itself from the East

---

145 Kapcia, 74.
146 LeoGrande, "El Partido Comunista de Cuba y la Política Electoral: Adaptación, Sucesión y Transición," 5.
147 Bain, 27–28.
148 LeoGrande, "The Communist Party of Cuba since the First Congress," 405.
149 It is possible to participate in politics in Cuba and become a member of elected bodies without being a member of the PCC. According to Kapcia, "Officially, the OPP [representative electoral system of Cuba] existed beyond parties." Still, he also points that that "Inevitably, the more powerful the Party became nationally and locally, the more likely it was that those selected [as candidates to Popular Power organs] would be Party members already or would soon be invited to join." See: Kapcia, 79. In local and provincial elected bodies as well as in the National Assembly, there are deputies who are not members of the Party, although the proportion of delegates that are not Party members is low in the National parliament. Still, it is worth taking into account that they can be elected, and also that the Parliament fulfills its tasks—to enact laws, prepare budgets, and others—without the PCC intervening *as an institution*. In other words, there is a *separation of functions*, although it would not make sense to talk about separation of powers. The National Assembly is obliged to work on the basis of the general political line of the Party, and in practice the people who make up the highest levels of leadership, the Council of State (represents the parliament between its sessions), and the Council of Ministers (government), are Party members.
150 Peter Roman, *People's Power: Cuba's Experience with Representative Government, Updated Edition* (Boulder: Rowman & Littlefield, 2003), 3. The author also comments that these elected assemblies oversee a large number of social and economic activities that are under their control. In this regard, "They have a much broader scope than their capitalist counterparts," where these activities are in private hands.
151 Bunce, 22.

European parties in terms of the separation between Party and State."[152] This does not imply a separation of powers such as in liberal democracy or accepting opposition within the state. There was, still, some separation of *tasks*, although perhaps not as clear as the original pretension. In the mid-1970s, "[t]he PCC led, the state administered, and the mass organizations maintained 'contact with the masses.'"[153]

The ideology of the Party and the State was contradictory, and not static. The process was marked by the continuous presence of a charismatic leader like Fidel Castro—in some ways more reminiscent of Latin American radical populists than his Soviet and Eastern European counterparts. The balance between the Party and the leader changed from one moment to another, and in the 1970s there was certainly some degree of the "depersonalization" of Cuban politics.[154] Pérez-Stable points out that the Rectification Process, announced in 1986, which implied a significant turn in national policies, was an initiative developed by Fidel Castro that was later adopted by the Party Congress. Pérez-Stable argues that this is a sign of the relative weakness of the Party vis-a-vis the leader (FC) at that time,[155] although precisely at that time, Castro called for a strengthening of the Party.[156] Even if this might be true, according to William LeoGrande, "organizationally and ideologically," the PCC "(was) stronger than what most European parties were on the eve of the transition."[157]

2 Review of the Existing Literature

This investigation draws upon and enters into contact with a series of previous academic works. Most of the works found to be relevant or useful to our enterprise could be grouped into four categories: 1) academic literature on Cuban politics and society, 2) literature on Cuba–Soviet relations, and 3) analysis of the Collapse of the Soviet Union written by Cubans, as well as 4) recent works of oral history realized in Cuba, even when these investigations are about other topics, as they share the methodology and the national context with our investigation. For practical reasons, this review will be limited to literature published

---

152 Fernando Martínez Heredia, interviewed by Eric Toussaint, 2015.
153 Pérez-Stable, 104.
154 Domínguez, *La política exterior de Cuba (1962–2009)*, 275.
155 Pérez-Stable, 123.
156 Ibid, 127.
157 LeoGrande, "El Partido Comunista de Cuba y la Política Electoral: Adaptación, Sucesión y Transición," 42.

in English and Spanish, but most works that fall into these four categories have been written in one of these two languages.

With regard to the first category, academic literature on Cuba and its politics, my main interest has been in works that in some way or another address the collapse of the USSR and its impact on Cuba. Although there is an immense amount of works on the history of Cuba, this literature is often not specialized enough to be of any use. Even so, some works written after 1991 contain data and analysis of interest to us, especially studies that try to gain further insight into Cuba's "non-transition" or "exceptionalism," an objective that is also shared by us.

Kapcia has made critical comments on the academic literature on Cuba written in recent decades. For instance, he observes that academic works on Cuba that were published during the 1990s tended to center their attention on the material crisis that the country lived through.[158] Another feature of this literature is that it often takes for granted that the Cuban system will soon collapse. It was not until the end of the 1990s that a number of books were published that discuss why no regime change took place.[159] As previously seen, Kapcia also affirmed that part of the literature tends to one-sidedly emphasize Fidel Castro at the cost of the underlying institutions.[160]

However, there are also monographs on Cuba written after the Collapse of the USSR that do not have these characteristics, and some of these have been very useful to us. I refer here to the "generalist" works of Marifeli Pérez-Stable (2012)[161] and by Antoni Kapcia (2010),[162] as well as books on specific topics, such as Julio García Luis's book on the Cuban press,[163] *People's Power* by Peter Roman (2005), on the political system,[164] and *The Structure of Cuban History* by Louis A. Pérez Jr. (2013),[165] about how Cubans see their history. Other books that should be mentioned are *Globalization and the Cuban Revolution* by José Bell Lara (2002)[166] and *Cuba* by Janette Habel (1989, updated in 1991).[167]

---

158   Kapcia, 640.
159   Ibid.
160   Ibid.
161   Pérez-Stable.
162   Kapcia.
163   Julio García Luis, *Revolución, socialismo, periodismo: La prensa y los periodistas cubanos ante el siglo XXI* (La Habana: Pablo de la Torriente, 2014).
164   Roman.
165   Pérez Jr.
166   Bell Lara.
167   Habel.

INTRODUCTION

One challenge is that very little literature exists that analyzes the role of the Communist Party of Cuba, specifically.[168] There is a lack of up-to-date studies of this institution and even serious journalistic coverage outside of Cuba, and from inside of Cuba, most of the information and analysis to be found comes from official documents and the official press, which has of course to be read critically. There are few Cuban academic studies on the political system and the Communist Party itself. I have been able to locate one compilation of texts made in Cuba in 2011, edited by Maria Julia Peláez Groba,[169] that centers on the Party. That book, however, focuses on the Party in its early years and merely gives a chronology of events of the 1990s. Still, the earlier mentioned "generalist" book-length studies on the country and on its political system and culture have been of some help to this investigation. There are also some non-monographic works that focus specifically on the Communist Party, such as a well-known article by Hans Magnus Enzensberger from 1970,[170] in addition to three texts written by William M. LeoGrande[171] at different moments in the history of the Revolution.

There are several works that deal specifically with Cuba–Soviet relations, from different fields of research. Due to the focus of this investigation, the most relevant are those that were written during or after the weakening and disappearance of Cuban–Soviet relations. In 2007, Mervyn Bain noted that since 1991, very little had been written about Cuban–Soviet relations during the period between 1985 and 1991.[172] This affirmation seems especially true when taking into account the *importance* of this period—as these were the final years of the greatly important Cuban–Soviet relations. Still, some books that have been of great help to us are the monographs of Carmelo Mesa-Lago,[173] Yuri Pavlov,[174] Michael H. Erisman,[175] Jorge Domínguez,[176] and Mervyn Bain.[177]

---

168   Kapcia, 647.
169   *Partido Comunista de Cuba: Evolución histórica (1959–1997)* (La Habana: Editorial Historia, 2011).
170   Enzensberger.
171   William M. LeoGrande, "El Partido Comunista de Cuba y la Política Electoral: Adaptación, Sucesión y Transición," (2002); "Party Development in Revolutionary Cuba," *Journal of Interamerican Studies and World Affairs* 21, n.° 4 (1979); "The Communist Party of Cuba since the First Congress," *Journal of Latin American Studies* 12, n.° 2 (1980).
172   Bain, 9.
173   Carmelo Mesa-Lago, *Cuba: after the Cold War*, Pitt Latin American series (Pittsburgh: University of Pittsburgh Press, 1993).
174   Pavlov.
175   H. Michael Erisman, *Cuba's Foreign Relations in a Post-Soviet World* (Gainesville: University press of Florida, 2000).
176   Domínguez, *La política exterior de Cuba (1962–2009)*.
177   Bain (2007).

While work on this study was going on, two books were published on cultural aspects of Soviet influence and heritage in Cuba, one by Jacqueline Loss and José Manuel Prieto[178] and another by Jacqueline Loss.[179] These texts place great emphasis on Cuban *perceptions* of the USSR and Cuba's relation with the USSR, just like our own work, but their interest is primarily in cultural aspects of the relations, and less in the political aspects (both words are here used in a narrow sense).

Except the last two books mentioned, most explore Cuban–Soviet relations in a more general fashion and are not exclusively centered on Cuban visions of the Collapse, although some do contain important insights on the subject. In the case of Bain's *Soviet-Cuban Relations 1985 to 1991: Changing Perceptions in Moscow and Havana*, perceptions on both sides are explored,[180] and in an article in the Mesa-Lago book, Domínguez analyses perceptions of the Collapse in the Cuban press and publications.[181]

Pavlov also deals with perceptions on the relations within both countries in the book *Soviet-Cuban Alliance 1959–1991* and shares much information obtained during his years as a representative of the USSR in Cuba, in a book that according to Bain could be described as something between a personal testimony and an academic analysis.[182] The works cited usually base their analysis on written sources, mostly official ones such as the press, speeches, and so on. No oral history has been published in which Cubans' perceptions of the Collapse constitute the central theme, although one major work is due to be published that will likely dedicate considerable space to the experience of the Collapse and the Special Period.

In general, it should be said that little oral history has been conducted in Cuba. I will briefly mention those works that I have been able to identify. Paul Thompson, founder of the Oral History Society, as I mentioned earlier, while of the view that little oral history has been recorded in socialist countries, cites Cuban *testimonial literature* as an exception. The quintessential example of this literature is *Cimarrón: History of a Slave*, by Miguel Barnet, first published

---

178 Jacqueline Loss and José Manuel Prieto, *Caviar with Rum: Cuba-USSR and the Post-Soviet Experience*, New directions in Latino American cultures (New York: Palgrave Macmillan, 2012).

179 Jacqueline Loss, *Dreaming in Russian: The Cuban Soviet Imaginary* (Texas: University of Texas Press, 2014).

180 Bain.

181 Domínguez, "The Political Impact on Cuba of the Reform and Collapse of Communist Regimes."

182 Pavlov.

INTRODUCTION

in 1966,[183] which recounts the testimony of a former slave, who was at the time 103 years old. The prestigious Casa de las Américas literary prize awarded in Havana since 1970 has included a category for testimonial literature, and some winning entries have been about the experiences of Cubans.

However, as previously stated, it should be said that little oral history has been done in Cuba, and the historical reasons for this should be mentioned. The historian and anthropologist Oscar Lewis was doing extensive work on the Cuban Revolution, but the authorities stopped the project in July 1970. Despite this, he managed to finish three books.[184]

Since the late 1990s, there have been at least one attempt to foment oral history amongst Cuban researchers; still, this does not seem to have produced much results.[185] According to historian Elizabeth Dore, between 1970 and 2004, no large oral history project was done on the island. More recently, though, there have been some works about terrorism suffered by Cuba[186] and sexual revolutions in Cuba,[187] as well as a book that brings together testimonies of former revolutionaries.[188] The major work that I mentioned was directed by Dore herself and is called "Memories of the Revolution." A book based on this research is forthcoming.[189]

The last category of literature that interests us and that has been cited in this study is literature on the Soviet collapse written by Cuban academics. Although this literature explores circumstances related to the Soviet Union and to a lesser extent the relationship between Cuba and that country (or aspects

---

[183] Miguel Barnet and Esteban Montejo, *Biografía de un cimarrón* (La Habana: Ediciones Huracán, 1968).

[184] Oscar Lewis, Ruth M. Lewis, and Susan M. Rigdon, *Living the Revolution: An Oral History of Contemporary Cuba: 3: Neighbors* (Urbana, Illinois: University of Illinois Press, 1978); *Living the Revolution: An Oral History of Contemporary Cuba: 1: Four Men* (Urbana, Illinois: University of Illinois Press, 1977); *Living the Revolution: An Oral History of Contemporary Cuba: 2: Four Women* (Urbana, Illinois: University of Illinois Press, 1977).

[185] In recent years, there seems to be a greater interest in Cuba in regard to the use of oral sources in history. In 1999, after a resolution from Minister of Culture Abel Prieto, the "Carolina Poncet de Cárdenas" Chair of Studies was created, "with the objectives of establishing a space for permanent theoretical discussion on Orality and on the use of oral sources in historical-cultural research." See: "Cátedra de Oralidad," http://www.perfiles.cult.cu/catedras.php.

[186] Keith Bolender, *Voices From the Other Side: An Oral History of Terrorism Against Cuba* (London: Pluto Press, 2010).

[187] Carrie Hamilton, *Sexual Revolutions in Cuba: Passion, Politics and Memory* (Chapel Hill: The University of North Carolina Press, 2012).

[188] José Bell Lara et al., *Combatientes* (Havana: Ciencias Sociales, 2014).

[189] Elizabeth Dore. *Cuban Lives: What Difference Did a Revolution Make?* (London and New York: Verse, forthcoming).

of this relationship, such as the Cuban perceptions of the collapse), academic literature on the Soviet Union produced in Cuba is in some cases of relevance for our project not only because it is a source of scholarly insight on the subject of Cuban–Soviet relations, but also because the interpretations in these books *are* Cuban perspectives on the Soviet collapse.

To put it in other words, in relation to this study, these works to some extent constitute primary sources in that they reflect Cuban perceptions of the Collapse, but they are also academic works and as such useful support literature. In many cases, there is a political motivation behind the elaboration of this literature, and this is sometimes expressed openly by the authors. For example, in the compilation of articles *El derrumbe del modelo eurosoviético: Una visión desde Cuba* published in 1994, Figueroa Albelo states that: "For Cuba, specifically, the study of the Collapse has a transcendence that exceeds the limits of an academic and simply theoretical exercise, because it is vital for the sociohistorical practice of building socialism."[190]

The mentioned book includes interpretations of the Soviet collapse by different scholars; for example, it offers a variety of perspectives on the changes and their causes. Some put emphasis on the lack of democracy in Soviet and East European socialism, while others center more on economic causes. There is a consensus that what failed in Europe was a "specific, bureaucratic, antidemocratic" type of socialism rather than "socialism as a system," not socialism as an idea or a project of liberation. The book's editors recognize that in Cuba it was difficult to analyze Soviet reality scientifically before 1991, as a "uncritical and apologetic approach of the Soviet and East European Socialism was an obstacle to [obtaining] a scientific view [...]."[191] One of the contributors acknowledges that the work, as it was published a few years after the events, should be seen as an early contribution to the debate: "The elapsed time is very short and the factual material has not been fully examined and systematized." One striking detail is that the authors emphasize that there are still regimes that declare themselves as socialist, such as China, North Korea, Vietnam, and Laos, and thus portray the Collapse as mainly a European phenomenon. This geographical delimitation of what is often referred to as the End of Communism is actually quite interesting, as it was typically absent from the Western academic debate at the time, although it is taken more seriously now, as

---

190   García Báez Román and Ramón Sánchez Noda, editors. *El derrumbe del modelo eurosoviético: Una visión desde Cuba* (Havana: Editorial Felix Varela, 1994), 3.
191   Víctor Figueroa Albelo, "La transición al socialismo y el derrumbe del socialismo de estado," in *El Derrumbe del Modelo Eurosoviético*, ed. Román García Báez (Havana: Editorial Felix Varela, 1994), 79.

suggested by the title of the book *Why Communism Did Not Collapse*, published in 2013.[192]

The first book or booklet published in Cuba on the process of the disintegration of Soviet and East European socialism was titled *The Collapse of Socialism in Eastern Europe, Causes and Consequences*,[193] but unfortunately I could not locate a copy. The publication was prepared by anonymous researchers at the Department of International Relations of the Central Committee of the PCC, representatives of the political leadership of the FAR, and the Center for European Studies (CEE). It was published in February 1992, and according to journalist Tania Díaz Castro, at the time it was circulating among military personnel of higher and lower rank. Díaz Castro gives the impression that the book emphasizes, to some extent, the internal causes of the Collapse, that is, problems internal to the USSR, such as the "excesses" of Joseph Stalin, and "errors" such as the imposition by force of socialism in Eastern Europe, violations of socialist legality, the tendency of ageing in the country's leadership, a lack of dynamism or initiative, a growing state bureaucracy, and others. Despite the title of Díaz Castro's article, the booklet seems to go a bit further than just blaming Stalin for everything, as it also mentions persistent problems that did not go away after Stalin's death and that some might attribute to the model itself, more than just the deviations or "errors" of certain leaders. Some problems have clearly also been present in Cuba.

I should moreover mention a chapter of the book, *Vision desde Cuba*, published in 1997, "Note on the crisis and collapse of the model of socialism implanted in the USSR" (our translation from Spanish), by Cuban sociologist José Bell Lara. This text describes the Soviet Union as a deformed workers' state ruled according to the interests of the bureaucracy. Perestroika was, according to Bell Lara, a proposal to reintroduce capitalism wrapped in socialist "clothing," but in it was also a product of the very same Stalinist project that it intended to criticize (Perestroika was, according to the author, a proposal made by the bureaucracy that arose as a result of Stalinism). The text was revised and published again in 2006, with an extension to its title: "Twenty years after Perestroika" (translated from Spanish).[194]

---

192 Dimitrov.

193 Original title: *El derrumbe del socialismo en Europa del Este, sus causas y consecuencias.* Do not have detailed bibliographical information.

194 José Bell Lara, "Nota sobre la crisis y hundimiento del modelo de socialismo real. A veinte años de la Perestroika," *Revista Cubana de Ciencias Sociales*, No. 36/37; José Bell Lara, "Nota sobre la crisis y hundimiento del modelo de socialismo implantado en la URSS," in *Visión desde Cuba*, eds. José Bell Lara and Clara Pulido Escandell (Madrid: SODePAZ, 1997).

More Cuban perspectives on the Collapse can be found in *Eastern Europe: The Collapse* (title translated from Spanish), by Francisco Brown, and *Russia, from Real Socialism to Real Capitalism* (title translated from Spanish) by Ariel Dacal and Francisco Brown.[195] In these titles, including Bell Lara's, one can also find the description of a Revolution betrayed by a bureaucracy that had been allowed to accumulate power, an explanation not unlike that of Leon Trotsky, who wrote that the Russian revolution had allowed a bureaucracy to accumulate power and that this bureaucracy had betrayed the principles of the Revolution, which is interesting considering the highly negative view of Trotsky in official Soviet history (which was, in this case, replicated in Cuba). It is furthermore noteworthy that the latter book even has a prologue written by Alan Woods, a well-known Trotskyist theorist and activist from Great Britain.

In 2014, the former Cuban Minister of Economy José Luis Rodríguez wrote the book *The Collapse of Socialism in Europe* (my translation). This monograph focuses on economic issues and causes of the Collapse.[196] There is also the book *Eastern Europe: From the Collapse to Neoliberalism* (my translation) by Iván Emilio León,[197] which was published by a Cuban state editorial house in 2011. It is an anthology consisting of contributions by non-Cuban authors, and therefore they are not Cuban interpretations of the Collapse, but its publication in Cuba where the state has a monopoly on book publishing, indicates an interest in the international debate on the subject or more specifically critical left debates on the issue, and shows that Cubans interested in the subject also have access to these takes on the topic.

The majority of other contributions, those that have not been mentioned so far, are from 2000 and later. Orlando Cruz Capote has a contribution on the Collapse in the *Cuban Journal of Social Sciences* in which he discusses the possibility of a "hidden political agenda" among some members of the Soviet leadership.[198] The Cuban magazine *Temas* organizes a monthly panel that is open to the public ("Ultimo Jueves"), and one of these events was entitled "Why did socialism fall in Eastern Europe?," which was published together with other

---

195   Francisco Brown, *Europa del Este: El Colapso* (Cuba: Editorial Ciencias Sociales, 2002); Ariel Dacal and Francisco Brown, *Rusia del socialismo real al capitalismo real* (Cuba: Editorial Ciencias Sociales, 2005).
196   José Luis Rodríguez García, *El Derrumbe del Socialismo en Europa* (Cuba: Editorial Ciencias Sociales/Ruth Casa Editorial, 2014).
197   Iván Emilio León, *Europa Oriental: Del derrumbe al neoliberalismo* (Havana: Ruth Casa Editorial, 2011).
198   Orlando Cruz Capote, "Unas notas y dos visiones sobre la Perestroika y sus consecuencias," *"Revista Cubana de Ciencias Sociales, n.° 36/37," Revista Cubana de Ciencias Sociales*, No. 36/37.

debates in a book compilation.[199] The debate reflected a wide range of views, too many to list in detail; however, most tend to coincide in emphasizing internal factors and in tracing the origin of the causes of the Collapse to the early years of the Soviet Union, during the Stalin years or even earlier. The article "The role of politics in the collapse of Soviet socialism" (my translation) by Oscar Julián Villa Barroso, however, makes reference to a Fidel Castro statement where the Cuban leader said that the collapse of the USSR was an act of suicide, that is, not provoked from outside forces. Villa Barroso himself concludes that a sector of the Soviet elite, led by Gorbachev, helped promote that change.[200]

In recent years, two degree theses of journalism have also been written on the subject, the *licenciatura* of Carlos Díaz Hernández and Mabel Machado López of the Faculty of Communication of the University of Havana,[201] and the master thesis of Julién Richard Ruíz.[202]

Our work is different from all the above-mentioned ones as it has another object of study, which is not the Collapse of Soviet and East European socialism as such but the views or perceptions of the Collapse on the part of the Cuban Communist Party and individual members of this party. Even so, the authors of the cited works sometimes include references to the interpretations of other Cubans, and thus we sometimes share the same object of study. The renowned Cuban academic Desiderio Navarro (1948–2017), for example, as one of the participants in the *Ultimo Jueves* debate panel, made an interesting observation on the debate surrounding the Collapse in Cuba. He stated that in Cuba, one had a misleading image of Soviet society that was created and reproduced massively, and this gave birth to beliefs "at a popular level" according to which the Collapse was the product of Gorbachev allegedly being a CIA agent (these perceptions gained strength, according to Navarro, because people were not familiar with the structural problems that the Soviet Union suffered from, and thus it was more tempting to look for possible traitors as an explanation). He characterizes this view as not Marxist.[203]

---

199   Denia García Ronda, "¿Por qué cayó el socialismo en Europa Oriental?," in Ultimo Jueves (Havana: Instituto Cubano de Investigación Cultural Juan Marinello, 2008).
200   Oscar Julián Villa Barroso, "El papel de la política en el hundimiento del socialismo soviético," *Temas*, April–June edition (2014).
201   Carlos Díaz Hernández and Mabel Machado López, "Palabras sobre la 'glásnot' (sic): la llamada transparencia y la narrativa periodística sobre la historia soviética," Revista Universidad de la Habana, No. 274 (2012).
202   Julién Richard Ruíz, "Kilómetro 0. La desintegración de la URSS, una visión desde Cuba. Tesis de licenciatura" (Facultad de Comunicación, Universidad de la Habana, 2012).
203   Ronda, 29.

This literature review is not intended to be a complete bibliographic systematization of everything that has been written; rather, we have prioritized works considered to have certain points of contact with our study and have tried to give the reader a general idea of the literature on the Collapse that exists in Cuba.

With regard to the academic debate in Cuba, it should be said that a particular difficulty soon became apparent: Many contributions are not online, and they are not easy to locate. Sometimes their circulation was quite limited, as paper was strictly rationed during the Special Period. It should also be noted that although the debate was limited, parts of it may have taken place at a very local level and in relatively closed academic circles, which means that little of it is preserved or easily locatable.

3 Definitions and Terminology

Before proceeding to the first chapter where I will present the analysis of our written sources, some definitions, delimitations, and clarifications are necessary. First, when I started this investigation in 2013, I wanted to limit myself to analyzing the views of Cuban communists of the Collapse of the Union of Soviet Socialist Republics, leaving out the republics in Eastern Europe.[204] I thought that this was necessary for the project to be practically manageable.

At the beginning of my field work, however, I discovered that the disappearance of Soviet and East European socialism is usually treated in an "integrated" manner by Cuban communists, just as one often speaks of the "fall of communism" in the western capitalist world; that is, as an event that encompasses

---

204 This is reflected in the interview guide (see Appendix 2). The attentive reader will see that there is slightly more emphasis on the USSR (not Comecon states in Eastern Europe) in Part 2 of this work, than in the first part. This is partly because in the interviews I asked more questions about the USSR specifically—I asked few questions about the other European socialist states, because at the beginning of the field work, I still held the idea that it would be better to study only the relations between Cuba and the USSR. Moreover, it seemed that most of the respondents remembered the USSR better than what happened in other countries. Of course, this makes sense as it was the main trading partner of Cuba and the main country within the socialist community. Even so, when I did our analysis of the press, most of the topics that I was able to identify, following the selection criteria that I have laid out in Part 1, happened to be events or processes in Eastern Europe and not the USSR.

both Eastern Europe and the former USSR.[205] Of course, most of Eastern Europe was very closely tied to the Soviet Union between 1945 and 1989, and its countries have been described as the USSR's external empire, or more commonly as satellite states.

When I asked our interviewees questions about the USSR, sometimes we received points of view, analysis, or examples that had to do with Eastern Europe and not the Soviet Union. One of my informants, sociologist Jorge, even compared the relation between the USSR and Eastern Europe to that of a spreading disease: socialism in the USSR, he said, was the "main tumor" and its local variants in Eastern Europe, its metastasis. Accordingly, I opted for the term Soviet and East European socialism and included in these all the state socialist countries that were in 1989 part of the Council of Mutual Economic Aid (Comecon) and the Warsaw Pact in Eastern Europe. In other words, the countries of the so-called Eastern Bloc: Bulgaria, Czechoslovakia, Hungary, Poland, East Germany, and Romania (despite the frictions that existed between Romania and the USSR). We did not include Albania or Yugoslavia. Albania distanced itself from Comecon and the Warsaw Pact in the 1960s, and Yugoslavia never became a full member of either of the two organizations.[206]

In Cuba, people often refer to the *campo socialista*, the socialist camp, or the Socialist Bloc. In Fidel Castro's speeches and other available documents from the epoch, *campo socialista* normally refers to the socialist countries in Eastern Europe *excluding* the USSR. However, a quick search at contemporary *.cu domains reveals that today it is often used to encompass both the Soviet Union and the so-called "people's democracies" in Eastern Europe. Sometimes the concept even includes Asian socialist countries such as Vietnam (for instance, Ecured, the Cuban encyclopedia, does so in its article "Campo Socialista"[207]). In my analysis, "Socialist Bloc" reflects the same geographical delimitation as "Soviet and Eastern European socialism"; however, in the sources, the term is used both including and excluding the USSR, but never includes Asian countries, except former USSR republics.

The USSR was, we recall, the hegemonic promoter and member of Comecon and the Warsaw Pact, and that state, organized as a federal union, consisted of 15 republics: Russia, as the largest and most powerful, but also (in alphabetical

---

205 This perception of course came gradually, and in early to mid-1989, most Cubans would probably not have recognized a "crisis of socialism," but rather have seen the profound crisis in countries such as Poland and Hungary more as local situations.
206 Cuba itself was a member of Comecon between 1972 and 1991, but not of the Warsaw Pact.
207 "Campo Socialista." *Ecured*, https://www.ecured.cu/Campo_Socialista.

order), Belarus, Azerbaijan, Georgia, Turkmenistan, Ukraine, Uzbekistan, Tajikistan, Armenia, Kazakhstan, Kyrgyzstan, Latvia, Lithuania, Moldova, and Estonia. In this study, the terms Soviet Union (colloquial name), Union of Soviet Socialist Republics (official name), and USSR (abbreviation of the official name) are used as synonyms. Some respondents in the interview part may confuse one territory with another or use another terminology. For example, some respondents use the Spanish nationality adjective "ruso" (Russian) as a synonym for "Soviet," or Russia instead of the Soviet Union; these are common practices in everyday speech in Cuba.

The use of the word "communism" to refer to the societies that this study center upon would seem problematic to us. Not only because they were not classless societies like the one Karl Marx had proposed as a long-term goal; these states did not even consider themselves to be communist societies. The authorities referred to their societies as socialistic, that is, as countries that were in a transition to communism or the class- and stateless society, in accordance with a common reading of Marxist ideas, and the population also commonly used the word socialism to describe their system. Although it could certainly be questioned whether these countries were *really* even socialist, and some informants in this study also suggested that they were not, at least, I am convinced that at some point, it was the real intention of these countries to create socialism. They are often referred to as socialist in the academic literature, and I find that they had more in common with the society described by Marx as socialist than to what he described as communist. Although the term is not ideal, I opted to use the word "socialism" and derivations such as "socialist,"[208] to refer to the societies that this study centers upon, occasionally adding "state" in front of "socialism" in the analysis to underline the centralized character of these systems. One further reason to use "socialism" is that it was the term that made the best sense to use during the interviews. The use of "communism" to refer to Soviet and Eastern Europe, as well as Cuba, is strongly associated with an American cold war discourse that our informants would probably find alienating.

---

208 "Socialist country," "socialist economy," etc.

PART 1

The Collapse According to Granma (1989–1992)

CHAPTER 1

Written Sources on the Collapse

In this chapter, I present the analysis of the written sources of our study, almost all published between January 1989 and March 1992—in other words, the period contemporaneous with the Collapse. Specifically, the selected sources consist of selected materials from more than three annual volumes of the newspaper *Granma*, officially known as the official organ of the Central Committee of the Communist Party of Cuba.[1]

Ever since it was founded in 1965, the newspaper *Granma* occupied a privileged position in Cuban society. Harbron affirmed that unlike in what he refers to as "all other totalitarian regimes of our era"—a group in which he explicitly includes the Soviet Union and Eastern Europe—"Castro's Cuba does not possess a single ministry of information and propaganda."[2] However, in his opinion, "*Granma* is, in effect, the substitute for the information ministry"[3] and therefore guides the work of other media, including radio and television. This protagonist role probably became further accentuated from about 1990, during the early years of the Special Period, because at that time frequent blackouts affected people's ability to follow television and radio transmissions. In addition, television broadcasts were reduced; by 1992, they had decreased by 34.9% (speech by Carlos Aldana, *Granma*, March 17, 1992). With respect to the written press, at the beginning of the Special Period there was at least one newspaper for each of the (then) 14 provinces of Cuba, but each one consisted of only a few pages and, being local newspapers, their coverage of national

---

1 As already mentioned in the introduction, I have also read a number of speeches by Fidel Castro and old magazines (*Cuba Socialista, El Militante Comunista*). Some other official Cuban publications have also been of use to our study. Notably, books with speeches and documents published by the PCC, for example one titled *IV Congress of the Communist Party of Cuba, Santiago of Cuba, October 10–14, 1991: Discursos y documentos* (Havana: Editorial Política, 1992). Like the *Granma* newspaper, these sources were produced by—or under the supervision of—the Communist Party of Cuba. These documents have served primarily to familiarize ourselves with the epoch and its political actors, so with the exception of some of the speeches I will generally not cite or make references to specific items of information in these materials.
2 John D. Harbron, "Journalism and Propaganda in the New Cuba," in *Cuban Communism*, eds. I.L. Horowitz and J. Suchlicki (New Brunswick: Transaction Publishers, 1998), 449.
3 Ibid.

and international events was obviously limited.[4] Due to the shortage of paper, *Granma* became the only *daily* newspaper in Cuba from 1991.

Our written sources will allow us to inquire about the perceptions and criteria of the Party about the changes in Eastern Europe and the Soviet Union, but they also help us gain some rough insight into what kind of information most of our interviewees had daily access to at that specific moment. So, how did *Granma* present and assess some important events and processes that reflected problems and changes in Eastern Europe and the USSR (1989–1991)? How did *Granma* present and evaluate the Collapse as the events were unfolding? Furthermore, how can these visions help us understand the position of the PCC and its members in the face of the Collapse?

This chapter is organized into four sections. First, I briefly discuss the Cuban press, its history, its role in society, and its readership. For this, I will rely primarily on the existing academic literature on the subject. Second, the methodology will be explained including a general description of the sources and the criteria for selecting sources, plus the procedure that I followed during the core part of the analysis. Third, an analysis of the press will be presented. During this section, I examine A) how six historical events or processes were presented; these events are considered to lead up to or be part of what eventually would be referred to as the Collapse, in all cases events or processes that reflect important problems and tensions in those societies,[5] and B) some materials that contain assessments or interpretations of the Collapse and that were published during the first three months of 1992, that is, just after the dissolution of the USSR, an event that could be said to be a sort of "concluding chapter" in the Collapse of Soviet and East European socialism. The present chapter wraps up with some preliminary conclusions.

1 The Cuban Official Press

Several authors have written about media of mass communication in Cuba, for example, John B. Harbron; Julio García Luis; Marie Laure Geoffray and Armando Chaguaceda; Maria Margarita Alonso and Hilda Saladrigas; and James W.

---

[4] James W. Carty Jr., "Mass media in Cuba," *Caribbean Studies* 6, issue on Mass Media and the Caribbean (1990): 134.

[5] These events or processes are: 1) the semi-competitive elections taking place in Poland (1989), 2) the debate on the future of the ruling workers' party in Hungary (1989), 3) the GDR migration crisis (1989), 4) the fall of Nicolae Ceaușescu (1989), 5) the debate on economic reform in the USSR that began in August 1990, and 6) the coup against Gorbachev (1991).

Carty Jr. In this section, I will briefly discuss and draw from some of their contributions.

Also, there is a body of literature on media in state socialist countries. I thought, as I approached this project, that becoming familiar with this literature would be interesting because of similarities between media in Cuba and other Comecon countries, even if Cuba is geographically and culturally part of the Western Hemisphere. However, Colin Sparks warns that much of the literature on the media in socialist countries is based on some precepts that have been refuted in recent years. Many works rely on the classic *Four Theories of the Press*,[6] where a distinction is made between three different Western media systems and one "communist." However, according to Sparks, "[c]ontrary to what was widely believed, there was no single, uniform and monolithic communist media system."[7] No such thing exists, he claims, as a "Leninist theory of the press" or "Soviet communist theory of the press," concepts used in earlier literature. Furthermore, according to Sparks, the media systems of the socialist countries were different one from another, they were open to Western influences, and they changed over time, so these media systems were "not the static articulation of central theories or values."[8] This claim seems to be consistent with the findings of Ágnes Gulyás, who in an article on media in Czechoslovakia, Hungary, and Poland shows that there are both similarities and differences among the three countries' media systems,[9] and that in all three cases, the economics of their media and their media systems changed over time.

But there were also some constant features. For example, in all cases bureaucratic coordination had replaced market competition, and production and distribution were organized by state monopolies.[10] Also, the general perception is that media in socialist countries "were integral parts of the power structure and were used as means of control and propaganda" and that criticism of the regime was not allowed.[11] There was not much legislation in place with regard to media, rather what existed were informal rules, a situation that

---

6   Fred S. Siebert, Theodore Peterson, and Wilbur Schramm, *Four Theories of the Press: The Authoritarian, Libertarian, Social Responsibility, and Soviet Communist Concepts of What the Press Should Be and Do* (Urbana: University of Illinois Press, 1956).
7   Colin Sparks, "Media theory after the fall of European communism: Why the old models from East and West won't do any more," in *De-Westernizing Media Studies*, eds. James Curran and Myung-Jin Park (London: Routledge, 2000), 40.
8   Ibid., 32.
9   Ágnes Gulyás, "Communist media economics and the consumers: The case of the print media of East Central Europe," *International Journal on Media Management* 3, no. 2 (2001).
10 Ibid., 77.
11 Ibid., 74.

made it possible to exercise a "stricter control" over media content.[12] Another characteristic is that there was a high level of subsidies, and a strong culture of books and press had developed, something that was reflected in the high percentage that read newspapers and followed other media.[13]

In general terms, I find these characteristics also applicable to Cuba during the years 1989–1992.[14] In Cuba, the press, radio, and television are still under the control of the Communist Party, and in 1989–1992, internet access had not been developed in the country. In his article written on the Cuban media, that was first published well before internet became widely used on the island, John D. Harbron, describes the print and electronic mass media of Cuba as centralized in the sense that they follow the line established by the PCC but also as decentralized as they are controlled through "a bureaucratic expansion of media outlets that fulfill the special publishing responsibilities of various government agencies."[15] Harbron refers to the existence of supervisory agencies such as the Union of Journalists of Cuba (UPEC), the Cuban Institute of Radio and Television (ICRT), and the Department of Revolutionary Orientation (DOR).[16] The basic function of the DOR was ideological coordination "among the editors, publishers, and television and radio station managers as promulgated by the central committee of the Party."[17] The author also cites a study by John Spicer Nichols, according to which, in the early 1980s, 32 (71%) of 45 people with decision-making power over media policies in Cuba had "at least one significant affiliation with the Cuban power structure," and 25.2% of all journalists were Party members.[18] It is likely that the latter percentage was even higher in *Granma*, as it is the official organ of the Central Committee of the Communist Party of Cuba, and it is probable that this number increased

---

12 Ibid., 75.
13 Ibid.
14 Since then, there have been significant changes in Cuba's situation. Mostly, this is due to new information and communication technologies that have favored independent publishing and access to information from outside of Cuba, which again has had a certain impact on state media as it also has had to adapt to the new technologies and the new media landscape. One could argue that major traditional media such as *Granma* have changed surprisingly little. I will describe some changes regarding access to information in Cuba in Chapter 5. With regard to legislation, Cuban journalists have for years criticized the absence of a Press Law. In 2015, journalist Fernando Ravsberg reported that a law was under way that would regulate this activity. See: Fernando Ravsberg, "Ley de prensa" http://cartasdesdecuba/ley-de-prensa/.
15 Harbron, 446.
16 Ibid.
17 Ibid.
18 Ibid., 447.

furthermore amongst journalists who were trusted with covering issues of strategic importance to the Cuban state, such as the USSR and Eastern Europe.

With regard to the content of the press, a common denominator with the media in Eastern Europe is that "sensationalism, crime and human interest stories were disapproved of and neglected unless there was a lesson to be learned."[19] My observations indicate that the Cuban press is also similar in this regard. Carty Jr. wrote in 1990 that the Cuban press usually "interpret domestic and international events and trends from the Marxist–Leninist perspective in a systematic and rigorous manner."[20] He argues that "The few interviews of the public by print reporters produce only syrupy endorsements [...]. There is insufficient feedback from the public regarding their deep views."[21] Furthermore, he criticized the lack of "much needed editorial comment."[22] Harbron describes a tame but not always uncritical press and wrote that "*Granma* can be critical of the activities of state agencies when Castro and the Party brass decide it must be so."[23]

Although I broadly agree with the claims of Carty Jr. and Harbron, this study will show that in the context of the Collapse, there are quite a few cases where the data do not fit these general descriptions. The newspaper did not always systematically and rigorously interpret events, as Carty Jr. suggested. While what Harbron wrote on criticism may be true for internal affairs, in the coverage of the Collapse, the relation between "official views" and what was published was sometimes more contradictory.

A brief look at some key moments in the history of the Cuban revolutionary press can help us understand it better. It is important to note that there have been some changes over time. Notably, until the mid-1960s, the press was more critical, and there was a limited and short-lived opening of the press in the late 1980s. Although this does not invalidate the general observations by Carty Jr., these nuances are of special importance to us as our study centers precisely on that period.

With respect to the early years of the Revolution, it should be remembered that the coup by Fulgencio Batista in 1952 interrupted the Cuban constitutionality. The Batista regime imposed censorship and persecuted the press. However, newspapers were private, and there were some that maintained a critical

---

19 L. John Martin and Anju Grover Chaudhary, *Comparative Mass Media Systems* (New York: Longman, 1983), in Gulyás, 74.
20 Carty Jr., 134.
21 Ibid.
22 Ibid.
23 Harbron, 449.

line toward Batista's government, especially (but not exclusively) the magazine *Bohemia*.[24]

After Fidel Castro took power in 1959, most of the private press disappeared within about 18 months, although not because it was directly shut down by the government—with some exceptions, such as the pro-US *Diario de la Marina*, which was forced to close. Rather, the disappearance of private print media was largely related to other factors. One of them was the appearance of publications edited by the revolutionary state, which meant that the private press had to compete with state media that were subsidized and probably attractive for many as it was associated with a popular Revolution. Other factors were nationalizations in other sectors, which meant there was no longer a private sector that could buy advertising space, as well as the abandonment of media by the owners, sometimes attributed to acts of sabotage against the Revolution but perhaps often because they feared that the Revolution would not be reversible and would not have room for them.

Private media was also affected by sabotage actions by workers who opposed the conservative editorial line of the editors. One well-known phenomenon at the time was *la coletilla*, small texts expressing revolutionary messages that the workers included without authorization just before the newspaper went to print and that questioned the official line of the newspaper.[25] Furthermore, one factor needs to be mentioned that was probably of much greater importance than these acts of sabotage: Migration in the early years of the Revolution caused the middle class to shrink, a group with a high number of newspaper readers.

Still, during the first half of the 1960s, Cuban journalism was "extraordinarily rich in experiences," according to the Cuban revolutionary journalist and researcher García Luis.[26] Cuban journalism, it should be specified, was not pluralistic in the sense that the word is used in many other countries, but one that was positioned politically "within the Revolution," as Fidel Castro had asked in his *Palabras a los intelectuales* ("Words to the intellectuals") in June of 1961, only a few months after the Bay of Pigs invasion in the month of April.

García Luis asserts that this relative pluralism and the wealth of experiences started disappearing in 1965, when the government restructured the daily press. In the words of García Luis, there was "a frank setback" in "professional content and journalistic creativity [...]."[27] *Granma*, a newspaper that emerged

---

24 García Luis, 76.
25 Ibid., 78.
26 Ibid., 79.
27 Ibid., 81.

in 1965 and has since then been the main newspaper of the country, developed a close link with the political leadership of the country, with visits every night of key figures to the premises where it was made.[28]

According to García Luis, "The Revolution configurated the institutional press model upon totally endogenous bases, in moments of sharp political contradictions with the Soviet Union, when the levels of trade and cooperation with that country still did not indicate the high degree of dependence that it would reach years later";[29] however, although apparently there was no condition from the Soviets that Cuba should implement media policies similar to those in the USSR, that model was an "underlying paradigm"[30] and a "source of reference,"[31] and this may have contributed to "the adoption of similar structures and systems of relations" in the Cuban press.[32]

As mentioned, in the 1970s, Soviet influence increased in Cuba. In 1975, Cuba adopted a Constitution and an institutional framework that closely resembled the Soviet model, although it also has its particularities. However, integration with the Soviet Union and Soviet influence increased during this decade. This decade also saw a period characterized by strong censorship and the marginalization of artists, the so-called "Five gray years" or *Quinquenio Gris* (1971–1976).[33]

However, García Luis believes that the negative changes within the press should not be understood in the context of the process of increased Soviet influence that took place in the 1970s or in the context of the *Quinquenio Gris*: "Nothing exceptional happened in the press during those so-called *five gray years*," he claims, "except for a sustained setback and loss of efficiency, because in the press, the fundamental rupture had already occurred [...] since 1965 one had begun to implement some lines of direction (*líneas*) that were similar to the Soviets in the media management system."[34]

---

28   Ibid. Curiously, one private newspaper, *El Mundo*, survived all of these changes. This newspaper followed market patterns and had a somewhat different profile than the country's hegemonic press (for example, it published private business ads until 1968). Still, it did not oppose the Revolution or the government. It disappeared in 1969, after a fire took place at its premises. After that, all major media were controlled by the Party and the Cuban State.
29   Ibid., 84.
30   Ibid., 85.
31   Ibid.
32   Ibid.
33   This term is controversial. Some Cuban artists have expressed the view that this situation lasted more than five years, and that it was worse than what the adjective "gray" would suggest.
34   García Luis, 115.

Some scholars have remarked that there was an opening in the media toward the end of the 1980s. Geoffray and Chaguaceda state that there was a "short and accidental spring that permitted a certain criticism in print as well as audiovisual media, a spring that was essentially interrupted with the economic crisis of the 1990s [...] and the reinforcement of the siege mentality which the end of the Soviet bloc implied [...]."[35]

While I agree with this affirmation, I believe that this process was not *only* accidental, although it might have been to a large degree. It is true that the liberalization processes that took place in the Soviet Union and in some countries in Eastern Europe had an impact on Cuban intellectuals and their journalism. With Gorbachev's *Perestroika*, the reporting of press agencies and leading media in the Soviet Union became more critical and open, and the Cuban press depended to some degree on information from these sources. The Soviet publications that were sold on the island until 1990 also changed their political and editorial positions toward more pro-reformist and even anti-socialist stances. Academics and leaders who had been to the USSR or in other ways had become influenced by reformist ideas tried to introduce a greater media openness than perhaps the authorities would have been willing to accept at the time, taking advantage of calls by Fidel Castro for rectifying past errors, a discourse that had been strong since the mid-1980s.

So to some degree, one could certainly speak of "openness" as accidental or something not desired by Cuban authorities. But while the government was certainly not in favor of any radical opening of the press and in general distanced itself from reforms in the Soviet Union, the policies of the Cuban government were a bit more contradictory with regard to the press. García Luis shows that various organs and leaders of the PCC did make quite frequent calls

---

[35] See: Marie Laure Geoffray and Armando Chaguaceda, "Medios de comunicación y cambios en la política de información en Cuba desde el 1959," *Temas de Comunicación*, no. 29 (2014): 178. This criterion is echoed by people familiar with the subject as journalists in Cuba. Fernando Ravsberg, who had been for many years a correspondent for BBC Mundo in Cuba, during a brief and informal exchange told the author of this study that in the late 1980s, there was a tendency toward increasing openness in the Cuban media. This criterion is also shared by Cuban novelist Leonardo Padura, who worked in the Cuban press at the time. In an interview with the Argentine newspaper *La Nación*, he refers to a "springtime" in journalism in the 1980s, which he says ended in the early 1990s: "It was a very special 'parenthesis' in the development of Cuban journalism, during which a number of conditions were in place—as one usually says, objective and subjective—that allowed for a different journalism." He attributes the end of this stage to the lack of paper, which seems to us to be only part of the explanation. See: Leonardo Padura, interviewed by Astrid Pikielny, 2014.

for a more critical and autonomous press, although one should keep in mind that these were not followed up with new laws or other more fundamental changes. Such calls were issued in 1976, 1979, and 1980,[36] in the latter case in a speech given by Raúl Castro on behalf of the Party leadership. During Rectification, which began in the mid-1980s, the leader of the Revolution Fidel Castro also called for a more critical press, on at least two occasions: in 1986 (Congress of the Union of Journalists of Cuba) and 1987 (during the II Plenary of the Central Committee).[37] García Luis believes that there was some optimism in the circles of the press and that, during the late 1980s, "there was an effort to realize the so-called *new information policy*."[38]

This "spring" did not last for long. In 1992, the Cuban authorities acknowledged that they had reinforced control over the media, justifying this with the very difficult circumstances that had arisen due to the crisis and the Collapse of Soviet and East European socialism. In a speech on Cuban Press Day (see *Granma*, March 17, 1992), then member of the Political Bureau Carlos Aldana made it very clear that the time for openness was over. Aldana, who had formerly been associated with pro-Gorbachev positions, now gave a speech in which he referred to the "harmful presence" of a discourse that was "supposedly one of renewal." He said that a more restrictive line was now necessary:

> [...] neither can we ignore the ideological influence—upon press workers, people in the cultural sector, and amongst intellectuals in general—of that presumably renovating discourse whose proposals not only remained in theory, but in practice created the opposite [of its proposed goals]. We understand the confusion caused by that glare; its most immediate effect was the abrupt appearance in our sphere of society [the media] of an agenda that is strange to our reality, according to which we had to rectify errors that had not been committed here.

---

36 García Luis, 119–120.
37 Ibid., 125–126.
38 Ibid., 127. Decades later, demands for a more critical press were still being raised. At the 2013 Congress of the Union of Journalists of Cuba (UPEC), the vice president of the organization, Raúl Garcés, acknowledged that "We have gradually adopted a model which portrays reality by contrasting the alleged 'hell abroad' with Cuba's supposed 'domestic paradise.' We have often substituted reasoned argument with propaganda." See: Fernando Ravsberg, "Creating a New Media Model on the Go," *Havana Times*, July 25, 2013. The song "Catalejo" by the popular Cuban group Buena Fé is also commonly interpreted as a criticism of a culture that tends to emphasize problems outside of Cuba and minimize those within the country: "I have a telescope with which I can see the moon / I can see Mars and Pluto too / but I cannot see my little toe" (loose translation).

Aldana acknowledged in his speech that the journalists had not been enthusiastic about the idea of reversing the relative opening of the previous years: "We are not oblivious to the political cost and misunderstandings that we have been subject to in the sector" and suggested that policies could change again, at a later point: "The current circumstances force us to a period of special journalism, of journalism oriented towards resistance; we are convinced that this stage is as transitory as the resistance, as we will reestablish the situation [of a certain normality] in the country, we will return to our goal of improving the work of the press."

Besides the impact that this new and more restrictive policy had on the quality of the press, the Special Period also meant that the press was reduced in more quantitative terms. From 1989 to the beginning of 1991, *Granma* was published six days a week, generally with six and eight (full size, approximately 60 cm) pages, except for special occasions such as a significant event or an important speech (speeches are sometimes published in an integral manner in the Cuban press). As of March 1991, the newspaper stopped circulating on Mondays, except during the Pan-American Games that were held in Cuba in August of that year. On December 27 of that year, it was announced in a small note on the newspaper's front page that the number of pages would be reduced to six pages twice a week and four pages three times a week due to problems in the supply of paper from the Comecon countries. As of March 17, 1992, the newspaper changed its format into a tabloid with eight (occasionally 12) pages, which implied a further reduction in content as there was much less content on each page than before. These changes may have further contributed to limiting the degree of diversity in the newspaper.

Even if the Cuban press is characterized by a series of control mechanisms and impositions from above, as well as a culture of self-censorship, one should not overlook that journalists are also professionals, as well as human beings with ideals and desires, a relation to society, and so on. In Cuba, journalism studies last for five years. This career choice serves, surely, as a political filter and a mechanism to instill certain political values in students. However, it would be a mistake to reduce these courses to merely a mechanism of political indoctrination. During those five years, the students learn the techniques and principles of the profession and an ability to analyze, which sometimes are in tension with outside expectations or restrictions and pressures on the work of the journalist.[39]

---

39   Years before starting my investigation, I had a conversation with a Cuban student of journalism that was revealing. She said that in her classroom, the students had to read and discuss a text about how media manipulates the public, written by Noam Chomsky.

WRITTEN SOURCES ON THE COLLAPSE 53

The Cuban public has a high educational level and when their media is openly controlled by the state, this can create a more skeptical and critical reader who knows how to read between the lines. The Cuban researcher María Margarita Alonso argues that the low saturation of information and the lack of publicity can influence how readers are interacting with the media.[40]

Finally, media penetration from the Western capitalist world must be mentioned. The media isolation of socialist countries has sometimes been exaggerated. Sparks goes so far as to claim that the media systems of Eastern Europe, "far from being isolated and closed against bad imperialist influences [...] were, for the most part, surprisingly open."[41] In the case of Cuba, the country of course exists in the middle of a world dominated by capitalism, and an important part of the information transmitted or published by official media came from the Western world including the United States. It should be enough to mention that in 1988 the Cuban television broadcast a total of 288 US films (*El País*, April 8, 1990, citing Cuban "official data").[42] Because of the geographical

---

Although Chomsky's works deal mostly with media in capitalist societies, she told me that during the classroom discussion some other students began to question whether the Cuban press did not also resort to some of the techniques of manipulation described by Chomsky. After this investigation was concluded, another study came out by Anne Natvig, which suggests that this episode should perhaps not have been that surprising. These confirm that journalism studies in Cuba are not so unlike similar programs in other Western countries, and that they are of a certain quality. Natvig furthermore found that students often find it difficult to remain true to their professional ideals as they graduate, and have to work within rigid and politically controlled media. See: Anne Natvig, Cuban journalism students: between ideals and state ideology. *Journalism Education 2018*; Volume 7 (1), pp. 19–28.

40 Maria Margarita Alonso and Hilda Saladrigas, *Teoría de la Comunicación: Una introducción a su estudio* (Havana: Pablo de la Torriente Editorial, 2006).
41 Sparks, 32.
42 Back in the 1970s, the North American cultural influence was more limited, and, on the other hand, that from the Soviet Union was greater. But not even during the epoch of the strongest "Sovietization" in Cuba were Western influences eliminated from the media. And by 1986, most films screened at Cuban cinemas were probably from the Western capitalist world: About 20 films from North America, 28 from the USSR, 100 from Europe, 12 from Latin America and "a few" from Africa, according to Rafael Hernandez et al., "Political culture and popular participation in Cuba," *Latin American Perspectives* (1991): 43. (The word "probably" is added since is not clear how many of the European movies were from Eastern and Western Europe, respectively.)

It should also be remembered that Cubans share a common language with many of their neighboring countries, and thus there are no major linguistical obstacles to understanding the information disseminated through media in Spanish-speaking capitalist countries. This was not the situation that Russians found themselves in, as mainly their mother tongue was spoken within the Soviet Union.

location of Cuba, radio signals from "the entire hemisphere" could be heard on the island.[43] Satellite dishes were not common in the 1980s, but in more recent years they began to proliferate and have an impact,[44] despite being an expensive and forbidden technology.

Another important factor is the consistent work that was done to influence Cuban opinion from outside of the country. In this sense, it should be taken into account that influential parts of the diaspora as well as the US authorities have been trying to influence the population on the island ever since the early days of the Revolution. Geoffray and Chaguaceda, citing other works, assert that despite the "hegemonic state monopoly" and the lack of competing media, the Cuban diaspora "has built its own communication network: television channels, newspapers, radios and several tabloids."[45] This diaspora is "inserted into national networks of power and powerful communication media" and thus has been able to "circulate hegemonic narratives about Cuban reality in the US and internationally."[46] Notably, in 1983, the US government created the Radio Martí station, and since 1990 there has also been a television channel (TV Martí) transmitting to the island with the declared purpose of influencing its citizens and promoting political change. The Cuban authorities try to block these signals, but the radio station seems to reach a considerable number of people. In 2003, only 2% of Cubans said they had seen or heard these transmissions.[47] However, the real figure might be higher because it is a channel managed by what is often referred to in Cuba as *el enemigo* ("the enemy"), a channel with very clear political aims, and although its existence was not a taboo, many people might have been reluctant to admit to listening to it.

In any case, it must be taken into account that people talk to each other—in Cuba, one sometimes even refers to the important rumor mill as *Radio Bemba*, bemba meaning lips—so that stories or ideas presented by Radio Martí certainly circulated more broadly than just among its active listeners.

Having given a certain background on relevant subjects, we are approaching our analysis of how the Collapse of Soviet and East European socialism was reflected in the Cuban press over a period of approximately three years. However, to understand this coverage and to even have some idea of how it

---

43 Hernández et al., ibid.
44 Geoffray and Chaguaceda, 185.
45 Isabel Molina Guzmán, "Competing discourses of community: Ideological tensions between local general-market and Latino news media," *Journalism* 7, No. 3 (2006); Gonzalo R. Soruco, "Cubans and the mass media in South Florida" (1996): in ibid.
46 Ibid.
47 "Informe: Sólo un 2% de los cubanos ha visto o escuchado transmisiones de Radio y TV Martí desde 2003," published by Cubaencuentro on February 5, 2009.

might have been received by the public, one also has to take into account how the USSR was covered by Cuban media *before* 1989. Historian Rafael Rojas has stated that "From 1961 to 1989, the vision of the Soviet Union transmitted by Cuban media was apologetic."[48]

Rojas furthermore observes that the information on Soviet culture that was reflected in Cuban media had been censured twice: "[...] first in Moscow and then in Havana."[49] While criticism of the past government of Joseph Stalin was allowed, the debate of the CPSU in the five-year period of 1985–1990 included criticism not only directed toward Stalinism, but also self-criticism or critical appreciations of the period of Leonid Brézhnev at the helm of the Party (1964–1982), a period often referred to as the period of "stagnation"; however, this criticism or version of history was not adopted in Cuba.[50] Nor were the main authors of a critical Marxism that emerged in the 1980s within the USSR read in Cuba, according to Rojas.[51] What was published was the vision of the Soviet authorities.

Rojas maintains that "[...] between 1986 and 1989, during the three decisive years of Perestroika and Glasnost, there was a radical inversion of the Soviet referential field in Cuban culture: From being a metropolitan and paradigmatic place, a source of values and languages of legitimacy, it suddenly became a subversive, dissident city, exporter of ideas and preferences (*gustos*) that were destabilizing for Cuban socialism." When it was announced that Cuba would cease distribution of *Novedades de Moscú* and *Sputnik*, in August 1989, this was "the climax" (*el momento culminante*) of this "inversion."

Regarding the coverage of Gorbachev's reforms, Mervyn Bain argues that the Cuban press did cover the problems that arose as a result of the reforms

---

48   Rafael Rojas, "Souvenirs de un Caribe soviético," *Encuentro Magazine* 48–49 (2008).
49   Ibid.
50   Ibid.
51   Desiderio Navarro (1948–2017), founder and during many years the editor of the Cuban journal *Criterios*, wrote on the (non-)reception of Soviet theoretical debate in Cuba: "It is sufficient to compare the 'offer,' the 'stock,' 'the catalogue' of the Soviet publishing and cultural world in terms of theoretical thinking with what was published in Cuba from the early 1970s to the mid-1980s and even later (when there are major changes in the correlation of forces in the local ideological sphere) to realize clearly that [he mentions a few exceptions from this rule, notably some articles published by Criterios] what was chosen from that offer was the most dogmatic or conservative of what was produced by the Soviet academic nomenclature—which was almost always, at the same time, the most mediocre, inert and intranscendent of the Soviet theoretical production." *El pensamiento cultural ruso en Criterios* (Havana: Centro Teórico-Cultural Criterios, 2009), 15–16. However, Navarro believes that a gradual "thaw" began in Cuba "from [19]83, and especially 87." See: Ibid., 21–22.

but not the problems that had led to the reforms in the first place.[52] According to Domínguez, Cuban leaders impeded access to new ideas about politics or economics coming from Moscow but also argues that some aspects of these reforms had little obvious relevance for Cubans. For example, Cuba had already seen changes in its intellectual life that anticipated Glasnost.[53] A first sign of an opening in the cultural sector came back in 1976, after a period of great closure and intolerance, when a Ministry of Culture was established with Armando Hart at its helm; a politician known for more inclusive positions.[54]

Domínguez also shows that in the late 1980s, there were certain differences in how Cuban print media related to the ideas of reform communism. Journals could be found that disseminated reform communist ideas and reported on what happened in "communist" Europe. An example of this is *Temas de la economía mundial*, published by the Centro de Investigaciones sobre la Economía Mundial (CIEM), which, according to Domínguez, showed an interest in Gorbachev's experiments, but only during the early years of these reforms. *Cuba Socialista*, on the other hand, was an official Communist Party magazine that, according to Domínguez, "respond[ed] to party directives and follows a political logic," and it never showed an interest in Soviet reforms.[55] From 1988, the publication published almost no Soviet authors at all.[56]

Also, among major newspapers and magazines, it is possible to identify differences in the treatment of reform communism, especially with regard to the exact moment when each one of them definitely distanced itself from these types of policies, because all of them eventually did. According to Domínguez, the magazine *Bohemia*, the one with the highest print numbers in Cuba, published materials with a favorable view on reform communism until at least February 1990, four months after the fall of the Berlin Wall.[57] On the other hand, the newspaper *Trabajadores*, the organ of the Cuban trade union federation (Central de Trabajadores de Cuba, CTC), clearly opposed reform communism by October 1989.[58]

---

52 Bain, 101–102.
53 Domínguez, "The Political Impact on Cuba of the Reform and Collapse of Communist Regimes," 102.
54 Later, in the 1980s, he was also seen as one of the leaders representing a friendly attitude toward reform socialism. Ibid., 103.
55 Ibid., 115.
56 Ibid., 116.
57 Ibid., 122–123.
58 Ibid. After this investigation concluded, I was informed by someone well informed on the topic of Cuban media that *Juventud Rebelde*, the newspaper of the Union of Young Communists (UJC), had somewhat more reform friendly positions than *Granma*. However, during a brief and not less than systematic comparison of some topics regarding the

Until the beginning of 1990, the previously mentioned Spanish-language Soviet publications were still circulating in Cuba, even though the Cuban authorities had announced in August 1989 that they would be withdrawn from the shelves. These publications could be said to advocate for major reforms and possibly even capitalism, although not under that name. Some books and brochures were also published by Cuban editorials that defended reformist ideas. Notably, Mikhail Gorbachev's speech to the National Assembly of Popular Power in Cuba, on April 4, 1989,[59] which presented some of his views, was published by the Cuban *Editora Política*, a publishing house, which, according to Cuban online encyclopedia *Ecured*, has as its task promoting propaganda.

Even though this synopsis shows that there was some variation in how publications available on the island treated the changes in the Soviet Union and Eastern Europe, I have centered my attention primarily on *Granma* because, among other reasons, the others did not have the same impact on the population (it was the daily newspaper with the broadest circulation), nor did they have the same authority as a voice of the Party, and our main interest in this study is, as stated, Party perceptions.

Collapse at the start of this investigation, I did not detect any significant differences in their coverage. *Juventud Rebelde*'s coverage of the Collapse and other issues at the time might be worth examining more closely, since Cuba's young communists were often more reform friendly.

59   Fidel Castro and Mikhail S. Gorbachev, *Una amistad inquebrantable* (Havana: Editora Política, 1989).

CHAPTER 2

Granma and the Written News as a Method

As I have already pointed out, the main written sources have been selected from old editions of the *Granma* newspaper. The editions used for this study were published between early January 1989 until the end of March of 1992 and were located in the newspaper library of the José Martí National Library and the archives at the building where *Granma* and other major newspapers are edited, both located by the famous *Plaza de la Revolución*, where the government and important departments are also located. I was allowed to enter together with my collaborator Raynier Hernández Arencibia, who used a camera to digitize all the newspapers, a total of approximately 9,000 pages.

First, I went to the José Martí National Library because it took several weeks of bureaucratic formalities to get the necessary documents to be able to access *Granma's* official archive. Some older copies of *Granma* at the National Library were physically damaged, apparently by a sports fan who had more or less systematically cut out news stories to his or her interest, and the sports section was sometimes located on the obverse page of the international news section. Upon receiving permission to access the archives on *Granma's* premises, it became clear that their copies were in excellent condition. Due to time constraints, however, it was not possible to digitalize for a second time the editions of 1989 and parts of 1990; our collaborator had already photographed these at the National Library newspaper archive. The damages, however, are only present in some editions, and although I cannot guarantee that I have seen all relevant materials, there is little reason to believe that there were any removed materials that would significantly change the results.

In parallel with digitalization, I spent between two and three months sifting through the newspapers to familiarize myself with *Granma*. During the process of reading, I pursued a simple list of relevant headlines and descriptions on anything that was written on Eastern Europe (excluding the USSR) between early 1989 and late 1990. Everything was included unless it had clearly no obvious relevance to our research, such as was the case, for instance, with most stories on sports. Keywords were added to entries, to later facilitate the search of materials dealing with a specific topic. I noted down the size and location of materials within the newspaper whenever a topic seemed to be "downplayed" or "highlighted." Though this might seem excessive, the process helped in gaining an overview and made it possible to eventually select more specific topics that the study could focus on.

When studying the coverage of the USSR, at an early point I decided to concentrate on two specific events in this country that took place over more or less short periods of time—which will soon be identified—and deemed it unnecessary to compile such a thorough table of the complete USSR coverage.

In the same sense, with regard to the assessments of the Collapse in early 1992, it was not necessary to create tables or any other particular techniques to organize the materials, as the number of texts with relevant information was relatively limited. Accordingly, in the latter cases, we mainly conducted a chronological review of any relevant materials, sifting through the editions and making notes along the way.

According to Francisco Alía Miranda, one of the historian's main tasks is to select materials, a task that is not separate from the analysis itself; rather, it takes place during the process of analysis.[1] It is necessary to select the topics and texts to be analyzed (in our case, news, articles, etc.), but the continuous work of selection does not cease there because the researcher must constantly eliminate units of significance that are not relevant for the analysis.

Of the 9,000 digitized pages, only a relatively small number contained relevant information for the study. But even if everything that had no direct relation to the Collapse was removed from the corpus, the amount of material would still be too big to be manageable. The decision was therefore made to analyze only some specific and highly relevant events that were presented and treated by the newspaper.

I therefore selected events with the help of set criteria as well as existing academic literature on the collapse of Soviet and East European socialism:

We are mainly interested in *events and processes that have been highlighted by academic literature as key milestones in the dissolution of the Socialist Bloc.* These should be *events or processes that, at the time they took place, could be identified with relative ease as elements that were to impact the future of Soviet and East European socialism, in some way or another.* We included these criteria as there might also have been events and processes whose significance could not be expected to have been easily visible to their contemporaries.

Based on these criteria, I chose a total of six events or processes:
- Elections in Poland (1989).
- Debates in Hungary on the future of the ruling Hungarian Socialists Workers' Party (1989).

---

1 Francisco Alía Miranda, *Técnicas de investigación para historiadores: las fuentes de la historia* (Madrid: Síntesis, 2008), 55–56.

- Increasing illegal migration and opening of the borders of East Germany (1989).
- Rebellion in Romania and the execution of Nicolae and Elena Ceaușescu (1989).
- Debates in the USSR with regard to or surrounding the Shatalin Plan, a radical proposal for economic reform (1990).
- The short-lived coup against Gorbachev (1991).

In addition to analyzing coverage on these six topics, I identified and analyzed the comments and assessments published in the *Granma* newspaper between January and March 1992 about the Collapse. Although the Soviet Union had already changed largely before its end in December 1991, and severe crisis was evident long before this moment, one should recognize that the moment of the USSR's formal dissolution represented a sort of closure of a chapter, since the USSR, the most important country in the socialist community, had formally ceased. This also meant the dissolution of Cuban–Soviet relations. It seemed logical to us, therefore, that more holistic appreciations would appear during those early months of 1992, representing an effort to assess what could by then be more clearly perceived as the end of the Socialist Bloc.

For the analysis of the selected materials, I have relied on the book *Técnicas de investigación para historiadores: las fuentes de la historia* by Francisco Alía Miranda, which proposes the Documentary Analysis of Content (Análisis Documental de Contenidos, ADC) as a methodology for the analysis of newspaper texts.

The ADC is not characterized by "rigid norms"[2] and requires that the analyst "assume his protagonism, adopting the necessary strategies for each situation [...]."[3] However, the use of this qualitative technique generally follows three phases: 1) reading/comprehension, 2) analysis, and 3) synthesis.[4] The first phase, reading/comprehension, consists of establishing a hypothesis and of decoding, that is, interpreting and representing the information contained in the text. During what Alía Miranda calls the analysis phase, the text must be segmented and irrelevant units of significance removed, and thereafter it must be interpreted again. In the synthesis phase, according to Alía Miranda, the researcher should "compose the information that results from the analysis,"[5] a phase that normally concludes with the writing of a text.

---

2 Ibid., 55.
3 Ibid.
4 Ibid., 55–56.
5 Ibid.

Alía Miranda also gives some methodological recommendations that I have tried to keep in mind. He maintains that the use of the press as a historical source requires a "strong critical spirit";[6] it is necessary to know the history of the newspaper and its interests, and "never forget [...] that the press, in addition to information, political opinion, literature or feature, is ideology." Miranda further presents recommendations for the use of the press as a historical source, which he summarizes in seven points.[7] I include the list as some points have served as guiding lines as I worked on the analysis, but also as a means to highlight some important differences between the Cuban press and other countries and to underline some things to keep in mind when analyzing Cuban newspapers.

1) The historian, according to Alía Miranda, "must always keep in mind the conditioned retrieval of the information that is displayed in the journalistic text. Most readers read what the newspaper wants them to read."[8] We must carefully examine the use of visual space in print newspapers. Alía Miranda argues that "the journalist guides the reader, and the historian must be aware of this type of alteration." The Gutenberg Diagram states that the reader usually begins reading in the upper left corner, before "entering" the page.[9] "The eye tends to move diagonally towards the lower right corner," that is, there is a "reading gravity line," although there may be "optical magnets" that draw the reader away from this line.[10] On the other hand, the headline occupies the most prominent place of a news story, and it contributes, together with the lead paragraph or intro, "to guide how the newspaper is read."[11] The location where the text has been placed on the page, as well as the page number, can affect the reader's attention. If there is a lot of news on the front page, the reader "might place their attention on some story or another"; however, if there is only one, there is no doubt about which one will become noticed.[12] The extension or length of a news story or any other text also implies a need for assessment.[13]

2) "The understanding and social behavior that arises from the choice of informational texts is influenced by ideologies and by the belief system, often

---

6   Ibid., 326–327.
7   Ibid., 327.
8   Ibid.
9   Ibid., 330–331.
10 Ibid.
11 Ibid.
12 Ibid., 332–333.
13 Ibid., 330–331.

implicit, of transmitters and receivers, of the media and its consumers."[14] We recall in this regard that *Granma* played a key role for more than two decades in creating an embellished image of the Soviet Union in Cuba, an image that left a mark on people, even if the coverage eventually changed. Both the readers and journalists were formed ideologically in a world in which *Granma* played a central role.

It could be added that some texts in *Granma* are strongly politicized, so much that it may be seen as blunt indoctrination by a foreign observer, and there are certainly also Cubans that would make similar claims about their press. But by other Cubans, these texts would be considered credible because they fit into their worldview. Also, the explicitly political charge of some newspaper texts might be seen as more sincere than the apparently objective, but not neutral, approach that is common in liberal media. Even a part of *Granma's* more critical readership, which could be expected by foreigners to reject the coverage when clearly discursive or with a strong bias, might rather see such materials as a means of "raising socialist consciousness" in the population, as a justifiable mobilization of nationalist sentiments in a conflict situation, or even as a necessary counterweight to hegemonic values and information inherited from capitalist Cuba and that is entering the country from the outside.

3) "The editorial expresses the opinion of the newspaper [...]. It must be, therefore, the main focus of the historian in regard to obtaining the opinion of the political, social or economic group behind the newspaper."[15] This advice helps little in the case of *Granma*, as it contains few opinion articles. We will see, however, in the subsequent analysis, how the newspaper expresses its position in other ways.

4) Alía Miranda refers to the section of letters as "the freest in the newspaper."[16] In the case of *Granma*, in 1988 the readers' letters section was closed, and in 1989–1992 there were hardly any such letters (although there are currently).

5) "One should not think so much about intentional lies as much as half-truths, things concealed intentionally, in the things that are not said. The information is usually modified by means of silence, the highlighting of information by the use of headlines, use of location (page and place), through photo captions. The newspaper cover is a fundamental element, because the readers'

---

14   Ibid., 327.
15   Ibid.
16   Ibid.

first look is directed at it."[17] Alía Miranda seems to base these observations on the commercial press and especially the Spanish one, but these suggestions are also worthwhile in our case.

6) Alía Miranda discusses the *monadic* and *dyadic* conceptions of the press. The first considers the credibility of the press as a "function that is exclusive of the information source,"[18] while the latter emphasizes "a systematic interaction between source and audience."[19] I am inclined toward the second position, even in the case of Cuba where the press is controlled by the Party, since to some degree it does depend on what the public thinks; in this sense, one should take into account what Alía Miranda calls "the cognitive context and the criteria or scale of truthfulness (*baremo de veracidad*)" that the readers possess,[20] to the extent that this is possible.

7) He also warns that "[...] censorship has been important in the history of Spain, but we cannot get obsessed with that. More than censorship, we must not forget self-censorship."[21] This point is also very relevant for the study of the Cuban press. *Granma's* journalists or the people that select the contents of the newspaper may have been concerned about the reactions of other actors when doing their work: What will the director say, what will the Department of Revolutionary Orientation say, what will people say, and even, what would an eventual anti-communist post-Fidel regime say, or what would a potential employer in a reformed or capitalist Cuba say (by the early 1990s, Cuba was in crisis, and it is likely that many must have thought of regime change as a real possibility)? On the other hand, for many media workers, there was clearly a feeling of fidelity and solidarity toward "sister" parties and governments that were part of the international communist movement and one did not want to harm or disrespect these entities or tension Cuba's relations with key allies, especially in a situation that could be perceived as delicate and threatening.

Another key contextual element is that Cuba had been under strong US pressure for several decades. In this context, a culture had arisen in press circles that prioritized unity and the need to protect the country above all. In this sense, the warning to not "give weapons to the enemy" (*darle armas al enemigo*) is common in Cuban press circles and political circles in general. For instance, reporting on internal conflicts or social problems could help the "enemy" legitimize a policy of aggression, such as the US embargo or blockade, or give them the means of interfering more efficiently.

---

17   Ibid.
18   Ibid.
19   Ibid.
20   Ibid.
21   Ibid.

Before presenting the analysis, it should be clarified which types of newspaper texts will be analyzed and their respective role in *Granma's* coverage of the Collapse of Soviet and East European socialism. Here, we distinguish among three main genres, based on the typology of Daniel Jorques Jiménez, cited by Alía Miranda:[22]

1) *Overview or outline information texts (Textos informativos de relieve).* These first appeared in the Anglo-Saxon world, and they "focus on the priority explanation of the event as such."[23] They are divided into three types of texts: News in brief, Explanatory news in brief, and Interviews.

The coverage of Eastern Europe and the USSR between 1989 and 1992 consists mainly of overview information texts. The number of interviews is not great, but beginning in April 1989, there are some interviews with directors of official communist or workers' party newspapers in allied socialist countries. They are representatives of sister parties that for the time being still have a hegemonic position within each country of the "socialist community." These interviews give a more or less critical and realistic review of some key problems and conflicts in their countries and stand out as particularly frank and informative, because *Granma*, most of the time, reproduces news stories without offering much comment but probably also because public discourse had, by 1989, become more openly critical in those countries than what was common in Cuba at the time, and this was reflected in the way these foreign Party representatives expressed themselves.

Still, the news in brief and how it was presented can also give valuable information how the PCC, its members, and Cuban journalists perceived events in the Soviet Union and East Europe and on the strategies employed by the newspaper and the Cuban state to defend its interests and ideology.

2) *Detailed information texts (Textos informativos de detalle o precisión).* These are texts that "focus their interest in the explanation of the data" and are "closely linked to a primarily Latin conception of written journalism."[24] They can be divided into three types: [In-depth, detailed] news report (*reportaje*), criticism/review (*crítica*), and features (*crónica*).

It is striking that *Granma* contains few texts of this type in general and very few regarding the situation in the USSR and Eastern Europe, despite the fact that the readers must surely have been interested in understanding what was going on. By 1989, there were still some reports that gave an embellished vision that was not representative of the state of things in the socialist countries; take, for example, one that told about a visit to an apparently successful soap

---

22 Ibid., 334.
23 Ibid.
24 Ibid.

factory in the USSR (March 7, 1989), which was published just before Gorbachev's visit to Cuba. During subsequent months and years, there were no close-ups on "everyday life" in the Soviet Union, not even embellished accounts such as the one from the soap factory, and most news stories on politics would probably be closer to "Explanatory news in brief" than to reports.

Some texts that could be described as criticism (*crítica*) or chronicles talk about Eastern Europe and the USSR, but they are few.

3) *Opinion genres* (*Textos de acumulación*). These types of texts code and interpret the information and thus also underline the importance of what is happening. In the view of Alía Miranda, these represent an elitist approach where "the original knowledge of the event is a privilege of the journalistic class," and the journalist is "a depositary of a kind of fiduciary commitment of ideological, moral and civic responsibility on behalf of the community of citizen-readers." Its main subcategories are: opinion columns, editorials, and analytical articles.

Although there are some texts of this type in *Granma*, not many dealt with the process of the dissolution of Soviet and East European socialism. The speeches of Fidel Castro provided some explanation; these were at times published in an integral manner in the newspaper, but most of them touched upon other issues and not so much on Soviet or East European affairs. There were some other opinion texts, notably "Sendero Borchornoso I" ("Shameful Path," possibly a word play on the Peruvian Maoist guerrilla group "Shining Path," September 18, 1989) and "Sendero Borchornoso II" (September 19, 1989), which have been cited in other studies, that criticized the attitude of a group of Hungarian journalists toward Cuba and did so in a very direct way. They were striking because they covered a large space in the newspaper and because it was the first time for *Granma* to speak so clearly and so extensively about the forces in Eastern Europe and the USSR that were taking advantage of the media openness in their countries to criticize an allied country; they viewed Cuba as backwards and rigid as it had not embraced reforms.

There was also an opinion text when the decision was taken to withdraw and stop the circulation of the Soviet pro-reformist magazines *Novedades de Moscú* and *Sputnik*, only a few weeks earlier (September 4, 1989), and there are some others. Although *Granma* generally was not fond of opinion columns and editorials in general—speeches, synopses of speeches, and analysis articles were a bit more common—the generally low number of any texts that tried to assess what was happening in the Soviet Union and Eastern Europe could have been a way of downplaying the importance of events.

On the few occasions when *Granma* published opinion columns or analysis that touched upon the situation in other socialist countries during the period that we study, they were written by foreign or local specialists, although there is little doubt that they would not have been published if they were not also close to positions that existed within the PCC leadership and amongst *Granma*'s editors. Since these comments were not presented as official criteria of the newspaper, the newspaper avoided having to answer for their content.

One visual characteristic of *Granma*'s coverage of the Collapse is that when there are several news pieces on a specific country on the same day—this was especially common in its coverage of the USSR—*Granma* often visually grouped these into a large box or rectangle. These boxes always had a main headline that introduced the content of the first of the "news in brief" items contained in the box, or several of them. Sometimes, the first news in brief item within the box was of a more explanatory character, while the others were pieces of information on different events taking place in the USSR. News in brief items also appeared at times within the column "Direct Line" (*Hilo Directo*). I conclude this discussion of method with an illustration that shows (see Figure 1) how this latter style of presentation is visually structured.

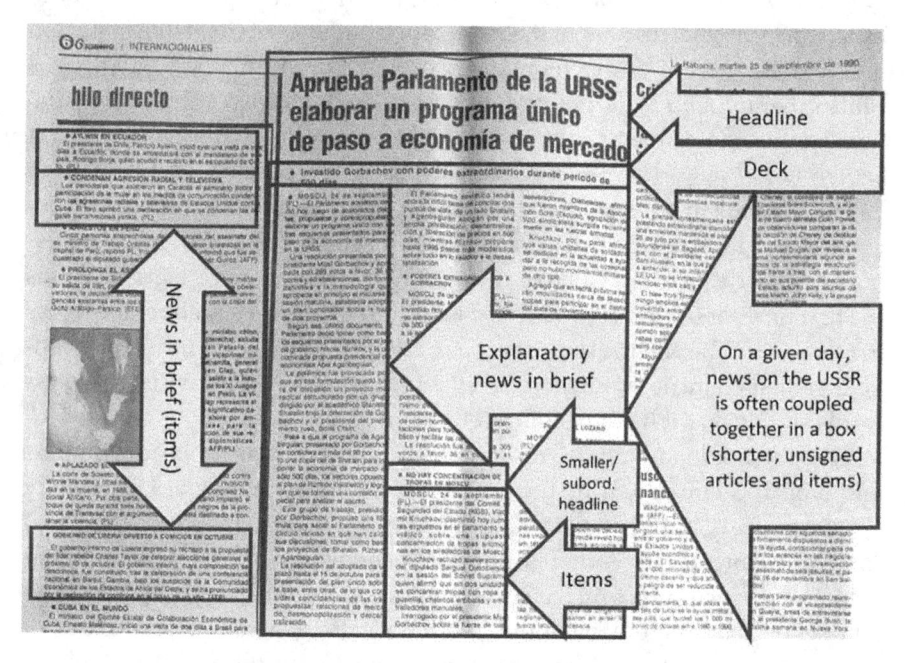

FIGURE 1   *Granma*, September 25, 1990; the upper part of the internationals page, with its "Soviet box" in the middle, and "Direct link" (Hilo Directo) on the left

CHAPTER 3

Analyzing the News Accounts

This chapter sets out to analyze *Granma's* coverage of six historical events and processes, four of which occurred in Eastern Europe (all taking place in 1989) and two that took place in the Soviet Union (in 1990 and 1991, respectively). Furthermore, I analyze some materials published in the newspaper during the first quarter of 1992 that can shed light on how the PCC and actors belonging to the organization saw, portrayed, and responded to the fall of Soviet and East European socialism right after the Collapse.

I will refer to many texts published in the *Granma* newspaper. To avoid repetitions, I only refer to the date of publication of the news.[1] Unless otherwise indicated, the materials are from *Granma*. I have specified the name of the newspaper, the page number, and the name of the article only where necessary for reading and explanation or where it is in some way relevant for analysis.

1 The Crisis of Socialism in Eastern Europe

1.1 *Example 1: Elections in Poland—A Correspondent Leaves Her Mark*

In Poland in 1989, open discontent and conflict with the authorities were not new occurrences. Resentment toward Soviet influence had already been present in the post-war years but had increased over time, together with criticism of the government and the system. The opposition Solidarity trade union was founded in the early 1980s and gained millions of adherents, an unprecedented situation in the socialist community. Between December 1981 and July 1983, the government imposed martial law. As the 1980s were fading, in 1988, a series of strikes increased pressure on the governing elite.

In 1989, the opposition gained power. Following a dialogue between the government and the opposition, in June of 1989, semi-competitive elections were held for the first time. These ended with the election of a new parliament, which had a considerable opposition presence. In July and August, according to a pact between the opposition and the socialist party PUWP, a president

---

[1] Every day, at least two editions of the newspaper were published. We have analyzed the second edition published on each day, occasionally the third. According to the archivist of the *Granma* newspaper, the first one was for distribution in rural areas, and it was printed before the sports results were ready. Apart from that they are the same, she informed us.

representing the ruling party and a prime minister of the opposition were appointed. It was unprecedented that a Comecon country, officially socialist, had a non-communist prime minister.

Granma gave considerable coverage to Poland's internal crisis during the first half of 1989 and also to the elections that took place in the summer of that year. The coverage was relatively clear and understandable, and detailed enough so that the reader could easily understand—without much prior knowledge of the country and its political situation—that a serious crisis was taking place there.

It is worth pointing out that by mid- to late 1989, *Granma* had yet given few suggestions that a major "crisis of socialism" was in the making, although it continuously reported on problems in the Socialist Bloc. Most of the coverage still treated the problems in Poland and Hungary as more or less isolated situations, first in one country and then the other, and later that year as something that was affecting Eastern Europe but would not necessarily mean the end of the USSR as well.

Yet José Machado Ventura, a leading politician and veteran of Fidel Castro's insurrection, warned in a commentary on June 8, 1989 that "as the danger of a World War gets more distant, the efforts of capitalism to try to defeat socialism in the field of ideology will get more persistent." He also suggested that Soviet and East European socialism had internal weaknesses, allegedly products of their own mistakes. And as has been seen in the introduction to this thesis, one and a half months later, on July 26 the same year, Fidel Castro made his famous warning that the Soviet Union could disappear. However, the rest of *Granma* did not immediately change its tone even after these warnings, and they do not seem to have had any strong immediate repercussions on what was being written on Eastern Europe and the USSR. Most of the time, the news was still being narrated and presented without much comment, giving a sense of normality, despite the news stories themselves reflecting strong symptoms of discontent.

The lack of comment may be in part a media strategy, to avoid the spread of pessimism and critical views on socialism, but it probably also suggests that most of the Party and most journalists did not, by mid-1989, fully appreciate how serious the problems were, much less foresee an outcome such as the one suggested by Fidel Castro. The coverage of Polish politics and society clearly reflected some of the problems that caused many Poles to reject their government, even when the country was an ally of Cuba. It is possible that *Granma* had practiced an "embellishing" coverage of Poland in previous years, but by mid-1989, it was neither embellishing nor very critical. Still, there was a certain level of detail and openness to the events themselves. In the news, some slogans

ANALYZING THE NEWS ACCOUNTS

and demands of the opposition were reproduced, although little space was given to the reasoning or arguments behind these slogans and demands. Yet the desk in Havana was more restrictive than the correspondents and apparently tried to "hide away" incoming news that it did not like. News items that it considered to be negative—events that did not favor the ruling Party or the system in place in Poland—were often placed at the bottom of a page to indicate disapproval or so that the reader would perhaps not fix their attention on it.

Let us examine some examples of the coverage.

There were *some* materials in 1989 that highlighted the links and collaboration between Cuba and Poland and also certain Polish achievements. In addition to being rare, this type of news received little space in *Granma*, but its mere existence reminds the reader of the official links between Cuba and Poland and also recalls the type of embellished stories based on official information from the Socialist Bloc that was common until the late 1980s. On April 22, 1989, a short feature or report called "URSUS: A Polish industrial colossus" was published, but after the semi-competitive elections that took place later that year, there were no more major stories of this type, just some news in brief items that mentioned official exchanges, such as: "Alicia Alonso acclaimed in Warsaw" (May 31, 1989), referring to the *prima ballerina assoluta* of Cuban ballet, or "Medal awarded to the Ambassador of Poland" (July 14, 1989).

On July 22, 1989, the newspaper featured a story entitled "Evening for the 45th anniversary of Poland," which recalls the links between Polish ruler Wojciech Jaruzelski[2] and Fidel Castro. Jesús Montané of the PCC's Central Committee, expressed his wish that the "Polish brothers present here" could "overcome the difficulties." So, these materials made clear that Cuba still had a position in favor of the governing Polish United Workers Party (PUWP) and that, at the same time, they openly recognized that their Polish allies were in a difficult situation.

Granma also published news and correspondents' stories on the internal situation of Poland throughout the year, many of these prepared by the Cuban press agency Prensa Latina. The political tendency and the tone of the materials varied, but enough information was given about the crisis in Poland so that a reader who actually noticed and read those texts should have been easily able to understand that there was a serious crisis in the country and to understand some of the main lines of conflict. For example, on February 22, 1989, there was a news story on page 4 that referred to about 800 ongoing labor disputes in Poland. The story has a descriptive tone but dedicated most space to

---

2   The leader of Poland since 1981, Jaruzelski was replaced as the Party leader on the July 29, 1989 and resigned as president of the country in December 1990.

the Polish government, the framework of which was reproduced in the third person. On February 25, on page 7, an article was published that referred to the positions of the different political forces in Poland; but again, the newspaper clearly expressed an affinity for the government's posture. It is entitled "Warnings on the dangers of the Round Table in the country," referring to a mechanism for dialogue between the government and the opposition. In this story, Polish Prime Minister Rakowski was referred to as saying that a part of the opposition wanted to create the conditions to change the country's political system.

There was some coverage on the activities of Lech Walesa, leader of the opposition Solidarity labor movement, which by the early 1980s had many millions of adherents, despite it not being recognized as an official union.[3] In general, it could be said that some news on the Polish crisis was descriptive in form, while other items had a biased or tendentious tone in favor of the government. The latter might have conditioned the reading of even the news that described events and situations in a more neutral manner.

One example of a strongly biased tone can be found on February 16 when it was reported that Walesa had called for the reduction of the country's military expenses, "to weaken the Polish defense." When the governments of East Germany and the USSR also wanted to cut their military expenses that same year, such "anti-national" motives were not attributed to their leaders by *Granma*. In a news in brief item published on August 8, 1989 ("Kiszcak tries to form a government in Poland"), Walesa was generally portrayed as a negative figure; there was even a headline that read "The PUWP rejects Walesa's divisionist proposal" (August 9, 1989), suggesting that Walesa wanted to divide the people of Poland. But perhaps there was at least one exception to this assessment of Walesa: On June 5, 1989, in a story written by Cuban correspondent Mirta Balea about the ongoing parliamentary electoral campaign, the union leader was presented as a constructive actor who questioned the "aggressive language and stance" of other Solidarity candidates. Even so, the general tendency in *Granma's* coverage was that Solidarity received a more benign treatment than Walesa, something that might be attributed to Solidarity being a mass organization and

---

3   In her reference to I. Barlinska, *Civil Society in Poland and Solidarity* (Madrid: Center for Sociological Research, 2006), 13. In this work, Barlinksa cites sources according to which Solidarity had 10 million members before the introduction of Martial Law by Jaruzelski in 1981. It had the support of approximately 25% of the population during that same decade, similar to the support that the government had. Many citizens did not support or did not fully support either of the two.

therefore something that would be difficult for a communist newspaper to question.[4]

The same story on June 5 gave important information on the upcoming parliamentary elections. It said that the polls were the first since 1947 where the opposition could present candidates. It specified that they could present candidates for "35% of seats in the congress and for a 100% of the senate seats [of the newly created senate]"; that is, the story spoke clearly about the exclusion of the opposition within the electoral system that had existed until then—it is noteworthy that this is stated so frankly as the story is about an ally of Cuba. The text also mentioned the limitations the opposition still faced.

The parliamentary elections took place on June 4. All news on this subject was prepared by Prensa Latina, and the news was in most cases relatively detailed. Still, it is striking that the stories always appear at the bottom of a page, which could be a way for *Granma's* editors to give less visibility to Prensa Latina's correspondents, who had been sent on an official mission, yet did not simply echo the positions of Cuban and Polish authorities.

On June 5, Mirta Balea referred to the celebrations and the various electoral activities of Solidarity and reported that they already had hopes of winning. The correspondent states clearly that Communist Prime Minister Mieczysław Rakowski is in serious difficulties. The news in brief item, with the long headline "It is recognized that there has been a setback in the parliamentary elections in Poland" (June 6, 1989), is of small or medium size and appears almost at the end of page 4, and because of the location, the reader could easily not notice it, or might think that this is not important news.

The next day, the story, "The Polish cabinet will resign" (June 7, 1989), was published. This text is longer, just over 50 lines, but it has been placed at the bottom of the last page, and as such, by being presented again as though it was an event of lesser importance, this physical location might even be a signal that this is something the Cuban Party would prefer people not to talk about so much. Rykowski, a spokesman for parliament, is quoted while speaking about the procedures for appointing another government and says that the "setback suffered by the government coalition reflects the rejection of mistakes made in recent times" and that the elections were "a plebiscite, and the vote results, an emotional reaction." He questions whether "the sum of personal decisions really reflects the general feeling" and calls for "understanding" and for a shared

---

4   Also, while Solidarity had, toward the late 1980s, swung toward liberal positions, some consider its early ideology to be a variant of socialism—although this is a matter of controversy.

government.[5] On June 17, 1989, *Granma* gave voice to the Polish government, which then attributed the defeat to "inconsistency at the time of introducing reforms."

Despite the tendency of "hiding away" certain stories, *Granma* gave quite broad coverage of the first round of the parliamentary elections and also of the subsequent dialogue between PUWP forces and Solidarity—not always in a neutral manner, but without omissions or distortions that could have made it impossible to understand the conflict, despite these topics being of a somewhat delicate nature as Poland was an ally and had a system similar in many senses to the Cuban one. The position of the Polish government was given priority, but the opposition was also heard quite clearly.

On the other hand, little is said about the second round of parliamentary elections that took place on June 18, 1989. In the item "Low participation in second electoral round in Poland" (June 19, 1989), however, it is explained that only 25% of the electorate participated, so not only *Granma* but also the Poles do not seem to have considered this a major event.

After the parliamentary elections, *Granma* began to publish a series of news items about the *presidential* elections, during which the two chambers of parliament would choose the future president, a position that had not existed until then. *Granma* referred to Jaruzelski's resistance to running by stating that he "had declined to accept that responsibility, claiming that his person was associated with the state of exception implemented in December 1981" (quote from *Granma*, July 19, 1989). Even so, he ended up being elected, and a day after the parliament elected Jaruzelski as president, a news item from Prensa Latina (July 20, 1989) was published that says the president had "very broad" powers that include "the right to proclaim the state of war and exception and dissolve Parliament [...]"; this may be an allusion to the state of exception in 1981–1983. *Granma* does not mention that more than 100 people were killed by the Polish regime after the introduction of Martial Law,[6] although the newspaper might have reported on this before 1989.

However, more than a year later, in 1990, *Granma* did publish a short commentary by Uruguayan leftist essayist Eduardo Galeano in which he refers to Jerzy Popieluszko, "a priest killed by state terror in Poland in 1984 [...]" (under the headline "The theory of the end of history becomes fashionable. Contempt

---

5 On June 7, 1989, *The New York Times* published a story titled "Solidarity and Warsaw Search for a Way to Govern Poland," where it states among other things that "Solidarity and the Communist Government appear to be moving toward greater cooperation in the face of the opposition's success in outpolling the Communists in Sunday's national elections." So, this is not a matter of *Granma* downplaying the probability of radical change; a compromise solution was still considered to be an option by observers, not only in Cuba.

6 BBC News, "Poland marks communist crackdown," *BBC News*, December 13, 2006.

as destiny," October 16, 1990). Galeano's essay probably was published not because of this comment but because of other opinions it contains—it might even have been published *despite* these comments. But even so, *Granma* did eventually publish an essay written by a respected friend of Cuba in which he accuses a then former ally of Cuba of "state terror." Publishing such explicit criticism in 1989 when Cuba's allies were still in power in Poland would probably have been unthinkable since *Granma* is the official organ of the Cuban Central Committee. When it was published in late 1990, it was also a way of indirectly saying that *Granma* was not afraid to talk about the evils of Poland. Another way of distancing oneself from what happened, it had little to do with Cuban reality. But let us return to the news as events were still unfolding.

Other news items in the summer of 1989 indicate the realignment of Poland toward the West. The visit of George W. Bush (July 12, 1989) and other events related to this were mentioned (for example, "Withdrawal of Soviet troops from Poland has started," July 17, 1989). Despite promises from the new Polish government to remain in the Warsaw Pact (August 26, 1989), the country soon took steps to align itself with the US and the International Monetary Fund (IMF). There are no assessments from *Granma*; they just describe what is happening.

The most notable and perhaps surprising moment in the coverage of the Polish crisis—perhaps except the inclusion of Eduardo Galeano's text a year later—is a story published on August 25, 1989 (see Figure 2). That day, there is a box with several articles or items on Poland. It is striking not only because the news that is contained in the box gives quite broad coverage on a key event that is not favorable to the Cuban government—the election of a non-socialist prime minister in a country that forms part of the "Socialist Camp"—but because parts of it are written in an ambiguous tone and contain phrases that could be intended as veiled messages in support of the Solidarity union. The coverage is published on the last page of the newspaper and has a main headline reading: "Tadeusz Mazowiecki elected as Prime Minister of Poland."[7] The box covers approximately three-fifths of the page, and it contains information on the issue from different agencies: Prensa Latina (Cuban), TASS (Soviet), EFE (Western), and the Soviet Foreign Ministry. So, there is not only quite broad coverage, but the use of sources is quite plural.

---

7 The Jaruzelski government was forced, at that time, to accept a prime minister appointed by the Solidarity union, due to the results of the parliamentary elections and since two parties that had always supported the ruling Socialist Party now gave their support to the Solidarity parliamentarian group.

FIGURE 2   *Granma*, August 25, 1989; "Tadeusz Mazowiecki, elected first minister of Poland"

The first element that attracts the reader's attention is a photo of protesters with three banners of the opposition union Solidarity. There is a caption under the photo that reports the protesters' demands: "Polish doctors, nurses, and health workers protest in Warsaw over the dramatic economic situation, shortly after having what they called a 'white march.'" *Granma* is a newspaper that most of the time presents demonstrations in other parts of the worlds as something positive, in accordance with a socialist ideal of representing the masses that demand justice. The Cuban press also refers, quite often, to health personnel as heroes (though typically referring to Cuban health personnel). Thus, the reader who only looks at the photo and for a moment disregards *Granma's* historical position on Polish politics, could easily get the impression that the government has a positive view of the Solidarity union, that they see them as "the ones below," that is, "the good ones," despite this union protesting an allied government of Cuba for years. There is no information that suggests that the marchers have been manipulated, even if one could have expected *Granma* to play this card, as it often suggests that the Cuban opposition is financed and/or controlled from outside. At least by now, it has also been documented that

Solidarity received financial support from US authorities,[8] although this obviously does not mean that it was not also a mass movement.

The first piece of news within the box comes from Prensa Latina and is written by Cuban correspondent Mirta Balea. Although the Prensa Latina journalist prefers a neutral or descriptive tone, for example, when she reports that the nomination of a non-socialist president is something "unprecedented in socialist countries," she also occasionally uses words that could indicate approval of the changes (such words have been bolded): "the **concerted** alliance," "[the] Polish **legal** opposition" (the word "legal" has positive connotations in most contexts, although it can also be simply a way of accounting for the legal regulatory horizon), "*the historical moments* that the country is experiencing," and "[the non-Communist Prime Minister said] that his government will be *open to all the country's forces.*"

The new prime minister is cited when he clarifies that Poland will continue in the socialist community and the Warsaw Treaty, which can also make the reader think that this transition is not against the interests of Cuba and the USSR.[9] The credibility of this claim is not questioned, it is simply reproduced.

However, the tone changes in a second story (also from Prensa Latina but in this case, the author is not identified). It warns that the Solidarity union tries to "exclude the PUWP" from the executive. It also mentions that there is a "tense social and labor panorama" in the country, and this is "fundamentally" attributed to the application of an adjustment plan imposed by the IMF. It is mentioned that Mazowiecki, the new prime minister, wants to approach the US, a country whose foreign policy is viewed critically by the majority of Cubans. Even so, not all readers read all the news, and the first news in brief item certainly gives an impression of the new political actors as constructive ones.

For its part, the TASS news in brief item that follows, within the same box, describes a long list of economic and social problems faced by Poles and attributes these problems to "the so-called market economy mechanisms," but if one reads these lines without knowing the Solidarity movement well, one could be left with the impression that the protesters in the photo (from Solidarity) are actually opposed to these "so-called market mechanisms," because,

---

8   The vast majority of its members did of course not have any links to the US government, nor were they necessarily supportive of that government. The information on outside financing of the Solidarity movement comes from the following article: Gregory F. Domber, "The AFL-CIO, The Reagan Administration and Solidarność," *The Polish Review* 52, No. 3 (2007).

9   *Granma* later informs that, in the new non-communist government, the once almighty PUWP retained the posts of the Minister of the Interior, the Minister of defense and the Minister of international cooperation (*Granma*, September 8, 1989).

as we saw, they are demonstrating because of the economic situation of the country. Under the smaller heading "Declarations of Walesa" (introducing a news in brief item by EFE), almost at the end of the box, the famous union leader warns that his allies "could not allow the resurgence of the monopoly of the PUWP after the agreement at the round table [dialogues between the government and the opposition]." There is talk of the need to defend reforms and receive help from the West, but little space is given to Walesa's agenda. At the end, *Granma* has included an "Opinion of the Soviet Foreign Ministry" that recognizes Mazowiecki, the new prime minister, as an interlocutor.

A close reading of the coverage on the 25th reveals enough elements to suspect that correspondent Balea could have sympathies with the Polish radical opposition or at least with some parts of this opposition and possibly is trying to use her position as a foreign correspondent to show the Cuban public that they might be worth listening to. Of course, this does not necessarily mean that she was against the *Cuban* government (Poland and Cuba were, despite everything, different realities).[10]

If this is correct, it shows that there was not only some support for Soviet and East European communist reformers within the Cuban press sector, as we saw in the introduction. In this case, the opposition that we are talking about had actually been created outside of the hegemonic Party in Poland. Cuba itself did not and does not permit opposition organizations, so this would certainly be seen by the government as a very bad example. It was an opposition that had been created outside of government-endorsed organizations. So it is possible that at least one Cuban press worker had some sympathy for a radical opposition in an allied country of Cuba's or thought that they merited some respectful coverage as they had won an election against many odds. It should still be said that at that time it was not yet known exactly how extensive the changes were going to be, and few if any expected changes in Eastern Europe to happen as rapidly as they eventually did.

Also, despite the somewhat ambiguous coverage on August 25, 1989, it could not be said that the correspondent of Prensa Latina in Poland was producing news favorable to the opposition in general, and otherwise in *Granma*, the

---

10   This practice of introducing subtle messages that criticize the socialist system also took place in other Comecon countries. According to researcher Tiiu Kreegipuu, in the Estonian Soviet Socialist Republic, in the absence of an alternative press to that of the ruling Communist Party, some journalists critical of the government tried to introduce "new topics, styles and focuses" into the official press. Kregipuu also argues that the public got used to reading "between and behind the lines" in search of "alternative messages." See: Tiiu Kreegipuu, "The ambivalent role of Estonian press in implementation of the Soviet totalitarian project" (University of Tartu, 2011), 55–56.

coverage clearly reflected a loyalty toward Poland's former leaders, although little indicates that there was great enthusiasm for them. Moreover, to understand how these articles might have been received, it is important to look at the context in which each individual article was presented. When cut out and read in an isolated manner, the coverage of Prensa Latina of Poland on August 25, 1989 might seem ambiguous, possibly even giving a slightly favorable image of the Solidarity union.

But on the same page, the newspaper also published other news or articles with headlines such as "Panama asks for solidarity" (accompanied by a drawing of a US soldier who walks on a rope with hanging letters saying "Provocation"), a story about drug traffickers in Colombia (an important US ally) and another negative piece of news about UNITA (US allies) in Angola. That is, the news was published in a context where the US government figured as a threat to the world. *Granma* had just reported on Poland's tendency to build closer ties precisely to the US, so any reader that trusted the newspaper would generally be at least a bit skeptical about the direction of developments in Poland. Solidarity's more pro-Western views were also known.

Also, on August 28, just three days after the report by Mirta Balea on the new Polish prime minister, *Granma* published a kind of interpretive historical chronicle on World War II that would undermine any idea that the newspaper had any illusions about the new Polish government. The chronicle is about the Nazi invasion of Poland and how this represented a step on the way toward Hitler's goal of invading and controlling the USSR and goes under the heading "From Hitler's swipe to the East...." Besides this headline, there is another one that appears typographically as a continuation of the headline of the historical chronicle, that reads "To the dangers of today." It introduces another text that talks about the dangers of modern-day Western capitalism and fascism. In the text about current developments, there are photos of neo-Nazis in the US and of police in West Germany attacking anti-fascist protesters, and the USSR is presented as a guarantee against the ambitions of warmongers in the West.

So, in other words, while *Granma* allowed the publication of news from Poland that was sometimes presented with a diverse focus and with a generally descriptive and less militant tone, in other parts of the newspaper, it also published materials that presented the changes in Eastern Europe as processes being promoted or exploited by fascist forces and that suggested some continuity between the Nazi expansion and the current arrival of non-socialist forces to power in Poland in 1989.

So, how do we explain this contrasting shift from an apparently more or less open attitude to changes in Poland, to suggestions that Poland is under a fascist threat? To some extent, this has to do with the differences in genres; it is not surprising that news in brief items and the news articles that predominate on the international page put a greater emphasis on describing what is happening than giving an opinion. It might also be partly explained by the physical distance between *Granma* in Havana, which sees the events in Poland from afar and interprets them within the scheme of imperial pressure, and the correspondent in Poland, who centers her focus on the visible Polish political reality on the ground. Seen from the streets of Poland, there were—independently of which outside actors might have tried to interfere and what one might have thought about the different internal actors—a crisis and a desire for change among a large part of the population. Also, this could suggest some contrast between the individual journalists, and perhaps especially those at Prensa Latina, and those trusted with editing the newspaper and writing commentary on significant issues.

Finally, it should be pointed out that after the change of government, *Granma* started publishing a considerable quantity of news about the evils of the new Poland. Even Mirta Balea has a small report on the disastrous state of Polish cinema as capitalism gains ground, and alleges how filmmakers now depend on private financing and that "[t]he 'censorship of money' is capable of replacing any other type of censorship" ("Polish cinema, full of questions," October 16, 1990). The message conveyed by *Granma* is that capitalism has not been good for Poland and the Poles.[11]

To summarize, there was relatively detailed coverage of the Polish elections in 1989 in *Granma*, although the topic was not highlighted by the newspaper. It was mostly covered in the form of news, and most of its contents were produced externally by the news agency Prensa Latina. These contents mostly drew on observation and description of the events, rather than assessing or explaining the events explicitly. Although the general coverage and even the Prensa Latina materials are often colored by the fact that Cuba had official links with Poland, the correspondents at that time seem to have had a certain autonomy with regard to the Cuban authorities, and the situation in the country they were working in seems to have allowed them a certain freedom. There is a certainly a tendency of focusing on Cuba's allies in Poland—at least until more fundamental changes took place in the summer of 1989—but this does not mean they are the only forces that are mentioned, and Mirta Balea's contributions sometimes describe problems of the country and opposition activities,

---

11 Currently, Mirta Balea appears to live outside of Cuba and writes a blog that is very critical of the Cuban government and its allies. In a blog post, she referred to Polish socialism as the "true enemy" and praises Lech Walesa: http://lasnoticiasdemirta.blogspot.no/2011_08_01_archive.html.

while also briefly mentioning previous and current democratic limitations in Poland. As we have seen, on one very particular day, the news article even seems to have reflected a certain veiled support for the opposition or at least to somehow discreetly recognize positive aspects of the elections, of the new leaders, and of the street protesters.

The news coverage, however, contrasts strongly with the little commentary there is. What there is seems to have been written or hand-picked by *Granma*'s editors. Only a few days after the news story that could be seen as somewhat sympathetic to the changes, *Granma* dedicated a whole page to some materials where it is indirectly suggested that Poland is under a fascist threat. By that time, a message is being conveyed, also through the publication of numerous news in brief items on new social problems in Poland, that the PCC considers what is happening to be very negative and that it sees Western influence as a factor behind this, or at least that is the explanation it wants to present to the public. Only discreetly is it suggested that there is anti-Soviet sentiment in this part of the world, but the reasons for this are not made very clear.

On the other hand, in late 1990, the newspaper published an essay by Eduardo Galeano that was critical of the introduction of capitalism in Eastern Europe but also accused the old Polish government of "state terror." Although not signed by *Granma* itself, this seems like a way in which the PCC recognized, one year later, abuses by the former Polish government, at least giving the reader a perspective that challenges the "blame it on the West" variants; yet this commentary only implies a critical view of certain decisions or practices, not of the Polish system itself.

Publishing this comment from an outsider could also be a way of saying that Cuba is not (that) afraid of talking about these things, since Cuba's situation is (significantly) different. Together with the editors' decision to permit relatively open news coverage as events unfolded, this suggests that the PCC recognized that both internal and external causes were in play as the system collapsed, although the latter was suggested in a major chronicle, and there is never any explicit analysis of why the government and system fell. In 1990, *Granma* published many news items that suggest that, whatever problems they used to have, the people of Poland were now suffering from capitalism.

1.2   *Example 2: The Future of the Hungarian Party—Observing the Reform Debate with Curiosity*

As the 1980s came to an end, the ruling socialist parties in Eastern Europe underwent major changes. Within the parties, factions arose or became strengthened, and the practice of democratic centralism was broken. Ideological changes accelerated and the parties yielded or were forced to give up their role as monopolistic parties.

Hungary had been through a process of reforms and by 1988, multipartyism was already developing in the country at the margins of the ruling party, then known as the Hungarian Socialist Workers Party (HSWP). In October 1989, the parliament adopted legislation that permitted multiparty parliamentary and direct presidential elections. In parallel, in 1989 there was intense internal debate about the future role of that party. *Granma* gave considerable space to these ongoing interchanges. One important question or dilemma was whether the HSWP should continue to play the role of a vanguard (socialist or communist) party. This was not a minor question since the ruling parties in Eastern Europe and the Soviet Union, as well as the one in Cuba, were characterized by an enormous power over politics and the economy, and their renunciation of this privileged position was a key step in dissolving the hegemonic system in all Eastern European countries.[12] It is also of particular interest to analyze how *Granma* covered these debates, since the Cuban authorities always strongly emphasized the importance of the single or unified party model as a guarantee of national independence and the building of socialism, and very much so in 1989.

This can be noted, for example, in the tendency of *Granma* to constantly reproduce certain statements of Soviet leader Mikhail Gorbachev at that time (1989), in which he underlined the importance of the Communist Party and/or warned against forces contrary to its leading role in society. A review of *Granma* in 1989 shows that there were news stories where this message was repeated on the following dates: January 9, 1989, February 16, 1989, March 30, 1989, July 3, 1989, July 18, 1989, August 21, 1989, September 15, 1989, September 21, 1989, September 26, 1989, September 19, 1989, November 18, 1989, and others. These stories had headlines such as "Gorbachev rejects criteria on multiparty and private property," "Gorbachev rejects intents to damage the prestige of the

---

12 According to Martin K. Dimitrov, the elimination of the Communist Party's leading role in society was one of the fundamental steps leading to the collapse of Soviet and Eastern European socialism between 1989 and 1991. Empirically, Dimitrov argues, the collapse began in these countries when they could no longer "orchestrate" electoral outcomes. The process then continued with the decision to remove the language about the leading role of the Communist Party from the constitution ("thus legalizing opposition parties") and ended "when the first free multiparty elections are held or when the country disintegrates." The end of the Party's power monopoly is, in other words, a fundamentally important step within the process of collapse. See Dimitrov, 16–17.

CPSU," and "The CPSU, the only one capable of ensuring socialism in the USSR."[13]

Both in the case of the USSR and in the case of Hungary, *Granma* presented different criteria from their internal debates on the issue of the role of the Party, although it clearly favored criteria that were expressed by actors *within* the ruling party and criteria that were authorized by the official press in each country (a press still controlled by the Party, but that was more open by 1989, both in the USSR and Hungary).

In the coverage of the Hungarian debate, *Granma* gives prominence to the defenders of the thesis of democratic centralism and the single party but also frequently reproduces what the reformists say. For example, in February 1989, *Granma* gave some space to the debate on a new constitution in Hungary, which suggested a change in the role of the Party in society. On February 2, 1989, a headline suggests that there will be a politically "hard struggle" in Hungary and that the HSWP will have to fight for its survival as a hegemonic or vanguard party since it has accepted the introduction of a multiparty system. On April 25, the topic also appears, with another warning that is actually presented in the shape of a headline: "There will be a response to attempts to divide the HSWP, says Grósz (Károly Grósz, General Secretary of the Party)."

Granma also referred to a debate on whether to tolerate so-called reform circles within the Party or not. On May 9, a story is published about a group called the Centrist Platform, which has just been formed within the HSWP. In a (somewhat shorter) story on June 27, a headline announces that "The HSWP exposes its strategy on the reform process in Hungary." The party argues that ongoing reforms *do not* represent a counterrevolution and that the country is heading toward a mixed economy and democratic socialism with several parties. It argues that it wants a synthesis of communist and social democratic values (!) and is opposed to anti-Soviet attitudes.

On August 23, 1989, the reader was exposed to the headline "New party in Hungary" and on August 24, 1989, it was mentioned that the HSWP monopoly of power had been abolished in Hungary. It was presented only in a brief item, which could be an indication of *Granma's* disapproval of what was happening.

---

13   In the story published on September 19, 1989, *Granma* correspondent Nidia Díaz quotes readers of the Pravda newspaper that express support for the Communist Party and claims that the people are confident in the Party. One interesting detail is that one of the readers says that the Party is "the only force at this stage." This could reflect a more extended idea in state socialist countries that the one-party system was a necessity in a certain historical phase, more than something to be in place forever. At least one of our Cuban informants in the second part of this thesis expresses a similar idea, with regard to his own country.

The small space used for the news may also have corresponded to a desire to "hide" the news, from fear of ideological contagion, as reformist ideas had some impact in Cuba.

On August 30, the following item appeared: "The HSWP accepts to give up [hand over, cede] its functions at workplaces, teaching and service facilities." This event was not explicitly valued by the newspaper, but the verb give up (in Spanish: *ceder*) could be read in the sense that a concession has been made, that one has given up on something within the framework of an ongoing conflict, or that this is a step backwards. The next day, the newspaper explained that the HSWP has announced that it will have local branches in the neighborhoods, rather than at the workplaces, as until then. It is stated in the news story that the working hours are meant for working, but the story also gives voice to actors who believe that this will undermine the HSWP. On September 1, *Granma* again referred to the debate and the transition to multipartyism.

There are some obvious parallels between Cuba and Hungary that make the publication of these stories very noteworthy. Not only had there been a one-party system in both countries for decades, but in Cuba, the Party branches are organized in workplaces, except in the case of retired people, who are organized at the neighborhood level. So here, *Granma* practically hands out an argument to any reader of the newspaper that does not agree with the right of the Communist Party of Cuba to have—as the only Party permitted—a presence in any workplace. The journalist actually uses the phrase "depoliticize the production facilities" as a description of what has been proposed. This phrase could sound like something positive to anyone who is a follower of the ideas of multipartyism and who will generally believe that the state should facilitate competition on a more or less even level between political parties.

However, "to politicize" the workplace (or any other part of society) is likely to be a positive thing for people with a Marxist–Leninist view of society. People of this ideology might consider that a neutral state is not possible, at least not in any current society, because it is always an expression of class interests, and having different political parties in a socialist country or one that is transitioning to socialism might be seen as something that could fragment popular will while real power is not elected and is located somewhere else (for instance, in economic elites). According to this point of view, the workplace would then be an important space to be conquered, politicized, to "build socialism." In this sense, it is interesting that *Granma* publishes not only the demands of the reformists but also cases of rhetoric that might sound attractive to people that are or could become critical of the PCC's monopoly.

In parallel, *Granma* covers other political-ideological debates that were taking place in Hungary. On August 29, a news story is published under the headline "Hungary: Groups within the HSWP question program proposal." Journalist Miriam Castro of Prensa Latina cites criticism of the new program proposal of the Hungarian ruling party, both from the left and right oppositions within the Party. The Marxist Unity Platform states that the party they belong to has already eliminated Marxism–Leninism, that it has forgotten the progress that the country has made under socialism, and that they have renounced being socialists. The journalist writes that this tendency or platform within the Party has the "strongest tone" and explains that it is "one of the wings of the HSWP that the reformists describe as conservative or fundamentalist." She also cites the Reform Circles within the HSWP, another tendency, that "consider that the proposed program does not guarantee renewal and the changes that are necessary for the Party in the future, and at the same time, position as a deficiency of the document the non-inclusion of agriculture as a topic." If true, the reformers seem to be pointing out a very large deficiency in the HSWP's program (the lack of a policy for something as fundamental as agriculture). So, the journalist, by including these criticisms, presents the reformists as at least people that have some valid points, despite the Cuban party generally being opposed to reformists.[14]

The fact that *Granma* allowed mention of these debates reflects a certain professionalism. The newspaper not only referred to a democratic debate in another country but also gave some space to people that wanted to modify radically or dismantle a system similar to the Cuban one. This was of course not the case for all countries; as we will see, the coverage of East Germany was very different, and it might not have happened if the debate in Hungary had taken place at another moment: There was a partial opening in the Cuban media that took place at the end of the 1980s. As previously seen, this was partly "accidental" since reformist ideas were present amongst Cuban journalists, but also difficult to avoid since new ideas began to arrive from allied countries in Eastern Europe as well as the USSR, from which information arrived through different mechanisms and agreements. So, sources in the USSR and Eastern Europe started reflecting a greater degree of diversity and criticism in the societies themselves.

Also, since Hungary had really accepted a certain pluralism both in politics and its media, there was not a high risk of provoking Hungarian leaders by publishing different views on the Hungarian reality, as they had already

---

14   On that same day, there is also a news item regarding the national Round Table *in Poland* where the parties decided to eliminate socialism from the constitution, underlining that the Hungarian debate is taking place under very special circumstances—for the first time, another Eastern European country is actually abandoning socialism.

accepted these criteria as more or less legitimate in their own society. There was more coverage during the autumn.

On September 8, a short news item appeared in the column "Direct link" under the following headline: "A new dialogue is necessary in Hungary." Except for this, there is some silence on the situation until September 20. On that day, a news article appears entitled "HSWP achieves agreements on changes in Hungary with other political forces." It mentions that a national Round Table has started working—like earlier in Poland—and that the parties had decided that the population should elect the president directly. *Granma* does not highlight or show any sign of approval of these events and gives it little visibility, but neither does it distort or censor the information.

The important HSWP congress took place on October 3, 1989. On this day, *Granma* reports on some demands made by the reformist wing, including to change the name of the dominant party, and promises of a "democratic socialism." A few days later, on day nine of the same month, *Granma's* readers were made aware that the HSWP had disappeared and that a new socialist party had emerged in Hungary. This news, although it would have been of great interest to the main organ of the Central Committee of the Communist Party of Cuba and to the Cuban public, is presented almost at the bottom of the page. The article mentions that the new Hungarian party had distanced itself from a series of ideas or practices that had until recently been considered sacred: the thesis of the dictatorship of the proletariat, democratic centralism, and being a "state party."

On October 10, on the last page of the newspaper, there was a very detailed description of the new parliament and its leader Rezso Nyers, and one could also read about some events of the Party Congress, as well as conflicts and uncertainties facing the new Party. For example, it stated that it is not known what will happen to the organization's properties. It mentioned that a new communist party has been founded by people who have left what used to be the HSWP. It is claimed that there were many irregularities during the congress, which can be a way in which *Granma* delegitimizes the changes in Hungary, but the newspaper also extensively featured the new leader of the HSWP, as it published a long biography of his life. This way, *Granma* essentially complies with its informational duties, but also questions the legitimacy of changes in the HSWP and avoids distancing itself too much from a former communist or workers' party that could still play an important role in Hungarian politics. This would not serve Cuban interests.[15]

---

15   Recall that it might not have been convenient for the Cuban government to break links with countries that separated themselves from "real socialism," especially considering

On October 4, 1989, it is reported that there is a debate on the new name of the HSWP. Some want to avoid the word "communist" and advocate the use of words such as "socialist" and "Hungarian." They complain that the word "worker," which had formed part of the name, excludes intellectuals. *Granma* reproduces the proposals for a new name. Imre Pozsgay, a key figure of the reformist wing, already refers to the new party as the *Socialist* Party, it is reported.

On October 19, a medium-sized explanatory news in brief item appears on page 4 of the newspaper, which reports that the Hungarian parliament "today decided to ban the presence of political parties in the workplace, and legalized opposition parties," citing the Western AP news agency as a source. The story also reports, among other things, that a new law establishes that political parties can "function freely" and "establishes that no party can accept contributions from a foreign State." The body text as such could be described as informative and its tone is neutral; however, the headline could be said to distort what the news is about: "The Hungarian Parliament decides to prohibit parties at workplaces," which could suggest that Hungary puts restrictions on political activities, rather than focusing on the introduction of multipartyism. The headline might have been added by someone other than who wrote the story.

After the first news in brief item, another story appears, this time from Prensa Latina, with a shorter title: "Alleged fascist party under investigation [in Hungary]." The inclusion of this story underlines possible negative side effects of permitting several parties and as such could serve to "vaccinate" Cubans against multipartyism.

Several weeks later, the action of HSP (formerly HSWP) to "renounce from Leninist principles" (November 10, 1989) was reported, that it was now against the principle of democratic centralism and that it wanted to implement a multiparty system.[16] From late autumn of 1989, *Granma* gave less attention to Hungary, and when it did publish stories on the country, they were covered in the same way as *Granma* often covers capitalist countries—by highlighting their social problems.

Jorge Domínguez maintains that the Cuban government "flooded" the country's media with "stories of misery" from the new Eastern Europe and the

---

that it was (and is) a country under US embargo/blockade and therefore not in a position to antagonize potential trading partners.

16 On October 24, 1989, *Granma* also reported on the last page of the newspaper that the Republic of Hungary had just been proclaimed, and on November 4, that the Socialist Party of Hungary had applied for membership in the Socialist International (the international union of Social Democratic parties) and on the 7th of the same month, it is reported that another social-democratic party has emerged in the country. On November 21, it is also reported that a Green Party has been founded.

USSR,[17] something that may be even more true in the coverage of that region from 1990 onwards. But even in the last quarter of 1989, there was quite a lot of coverage of social problems in those Eastern European countries where the transition to capitalism had come far. In the case of Hungary, a news in brief item was published on the last page of the newspaper with headlines such as "Hungarian unions dissatisfied with the government's economic program" (November 11, 1989) and one about a private university that would open where the annual registration fee is US $1,725 (December 2, 1989). These stories would have served as a warning to Cubans, who were born in a state that considers itself to defend the rights of workers and which offers free education, often hailed as one of the greatest achievements of the Revolution.

Other consequences of the transition were also covered, such as the emergence of new parties in the form of news in brief items that typically had a descriptive tone. There was no real analysis of what had happened in Hungary; instead, the newspaper moved on to other topics. However, the emphasis on social problems was a warning to readers that reforms should be avoided and that socialism might not be perfect, but it had to be defended.

As noted, even at a moment when the space for reformist ideas in Cuba had long ago peaked, according to the existing literature on the topic, news items continued to appear to reflect a certain curiosity about reformist ideas among some journalists or correspondents. While the general coverage leaves little doubt that *Granma* did not like reforms, it permitted the publication of some individual news stories that gave some space to convincing reformist arguments and proposals.

Of course, political pluralism is seen by many people around the world as an important historical advance and a basic characteristic of democracy. Allowing opposition parties—or even "just" permitting various factions within a ruling Party, one change that took place in some Eastern European countries before regime change—may be associated with the greater existence of different political criteria, greater freedom of citizens to choose policies, and the introduction of democracy. Multipartyism could be seen as positive in the sense that it creates competition for power, as a guarantee against abusive governments, and there are surely other arguments. If one assumes that most Cubans that read *Granma* at the time shared these basic assumptions on the issue, or even that they *would* find multipartyism convincing if they just had access to some basic information on the matter, then logically, the Communist Party of Cuba should at least be extremely afraid of a debate on the issue. In accordance with that logic, the Party and *Granma* editors could at least be tempted

---

17   Domínguez, *La política exterior de Cuba (1962–2009)*, 298.

to censor or misrepresent any news or analysis that questioned the viability of the one-party model, to prevent Cubans from being seduced by such ideas.

However, its treatment of the topic is more contradictory. On the one hand, it does try to prevent these ideas from gaining hold in Cuba through a number of means that have been detailed here, and in some situations it could also be said to misrepresent, even deliberately, news about reforms. It also publishes materials warning against such ideas, such as Fidel Castro's speeches that contain criticisms and arguments against multipartyism. On the other hand, in the coverage of Hungary on various occasions, it quite generously reproduces arguments in favor of dismantling the one-party system.

While it is true that this might be the exception more than the rule in the coverage of Eastern Europe and the USSR—and that in the coverage of some other countries there is little or no space given to the reformists except for when they gain such strength that it is more or less unavoidable—it should also be taken into account that *Granma* usually reported on electoral contests in multiparty systems in other parts of the world. For example, on November 13, 1989, an entire page was devoted to covering the Brazilian presidential elections, in which the main candidates' stances on important topics were reviewed. Again, since Cuba did not and does not allow multiparty elections, a foreign reader might expect *Granma* to be even more restrictive with regard to publishing "favorable" or even "neutral" accounts on proposals for liberal democracy. However, this was not always the case.

This shows that the PCC was wary of these ideas, but most of the Party elite were not panicking. Furthermore, there was some room for different ideas and not all spaces in the newspaper were excessively ideologized or politically controlled. One could say that the coverage suggests that the government understood that a considerable number of Cubans could be open to reformism and even liberal democracy but that most were not likely to uncritically embrace them.

To try to understand Cuban perceptions of multipartyism, one would have to take into account the country's history and ideology. Long before Fidel Castro came to power, there existed a strong myth in Cuba—documented in detail by historian Louis Pérez Jr.—with regard to the importance of unity. As shown in the introduction, when the one-party system was installed, it was often argued in reference to José Martí and a history where the lack of national unity at earlier moments in Cuban history was perceived as something that had made the country a victim of foreign interference and repression. This had some historical foundation, as in the second half of the late nineteenth century, divisions among Cuban patriots affected the effectiveness of military actions against Spain during the two Wars of Liberation (1868–1878 and 1895–1898).

Furthermore, experiences with multipartyism during the first half of the twentieth century were contradictory, and people often associated election politics with corruption and vote buying, false promises, US interference, and other negative treats. Even after Fulgencio Batista's 1952 coup, there were a number of legal parties, yet there was little doubt that in this case, "multipartyism" was a facade. Moreover, the ideas of liberal democracy were often associated with the US, but that country's rhetoric seemed shallow as its leaders had helped uphold two dictatorships in Cuba. In 1989, many Cubans could personally remember some of these experiences.

Although most Cubans are aware that there are other countries where multipartyism has given quite different results, in light of their own experiences, introducing such a system was probably seen by many as dangerous and a potential setback, especially in light of the pressures from the US and the situation in neighboring "democracies" that had not been able to solve basic problems. It is notable that the government, even in 1989–1992, often went on the offensive on these questions. Fidel Castro has used the term "pluriporquería" ("multi-rubbish") in his speeches. While this rhetoric has been toned down over the years, even more recently, multipartyism has been described as an "institutionalized power auction" even by Cuban intellectuals with critical positions, such as sociologist Aurelio Alonso.[18]

In the case of Hungary in 1989, largely independent of official Cuban positions, *Granma* allowed the reader a certain look into what the reformists proposed. There were sympathies amongst some journalists, and some might have considered it a duty to report on debates in allied countries that, independently of one's opinion, touched fundamental issues. This does not imply that coverage was always this open; as we will soon see, there were cases where the coverage had entirely other characteristics.

There are several reasons for this, but in the coverage of the USSR and East Europe in general—there will be more examples of this—one notices that there is sometimes more openness when a country is transitioning, and there is some level of open conflict. Such situations imply a larger diversity of actors and actions to cover, and strategically, for an official newspaper that is in practice representing Cuban official positions, it is a situation where it is risky to reproduce the triumphalist narrative of one actor, as it does not know who is going to win. In these cases, *Granma* sometimes avoids comment and opinion and simply reports. It could be said to adopt a wait-and-see approach. Yet not everything is political strategy, even in *Granma*.

---

18 Angel Marqués Dolz, "Un hereje en el convento. Conversación con Aurelio Alonso," *On Cuba*, July 17, 2015.

Sometimes, *Granma* seemed to just reproduce whatever news came in. Let us give an example of this: In April 1989, a story was published in which the Secretary General of the HSWP reported that "the [Hungarian] economy is still confusing" ("Grosz considers it necessary to improve Hungary's image in the Socialist Bloc," April 17, 1989). A few days later, a short news story appears that is called "Rumors of economic emergency in Hungary are undermined" (April 24, 1989), and finally, a month later, *Granma* publishes another story in which it is reported that Prime Minister Miklós Németh "described the situation of the Hungarian economy as characterized by chaos" (May 24, 1989). There is clearly no political plan guiding specifically what explications or news to emphasize; the news coverage includes any that comes in, and whomever is at work one specific day might determine the headline.

In summary, it could be said that *Granma* showed considerable interest in the debate about the future of the ruling party of Hungary, taking into account its own ideology and the situation as a whole. There was little interpretation or assessment but more of an approach where the journalist tried to report on what was happening. *Granma* certainly put more attention on the opinions of Hungarian communists that opposed reform, but significant space was given to the interchange of words between political actors (within the ruling party), and thus also reformists' arguments. Publishing the arguments of the reformists, sometimes in their own words, would have been seen as dangerous by some Cuban party members, since they reflected proposals to change policies in Hungary that also existed (and exist) in Cuba and that were promoted by an internal opposition and by the US. However, in the case of Hungary, *Granma* allowed this debate to be heard, and this shows the relative degree of openness of the Cuban media at the time and also how much the particularity of the situation in the country and each journalist could influence the coverage at certain determined moments. The relative openness suggests some level of professionalism but could also reflect that the newspaper's editors knew that Cubans were not likely to uncritically embrace reformist ideas.

In the sources analyzed here, *Granma* does not say why regime change took place in Hungary. As we have previously seen, the newspaper did suggest that there was a reactionary offensive in Eastern Europe and it had also suggested that reforming socialism was a bad idea, something that Hungary had been doing for years. However, by giving notable attention to internal political debates in Hungary in 1989, *Granma* showed that many people there, and even Party members, genuinely believed in more political pluralism. It gave the impression that these ideas were being advanced by people that believed in them within the country as opposed to being imposed by imperialism. As soon as it became clear that reformed socialism was no longer an option in Hungary, as the country more openly started transiting toward capitalism, the newspaper moved on to other topics. It lost interest in the Hungarian political debate, and the editorial emphasis was now on the social problems brought about by the changes. If there is an underlying message at that later point, it is that it would be necessary to be careful with the reforms, even if they are well-intentioned: Worse than imperfect socialism is capitalism.

1.3 Example 3: Migration Crisis in the GDR—The Uncritical Repetitions of an Ally's Discourse

According to sociologists Stephen Pfaff and Hyojoung Kim, most scholars agree that the regime of the German Democratic Republic (GDR) began to falter in September 1989 in light of the massive migration of its citizens.[19] After the events known as the Fall of the (Berlin) Wall on November 9, 1989, the fall of the state accelerated.[20] Pfaff and Kim consider, however, that it was a mixture of migration and popular protests that gave the "fatal blow" to the GDR.

In this section, the focus will be on *Granma's* coverage of East Germany's migration crisis. *Granma's* coverage of the issue of migration from the GDR is especially interesting because, as researcher Silvia Pedraza has pointed out, there are "many parallels" in the respective situations of Cuba and the GDR, such as its proximity to a capitalist country with a higher level of consumption,[21] although there were always important differences as well.[22] The existence of important coincidences, still, could have made the issue a delicate one for the Cuban authorities.

We recall that the emergence of the GDR and its migratory situation have their historical roots in the division of Germany by the great powers after the Second World War. East Germany in its early days suffered from high migration to the West until a series of physical and legal restrictions were implemented to stop that movement. Beginning in 1952, the inter-German border was monitored for this purpose, but in practice it was possible to move freely between East Berlin and West Berlin until 1961, the year in which the Berlin Wall was

---

19 Steven Pfaff and Hyojoung Kim, "Exit & Voice Dynamics in Collective Action: An Analysis of Emigration and Protest in the East German Revolution," *American Journal of Sociology* 109, No. 2 (2003): 415.
20 Ibid., 418.
21 Silvia Pedraza, "Democratization and Migration: Cuba's Exodus and the Development of Civil Society," *Association for the Study of the Cuban Economy* (ASCE) (ed.): *Cuba in Transition* 12 (2002): 255–256.
22 Bert Hoffmann, "Cuba's Dilemma of Simultaneity: The Link between the Political and the National Question," in *Debating Cuban Exceptionalism*, eds. Laurence Whitehead and Bert Hoffmann (New York: Palgrave Macmillan, 2007), 101–121.

built.[23] Although a number of changes were made to migration policies during the next few decades, it was not until November 1989 that radical change took place. For Pfaff and Kim, until then, "the stability of East Germany had depended on the constraint of individual mobility."

In 1989, three important changes took place in regard to migration:

1) In May, Hungary permitted the dismantling of physical boundaries on their borders with Austria. East Germans could already travel as tourists to Hungary, but from now on, they could also cross the border between Hungary and Austria. During the first months of the year, 5,000 GDR citizens left illegally that way; in July and August, more than 30,000 followed.

2) Groups of GDR citizens began to occupy embassies of the Federal Republic of Germany (FRG) in other socialist countries, demanding that they be allowed to go to the West. East Germany accepted that migrants could go by train to the West, but they would then be stripped of their GDR citizenship. The GDR also closed the possibility of traveling to Czechoslovakia without a visa.

3) On November 9 of the same year, there was a press conference of the ruling party during which a member of the Political Bureau—Günter Schabowski—announced that all travel restrictions were immediately removed (possibly by mistake). The announcement made many East Berlin citizens go to the border crossings of the Berlin Wall, demanding they be allowed across the border. Under popular pressure, orders were given to open border crossings, and citizen groups began to knock down parts of the wall. These events are known as the fall of the Berlin Wall, although in a physical sense, most of the Berlin Wall was still intact for a while longer.[24]

Granma's coverage of the GDR during the first half of 1989 tended to paint a very favorable picture of this society, considerably more so than other Socialist Bloc countries, and the coverage was largely based on the more or less direct reproduction of government sources or mimicking its narrative closely.

Some news that appeared in *Granma* were reports that went around the world, such as GDR leader Erick Honecker's assertions that the Berlin Wall would be intact for a hundred more years (January 21, 1989). Other times, *Granma* reported on solidarity activities of the GDR, on their assistance to the Third

---

23 The Berlin Wall is the most known part of the inter-German border, but physically, only a small part of it.

24 During the months after November 9, 1989, other major events took place, notably the free elections in March 1990, which the SED lost, and on October 3, the GDR ceased to exist. The following analysis does not include the entire unification process, but focuses mainly on the coverage of the migratory crisis up to and right after the fall of the Berlin Wall.

World (April 26, 1989), and that there were 6,000 foreign students in the country (July 24, 1989), all issues that should generate sympathy in Cuba, as it was a country that defined itself as part of the Third World. On January 7, a very short news item claimed that the GDR is one of the countries in the world with the least crime. Other suggestive headlines are: "The GDR will maintain its socialist development strategy" (June 23, 1989), and "[Arising] from the ruins we have become one of the ten most industrialized countries in the world" (June 6, 1989), the latter being the headline of an interview with a (smiling) member of the Political Bureau of the Socialist Unity Party of Germany, written in a triumphalist tone. Other materials underline the good state of relations between Cuba and East Germany, such as "RDA–Cuba Trade Exchange Protocol for 1989" (January 27, 1989), "Honecker receives Risquet [Jorge Risquet, Member of the PCC Central Committee]" (April 18, 1989), "Lionel Soto visited a petrochemical combine (enterprise) in the GDR" (June 10, 1989), "Professor Schneidewind speaks to *Granma*: Towards greater health collaboration between the GDR and Cuba" (April 6, 1989), and "GDR will supply Cuba with modern automatization system" (June 14, 1989).

The coverage contrasts strongly with that of the Federal Republic of Germany (also known as FRG, BRD, and West Germany), where social problems and neo-Nazis were recurring themes. West Germany was presented as an aggressive state, as opposed to the peaceful GDR (see, for example: "GDR border facilities are shot at from the FRG," August 19, 1989).

Many of the news items are signed by the newspaper itself or by Prensa Latina, but most of the time, both of them seem to mostly use official GDR sources, such as the official news agency Allgemeiner Deutscher Nachrichtendienst (ADN), the newspaper of the ruling party *Neues Deutschland*, and speeches given by the leaders of the country. Occasionally, materials produced in the GDR are reproduced even without adding any further content. An example is a speech by Erick Honecker in which he emphasizes the development of the GDR and the absence of unemployment (June 8, 1989), or a news in brief item that appeared under the following headline: "Commentary by Neues Deutschland: Internationalism [in this case, a euphemism for Soviet military intervention] was the only way out of the 1968 crisis in Czechoslovakia" (August 21, 1989). This news is given in a context when there were already considerable signs of instability in Eastern Europe, and therefore the GDR may have been perceived from Cuba as a more stable and more successful socialist country than some neighboring countries, especially Poland and Hungary.

Granma refers to the *ideological* affinity between Cuba and the GDR at various times; for example, on October 6, 1989 the newspaper uses the term "(to) perfect" (*perfeccionar*) to refer to changes that were occurring in the GDR. To

Cubans, this word would be very familiar as it was widely used during Cuba's Rectification of Errors and Negative Trends during the last half of the 1980s. *Granma* was interested in showing a positive face of the GDR in order to reinforce its own position, which was that socialism does not need to be reformed; it should be perfected by rectifying errors.

Besides ideological affinity, another factor that may have contributed to the strikingly positive, "one-dimensional" coverage of the GDR is as follows: In that country, during most of 1989, no legal opposition existed, neither was there legal opposition media. Therefore, the number of political actors and professional sources of information was limited to those authorized by the state. In other words, there was little open conflict, critical journalism, and protests to report on, and the information leaving the country was very much controlled by the authorities. Although the official sources quoted from the GDR did mention increasing migration, certain anti-government demonstrations, and other sensitive issues, they were presented in a certain manner; that is, GDR authorities had given the news a spin.

In addition, since *Granma* had given such a positive coverage of the GDR for so many years, probably since the founding of the *Granma* newspaper itself, it was somewhat trapped in a narrative and was faced with the challenge of how to present the news as stronger symptoms of discontent emerged during the second half of 1989. In the case of other Socialist Bloc countries that had been through reforms, it could be said that the problems were due to the negative effects of market reforms or political pluralism; in the case of the GDR, however, there had been no reforms and *Granma* had even highlighted it as a particularly well-functioning socialist society.

With regard to the migration issue, *Granma* mentions that a wave of migration began to emerge in May but very timidly in the beginning. For the time being, the newspaper closely followed the official narrative of East Germany. According to this narrative, illegal migration is the result of an attempt to weaken the Socialist Bloc: "West German support for emigrated Germans, so that they can attack [question, slander] Czechoslovakia, is criticized" (May 16, 1989). Although migration from the GRD had reached considerable levels by July, it was not until August that broader coverage can be observed in *Granma*. In addition to referring to alleged Western incentives to East German migrants, *Granma* initially described the migrants as irresponsible people (they are adventurous, they do not respect the laws). It also alleges that there are legal possibilities for people wanting to migrate, so the act of migrating without authorization is portrayed as something that doesn't make much sense and as a suspicious act. Cuban readers might have seen through this argument, as Cubans were also familiar with a situation in which they could theoretically travel if they had the money and all the permits, though in reality they did not have the money and the permits were out of reach for most, so they might not have easily accepted the supposition that East Germans had real possibilities of travelling freely.

The coverage of East German emigration was highly politicized, and explicit or implicit assessments were more frequent than in the cases that we examined so far. In the news-commentary "FRG: A game uncovered" (August 22, 1989), by Arsenio Rodríguez—a relatively long text that covered the fifth part of a full page—migration to West Germany via the territory of other countries was described as "a situation created by West German diplomats abroad." The journalist argues that there may be a link between the migratory phenomenon and the 40th anniversary of the GDR on October 7, 1989. There is talk of a deliberate plan to create problems for the country ("Day X"). Migration from East Germany is also presented as a "rejuvenation cure" (as West Germany apparently wants young migrants to counter an ageing population), and the West German press is accused of not mentioning the possibilities that the GDR has given for its citizens to travel abroad and to facilitate the reunification of families. According to *Granma*, "from January 1 to July 31 [1989], three and a half million GDR citizens traveled [legally] to non-socialist countries. Of these, 3,266,000 visited the FRG and West Berlin." There were "yearnings for an exodus to take place [from East Germany]" ("The departure of citizens from the country is solely a responsibility of the GDR," August 16, 1989).

While West German authorities allegedly yearned for people to migrate from the East, it also had no capacity to receive the migrants. On September 14, a comment by *Rude Pravo*, the official organ of the Communist Party of Czechoslovakia, was cited, according to which there were neo-Nazis who invited East Germans to leave their country. This information might have been based on something that had really happened somewhere—or it might not—but in any case had little relevance for understanding the migratory wave as a whole, and the news story could certainly be said to demonize both the FRG and to stigmatize migrants.[25] The news story "The GDR proves how the FRG promoted exodus" (September 20, 1989) accuses the latter state of using false

---

25   The topic of West German interference is combined with accusations every now and then of ties between West Germany and Nazis and fascists. On November 9, 1989, *Granma* reports on anti-socialist acts in the GDR that are supposedly directed toward foreign media. They mention the presence of the Western press and the participation of a Bluem who has links with Chilean dictator Augusto Pinochet, and in it the newspaper also refers to the fascist danger in Germany. Although fascism is a real threat, here, *Granma* recurs to a tactic of guilt by association. It is suggested that since some fascists participate in the campaign against the GDR, all participants are fascists.

promises and manipulation. It quotes as a source the newspaper *Neues Deutschland*. On the other hand, according to *Granma*, the world was rejecting the policy of promoting illegal migration from the GDR: "Strong criticisms of the FRG for hosting citizens of the GDR in its embassies" (August 18, 1989). According to the short news story, "Hungarian Foreign Minister offers his assessment of the situation with citizens of the GDR" (August 26, 1989), the mentioned politician defends the position of the GDR and says that Hungary "will reject passports given by the embassy of West Germany to citizens of the GDR, so that they can abandon their homeland."

Yet as of September 11, Hungary officially allowed East Germans in its territory to travel legally to the West against the desires of the East German authorities. The headline "The GDR denounces Hungary's violation of migratory treaties" (September 12, 1989) demonstrates that Cuba sympathizes with the position of the GDR. This news story also includes the official version of Hungary but states that the GDR gives Hungary a chance to *correct* (*corregir*) its policy, and, therefore, portrays East Germany as a generous state. That same day, *Granma* also reports that there has been criticism of the Hungarian decision to authorize that citizens of the GDR who are in Hungary as tourists can emigrate to West Germany via Austria. *Granma* uses the term "human trafficking," and it is stated that the GDR citizens emigrating to the West through Hungary are a minority, only a small part of "a quarter of a million GDR citizens that enjoy their vacations there [in Hungary] every year."

The newspaper also reports that West Germany has closed three embassies in Eastern Europe because "it was not prepared to receive, due to its internal problems, the citizens of democratic Germany (*Alemania democrática*; in Cuba, this is a common way of referring to the German Democratic Republic, or East Germany)."

But the really striking thing about this news item is not its denial of problems in the GDR, but that they "project" this crisis upon the neighboring republic, West Germany. Although problems of unemployment, neo-Nazis, and so on undoubtedly existed, the part of the phrase that states that West Germany "was not prepared to receive, due to its internal problems" makes it look like the West is the part of Germany that is in a terminal crisis. *Granma* continues to follow up on the issue in shorter news stories, such as "GDR citizens abandon the RFG embassy in Czechoslovakia" (September 14, 1989) and others. On the same day, the newspaper cites *Junge Welt*, a newspaper of the Freie Deutsche Jugend, or communist youth of Germany, which laments Hungary's role but calls for preserving good relations between that country and the GDR. *Junge Welt* again states that the migrants are relatively few and suggests that they have been fooled by capitalism.

However, the numbers continued to increase. On October 4, 1989, *Granma* reports that there are 5,000 at the West German embassy in Czechoslovakia, and on October 6, it can inform the reader that 8,000 citizens are being evacuated from that embassy. In a news article on October 5, migrants are described as irresponsible as they take their children with them during the transit. The news also says that there are many people sleeping in the streets near the embassy. This information might have been included to show the Cuban audience that emigrating is not simple.

On October 19, it was reported that 100,000 people had already migrated from East Germany. The news in brief item specifying the number of migrants occupies little space and could easily have been ignored by readers. The information could be said to be somewhat discontinuous, since before this figure was presented, the numbers cited were in the thousands. However, it should be underlined that *Granma* did report (very discreetly) on what was happening, despite this being a delicate issue, in several ways.

The newspaper also devoted considerable space to stories of migrants from the GDR who were disappointed or suffered different types of problems after arriving in the RFG. Caritas, the Catholic charity, allegedly claimed that the East Germans were not real refugees, and writer Dieter Lattaman stated that the migratory flow broke with an existing agreement (September 13, 1989). *Granma* also cited a source according to whom the politics of accepting refugees was selective, because at the same time the West said no to many Yugoslavs. It is also stated that these policies implied an incitement to flee.[26] Western sources are used in these cases, presumably because these criticisms cannot so easily be dismissed as propaganda if they come from "the other side."

On September 22, *Granma* reported that migrants have a bad impression of West Germany. "The first impression—of tents, collective pots, and rustic conditions—was not the best." The newspaper also highlights the existence of unemployment, prostitution, and drug use. The East German migrants are described as people who have their own cars and good clothes, they are well fed and have a high cultural level—in spite of this, they apparently got confused by Western propaganda and are now discovering the crude reality of West Germany.

In October, when a strong wave of protests within the GDR started accompanying the migratory wave, more self-criticism from the country's

---

26   This criticism is very similar to the one that the Cuban media always presented with regard to the US Cuban Adjustment Act, which gives Cubans who arrive in the US the right to become lawful permanent residents, a possibility not given to migrants or refugees from other countries.

government began to surface. *Granma* reported on October 13 that the East German governing party, the Socialist Unity Party of Germany (SUPG, more commonly known by the German acronym SED), was discussing how to create a "more attractive socialism," and they also recognized "some popular inconformity." They call for self-criticism on the issue of migration. The same day, it is also reported that youth are expressing their disagreement on issues such as freedom to travel, access to consumer goods, and so on. In a considerable change of tone, the GDR recognizes that its system is not as attractive as it should be and that there is discontent in the population, and a dialogue between the government and evangelist Christians is mentioned.[27]

These issues are repeated at other moments, for example, under the headline "Leaders of the GDR dialogue with protesters" (October 23, 1989), where it is again said that the protesters claim the possibility of traveling, a statement that contradicts the information that *Granma* had previously given, that people could already travel. On November 9, the then member of the politburo of the SED, Günter Schabowski, answered questions to the press about the immigration situation. As anyone familiar with the history of the Collapse of the GDR will be aware, he said—intentionally or not—that the borders would open immediately. That same evening, border guards started letting people through to West Berlin, and protesters also started attacking and making openings in the Berlin Wall itself.

Granma has subsequently been accused of not covering these events. For example, the Cuban journalist Regina Coyula, who writes for BBC Mundo, on July 10, 2015 quoted a Cuban economist: "If it had not been for Radio Martí [the US propaganda radio that transmits toward the island], I would not have been made aware that the Berlin Wall fell, but I found out right away and called all my friends. That news story went around the world, but in Cuba the national press did not give it the slightest importance." Let us examine how these events were treated.

On December 10, a short piece of text appeared on the newspaper's front page, which was continued on page 6. The part that appears on the front page covers less than ½0th of the page's surface and is placed very much toward the bottom of the paper and bears the headline "The GDR announces the opening of its borders." The title does not refer to the Berlin Wall as such, even though that construction was the best known and most symbolic part of the border system of the GDR, and the newspaper must have been informed before

---

27   *Granma* does not express criticism of the GDR, but does publish self-criticism coming from its own ruling party, and news on other sensitive issues if and when these have first been published by the official press in that country.

deadline that openings were being created in the wall by protesters, as people started doing this spontaneously during the evening of November 9. The small size, location (bottom), and absence of photos on *Granma's* cover are signs of disapproval, making it obvious that the editors did not want the news to attract too much attention.

Granma begins the story by saying that "the German Democratic Republic (GDR) today announced the opening of border points for citizens of the country that wish to travel abroad, Guenter [sic] Schabowski said" (see Figure 3). According to *Granma*, Schabowski "indicated that the measure will allow those who are interested in permanently abandoning the GDR, to avoid having to use third-country routes" and also that "Citizens can make private trips without explaining the reasons, and only need a visa and passport issued by the authorities [...]." A small part of the story had been removed from the newspaper that I acceded, apparently because someone had cut out whole segments of the sports page on the backside of the paper, but the newspaper does not dedicate much space to the subject and spends most of the story on page 6 to discuss other issues: Egon Krenz, the new General secretary of SED and his vision of Perestroika; economic reform in the GDR; a request for "free elections" by Hans Modrow, member of the Political bureau.[28]

On December 10, *Granma* makes no reference to the fact that protesters have demolished a part of the Wall, nor do they publish photos of this. Although immigration pressure and popular demonstrations have been reported on and will still be reported on for some time by the newspaper—the emphasis on November 10, 1989 is on the actions of the government and the ruling Party. As *Granma's* coverage of these events centers a lot on decisions taken from above, in some manner this gives the impression that the opening of borders was a more controlled and even premeditated event than it really was. The radical protesters are largely rendered invisible in the coverage.

On November 11, a third of the last page is covered by a box with information on the latest events of the GDR. The main head of the table says, "Support for the SED in a meeting in the GDR; Egon Krenz spoke." There is a small photo where a few cars that leave the GDR through a border crossing are visible. This contrasts strongly with aerial photos used by some Western media that gave a panoramic view of hundreds of cars leaving the GDR. The caption, however, acknowledges that "A large queue of cars was formed at the border post of Hirschberg, where hundreds of people crossed from the GDR into West German territory when the GDR government declared the borders open."

---

28 The newspaper also quotes Modrow saying: "We live in a time when the existence of our party, and socialism in the GDR, is at stake."

ANALYZING THE NEWS ACCOUNTS

FIGURE 3   *Granma*, November 10, 1989; the day after the Fall of the Berlin Wall, "The GDR announces the opening of its borders"

Thus, it is clear that *Granma* tries to minimize the news of the opening of the border to the degree that it is possible. In part, this might be to avoid the possibility that the events might inspire Cubans to demand the removal of travel restrictions and other reforms. However, for Cuban journalists and the Party elite, it must also have been embarrassing and difficult to accept that the German "model state" was losing control.

It is mentioned that there were tens of thousands of SED militants who demonstrated in Berlin supporting the new Political Bureau and that the newly installed general secretary of the Party, Egon Krenz, says that he wants "a revolution on German soil, which will bring us a better socialism," which advocates "free elections, radical reforms and for turning the SED into a great movement of the people." Krenz again touches upon the immigration issue and repeats the official narrative in which the authorities play the role of a constructive and auto-critical part:

> [Egon Krenz] also referred to the situation of the last hours that emerged at the border crossings with Federal Germany and West Berlin, following the facilities for travelling freely, put into effect yesterday.
>
> He said that this step is an expression that the renewal policy is very much for real. "We extend our hand to all who wish to move forward with us," he emphasized.

After briefly covering other issues such as the resignation of four leaders of the SED, at the end of the news box there is another news in brief item on the immigration issue, titled "New border crossings open." It states that the interior minister of the GDR "tonight announced the opening of eight new border crossings with West Berlin, amongst other measures that are meant to facilitate travel." According to the information, until that point 25 transit points had operated between the two parts of Berlin, "some of them with various limitations." It is reported that the new border crossings "will be ready before Monday."

The minister also reports that "the establishment of bus routes and the metro is being studied," and this would "facilitate travel, [...] only by presenting the corresponding identity documents." He says that Dresden, Leipzig, and Berlin are the cities "from where there are more trips to the Federal Republic of Germany and West Berlin" and that in the first 24 hours of opening the borders, "37,000 people passed through the transit places, and 2,500 decided not to return." Public opinion is being reported on but only through means of a summary: "Most of the people interviewed indicated that they returned and said that their purpose was to visit family members, while unanimously supporting the measure of the GDR authorities to open border points" [sources quoted are "local press" from West Berlin and the Federal Republic of Germany]. That is to say, *Granma* provides the reader with quite detailed information about the new possibilities for traveling, but still minimizes the topic of the street protests and the attacks on the Berlin Wall. Toward the end of the story, the following is said about this:

> [...] ADN [East German News Agency] indicates that the border with West Berlin was violated last night by citizens of both sides at the Brandenburg Gate, where several groups tried to damage the wall with iron bars.
> The border troops, it states, maintained a serene attitude, and convinced those gathered there to use the indicated steps to travel, because that place is not a transit point.
> West Berlin police, subordinate to the Senate (local government), helped restore order in the area where the violations occurred, ADN observed.

The last paragraphs portray the people that attacked the wall physically as problematic, since their actions are portrayed as unacceptable to both the East German and West Berlin authorities. This contrasts strongly with the portrait of these people engaged in civil disobedience as heroes, as a vanguard of liberty, in the Western press.[29] I include a photo of the relatively detailed coverage on November 11 (see Figure 4). The headline reads: "Support for the SED at rally in the GDR; Egon Krenz spoke."

Unfortunately, in the copy of *Granma* that we stored digitally and have permanent access to, it is not possible to read most of the GDR coverage that appears two days later, on November 13, because it has been cut out of the newspaper. Again, the apparently avid sports fan who has cut out articles from other editions has removed part of the sports news on the newspapers' page 7, which also makes it impossible to read some international news on the last page (page 8).

In the November 14 edition, however, there is wide coverage of the country's political situation, with *Granma* including information on protesters in Leipzig and their demands that the reforms be deepened. The coverage that day includes a reference to slogans such as "SED alone, no"—suggesting that there should be more than one party—and "Open borders do not guarantee freedom alone." *Granma* furthermore reports about the opening of another 12 border

---

29 An item also appears in a separate box, entitled "Kohl interrupts visit to Poland," which reports that the West German Chancellor "interrupted his visit to Poland for 24 hours, following the decision of the German Democratic Republic (GDR) to open its borders," and states that he expressed concern with regard to "the development of unpredictable events."

FIGURE 4   *Granma*, November 11, 1989; back cover, "Support for the SED [ruling party] at rally in the GDR where Egon Krenz gave a speech"

points, which, according to the newspaper, are "for citizens of the German Democratic Republic who since last Thursday travel freely to those territories." Also, it reports that "approximately two million people spent this weekend in West Berlin, and more than 400 thousand East Germans made visits to the FRG"; that the police, working extra shifts, have delivered more than four million visas in only two days; that civilian employees of the police as well as the Ministry of Interior are authorized to make private trips abroad; that prohibitions (unspecified) are lifted in restricted areas near the border with the FRG; and that the West Berliners "have received authorization to travel also by

ANALYZING THE NEWS ACCOUNTS

bicycle or motorcycle to the GDR and will be able to use all the border crossings allowed for cars and pedestrians." In other words, *Granma* gives relatively detailed information on migration, and it includes references to some political demands.[30]

So, during the autumn of 1989, the official narrative started falling apart, and coverage descended into a series of contradictions and "half-truths." It was at times clearly misleading. However, only a few days after November 9, it becomes more realistic.

With regard to the fall of the Berlin Wall itself, in a sense the events surrounding the opening of the borders are covered quite extensively, though the quality of reporting varies. The topic of the protesters attacking the wall itself is obviously one of a delicate nature for *Granma*, and although it mentions protests, the attacks on the wall and the consequences of the opening, the moment when they were allowed to carve the first openings in the wall, a moment quite obviously of great symbolism, is touched on only indirectly, and there are no photos. In this sense, one could say that there was censorship or distortion of events. Also, in general, these events do not receive a physical placement in the newspaper in correspondence to the importance of the topic and the interest that many readers must have had in the huge changes in a country that was a geographically distant but important ally of Cuba.

Granma had also previously that year recognized the importance of the topic of the Berlin Wall. It reproduced, for example, a short news item in which the US ambassador to the FRG states that the day on which the Wall is going to fall is approaching (May 1989). On another occasion, it quotes a member of the Political Bureau of the SED on the subject: "Referring to the repeated demands for the elimination of the construction that separates West Berlin from the capital of the GDR, the member of the Political Bureau of the SED reiterated that the 'wall' [it is put between quote marks] will exist as long as the causes that motivated its building in the first place, are not eliminated" (June 23, 1989). The newspaper publishes a short article titled "The Berlin Wall is 26 years old" (August 14, 1989), where it is stated that it has been kept in place despite what has been said on the subject. Even one of *Granma's* journalists, Juan Marrero, explicitly speaks about the Wall and describes it as a protective

---

30 On November 15, there are physical cuts in the newspaper that affect the reading of the last page, but apparently there is nothing from the GDR. In editions during the coming days (on the 16th, 17th, and 18th, as well as the 21st, 23rd, and other editions) there are reports on political events in the GDR, but now without addressing the issue of the borders.

measure against sabotage (in "GDR, four decades of struggle," October 8, 1989).[31]

Even as time goes by after November 9, *Granma* is careful not to reproduce the Western narrative of the "fall of the Wall," although by 1990 several news stories and commentaries are published that allude to this discourse and refer to walls (physical and metaphorical) of the capitalist world, apparently as an indirect "answer" to the Western narrative about the Berlin Wall. For instance, on May 21, 1990, a heading appears that reads "We are imprisoned in the Bush walls" (May 21, 1990). On February 23, 1990, *Granma* also published a news story with a photo caption that criticizes the wall between South Korea and North Korea, which was built by South Korea with support from the US and has otherwise been referred to as a tank shield. With this news, *Granma* acknowledges in some timid and indirect manner that the walls are undesirable but tries counterattacking, arguing that not only socialist countries build walls. The Berlin Wall is clearly a somewhat sensitive subject, maybe especially since Cuba had defended the GDR so strongly, but also probably because the opening of the Berlin Wall became a symbol for the fall of communism.

It should be said that almost a year after these historic events—on October 4, 1990, when the reunification of Germany took place—*Granma* published an extensive report (one whole page) with a coverage that was much more objective and less politicized than before. In this report, a chronology of the most important events in the history of the German division and reunification is included, and November 9, 1989 is listed as the day of the fall of the Berlin Wall. There is even a relatively large photo of a person who removes the symbol of the GDR, apparently from some public building. This more open journalism in the case of East Germany seems to go against the tendency described by some scholars of a Cuban press that became more closed as Cuba was entering the Special Period, but it might largely be explained by changes in Germany as a nation. Since there were no longer any close links that had to be defended, it would make little sense to invest much effort in defending the GDR as it faded away into history. Also, there was no longer one official version coming from East Germany/former East Germany, but many stories that had to be reported on.

---

31   The same journalist says that East Germany is a heroic country that has fought against a blockade, that is, they seem to create an identification between Cubans and East Germans, since Cuba is also under an embargo or a blockade. Interestingly, in most of the Western world, the issue of blockages, when talking about Germany, is more associated with the GDR blockade on West Berlin in 1947, which failed due to the introduction of an air bridge with Western support.

In an episode that echoes somewhat the publication of Eduardo Galeano's critical remarks on recent Polish history, in early 1992, *Granma* published a short interview with the famous (formerly East) German playwright, Heiner Müller, who criticized capitalism but also recognized the "schizophrenic effects of the wall." This, together with the more open coverage of the GDR during the last month of its existence in 1990, reflects a discreet but not explicit recognition that Cuban coverage of the GDR had been apologetic.

Having made it clear that politics trumped professionalism in the case of *Granma's* coverage of key events that led to the fall of the GDR, it should be said that the Western media have also perpetuated a number of myths on these events. It must have been obvious even immediately that these were events of a certain importance (because the Berlin Wall was a wall that divided a European capital and its inhabitants in two, and it was now attacked, because it was part of a border system where about a thousand people had died, because the wall was for many a symbol of the lack of freedom in Eastern Europe, because it was not known what was going to happen to the activists who were demolishing it, etc.). Still, it should also be said that they were events for which the final outcome was unknown. There were various assessments of their possible significance at a moment when most of the Soviet Bloc still existed.

To illustrate this, there were European newspapers that let the news of November 9, 1989 cover their entire front page the day after, but others did not. For example, in my own country, Norway, the main business newspaper, *Dagens Næringsliv*, did not dedicate any space to the subject on the cover on November 10—unlike *Granma*, which actually did so—and only a small part of its cover on November 11.[32] In his journal *Unterwegs von Deutschland nach Deutschland*, in his notes from early 1990, German intellectual Günter Grass still values the possibility of a German confederation, that is, months (!) after November 9 he did not see the unification of East and West Germany in a single state as inevitable.[33]

Contrary to what the best-known photos of the opening of the Berlin Wall might suggest, only a very small number of the citizens of East Berlin climbed the wall, and it is not clear how much immediate support the protesters had. Oral historian Lutz Niethammer, analyzing the results of the free elections in the GDR on March 18, 1990, points out that the former socialist party in power achieved only 17% of the votes, but that "The activist groups, whose demonstrations had been achieved in order to bring down the old regime, turned out

---

32 "Hvor var DN da muren falt?," *Dagbladet*, March 25, 2011.
33 Günter Grass, *Unterwegs Von Deutschland Nach Deutschland: Tagebuch 1990* (Göttingen: Steidl Gerhard Verlag, 2009).

to be a small radical minority without sympathizers among the inhabitants of the provinces and only exceeded the 5% barrier in the capital, East Berlin."[34] While *Granma's* suggestions that migrants and protesters were all naïve or irresponsible were unfair, the victors' narrative of the Collapse of the GDR as a fight where good won over bad, and as a nation gaining liberty, are questioned by many East Germans. According to a survey cited by Spiegel Online, in 2009, 57% of the population in Eastern Germany defended the former GDR ("Majority of East Germans Feel Life Better Under Communism," July 3, 2009).

I have already mentioned some possible reasons why *Granma* chose to align so closely with official GDR propaganda. One reason was uncritical admiration. It was probably also a question of old habits; one was accustomed to reproducing anything that came from an important ally, and one was not mentally prepared to admit many of the GDR's internal problems and tensions that were suddenly becoming more visible to the world. For domestic reasons, it was also very important to highlight the GDR as an example that socialism did not need to be reformed.

In addition to this, there may have been an attitude among editors according to which the GDR press "know their own reality better" in accordance with a common practice and/or principle within the international communist movement, where one does not interfere in allied states' affairs and generally accepts each country's official narrative on its internal issues. Since the GDR did not allow much public debate, it would have been seen as a matter of "disrespect" had *Granma* given much space to, let us say, the GDR's dissident voices. The GDR was at the time Cuba's second trading partner, after the USSR—and this was a delicate moment. Yet *Granma* did not always favor its allies' official versions, and this suggests that fear of offending an ally was probably not a main reason for the uncritical coverage of the GDR until late 1989. Even so, to some extent these preoccupations may have been present. It recalls an inherent problem of government-controlled newspapers (not referring to state-owned media in general), especially when there are no alternatives to this state press; what the press decides to publish can be interpreted as reflecting the official position of the authorities. This restricts journalists and editors in their work, and is a problem for the public.

In summary, in its coverage of the GDR migration crisis in 1989, *Granma* tends to repeat the versions of the GDR government and includes many

---

34   Lutz Niethammer, "Elecciones y fuente oral en la RDA (III-1990)," Historia y fuente oral: Revista Semestral del Seminario de Historia Oral del Departamento de Historia Contemporánea de la Universitat de Barcelona y del Institut Municipal d'Història, n.° 4 (1996): 155.

assessments in support of their positions. As has been shown, the coverage is very different from that of key events in Poland and Hungary, where there was more room for different sources and criteria, and where different types and styles of journalism co-existed.

In the case of the GDR's situation, there are a number of news in brief items that only "objectively" report the facts, for example when *Granma* publishes the number of people that have emigrated, but otherwise in its coverage of the GDR, *Granma* tends to include more commentary and subjective appreciations in news stories themselves, where migrants are often depicted as people who have been deceived by the West German government, which *Granma* tries to connect to a tradition of fascism, Nazism, and Western imperialism. It is not until the leading Party of the GDR begins to recognize some disagreement in the population—it does so clearly in October 1989—that this type of criticism begins to timidly reach the reader of *Granma*. Then it is acknowledged, for example, that serious limitations on travel had been in place, in contradiction of what had been reported shortly before. Fundamentally, migration is seen as a "game" induced by the RFA, as a product of pressures against the GDR, of false promises, and of Western propaganda. The coverage of the events surrounding the fall of the Berlin wall is striking, as it is described how the GDR authorities authorized the opening of its borders, but the protesters are barely visible.

The GDR government was always presented as generous and willing to rectify problems when necessary. The GDR was presented as a country with a functioning system that should become even better with the reforms announced toward the end of 1989. Also, at this point, when the GDR authorities started recognizing some demands and promising to fulfil them, *Granma* again repeated the message of its authorities.

No global explanation was given as to why the GDR collapsed. Still, news coverage together with analysis highlighted Western pressures, including false promises directed toward the citizens of the GDR, and to some extent, tensions related to the division of German were highlighted, more than problems with the East German model of society. While such factors may have contributed to the fall of the Berlin Wall and later, the fall of the GDR, it is clearly a very partial narrative and one that suits the Cuban state, as it does not have to critically examine state socialism. It emphasizes external pressures and thus underscores the importance of Cuban unity.

1.4 Example 4: The Fall of Ceaușescu—Ambiguous Reporting, Little Willingness to Defend the Regime as It Breaks Down

Among the nominally socialist countries in Eastern Europe, the case of Romania has its peculiarities. It is a country that had maintained a partially independent line in respect to the USSR. The pro-Soviet strands within the ruling Party were purged in 1952. The Soviet military forces withdrew from the country in exchange for Romania's participation in the suppression of the rebellion of 1956 in Hungary.[35] Subsequently, Romania decided not to support the Soviet invasion of Czechoslovakia in 1968, forged ties with the West and preserved the relations it had with China,[36] despite the USSR–China conflict. Nicolae Ceaușescu's regime had sultanistic characteristics.[37] Romania was also the only country in Eastern Europe where the transition to capitalism occurred amid widespread violence.

I do not have detailed information on how the Communist Party of Cuba perceived or expressed itself regarding Romania and its politics during the years before the events that led to the fall and execution of the Ceaușescus in December 1989. It should be noted that the coverage of Romania in *Granma* during most of 1989 is sparse and tends toward a protocol-based style in which the relations between the two countries are reaffirmed or highlighted "dryly," and very little is said about the internal reality of the country.

This might have to do partly with the character of the Romanian regime, as it was rather opaque, and *Granma* depended on official sources, but it could also be an indication that the PCC and especially some of its journalists were rather "lukewarm" toward Ceaușescu, and it was found to be preferable not to go much into depth on the topic. An educated guess, however, suggests that the differences between Cuba and Romania were less profound than those between the USSR and Romania, a relationship that was tense both in the pre-Gorbachev years and during Gorbachev's period.

Fidel Castro had a history of challenging official Soviet positions and the great power's intention to gain more control over Cuba, although most explicitly in the earlier years of the Revolution. This is a point Cuba had in common with Romania, although differences and tensions did not reach the same level as between Romania and the USSR. It is also quite possible that Cubans who visited the Soviet Union were receiving more critical information on Romania than what was presented in the Cuban press. This might also have been the case for journalists. The editor of an important cultural journal in Cuba once claimed to me informally that Cubans who were sent to Romania to study were often surprised by its unambiguously dictatorial traits. There were probably also critical perceptions at the Cuban government level. But the official

---

35 Bideleux and Jeffries, 551.
36 Ibid.
37 Houchang E. Chehabi and Juan J. Linz, *Sultanistic Regimes* (Baltimore: Johns Hopkins University Press, 1998).

position of Cuba was to comment little on the internal affairs of allied countries, and its priorities in the late 1980s seemed to be on preserving unity in the international revolutionary and communist movement above all.

The little news that was published on Romania during the month before December 1989, before violence and regime change took hold of the country, oscillates between a neutral and positive tone. Reporting on the country, however, was so brief and "routine-ish" in its style that one could get the impression that the country was not among *Granma's* priorities. Some news in brief items were published, such as "The Romanian delegation visited the CDR [Cuban neighborhood organizations]" (March 28, 1989) and "Ceaușescu criticizes attempts by the West to offer recipes to other countries" (July 28, 1989).

Granma did not comment directly on the internal problems of Romania, but on March 10, 1989, it included a reference to a statement from reformist Hungary that proposed condemning Romania for human rights abuses. It reported that Cuba's two most important economic partners, the USSR and East Germany, remained neutral during the vote (in other words, both a reform-oriented socialist country and a non-reform oriented socialist country refrained from defending Romania).

In October the same year, *Granma* reports briefly that Romania is trying to stabilize access to goods, so a conscientious reader who actually noticed this information would have understood that there had been supply problems. However, most stories on Romania in the newspaper were most likely ignored by many readers, due to their very limited size and discreet presentation. During the crisis in December, as widespread violence broke out, news coverage was much more detailed.

Romania was a strictly controlled and closed country until late 1989, when demonstrations and riots surged in the city of Timisoara on December 16, following the arrest of a Hungarian Protestant priest. Subsequently, the revolt spread to other parts of the country. A week later, on December 22, a member of the ruling Communist Party, Ion Iliescu, announced on radio and television the creation of what he called the National Salvation Front, composed largely of members of the ruling Party. According to the *New York Times*, at the time it was widely suspected that Iliescu had ties with Gorbachev.[38]

It could be said that the coverage of the *Granma* newspaper from those days of protest and social explosion until the death of Ceaușescu is confirmed little more than a week later goes through two short phases: There is a first phase from December 19 to 22, and another that only covers two days of reporting,

---

38   See, for example, "Upheaval in the East: A Rising Star; A Man Who Could Become Romania's Leader," *New York Times*, December 24, 1989.

from December 23 to December 25 (December 24 is Sunday, and there is no newspaper). On the 26th of that month, the death of Ceaușescu is briefly announced on *Granma's* front page, and some information is given about the official positions of East Germany and the Soviet Union regarding the new situation.

One difference between the two phases is that during the first (December 19 to 22), the news was produced by Prensa Latina, while during the second phase (December 23 and 25), the information coming from Prensa Latina was also extensively complemented with materials from different press agencies of the capitalist world and from the USSR. Both the Romanian governments and the opposition's actions and points of view were reflected during the first phase but at a time when Western media were, by then, publishing unconfirmed reports that suggested many deaths as victims of fighting and repression in the city of Timisoara; *Prensa Latina* and *Granma* first ignored these and quoted an official Romanian statement that mentioned no deaths at all.

During the second phase, however, the coverage was explicit about the violence and very explicit in general, and the rebel's views actually predominated since there was little on the Ceaușescu regime's position to report on, as the regime was disappearing. The coverage on December 23 and 25 was extensive, "pluralist" in that it introduced much information both from the capitalist world and the Socialist Bloc but also from Prensa Latina, and it gave a very wide and open view of the situation. I will limit myself to giving a summary of the coverage during its first phase (December 19 to 22) and then focus mainly on the coverage on December 23, since I consider that the coverage on that specific day reflects the spirit and general tone of the coverage during the second phase (December 23 and 25).

The events in Timisoara on December 16 were covered by *Granma*—though they appeared with a slight delay and downplayed accounts of violence. The delay is partly due to the fact that the 17th was Sunday and the newspaper was not published, but even on the 18th there was also no information on the matter [some cuts have been made in the paper by the aforementioned sports enthusiast, but the layout suggests that it is little likely that anything on Romania had been removed]. But from December 19 until December 22, 1989, there was some information on the internal conflict, by now spreading violently to Romania's capital Bucharest. On December 19, the topic was given about $\frac{1}{25}$th of page 4, on December 20 it received about $\frac{1}{10}$ of page 4, on December 21 nothing was said, and on December 22 the topic covered $\frac{1}{5}$ of page 7, a considerable amount of text taking into account the large page format.

On December 19, *Granma* published a Prensa Latina article titled "Traffic between Romania and Yugoslavia has been closed due to disorders." It said that the protests originated due to the arrest of a Hungarian-born pastor, Laszlo

ANALYZING THE NEWS ACCOUNTS

Tokes, "who in the past made statements about alleged human rights violations in the country (Romania)." The writer cited the Yugoslav consulate in Timisoara: "The protesters expressed their solidarity with the religious leader and used the opportunity to take other actions that the local authorities considered to be in violation of national laws." *Granma* also reported that security forces "intervened to disperse the demonstrators" and that they were able to restore calm. *Prensa Latina* was apparently observing events and did not commit itself strongly to one view, yet it also ignored reports of widespread violence in Timisoara, though as we will see, it might have had valid reasons at the time to believe that this information was false (even if it was not).

On December 20, there was further information from Prensa Latina but now in a very different tone. The heading says that "Romania will not allow that its laws are ignored or violated," and the information quotes a statement from *Scintela*, the newspaper of the ruling Communist Party of Romania. *Scintela* here maintains that the Romanian state is socialist and "stimulates the responsible participation of all citizens in the national work, but will not allow anyone to ignore or violate the laws." Curiously, on this day, the information more strictly adheres to the Romanian governments' position, suggesting perhaps that the Cuban correspondent(s), located in Romania, were afraid of reporting more freely as the situation became tenser. At this point, the paper still referred to the events in Timisoara as mere "disorders."

On December 22, there were several items coupled together visually in a box, notably an article entitled "The situation in Romania is extremely tense," from Prensa Latina. It gives information about Ceaușescu's speech on December 21, a speech that would later be remembered as his last. The story began by citing Ceaușescu, who called for "total unity to defend socialism," and said that "now we need more than ever to act in the spirit of socialist democracy and discuss all problems." He promised to improve the standard of living in the country and warned that the tense situation could lead to a scenario similar to that of Czechoslovakia in 1968—when the Soviet Union intervened to stop alleged dangerous policies and Western infiltration. It is recognized that Ceaușescu "was interrupted in his speech by unknown people" and that "he could not conclude his speech normally, for reasons still to be confirmed." *Granma* also included reports that a state of emergency had been reported in the county of Timis [on the border with Yugoslavia; Timisoara is its county seat] and on a request for an urgent meeting of the UN Security Council to discuss the situation.

There was also another Prensa Latina item titled "Demonstrations in the capital," where it was said that two people were killed and that "at night the automatic gunshots continued to be heard." Some descriptions attracted our attention:

Bucharest, December 21 (PL). Military and security forces today reinforced their positions at strategic points in this capital, while the university students reaffirmed their decision to continue on the street.

Leaflets distributed by citizens indicate that the students sent delegates to all the important points of Bucharest, including labor centers, calling for people to go out in the streets and city squares this morning to start a general strike.

From loudspeakers installed in the Intercontinental Hotel, in the heart of the city, young people make constant calls to the population, also, to join the demonstrations that started this morning after unidentified people interrupted a speech by President Nicolae Ceaușescu.

Thus, the coverage on December 22 began reproducing parts of what Ceaușescu said in what is now known as his last speech. The argument that was reproduced is very much similar to the discourse of the Cuban government (it focused much on unity and on defending socialism and/or the nation). If one read only this part, it could give or reinforce the idea that Cuba and Romania were essentially countries defending the same ideals and that Prensa Latina and *Granma* were trying to underline this common identity by quoting Ceaușescu as he used much of the same rhetoric as Fidel Castro.

However, the rest of the article suggested more critical positions. Prensa Latina described the government's opponents as "young," "universitarian," and "citizens." It is also stated that they called for "solidarity" with Timisoara's population. These are all positive words in many contexts, but especially in the context of a newspaper originated during the Cuban Revolution, which was produced in part because of the actions of young people and university students. In addition, in the Latin American context, university students are often associated with struggles for freedom and justice—as in the song "Me gustan los estudiantes" ("I love the students") by Chilean singer-songwriter Violeta Parra (1917–1967).[39] Therefore, the choice of words can be a subliminal message by the correspondent—not able to report openly from Romania and perhaps unsure what *Granma* would be willing to publish—to convey to the readers in Cuba that the demonstrators were worthy of support and struggling

---

39   The mentioning of the Intercontinental Hotel is probably more of a coincidence than a subliminal message, as this was a place where important events were taking place, and many journalists were reporting from the building, so it made sense to mention it. Still, for some readers it might have given further associations to the first months of the Cuban Revolution, when the rebels used the centrally located Hilton Hotel in Havana as the seat of the provisional government—what is now known as Hotel Habana Libre. Both are amongst the tallest buildings of their respective cities.

against a dictatorship. The further coverage suggests that this reading has some basis. As mentioned, on December 23—the day after the Ceaușescus fled the capital—*Granma's* coverage changed markedly.

Notably, the newspaper began to depend strongly on Western news agencies, as the Romanian propaganda apparatus had fallen apart. But Prensa Latina also wrote more freely on the conflict. The coverage on December 23 and 25 was remarkable mainly because of the multiple number of viewpoints; it consisted largely of a potpourri of small items of information, news notes or similar, all taken from different news agencies from different countries, often with somewhat contrasting versions.

Contrary to the case of the coverage of the migration crisis in East Germany, in this case there were very few explicit assessments; instead, the news tended very much toward a descriptive style. A good example of this is the coverage of December 23, which fills a third of the newspaper's last page. The information on Romania on that day is contained within a box that bears the main title "Confusing situation created in Romania."[40] Under the main headline, there is a summary of the news from Romania on that day: "* Different versions with regard to the whereabouts of Ceaușescu. * Heavy fighting is reported in Bucharest and other parts of the country. * Ceaușescu's son arrested. * A so-called National Committee for Democracy has been created."[41]

Under that summary in points, the first news item begins: "Bucharest, December 22. At the same time as the AP (Associated Press) reported that the whereabouts and status of Ceaușescu were unknown, other agencies reported that heavy fighting was recorded in the Romanian capital and other parts of the country." Then an IPS report was quoted. It reported on a story provided by Romanian radio that talked about "dramatic fighting" between army forces and units of the Ceaușescus' security apparatus. After IPS, some information from ANSA is quoted:

> ANSA, on the other hand, reports that a National Committee for Democracy was created today in Romania, following the collective resignation of Prime Minister Constantin Dăscălescu government and the removal and arrest of President Ceaușescu. The agency itself notes that this Committee is made up of military personnel that are not committed to

---

40   The coverage on this day is similar to the one during the two days that follow, although it is the one that uses the most Western sources.
41   The word "named" or "so-called" (*llamado*) has been added before the name of the "National Committee for Democracy," which *could* indicate disapproval of this organization, but it could also just be a way of underlining that, at the time, *Granma* still does not know what it really represents.

Ceaușescu, of workers, students and intellectuals, and that Ion Iliescu, former secretary of the Central Committee of the Party, who had been dismissed by Ceaușescu, announced its creation from the residence of the Party.

After summarizing the main political events of the day before in Romania, the newspaper turned its attention to the situation of violence in the streets of Bucharest, quoting yet other sources. From Moscow, the Western EFE agency, referring to what had been said on Soviet television, reported that in the streets of Bucharest there were hundreds of dead and wounded, due to the clashes, and the building of the Central Committee of the Romanian Communist Party had been semi-destroyed. There was information from ANSA that Belgrade (Yugoslavia) television showed scenes of the Romanian Presidential Palace on fire. Before this first part of the news in the box concludes, IPS was cited again, indicating that Ceaușescu had traveled by helicopter to the airport and, after being arrested there, "managed to continue on the road."

Then a note appeared bearing the title "Strong battles in the capital," and then "Radio and TV channels in danger," both presented by Prensa Latina. The text reiterates that clashes are occurring between military forces and security troops that remain loyal to Ceaușescu, but now in Bucharest. The note reports that:

> Elements still defending the deposed government of Nicolae Ceaușescu, said the sources [it refers to the new presenters of state radio and television], have again opened fire against the population in the Republic Square. At the same time, there is also shooting in the immediate vicinity of the radio and television buildings.
>
> In this setting it was announced that the population was called upon to face that aggression, to conserve the power of the people. [...]
>
> The streets of Bucharest are completely dark, illuminated at some moments by flares.

Here *Granma* essentially reproduces the version of Romanian television and radio events, now under control of people opposed to Ceaușescu. It describes the "elements addicted to the deposed government" as people who open fire on protesters and as committing an "aggression." At the same time, "flares" (in Spanish, *bengalas*, this might also be translated as sparklers) are often associated with celebrations.

After this report, another note appears that is titled "Provisional Government" (Prensa Latina). This note briefly tells us that a new government has been formed, with former Minister Corneliu Mănescu as its head, an important political personality who had been Minister of Foreign Affairs and also President of the UN General Assembly. A photo of the inauguration was included.

The next item contained within the same box is called "On the death of the Minister of Defense." Again, it has been presented by the Cuban-based press agency Prensa Latina. According to the note, an official statement from the new authorities urges people to "to trust in the justice [system]" and furthermore reports that former Minister Vasile Milea has just taken his own life, and, surprisingly, an explication is added; he (allegedly) had realized that he had acted as a traitor "at the service of imperialist circles." The announcement from the new authorities also asks that the people "help restore order and calm," and to "solve our problems in close unity." As we can see, the new authorities, along with the less-than-tasteful speculation on the reasons for Miles's suicide, adopt a socialist rhetoric ("imperialist circles"); here, it should be taken into account that Mănescu had a communist background.

There is also a short note titled "Son of Ceauşescu is arrested," from Prensa Latina. According to the information, the deposed president's son, Nicu Ceauşescu, had tried to take a group of workers as hostages in the region of Sibiu, which he governed, and that "unknown people" in the same region had tried to poison the drinking water of the population. This is an accusation that echoes old propaganda against Jews and others and that should obviously have been treated with a more critical attitude.

Finally, there is a fifth note entitled "Declaration from the USSR," citing the information from the *Granma* correspondents' office in the USSR, which explains that the Second Congress of People's Deputies of the Soviet Union—the new Soviet legislature that had been established by Gorbachev earlier the same year—had expressed its concern about Romanian events. At the end, it states that 32 deputies voted against the declaration and that 60 abstained out of a total of 1809 deputies.

We will not include a detailed analysis of the coverage on December 25, but it maintained the plural and open character of reporting and contained a new and more detailed report on violence: It referred to a story of 2,000 secret police paratroopers allegedly landing in Timisoara—it is not clear if this story was true—and recognized that fierce battles were taking place and that central authority controlled only the central plaza of the city. The Soviet agency TASS was also quoted claiming that there were "hidden snipers" in Timisoara. It stated that "the number of deaths and injured people is reported to be high," and Prensa Latina mentioned "thousands" of injured people and the need for blood and urgent humanitarian help.

Perhaps more surprising, though, is that Prensa Latina referred to the changes in Romania as a "social revolution"—those are clearly positive words in a Cuban context. *Granma* was also reproducing (through TASS) what the new leaders said, in their language: Ion Iliescu was quoted as objecting to "the leading role of the sole Party" and suggesting "a pluralist democratic system" with "free elections." Here, the newspaper reported on ideas that were in conflict with official Cuban politics and did not challenge what the new leaders of Romania said.

Finally, in *Granma's* edition of December 26—at the bottom right corner of the front page—there is a news story that covers approximately ½12 of the page, and which must have captured most readers' attention immediately. The heading says that "It is affirmed that Ceaușescu and his wife have been executed." The news story is characterized by a descriptive, "neutral" tone and says that the two were convicted "in a summary and secret trial" by "an extraordinary military court." The story briefly summarizes who the two were: "General Secretary of the Communist Party of his country and President of the Republic since 1975, in an interrupted manner" and, referring to Elena Ceaușescu, "Member of the political bureau of the ruling Party and Deputy Prime Minister." The article furthermore states that "Both of them were charged with a series of crimes and were held responsible for the crisis in that country," then it is reported that the Romanian capital "woke up to more calm" and that the new authorities have dictated a "program of actions to restore order."

It is striking how *Granma* again reproduces the version of the new authorities and that there is no real assessment or comment on the dramatic fall of a government that Cuba had relations and formal cooperation with until its end. The news story promised more information on page 5, but the only relevant information there was a note with the heading "The USSR denies that Romania has asked for military help."

Absences are as important as what was included in the coverage. Notably, there is no commentary or suggestion by *Granma* that echoed Ceaușescu's claims of imperialist infiltration in Romania, not even before the crisis in December. This could suggest that *Granma's* editors and the Cuban Party had for a time been critical of Romania, though never distancing themselves publicly from the regime. The lack of opinion, avoiding clear expressions of partisanship, emotional outbursts, and so on was a way of saying subliminally that the Cuba authorities were observing these events from a distance and that Romania's problems were not Cuba's.

It is true that *Granma* did not immediately publish the stories of deaths when violence first broke out in Timisoara. Being located in Romania, the

Prensa Latina office might not have been willing to publish such a story as this could put correspondents in personal danger as well as have some effect on Cuban–Romanian relations.

It is also possible that the correspondent genuinely believed that these stories were propaganda and had reasons to do so. Although there had been brutal violence in Timisoara, the details were at the moment impossible to confirm since no international correspondents were let into the city during the first days after the killings. Western media at an early point published stories of 300–400 deaths in Timisoara (*Verdens Gang*, December 20, 1989). Though the numbers were exaggerated, this news was in essence true: There had been many deaths. However, Western media also widely published photo material of a mass grave in Timisoara that later turned out to be a hoax and is now often used as an example of bad reporting where rumors are not verified. This had real world consequences as it contributed to accelerating the conflict but also regime change in Romania.[42]

It must be taken into account that *Granma* is also a newspaper that was and is extremely wary of anything that might resemble propaganda and that is launched again a nominally socialist regime and has often alleged that false information is used against Cuba to destabilize and try to legitimate intervention. It is indeed questionable that *Granma* did not immediately mention at least that these information items were circulating widely in the international press, even if it did not believe them. However, the belief that the information was not to be trusted was not totally unfounded, as the exaggerated numbers and the story of mass graves suggest. Romanian military prosecutors have more recently alleged there was also a deliberate spreading of false information and even false sound of shooting to create the conditions for the fall of Ceauşescu.[43]

One interesting detail is that *Granma's* coverage changed very quickly, as it became clearer how severe events were. By December 23, it wrote very explicitly about events, including a wide range of sources—perhaps a wider range than most Western media since they had their own correspondent, but also used sources from both capitalist and socialist news agencies. The number of deaths mentioned at this time was not too far off from the real numbers, while some media in the West repeated wildly exaggerated numbers.

---

42   AFP, "Misinformation from the archives: Timisoara's 'mass graves,'" *France 24*, Dec. 20, 2019.
43   Ana Maria Luca, "Romania's 1989 Uprising Was 'Orchestrated,' Prosecutors Say," *Balkan Insight*, December 18, 2017.

Granma's look at Romania had been that of a somewhat distanced ally for a time, but when the regime started to break down, it quickly distanced itself even more. Unlike in the case of the GDR, Cuba had not promoted Romania as a model of development, so its fall meant less in terms of loss of prestige, and while it shared some features with Romania, such as opposing reform socialism in general and in its independent national positions—Cuba had always distanced itself from any extreme cult of personality, by avoiding statues of living leaders and so on. At least the Cuban leadership must have been wary of the sultanistic characteristics of the Romanian regime, of its severe human rights violations and its lack of rational governance, such as when it decided to construct a megalomaniac Palace of the Parliament building in the midst of an economic crisis. It was a regime that had also received strong criticism from Romanian leftist positions.[44] Also, Ceaușescu had strong tensions with the USSR, Cuba's main ally and economic support at the time.

Actually, it might have been seen as a possibility at the time of the uprising that the new rebels could align with Gorbachev's USSR and try to reform the system, which would certainly have been more favorable for the Cuban government than the introduction of capitalism and possibly even to Ceaușescu's regime.

Cuban academic Esteban—one of the informants for the oral part of this study—told me during our interview that the differences in how the different Eastern Bloc countries were covered by *Granma* had to do with the perception that prevailed in Cuban political circles and Cuban society of each socialist country in Europe. For example, he claimed, "East Germany was seen as a kind of model state for us, and Bulgaria was seen as a model of agriculture for us." In this sense, when the fall of the Berlin Wall took place, it was not seen as something positive or necessary, but "as a failure of socialism, as something that ideologically did not favor us." Although practical and strategical reasons might also have influenced the decision to cover the crisis in a certain distanced manner, as suggested, it is probably true, as Esteban stated, that "what happened in Romania, when Ceaușescu and his wife were shot, the number of dresses and shoes that his wife had, the corruption and all that, this was perceived in a different manner [...] it was seen [in Cuba, by Cuban authorities] as a logical and clear consequence of the deterioration of Romania."

To summarize and conclude, although *Granma* talked about Romania as a friend and ally during most of 1989, it did not do so very often, and when it did,

---

44 Silviu Brucan, *The Wasted Generation: Memoirs of the Romanian Journey from Capitalism to Socialism and Back* (Boulder: Westview Press, 1993), 153.

ANALYZING THE NEWS ACCOUNTS

it was in a protocolar or routine way, without any apparent enthusiasm. It presented enough information to make it clear that other countries in the socialist community were critical or at least not overly enthusiastic about the situation in Romania. As protests broke out in December, it reported on events, but at first downplayed or ignored reports of widespread violence. To some degree it reported on both sides of the story, but it gave more space to government positions.

As the conflict spread to the capital, this changed in a matter of days. During the days before the executions, news on the Ceaușescu regime's repression was published as it came in, and the rebels were presented in a neutral or even positive manner. As the rebellion grew and the Romanian state apparatus changed hands, *Granma* continued to give quotes or refer to what the official sources said, but these now reflected anti-Ceaușescu positions precisely because the propaganda apparatus was now in the hands of the new rulers. At this point, these versions were largely complemented by general information on the situation that was coming from major news agencies in the capitalist West and also the USSR.

During all the year, reporting was very different from the enthusiastic elegies of the GDR both before the regime started collapsing and during these events but also from the more open, almost "Western-style" reporting on Poland, or the curious "listening" to the ideological debate on reforms in Hungary. Even if the Cuban authorities never did break with the old Romanian regime, the coverage suggests that Cuba wanted to distance itself somewhat even before open conflict broke out, and they did not respond in favor of or defend the falling regime.

The lack of any explanation or analysis still suggests that the topic was an uncomfortable one. The visual presentation and discreet placement of the news suggests that there was still some perception that the news was embarrassing for socialism or the Cuban government or that it could have some sort of negative impact on Cuba. After all, Cuba had relations and some cooperation with the old government, and as with all state socialist countries, there were structures, policies, and forms of rhetoric that were shared. Yet, by informing in a detailed and pluralistic manner on the crisis in December 1989, *Granma* retained a certain credibility (the GDR coverage shortly before might have raised some eyebrows as a society that had been presented as a model was suddenly the scene of major public protests). Since *Granma* did not make its position very clear, it is difficult to say if the PCC had conducted a detailed analysis on the causes of the Romanian collapse, but a subliminal message might be: Ceaușescu fell because of the regime's problematic practices.

2 The Crisis of Socialism in the USSR

2.1 Example 1: The 500-Day Program—Covering the Economic Debate Professionally But Making It No Secret Who Is the Adversary

Between 1987 and 1991, several proposals and plans for reform of the Soviet economy were presented. Marie Lavigne highlights six attempts.[45] First, in June 1987, the CPSU approved Perestroika, a "radical restructuring of economic management." Then came the program of "a mixed economy with planned market economy" presented by Vice Premier Minister Abalkin (in November 1989); Prime Minister Ryzhkov's proposal to introduce a "regulated market economy" (May 1990); the Stanislav-Shatalin Program to move to a market economy in 500 days (autumn 1990); the anti-crisis plan of Prime Minister V. Pavlov (April 1991); and finally, the Yavlinski-Allison Plan (June 1991), similar to the Shatalin program, but this time to be applied over the course of five and a half years.

We are going to analyze the coverage of *Granma* of the debate that arose in late summer-autumn of 1990, when two of the aforementioned proposals were debated: The radical Shatalin Plan (the 500-day Plan) and (a revised version of) that of Ryzhkov, which included elements of the earlier Abalkin plan and proposed keeping strategic parts in the hands of the state as well as introducing market reforms in a gradual manner. In Shatalin's proposal, much power would be transferred to the republics, and the word socialism does not even appear in the document.[46] For Cuban authorities, the Ryzhkov plan would clearly be the lesser evil.

The economic debate in 1990 took place at a time when Cuba had just entered the crisis known as the Special Period. In the Soviet Union, the economic debate took place in a tense and shifting environment. Soviet leader Mikhail Gorbachev, known for his often conciliatory approaches, ordered the Ryzhkov and Shatalin teams to work together, though without luck. By early September, he asked one of his advisors (Abel Aganbegyan) to draw up a conciliatory proposal, but this turned out to be almost identical to that of Shatalin (also one of Gorbachev's main advisers). The Russian republic, with Boris Yeltsin as an influential actor, put further pressure on Gorbachov as it symbolically approved the Shatalin plan. Then, Gorbachev asked Aganbegyan to draw up a "Presidential Plan," a merge of all the three proposals. This plan was approved by the Supreme Soviet on October 19, 1990. It followed the main line of the radical Shatalin Plan but did not include an application schedule.[47] During the

---

45 Marie Lavigne, *Del socialismo al mercado: la difícil transición económica de la Europa del Este* (Madrid: Ediciones Encuentro, SA, 1997), 155.
46 Edward A. Hewett and Victor H. Winston, *Milestones in Glasnost and Perestroyka: The Economy* (Washington, DC: Brookings Institution, 1991), 445.
47 Heyward Isham, ed. *Remaking Russia* (Prague; New York: Institute for EastWest Studies, 1995), 297.

debate, the power balance shifted much in favour of the radicals, yet this new document could be seen as a statement of intent rather than a concrete plan.[48]

A first observation of how the debate is covered by Granma is that a lot is written about it, but it is not highlighted visually. The debate taking place in the USSR is not something the newspaper ignores, far from it, but it is generally *not* presented with bold titles or photos, as the importance of the topic might suggest, and it is often relegated to the last pages in the newspaper.

To give some context, we should mention some specificities of the general coverage of the USSR in *Granma* during these times. The coverage of the USSR between August and October 1990 reflects many aspects of Soviet reality at the time, such as the economic debate, social crisis, anti-communist demonstrations, separatist attempts within the USSR, and other symptoms of discontent. Often, we recall, several pieces of information from that country were visually gathered and presented within a box,[49] which often occupied between the eighth and the third part of the international page and usually appeared at the top or middle of the page.

It should be remembered that *Granma* does not have advertising, it also generally avoids large photos and other "ornaments" typical of the commercial press (for example, white spaces). Also, in 1990, it was still a large-format newspaper. Therefore, measured quantitatively, we would be talking about a considerable amount of textual information that was dedicated to Soviet issues, and between August and October 1990, a significant part of this coverage of the USSR centered on the economic debate going on in that country. A noteworthy detail is that even when the news is clearly perceived as something that does not suit Cuba's interests, the box with news from the Soviet Union is generally *not* placed at the bottom of the page (something that was often done with the "bad news" of other socialist countries, suggesting that it was something the newspaper did not want to give much attention or did not approve of). Any major news regarding the USSR was of course in economic terms of great importance to Cuba, but this might also have been a way to signal Cuba's most important ally that it recognizes this debate as legitimate and wants to report on it.

---

48   Hewett and Winston, 444.
49   *Granma* also published materials that had to do with the Soviet Union *outside* of this visual box, but they did not deal with the economic debate. During August–October 1990, these news materials often talked about increasing and urgent problems in the supply of oil and other materials from the Soviet Union to Cuba, as the first state more and more entered a state of disorganization and became unable to fulfill its contracts. Brief news items regarding internal issues of the Soviet Union also appeared as short items in the stable column "Direct line" (*Hilo Directo*), but they were not about economic reform.

News about the internal events of the Soviet Union and Eastern Europe *do not usually* appear on the front page of the newspaper. This is also the case with almost all the news from Eastern Europe. This may be in response to an editorial policy whereby the newspaper's front page is preferably used to highlight information and news that may serve to serve the ideological and political objectives of the Communist Party, especially promoting certain values and prioritizing the successes of the Cuban system, which can inspire the population,[50] more than topics that could be seen as demoralizing or even stirring anti-socialist emotions, such as crises and conflict in allied countries.

Just leafing through the newspapers, however, reveals that the amount of information on the subject of economic debate is quite extensive. The first time there is information on the economic debate is August 30, 1990, and by October 20 the same year, the coverage of the debate concludes, as it is informed that the Soviet politicians adopt the "Presidential plan" that is based on the Shatalin Plan but is less clear on its implementation; after that, the topic receives limited attention.

I have identified news dealing with the topic of the economic debate on the following dates: August 30, September 3–7, 10–12, 14, 17–18, 20, 22, 24–27, October 2, 5, 7, 10, 13, October 15–18, 20, and 24. On some dates, the debate on the reform constitutes the main story within the "USSR box," other days it appears as a smaller item or substory more toward the end of the box, after information has been given on other things that have happened in the USSR, when updates on the debate are not are given briefly within another story. News on the subject is, as stated, relatively detailed. However, during the period, there are never really longer articles or features on the topic. At the beginning of the debate, most of the news material is supplied by Prensa Latina, but the official Soviet news agency TASS is also used as a source and occasionally also Western agencies: the AFP and ANSA. In October, there is also news signed by Nidia Díaz, correspondent for *Granma* in the Soviet Union.

A second observation is that Granma covers activities of all major actors and tendencies, although not in an equal manner. When reading the coverage of the economic debate as a whole, there is a tendency to prioritize the "conservative" sectors (those that are against the reforms) and the "moderates" (the tendency to which Soviet leader Gorbachev belongs, at least at the beginning of the

---

50 During these summer and autumn months of 1990, *Granma*'s front page is largely dedicated to topics of strategic or propagandistic interest, such as an initiative for reducing consumption and saving resources in Cuba, on major works in Cuba (works in progress or that have been inaugurated), the US war in the Middle East, activities and speeches by Fidel Castro, official events, sporting events, etc.

debate). The first one was of course closest to Cuba ideologically, but the "moderates" were more acceptable than the radicals, and Cuba's relations with the USSR depended upon the "moderate" Gorbachev government. Less, but still considerable space was also given to the "radicals" (pro-capitalist forces) and their proposals.

It is important to mention that at that time it was largely the radical forces (Boris Yeltsin, Stanislav Shatalin, and others) that had the initiative and were "making news"; therefore, giving more space to conservatives and moderates clearly reflects an ideological position against the radicals. There are still some cases where the radical forces' activities make up the center of the story, and where their demands are highlighted with large headlines. Two examples are the headlines "On Sunday they will demand the resignation of the Soviet government" (September 15, 1990) and "Protesters demand that the Government in Moscow resign" (September 17, 1990).

A third observation on the coverage of the economic debate in the USSR is that although a descriptive ("objective") style predominates, there are also materials with a more discursive tone. A descriptive style does not mean, of course, that the coverage is impartial. It should also be noted that occasionally, especially during the month of October 1990, some news *was* published where journalists broke with this impersonal, "objective" tone and quite explicitly express personal criteria.

Therefore, we will give some examples of the information that *Granma* has to offer on the different political tendencies that took part in the debate. We can use as an example the coverage on the first date when the economic debate was covered, August 30. This reflects some characteristics typical of most of the coverage of the debate. On the mentioned date, news of the USSR has been bundled together in a box under the main headline "Abalkin denounces that anti-socialist forces try to eliminate central government in the USSR" (Abalkin was vice president of the Council of Ministers in the USSR, and as mentioned, a central actor in the economic debate).[51]

The first news note within the box has nothing to do with the debate, though, and various notes appear with varying degree of relevance to us, as

---

51   The decision to give a preferential space to this type of criteria reflects the newspaper's political priorities, and the use of the verb *to denounce* (instead of for, example, "thinks") gives weight to what Abalkin says. The headline does not indicate that *Granma* identifies with Abalkin—he was the promoter of a social-democratic model for the Soviet Union. See: Hewett and Winston, 341. But by publishing this news, Cuba makes the reader aware that the USSR is in danger and by treating Abalkin as a trustworthy actor, they signal that his points of view (and those of Ryzhkov and Gorbachev) are respected by Cuba despite differences.

their headlines indicate: "State of Emergency in Armenia," "Variants of transition," and "Gorbachev–Yeltsin Dialogue"[52] (note that while the main heading is clearly politically charged, to convey a message even to those that do not read the full story, this is less apparent in the case of these smaller or subordinate headings). I cite the items that are most relevant to our analysis:

> Variants of transition
>
> Moscow, August 29 (Prensa Latina). Academician Abel Aganbeguian said here today that prior to the transition in the USSR to the market economy, more than 100 proposals from various Soviet republics, ministries and foreign scientists have been examined.
>
> Aganbeguian, who chairs a so-called independent commission that will consider the variants of the introduction of the reform, stated in a press conference that his group was presenting a report with numerous recommendations to the President of this multinational State and the government of the Russian Federation.
>
> Amongst the recommendations, he mentioned the stabilization of the economic life of the country, the creation of a free enterprise system and analyzing the quantitative evolution of the consequences of that transition.
>
> Referring to the two parallel programs […], the academic said that the program of the government [the one proposed by Nikolai Ryzhkov, our comment], was analyzed by the Supreme Soviet of the USSR in May, and is slow and palliative and does not foresee a rapid transit toward market prices.
>
> On the other hand, he pointed out that price increases should not be the first step. Previously we must achieve a monetary balance and pay attention to financial problems, added the academic.
>
> Aganbeguian also expressed concern because of the problems that the new reform would face, such as unemployment and the dismissal of workers.

The use of the word "so-called" in the second paragraph has clearly been put there to question the independence of the commission. This constitutes a valid and necessary "clarification" if one takes into account that the academic Aganbeguian was also an advisor to Gorbachev. But a more interesting

---

52   It is possible that the main headline ("Abalkin denounces...") was not prepared by the correspondents, but rather that the wording was prepared at the desk in Cuba to convey a specific message.

observation is that the newspaper reproduces Aganbeguian's criticisms of a more moderate plan for economic reform, the one that had first been proposed by Prime Minister Ryzhkov in May of the same year. According to Aganbeguian, that plan was "slow and palliative and does not foresee a rapid step toward market prices." Readers know that *Granma* is generally opposed to a market economy. However, an impartial tone is used when reproducing the ideas of Aganbeguian, who proposes a faster transition toward market prices. *Granma* signals that Aganbeguian is not impartial, which is true. But instead of omitting Aganbeguian's position, or disqualifying him, his claims are reproduced.[53]

In the news note "Gorbachev–Yeltsin Dialogue," a reference is made to comments by the head of President Gorbachev's press service: "[...] the spokesman recalled that tomorrow there will be held a joint meeting of the Presidential councils and the Federation, in which economic policy and the country's move to a market economy will be analyzed, among other topics." The newspaper, as this example shows, does not hide in any way that Gorbachev sees as his goal the introduction of a regulated market economy; that is, that he is no longer just promoting the moderate reforms he proposed in 1987, although it should also be said that at this point (August 1990), it was still not known that Gorbachev would very soon adopt an even more radical position (the final "Presidential Plan" reflected such radical positions, as, we repeat, this was essentially the Shatalin proposal without a time schedule). Therefore, some concepts are used that we do not think the editors like very much—such as "market economy" and "free enterprise"—because, on other occasions, they are described in *Granma* as misleading terms. *Granma's* ideologues would probably have preferred words such as "capitalism."[54] It is possible that the newspaper uses these terms as a way of staying true to the source. *Granma* does not hide, in this case, what the reforms are about or who support them, uncomfortable though the truth may be.[55]

---

53   Note also the serious, almost academic tone of the news.
54   Sometimes, for example in a story on September 15, the radical opposition is described as pro-capitalist rather than pro-market, as it usually defines itself.
55   Similar coverage is given to meetings between Gorbachev and Western leaders during these months—at this stage, they are often related to the ongoing economic reforms in the Soviet Union. The coverage of this news also tends to be written in a descriptive tone, without very explicit assessments. Let us take as an example the news coverage under the headline "Gorbachev-Bush summit held" (September 10, 1990). The headline is followed by various items. First, there is a joint statement by the two leaders on the Iraqi aggression in Kuwait, but then it is reported that "The president of the United States, George Bush, advocated in favor of the granting of assistance to the Soviet Union in the successful realization of the reforms that are carried out there," and Gorbachev is quoted questioning

Granma is careful to faithfully reproduce Gorbachev's criteria and gives quite a bit of space to these. This might be partly because Gorbachev's criteria are objectively important as he was the president of the USSR but could also be attributed to a desire to maintain good relations with the Soviet Union as an all-important ally.

However, in the issue published on Monday, September 3, *Granma* addressed the activities of the radical forces, and the impartial tone is maintained there as well. The main heading that day is "[Boris] Yeltsin demands resignation of the USSR government," and this is followed by a short, unsigned article or item.

> Yeltsin demands resignation of the USSR Government
>
> Moscow, September 2.—Boris Yeltsin, president of the Supreme Soviet of the Russian Federation, demanded the resignation of the USSR government presided by Nikolai Ryzhkov, as the first condition for the success of the reforms and the transition to the market economy.
>
> Yeltsin declared at a press conference that he demanded the resignation of Ryzhkov and his team at a joint meeting held by the Federal and Presidential Councils of the USSR and added that the same proposal was made by other participants in the meeting.

---

this as it "will create the opinion that the Soviet Union will be rewarded with one or another sum for this or that conduct." In a news item a week later, "Interview between Gorbachev and Reagan," (September 18, 1990), former President Reagan says that "Perestroika enjoys sympathy and support in the political and social circles of the United States." On the next day—October 19—however, reference is made to a speech by Gorbachev where he presents his transition plan to a market economy. Here, according to the newspaper, he "referred to the need to use financial resources from abroad, but, to go in such a direction, the Western partners need security that this spending be effective." In other words, Gorbachev by then had accepted that the West would give assistance only after knowing how it would be used, even if this practice made him look weak(er), and opened the way for political strings and pressures.

It seems that, at this point, *Granma* did not find it necessary to point out in each news item or story that Gorbachev's approach to the West implied great dangers. They simply quote what he is saying. Here it must be remembered that Cubans, as a developing country under major pressures by a neighboring imperialist power, have particularly strong reasons to interpret these statements in a negative manner. Because of the historical experience of Cubans, as well as years of socialization under an anti-imperialist paradigm, the editors of *Granma* knew that at least a substantial part of the Cuban population was going to interpret Gorbachev's "flirtation" with the United States as something unfavorable. Of course, pointing these things out in the newspaper could also have increased tensions between Cuba and the USSR.

The leader of the Russian Federation declared that the president of the USSR was trying to reconcile two different transit programs toward market economy, one drawn up by a group that both approved of, and another drawn up by the Ryzhkov government. He added that the Russian Parliament will begin tomorrow to discuss the project prepared by the group created by him and Gorbachev, and headed by the academic Stanislav Shatalin.

The Shatalin project, he said, was created taking into account the declarations of sovereignty of the republics, including the Baltic ones, and has the support of all of them. He added that this project could be approved in two weeks by the parliaments of the republics and begin to be implemented as of October 1st.

Yeltsin declared that the Parliament of the Russian Federation will examine only the Shatalin project and implement it regardless of what the leadership of the Soviet Union decides.

We see in the cited paragraph that *Granma* reproduces the criteria of the radical opposition without introducing assessments in this case, clinging closely to the language used by the radicals ("reforms," "transition," "market economy"). Although a descriptive and, on the surface, impartial style predominates, sometimes in the coverage of the economic debate, there is a more subjective tone. This can be noted in many of the main headlines—we could guess that they have been added by the desk, and some might not have been to the liking of all the journalists. But even in the body text itself, a more subjective style is sometimes used.

For example, on October 18, the main news story about the USSR is titled "Co-author of the 500-day plan [Gregor Yavlinski] renounces as Deputy Chief of the Russian government." Nidia Díaz writes that the objective of the plan that he had defended is "the radicalization of the passage to the market economy, against the social conquests achieved during more than 70 years of socialism in the USSR, and without taking into account the political risks implied by a sharp decrease in the level of life of the majority of the people, according to different opinions here." It is possible that the author has sent her contribution thinking of it as more of a comment than as a news note or a news story. However, it is presented along with the other news notes and thus breaks with the descriptive style that elsewise prevails. Using a phrase like "according to various opinions here"—the source is not specified—is not only subjective but actually rather typical of biased journalism at least when appearing in a news story.

There *might* be a slight increase in the use of a subjective tone toward the end of the debate on the Shatalin Plan in October, when the pro-capitalist forces had pretty much won the debate. However, the findings are contradictory, and it would make little sense to theorize much on the basis of a few editions of the newspaper, as this might be by coincidence. Still, it could also have to do with the increasing fear and strong antipathy toward what was happening; maintaining the distant view of onlookers is becoming more difficult. In the coverage on October 13, there is a more subjective tone, in the story "The battles surrounding the economic program in the USSR are aggravated." This refers to differences between Gorbachev and the so-called Interregional Group of Deputies, the latter dominated by the radical opposition. The journalist argues that "The position of Russian deputies put a dagger in the back of Soviet legislators, now engaged in the difficult search for consensus, before October 15th, to define how to undertake the radical turn of the economy." Of course, accusing someone of putting a dagger in the backs of others is definitely an explicit assessment of the events.[56]

Still, *Granma*'s views are mostly expressed in a more indirect manner, for instance by extensively citing political actors in other countries who hold views that are similar to *Granma*'s positions. An example of this can be found on October 5: "*Pravda* expresses: Private property is incompatible with the social demands of the Soviet people." In this case, the newspaper basically reproduces what a political tendency in the USSR says, the "conservative" tendency, which in this case speaks through the *Pravda* newspaper: "After highlighting that three main forces act in the Soviet political arena: the conservatives, the modernizers, and the liquidators of communism, *Pravda* recognizes that the latter two are the ones who at the moment 'carry the singing voice,' but (say) that their destiny will be ephemeral, because they will be swept away by the first wave of popular outrage."

The journalist reproduces *Pravda*'s language even without putting what apparently is the language used by the Soviet newspaper between quotation marks, such as "the liquidators of communism," so that the line between what is said by *Pravda* and what is said by *Granma* or the journalist becomes blurred. In other cases, the journalist marks a certain professional distance from his sources, but certain actors close to Cuba's positions may still be given authority through the journalist's use of verbs such as *underlines* and *points out*, instead of, let us say, *claims* or *says*.

A fourth observation is that the activities of the radicals (Soviet anti-socialists) are covered, but less space is devoted to their arguments. This underlines Cuba's position of considering their arguments dangerous and not favorable to most

---

56   The criticism is directed at *Russian* deputies. Let us remember that Russia is already a stronghold of the radical opposition within the Soviet Union.

people. When dealing with the Soviet radical opposition, there is a tendency to give more space to what they propose than to their arguments. This does not really come as a great surprise, because in Cuban journalism, there exists an unwritten rule that journalists should not "give weapons to the enemy," that is, facilitate its ideological and political agenda. Also, much of the adversaries' rhetoric is clearly perceived as false and manipulative.

We saw in the example of Yeltsin that the newspaper wrote on one of the radicals *demands* (that the Soviet government resign). This happens quite often, and their *proposals* and their *promises* to the population are also quoted and described. For example, on September 17, *Granma* reported that the Shatalin Program *proposes* "a complete restructuring of the economy, decentralization and liberalization of prices and an accelerated process of privatization in 500 days." A *promise* made by the radicals is reproduced on September 4, when the newspaper says that Russian Prime Minister Ivan Silayev promises to stabilize the Russian economy in 400 days and says that "during the remaining 100 days, one can expect a rise in the main indicators [...]."

What *Granma* gives less attention to are the *arguments* of the radicals. Fragments appear here and there, but the reader is not offered a detailed and "open-minded" account of how they argue in favor of their proposals, and their ideological universe is treated superficially and often with suspicion. Even if some of their proposals were to have some appeal to Cuban readers, because of the way they are covered, the Soviet radical opposition might easily have appeared to most *Granma* readers as naïve, less sincere, and occasionally difficult to understand, since whatever logic and argumentation exists in their proponents is given little attention.

However, as suggested, occasionally some of the radicals' arguments *are* mentioned or quoted. An example is the news story previously cited from September 3, where Yeltsin's demand was mentioned. *Granma* reproduces a claim that could be taken as an argument in favor of Shatalin's project: "It was compiled taking into account the declarations of sovereignty of the republics, including the Baltic ones, and with the support of all of them."

On September 4, a brief item titled "A programme is presented in the Russian parliament" is published, where it is said that the Russian Prime Minister[57] Ivan Silayev just presented "a so-called 500-day program that contemplates an economic reform in the largest republic of the Soviet Union" (still referring to the Shatalin Plan). Again, something that could be seen as an argument in favor of this proposal is given: "According to the Head of the [Russian, not Soviet] Government, the project was highly valued by foreign and

---

57   Again, this refers to the *Russian* prime minister. Silayev was an ally of Boris Yeltsin.

Soviet specialists," and by Stanislav Shatalin. This form of argumentation, the authority argument or *magister dixit*, is often considered a fallacy; however, Silayev apparently used it here, and *Granma* reproduced it.

In September, Gorbachev proposes, at a certain moment, a referendum on the privatization plans contained in the radical Shatalin Plan, "especially with respect to land" (September 18, 1990). On that occasion, *Granma*, not unsurprisingly, gave space to what Gorbachev has to say, but also quoted Shatalin, who rejected Gorbachev's proposal and argued that a referendum "[makes] the most difficult decisions fall on the backs of the population," the message here being that privatization is necessary and that the politicians have the responsibility of making decisions like this one.

On September 19, *Granma* again cites and paraphrases an argument by Shatalin that could seem rational and convincing, at least if one accepts the premise that privatization is necessary. He says that his plan needs to be implemented quickly, in 500 days, because "a human attitude will prolong the agony of the population, today virtually besieged by the shortage." This is an argument that has often been used by proponents of "shock therapy" economic reforms. However, since no space is given for Shatalin to substantiate the claim, and since the proponents of these therapies have been portrayed in a very negative way by the newspaper for a long time, printing this quote could also easily persuade the reader to consider them insensitive and inhuman.

As *Granma* does not cover in a more profound manner the radical opposition's ideas and arguments, the reader becomes more dependent on what he has learned during his life in Cuba (with the media often writing on the evils of privatization and during the late 1980s on the bad intentions or the naivety of the forces that want to have capitalism in the Socialist Bloc, about US interference in Soviet affairs, etc.). But they also could base their analysis on information acquired through other sources, and, for some, their own experiences (for example, older readers were familiar with capitalism and how it had manifested in Cuba).[58]

During the economic debate in the USSR in 1990, *Granma* reported on important activities and proposals of the radical opposition in the USSR, and, at least superficially, it presented their viewpoints and perspectives. It is important to remember that these are political forces that Cuba would not have allowed, and at the time, they were acting openly in an allied, socialist country.

---

58 There is also of course the possibility that the radical opposition in the USSR really had few arguments and a poorly crafted plan, because sometimes politicians do not have very coherent or elaborate projects, or they are guided by ideologies that are little grounded in reality, or even by petty interests.

The lack of a more detailed coverage of their arguments could suggest that the editors of *Granma* and thus the PCC increasingly feared that the radicals would win the debate and feared the impact of these changes on the USSR, on the world, and on Cuba. To some degree, they might also have feared that they could inspire Cubans to propose similar reforms, but again there were few signs that this fear had reached the level of panic. After all, *Granma* did occasionally reproduce even anti-socialist arguments, and more generally, they did allow journalists to cover what was happening and what the main actors proposed.

A fifth observation is that Granma gave ample space to "conservative" forces, that is, the forces that wanted to avoid reform. Contrary to what is the case with the radical forces, during the coverage of the economic debate, *Granma* devoted considerable space not only to the arguments, but in a broader sense reflected or opened up its pages to the viewpoints and reasoning of these actors.

On September 5, for example, the news stories of the day from the USSR are presented under one overarching or main headline: "The second part of the Congress of the Communist Party of Russia [not the USSR] has begun." Until 1990, Russia was the only republic of the Soviet Union that did not have its own communist party, and the branch of the CPSU that arose in June that year soon became a bastion of people opposed to pro-market reforms.[59] This party, which was eventually banned by (then President of the Russian Federation) Yeltsin on August 23, 1991,[60] received favorable coverage in *Granma*.

A news note on September 5 is entitled "Ligachev opposes private property." The reference is to Yegor Ligachev, known as one of the "conservatives" at the time, and *Granma* presents him as "a former leading figure of the Soviet Party." We will see that Prensa Latina did not even use quotation marks or similar when they repeated what he said, which in our opinion blurs the line between his opinions and the journalists' text, although it is not clear whether this is intentional:

> Ligachev opposes private property
>
> Moscow, September 4 (PL). Former leading figure of the Soviet Party Yegor Ligachev today ratified his opposition to the introduction of private property in the USSR, an aspect, he considered, contrary to any development logic.

---

59 Galina Michaleva, "The Communist Party of the Russian Federation (CPRF)," *Schriften des Hannah-Arendt-Instituts für Totalitarismusforschung*, No. 36 (2008): 437. Michaleva uses a different terminology than us and describes the Russian party as "a reservoir of reactionaries."

60 Ibid.

I am opposed because I consider it absurd to return, after 70 years, to what used to divide and isolate people, said the former member of the Political Bureau of the Communist Party of the Soviet Union (CPSU) before a group of journalists.

Ligachev, who participates as a delegate during the second stage of the Constituent Congress of the Communist Party of the Russian Soviet Federated Socialist Republic (CP RSFSR), showed confidence in the potential of socialism, in which—he pointed out—planning can be combined with monetary-mercantile relations.

He stressed that he supports dividing the state property, but, he added, the essential question is how this is done. If privatization is given emphasis, my position has been clear [against it] for a long time, he said.

Ligachev was on the other hand satisfied with the progress of the second part of the CP RSFSR Congress and praised the report presented by the first secretary of that organization.

Another example where *Granma* gives preferential treatment to the conservative forces is a short article that appears on September 7: "Congress of the Communist Party of Russia." *Granma* says that the congress had two "controversial" stages, but they dedicate more space to the second session, during which there was a debate about the program that the organization should adopt:

The delegates also analyzed a controversial program of action undertaken by the Russian communists, which emphasizes measures to clean up the republican economy and its passage to a regulated market economy. Its approval was postponed to next December.

The presentation of the project itself caused fiery disputes, dominated by Muscovites, who even proposed, although without success, that the congress be held during the first half of next year.

The defenders of that position argued that the action program had been published late (about 15 days before the forum) and that there had not been time for analysis in the group's grassroots organizations.

On the other hand, the meeting corroborated the heterogeneity of criteria in that organization of some ten million and five hundred thousand affiliates, which is grouped into several fractions, including those of the Marxist Platform, Democratic Platform and the Leningrad Initiative Congress.

Precisely—on the final day of the conclave, which lasted two and a half days—representatives of the Marxist Platform ratified their opposition to the introduction of economic reforms that would damage the social defense of the interests of the working class.

In that sense, they underlined the necessity of a popular consultation to be held, for deciding upon the conception of the passage to the market economy to be followed in this multinational State.

As we can see, *Granma* not only gives substantial coverage to the new party, which is a bastion of *resistance* to reforms, but also repeats the arguments and rhetoric of the "Marxist Platform" (it receives notable attention in the news story and gets the last word). Apparently, this is the wing in Soviet politics that was closest ideologically to the PCC at the moment, but they were not the leading force.

A sixth observation is that while Granma faithfully reproduces the criteria of the Soviet government, it does so in a rather distant and "indifferent" way. We have seen that a certain favorable treatment is given to the conservatives (anti-reformists) within the debate. *Granma* tries to "lead" its readers to sympathize with these forces. Still, since Gorbachev and his team are ideologically preferable to the radical pro-capitalist opposition, and for more pragmatic reasons, it is important to support them and hugely important to maintain good relations, as they are still in charge of the central government of the USSR.

Granma thus faces the challenge of maintaining good relations with Gorbachev, but at the same time, Fidel Castro and the PCC leadership hold the position that Gorbachev's policies are dangerous, viewed from a socialist perspective. The space for public endorsement of reformist positions in Cuba had by mid- to late 1990 become quite limited, still, Gorbachev had to be given a voice in the newspaper, and he was of course a reformist. So, the editors face the dilemma of explaining to the reader, without criticizing Gorbachev openly, that the situation is now very serious, and reforms are dangerous. It must do so without offending its Soviet allies and without providing ammunition to the actors in the Soviet Union who seek to reduce or eliminate ties with Cuba.

It does so in several ways; for instance, as Jorge Domínguez wrote, it is extensively covering new social problems of Eastern Europe and a Soviet Union in transition. Still, it does not cease to reproduce whatever Gorbachev and his allies say, as it has to do, but (as in some other cases that we have seen) it is done in a distant, "objective" style, without enthusiasm. Of course, it is somewhat difficult to give examples of this lack of enthusiasm, since what is notable is precisely the lack of open praise and so on. In the case of the GDR news, for instance, *Granma* was more explicit in portraying that country as a model, at least until more or less the fall of the Berlin Wall, and implying that its leadership was doing well. Of course, this is both a question of changing moments—it would be difficult to paint rosy pictures of almost any of these societies by the summer and autumn of 1990—but also different Cuban perceptions of the two countries, and more important to us, their leadership.

During the economic debate, *Granma* covers the positions of Soviet Prime Minister Nikolai Ryzhkov quite extensively; he is at this point in favor of the transition to a market economy but without some extremes of the Shatalin Plan, such as the time schedule. Ryzhkov is a central actor in the debate during September and October, although tensions had been increasing between him and Gorbachev.

Gorbachev himself is also, as previously suggested, given considerable space. Although the new "Presidential Plan" that attempted to reconcile different reform proposals was in practice close to the Shatalin Plan, it was much more attractive to Cuba, since Gorbachev wanted to introduce the reforms more slowly. Some Cuban leaders might have had hopes of the plan being stopped at some point, or even reversed, just as the triumphalist coverage of the new Russian communist Party suggested, but in any case Cuba would have some time to reorganize itself and find other sources of income if trade with the USSR were reduced because of internal reforms there (trade was state-to-state, so massive privatization would greatly affect trade). Gorbachev was also seen as a guarantor of a minimum of stability, as he defended an important role for the Soviet Communist Party in society.

But of even greater importance, Gorbachev still had good relations with Cuba and still maintained trade agreements with Cuba that were very much favorable to the latter country, despite internal pressures to change these policies and his policy of detente with the capitalist countries of the West, including the US. It was easy to see that any scenario that implied the radical opposition gaining power in the USSR could put Cuba in an extremely difficult position of isolation (of course, this became reality when the disappearance of the USSR finally occurred).

Granma does not hide the internal tensions in the Gorbachev government, but it was not necessary to point these out, as they were openly apparent and not hidden at this point even by the official Soviet news agency TASS. For example, as the economic debate was coming to an end, the official Soviet news agency, still close to Gorbachev, attacked Ryzhkov and claimed that he "seemed like an uncertain student (based on the Spanish translation: *un alumno inseguro en sus conocimientos*)" during a presentation. *Granma* published this, and only added briefly that the comment had an "unusual tone towards the leaders of the country." Ryzhkov was removed from his position the next month.

In this way *Granma* gave some space for the Gorbachev propaganda apparatus to express itself within the Cuban media, in this case, on Prime Minister Ryzhkov.

Granma would generally avoid giving any opinions that could be seen as critical of a press agency still under Gorbachev's control (although as we have mentioned, it did strongly oppose the appearance of anti-communist ideas and criticisms of the Cuban government in certain Soviet publications that were distributed in Cuba and even did stop their distribution). The discreet comment it added in this case could be a way of pointing out that the treatment of Ryzhkov in the Soviet press could be a hint of changes in the government, but it could also have been a way of helping the reader understand that the political debate in the USSR was not very healthy. This having been said, the practice is still to reproduce much of what is coming from these official press organs, in a routine way and without adding much comment.

A seventh observation: The visual presentation of the newspaper, such as where the news is located within the newspaper and the order in which it is presented, is often casual but frequently reflects ideology and the Cuban state's needs. This is also true with regards to the presentation of the economic debate in the USSR. We can see that the visual structure often underlines a message such as Cuba's anti-reformist stance but also the government's desire to maintain relations with other socialist countries and maintain internal stability. Sometimes it is very clear that *Granma* presents the news in a certain order to give a specific message to the reader.

We have said that any news items about the USSR on a given day are often visually presented together within a box. Often, between the end of August and October 1990, the first or second element within this box is a news story or a note on the debate on economic reforms. Then it is often followed by other texts, often on the economic and social crisis of the Soviet Union, about its approach to the United States, about sabotage or vandalism in the Soviet Union, or other symptoms of a major crisis. Some of these news notes suggest a return to the past (there are references to attempts by some parts of the opposition to rehabilitate the Tsar as a national symbol).

On October 5, 1990, the main headline in the "USSR box" reads as follows: "*Pravda* expresses: Private property is incompatible with the social demands of the Soviet people." But there are also subordinate headlines that appear within the box and introduce different short news items from the Soviet Union. On this day, they read as follows: 1) "A law project is described as anticommunist," 2) "*Pravda* criticizes the governments of Moscow and Leningrad," 3) "Theft of potatoes and legumes," and 4) "A Lenin monument is attacked." Here one can see how news items about anti-communist proposals are being mixed together with common crime, as well as a dynamite attack on a statue with clear political motives. The assessments suggested by the main headline are "supported" by later subtitles: First, it is said that reforms are bad, then (in the third and fourth smaller headlines) examples are given of chaos and crime.

On September 24, the first report is given on the refusal of Russian parliamentarians to give additional powers to President Gorbachev (which is proposed in the context of the debate on economic reform). The other headlines that follow are: "Russia and Moldova cooperate," "Latvia and Belarus sign agreements," "Pickets in front of headquarters of the KGB come to an end," "Attacks against statues of Lenin are condemned," and "The existence of more than 1,200 criminal groups is recognized." The latest news includes a comment from an KGB official saying that Soviet criminals take advantage of the new possibilities that cooperatives and joint ventures give them—both types of economic enterprises that the reforms had promoted—to have direct contacts with criminal partners abroad.

The same occurs in the "Soviet box" that is presented on September 19. On that day, the main headline reads "Authors of projects on market economy in the USSR respond to legislators," then comes a subordinate news note or story suggesting possible radical consequences of the reforms, through citing something that was actually in the news at the moment: "Solzhenitsyn proposes to disintegrate Russia and disband communists," referring to famous Soviet writer Alexander Solzhenitsyn. It is stated that Pravda published a proposal by Solzhenitsyn where he "proposes to face the problems of Russia with a mixture of anti-communism, machismo, religiosity and racism." The writer, who had just been given back his Russian citizenship, advocated for "the return of the woman to her home to care for their children, since work is for men." He also proposed to "end atheism in education" and "to disintegrate what he qualifies as a Russian empire, fundamentally for ethnic reasons [...] the Russians are unable to assimilate other peoples because—he says—they do not raise the level of other nations but rather lower its own."

On September 21, 1990, there is no news on the debate on the Shatalin Plan, but a big headline reads "The CPSU expresses its concerns with regard to the commercialization of culture." The article below the headline gives the voice of the Communist Party of the Soviet Union, which declared that the reform process has produced a more commercial culture. The Soviet Party considers that due to the profit motive becoming more important, the publication of "works of low artistic and ideological quality, and cheap sensationalism [...]" has been promoted. Furthermore, it mentions that one now has to pay for loans in libraries and other elements that most likely would be rejected by the average Cuban reader. By including an article such as this on the effects of the reforms, it is suggested that a deepening of the reforms, which is what is about to happen after the results of the economic debate, will not be good.

Let us take another example. On October 3, the news in the "USSR box" deals first with the relationship between the Soviet Union and Lithuania (which has just become independent from the USSR). Then another item appears on the law of organizations that "legalizes the already existing multipartyism in the USSR," then another item appears under the short headline "Memorial raised in honor of the second Tsar Nicholas"—clearly, the narrative order is not casual. It is suggested that the dismantling of the hegemonic system in the USSR implies a return to the past.

On the other hand, on October 10, the headlines regarding the USSR are "Plenary of the Central Committee of the CPSU has concluded" (main headline), followed by other articles or items: "The debates," "Warning of the Russian Parliament to citizens of the republic," and "Law approved on social organizations" (according to the text, "it is considered the legal basis for the full establishment of political pluralism in the Soviet Union"). Suggesting in a subtle manner that legalizing parties can have negative effects, the following item bears the headline: "Anti-Semitic leader a candidate for urban council of Moscow."

On September 15, the main article on the USSR has the heading "They will demand the resignation of the Soviet government on Sunday," although it also contains information on the economic reforms. Next to the box containing the information, there is a smaller news item titled "In the GDR: Alarming unemployment forecast." It is possible that *Granma* has positioned these articles to remind the reader that the Soviet Union is also at risk of having greater social problems, if it follows the path of Eastern Europe.

On September 19, the main title of the news box on the USSR has the headline "Project authors on market economy in the USSR respond to legislators." Next to the box is a story entitled "China revitalizes basic industries." It is possible that the position is coincidental, but it could also be a deliberate attempt to incite the reader to see the crisis of the USSR (which has fragmented power, while the economy has taken a turn for the bad) in the light of the situation in other countries like East Germany (where socialism has been more or less eliminated, and that apparently is going very badly, only weeks before the state itself ceases to exist) and with China (a country where, at least, no fundamental *political* reforms have been made, and that is, apparently, progressing).

There are also articles on the national situation in Cuba and historical articles, such as one titled "Cuba cannot again become a slave," on October 10, which deals with Cuban independence hero Carlos Manuel de Céspedes, who on that date in 1868 released his slaves and invited them to form part of the liberating army against the Spaniards—the Demajagua uprising.[61] However, the headline can also be read as a commentary on the possibility of Cuba following in the footsteps of other countries of the socialist community and once again being a slave to capitalism and imperialism.

Thus, there are important messages contained in the visual presentation as well as other materials that somehow enter into dialogue with the coverage of the USSR. These messages might be that Soviet reforms may lead to the restoration of the old Russian regime, a setback to an unpleasant past (be it capitalist, fascist, feudal, or religious, or some combination). Socialism in this narrative represents a historical advance, and the people who have turned away from it and have unleashed market forces after first undertaking the construction of socialism have reason to repent.

An eighth observation: Fidel Castro and external or internal commentators are allowed to handle the most explicit analyses. There are speeches by Fidel Castro, comments, analyses, and interviews during the summer and autumn of 1990 that touch in some way on the issue of economic reform, although they do not specifically go into the debate that is taking place in the USSR. Remember that there are hardly any editorials and that news on the Soviet Union is mostly quite descriptive in style, so these in a way fill the role of giving a more explicit and comprehensive ideological analysis.

An example might be the coverage on October 1, 1990, which takes place right in the middle of the economic debate in the Soviet Union. On this day, the front page of the newspaper is full of quotes from Fidel Castro's speech on the 30th Anniversary of the Committees in Defense of the Revolution (CDR), while four pages inside the newspaper are also devoted to the speech. On the front page is a quote by Fidel Castro saying "The morals of the patriots, the morals of the revolutionaries, the morals of the communists, are what have to

---

61 In the political discourse and symbology of the Cuban Revolution, references to this uprising are common. When Céspedes freed his slaves, this led to the first confrontation with the Spanish troops only a few hours later, an event known as the *Grito de Yara*. The rebels were defeated in 1878, and the *Pact of Zanjón* was signed, according to which they agreed to surrender. Still, one general, Antonio Maceo, decided to continue the battle; this became known as the *Protest of Baraguá* and is seen as a particularly heroic moment in Cuban history. In 1895, a new attempt at liberation took place, this time under the leadership of José Martí. However, Martí died at the beginning of the war and it ended as the USA—in 1898—decided to intervene militarily and occupy Cuba, using as a pretext the explosion of an American ship, the USS Maine, in Havana Bay.

prevail," and other quotes that emphasize specifically Cuban qualities, saying basically that Cuba's attitude will not be the same and suggesting implicitly that the crisis in the USSR and Eastern Europe is a product of some sort of weakness and a lack of revolutionary morals. Other affirmations by Fidel Castro suggest that Cuba is better equipped to defend its system and national interests and suggest that what is going on is a battle, including a battle of ideas: "We made this revolution on our own, nobody did it to us [...]," "We have the privilege of having one of the smartest, bravest, most heroic peoples [...]," "There will not be—and that is the characteristic of our socialism, of our system—a single homeless citizen, a single abandoned citizen," "Today, when some people want to tear down the Lenin statue, we feel that in our hearts and in our thoughts, the figure of Lenin is growing and becoming massive (*agigantarse*)," and finally there is a call for a combative attitude: "What we must do is to resist, fight, and win."

On September 12, still 1990, *Granma* publishes a summary of another speech that bears the title "We will never be discouraged, and we prepare ourselves to face all the difficulties, no matter how great they may be." The speech was given in the context of Fidel Castro being granted the title of Doctor Honoris Causa at the University of San Marcos in Perú. Castro warns that there is a "wave of neoliberalism and privatization" that "invades the world, including Latin America" and questions these policies. He speaks of "the uncertainty of the future of [Cuba's] economic relations with the USSR" and thus warns again about the seriousness of the situation, as he has done on previous occasions and very much explicitly on July 26, 1989. At the same time, he declares himself in favor of socialism and against capitalism and says that "If in those countries [Eastern Europe] several things have gone wrong, things are going much worse in Latin America and the Third World."

The inclusion in the newspaper of a speech like this, and other materials of the same ideological line, can contribute to sympathies with the pro-socialist forces in the USSR and in other parts of the world—to the degree that Fidel Castro convinces the readers, of course. Many of the *news* items on Soviet economic reform may be more or less "objective" synopses, but these materials serve to clarify what is the "correct" or official position.

In the middle of the debate on economic reform in the USSR, the newspaper also featured a long commentary from US sociologist James Petras, under the heading "Eastern Europe: The Language of Deceit" (September 17, 1990), where he argues that reformism in socialist countries uses lies, false promises, and techniques similar to those described by the novelist, journalist, and critic of totalitarianism, George Orwell ("inversion"), to get people to support their policies.[62] Although Petras refers to events that have already occurred in Eastern Europe, clearly the current situation in the USSR cannot be treated in isolation from what has happened in Poland, Hungary, the GDR, and so on. *Granma* also publishes a comment by Eduardo Galeano: "The theory of the end of history becomes fashionable. Contempt as destiny" (on October 16, 1990), in which he questions the idea of the end of history by Francis Fukuyama, who is described by Galeano as "a [US] State Department official."

Another example of a commentary that expresses similar points is one titled "Market economy: Fashion or 'discovery' for Eastern Europe," written by Elson Concepción Pérez (September 27, 1990). This commentary concludes that "The fashion is young and the 'discovery' too. But until today, more than one million workers in the former socialist countries of Eastern Europe have lost their jobs." By claiming that reformism is based on false promises or that the theories of its proponents are mere fashions, the commentator suggests Eastern Europe and the USSR are being deceived, that they will not be happy with capitalism, and also that in the long run socialism will succeed. He recognizes implicitly that there is some level of support for the changes but suggests that those people are making a bad decision that they may come to repent.

Finally, I would like to include as another example the interview "In Cuba there is an authentic revolution" (September 7, 1990), with the president of the Communist Party of Argentina. The Argentinean argues that some countries in Europe "have taken the course of a capitalist economy," and then emphasizes the differences between Cuba and the Soviet Union. Gorbachev would probably not have approved of the word capitalism—reformists and probably most radicals in the USSR instead used the term "market economy"—but this interview does not appear as an official comment of the Cuba authorities, and therefore *Granma* cannot be accused of attacking the Soviet Union.

The fact that all of these commentaries were published again indicates that there was some concern about ideological contagion from the Socialist Bloc, as *Granma* clearly tried to raise public awareness on the dangers of capitalism; however, *Granma* is also aware of the differences between Cuba and the USSR and tries to capitalize on the independent origin of its Revolution and suggest that Cuba will follow another path.

---

62 The word "inversion" apparently refers to the inversion of customary meanings—"war is peace." This is common in *newspeak*, the propagandistic language described by British novelist and essayist George Orwell (1903–1950) in his classic *1984*. Orwell is often remembered for his criticism of Stalinism, although he was also a critic of totalitarianism in general. *1984* was not published in revolutionary Cuba until 2016.

In summary, *Granma* gives a relatively wide coverage of the debate on economic reform that was taking place in the USSR between August and October 1990. It follows the three wings of the debate, and it cannot be said that it is censoring any of the tendencies involved or that Cubans who actually read this news suffered a lack of information on what was going on. However, *Granma* does give comparatively more space to the "conservatives" and the "moderates" compared to the "radicals" (pro-capitalists), despite the fact that the radicals were apparently on the offensive at the time. *Granma* made clear in often "indirect" ways which actors the readers should sympathize with and by listening quite emphatically to the so-called hardline communists, but for pragmatic reasons Gorbachev was also favored to some extent.

There are many reasons to suppose that in the PCC and to some extent also among *Granma's* leadership there prevailed a favorable attitude to the conservative wing of the Soviet leadership, despite journalists being a group that sometimes inclined itself toward reform socialism. Still, care was also taken to avoid directly attacking the moderates and not to harm Gorbachev, because as the PCC's official Cuban newspaper, what *Granma* published could theoretically have affected bilateral relations (which could have created more problems for Gorbachev but above all for Cuba).

The coverage also reflects the Soviet pro-capitalist opposition, but *Granma* gives limited attention to the arguments and reasoning from these actors; it generally prefers to present their actions, demands, and slogans more superficially. While the news coverage itself appears, most of the time, as relatively "informative" and apparently neutral, at least in terms of journalistic style, news coverage on the economic debate is sometimes accompanied by analysis or suggestively located articles and items that highlight social problems in the USSR and in Eastern Europe; these are there to remind the reader of the negative consequences that capitalism can have. Still, there was a certain compliance with the informative duty that *Granma* had as a fundamental source of news in Cuba. The relatively ample coverage of the debate on economic reform and the absence of more "desperate measures" in this case (such as outright censorship and major distortions) could suggest that the Cuban government's main fear at the time was that capitalist ideas could be imposed more strongly in the Soviet Union, something that could greatly harm the international revolutionary movement and Cuba, but that it was to a somewhat lesser degree fearful of an immediate ideological contagion within the Cuban population.

Although the many articles published by the newspaper against capitalism could indicate that this last fear also existed, the government and the editors knew that Cuban socialism enjoyed great support and that most Cubans found the changes in the Soviet Union partly alien to their reality, despite similar political and economic systems. In journalistic terms, an objective or informative style was what made sense as events were happening fast and perhaps sometimes were difficult to interpret at the time, but also in political terms, it was probably tactical to opt for describing what happened instead of assessing it much, considering Cuba's delicate position. Although no one could claim that *Granma* had not reported on these issues, it avoided a too-partisan coverage, which had lost credibility at other moments, such as in the case of the GDR's collapse, and mostly avoided attacks on actors that could become strategically important in the future.

2.2   *Example 2: The Coup against Gorbachev—At a Critical Point, Cuba's Perceived Strategic Interests Are Imposed on the Coverage*

The official Cuban attitude toward the USSR *coup d'état* on August 19, 1991, when Mikhail Gorbachev was put under house arrest in his holiday home in Crimea, and a group of eight Soviet communist leaders took power, has been studied or commented on by several academics. As the reader will be aware, the coup failed, as Gorbachev returned to power on August 21, although his position and the USSR were further weakened by the events, as were Cuban–Soviet links. In December, the USSR was dissolved.

According to Rafael Rojas, the Cuban official press expressed an attitude of approval for the coup. Mervyn Bain even asks whether Fidel Castro had prior knowledge of what was going to happen, based on the fact that five of the eight coup plotters had ties to Cuba. The material at my disposition does not give the necessary data to say whether the Cuban government knew or not about the plans, therefore we will not try to answer this question but analyze *Granma's* coverage based on the premise that the coup attempt took them at least "by some surprise." I include "some" since the situation was critical, and it was clear that anything could happen.

Recall that there is an eight-hour time difference between Havana and Moscow and that the coup was announced from the capital of the Soviet Union on the morning of September 19, at 6 or 7 a.m., according to different sources on the Internet. *Granma* closed its desk, according to the newspaper itself at 2:00 (in the morning) on that same date; due to the difference in time between Moscow and Havana they should have received the news about three or four hours before, if it arrived immediately, which is probable. On September 19, several editions of *Granma* were printed. This is normal and has to do with different editions being printed for distribution in different regions of Cuba. I only had access to the *third* edition of *Granma* on this first day where the coup is covered, but according to the newspaper's archive staff,

ANALYZING THE NEWS ACCOUNTS

there should be no difference between one edition and another, except with regard to the sports section.[63]

Information on the coup appears at the bottom of the front page of the newspaper of August 19, with the headline "Yanayev assumes presidential functions in the USSR," and a small box that states "Stop the press" (*Al cierre*). The text seems to be identical to the coup leaders' declaration, but a short introduction has been added:

> Moscow. August 19. (TASS)—The Soviet leadership made a statement today. In the statement it is said in relation to the inability of Mikhail Gorbachev to fulfill the functions of the President of the USSR and pass the powers of the President of the USSR, in accordance with article 127, point 7, of the Constitution of the USSR, as Vice President of the USSR, Gennady Yanaev,
>
> In order to overcome the deep and multifaceted crisis, political, interethnic and civil confrontation, chaos and anarchy [...] [sic]

This first part does not seem very well redacted, possibly because it was written under time constraints. Because of the way it is written, it is not completely clear to the reader where the coup leaders' statement begins and where the words of the news agency end, although the second paragraph seems like a straight quote, though without two dots or quote marks to introduce what is said by the new leaders.

Nor is it entirely clear whether the first paragraph comes from TASS or if it has been edited in some way by *Granma*. The text does not seem identical to any of the texts issued in English by TASS at that time (these were captured by a computer and/or communications enthusiast at the time, who published them online many years later),[64] but it is possible that TASS produced texts in Spanish that were different.

Although it might sound like a very distrustful interpretation, one could not disregard the possibility that the badly edited text was written this way on purpose by *Granma* so that it seemed to be written under pressure, which

---

63 I consider it unlikely that changes were made in the coverage from one edition to another one on the same day, as it would have given the impression that Cuba was hesitant on such a major event. In addition, this probably would have been commented on by journalists or academics abroad at a later time.

64 See: http://rainbow.chard.org/2011/12/23/tass-coverage-of-the-attempted-coup-in-USSR-19-august-1991/.

could serve as a pretext to later retract what had been published, if the coup were to fail.

The first reactions to the coup inside and outside of the USSR did not appear until after a few hours. That means that when the August 19 edition of *Granma* was going to print, the editors probably did not have much more information on the matter, for example, on the real situation of the deposed president. Even so, it would not have been difficult to understand from the information given by TASS that a coup had taken place, and *Granma* still reproduced the coup plotters' take on its front page without distancing itself from this in any way, thereby basically accepting the coup.

Even so, we have seen earlier that *Granma* tended to faithfully reproduce the news of TASS and the official viewpoint of the USSR, even when they did not match their own. Therefore, to some extent, if the coup would turn out to be a failure—which coups often do and which it eventually did—*Granma's* editors and the Cuban authorities knew they might to some degree be able to hide behind this long-standing practice as well as its position of non-interference in the internal affairs of socialist allies. It should also be remembered that the USSR had been seen as the leader of the communist movement since Lenin's time and that in reality none of its leaders had been elected in free, pluralistic elections, although this coup clearly did not follow socialist legality.

The way the statement is presented might say something about how *Granma* saw the events and how it wanted its own role to be interpreted. First, it should be noted that the statement is located at the bottom of the front page. As already observed, news that the editors do not like is often placed at the bottom of the page. In this case, the entire front page is covered by the news "Cuba Champion! 140 gold medals" with the extended headline "We honor our commitments with honor." The news of the coup came at the same time as the overwhelming Cuban victory in the Pan-American games that took place *in Cuba*. It is in no way strange that these stunning sports victories were scheduled to be the main story on that day.

However, considering the importance of a coup in the second most powerful country in the world on which Cuba was still very much dependent economically, it could seem curious that the news about the coup did not replace the sports story as the main or highlighted story. It is of course likely that the page was designed before the news of the USSR arrived, as indicated by the words "At the time of going to press," and it is possible that it was difficult to change the order of the news right before going to print. But it seems more likely that it was an intentional way of not highlighting too much the coup plotters' statement and thus not giving them too strong an endorsement. In such a situation, it would be dangerous for *Granma* to lean too far toward one side, since coups often fail. It could also affect the credibility of the newspaper since Cuba had close relations with the deposed state leader. Furthermore, *Granma* generally criticized coups as something bad and certainly would normally do so in strong terms when an allied government was the victim.

Still, even if *Granma* was not entirely enthusiastic about the coup, it did not have a lot of options. If it had written something critical about the announcement, it would have been a very strong statement against the coup plotters, since *Granma* had always reproduced whatever important messages came from TASS. While not recognizing the de facto Soviet government might have been the most correct posture in terms of political principles, had it done so, it would have jeopardized Cuba's economy and security, and it would have delivered a symbolic blow to the authorities in the Soviet Union—the coup plotters—as they were the real power at that moment.

It could have been possible, still, to include the message but report on it in a manner that did not seem to be an endorsement or a condemnation. *Granma* sought a route that, in fact, amounted to acceptance and, one could also say, like Rafael Rojas has claimed, approval of the coup government. But as Bain notes, Cuba was careful not to "burn bridges" with Gorbachev, and suggests that "the most striking aspect" of the official Cuban statement, actually published two days later, "was its noncommittal nature."[65]

A look at the visual presentation on the first day of the coverage underlines this. *Granma* places the news at the bottom of the page, which is something that it often does with news that it disapproves or finds "embarrassing" for the global movement of which it is part. It also somehow gives the impression that it is *accepting* more than cheering the events because it has no other option. This might be done partly to avoid internal tensions on the issue, as showing more enthusiasm about these events might have alienated Cubans skeptical about the coup, and it would look bad since Cuba had enjoyed good official relations with Gorbachev, despite differences. If they could choose freely, Cuban authorities would probably prefer that the coup plotters controlled the Soviet Union instead of Gorbachev, who was seen as not standing up to the radicals and the West. However, I will argue that the Cuban authorities' identification with the coup plotters was not necessarily total, and in any case they were aware that the coup itself as well as supporting the coup entailed political costs and major risks.

Although the coup plotters were ideologically closer to Cuba's positions than Gorbachev's, the Cuban government's affinity with them—they were often referred to as "hardline communists"—might have been more one of historical

---

65   Bain, 112–113.

and personal links since, according to Bain, several of them were associated with a "Cuban lobby" in Moscow—more than one of total identification with their political methods, ideology, and desires. After all, Gorbachev also had some upsides; despite the catastrophic situation and development in the USSR, he was still probably seen as a guarantor of Cuban–Soviet relations being preserved, at least in the short term. Despite the fact that Cuban–Soviet trade had decreased notably by August 1991 and was increasingly being conducted on market terms and in hard currency, Gorbachev, unlike the radicals, did want to continue some sort of relations. Also, the coup contained from the start the obvious risk of removing Gorbachev without achieving a new stable "hardline" government—this also became the final result: A debilitated Gorbachev and five of Cuba's main allies in Moscow out of the political scene. Shortly after Gorbachev returned to power, he announced the withdrawal of Soviet troops from Cuba—at a press conference together with US authorities—but even then he did not call for the relationship to be ended.

The coverage of *Granma* on August 20, 1991, the day after the coup, confirms and reinforces the impression that the Cuban government accepted the de facto government as legitimate, and removes whatever doubt anyone might have had that the publication of the news on the 19th was a simple act of confusion as the deadline was closing in. By the time that the first edition of the 20th of August was published, the editors already knew about the protests against the new Soviet government, mainly by pro-capitalist forces (Yeltsin). By then, the Cuban government had already had some time to analyze the situation, and the PCC's leadership would have reiterated and pointed out to the newspaper in more detail how *Granma* should respond. On this day, *Granma* published yet another statement by the coup plotters, alongside other news from the Soviet Union. However, neither *Granma* nor the Party nor the Cuban state had issued a statement on the coup.

On the 20th, the issue of the coup covers between half and a third of the front page of *Granma*. The news is presented in three columns located on the right side of the page, all of which begin on the top of the page and reach its bottom, under a headline superimposed over a red background: "Yanayev affirms that the strongest measures will be taken to get the USSR out of the crisis." A picture of Yanayev appears during his television broadcast, which presents him in a neutral manner. Items from TASS and Prensa Latina appear together in a box on the front page, and both give versions that are essentially accepting what is now the official line. First, in the message from TASS, Yanayev attributes the crisis in the USSR to Gorbachev's reforms. Then another Prensa Latina item appears, which says:

Moscow, August 19. (PL).—The acting president of the Soviet Union, Gennady Yanayev, reported today that the head of state Mikhail Gorbachev is resting in Crimea and did not rule out the possibility that he will resume his position.

At a press conference, Yanayev said that Gorbachev is very tired and unable to run the state.

During his meeting with journalists, he qualified the call for a general strike launched by Russian President Boris Yeltsin today as an irresponsible action and attempt to carry out political games in a situation that is difficult for the country.

Subsequently, another TASS item says that "the first reaction abroad [...] is also characterized by a certain understanding, because what most worries foreign states is chaos and anarchy in our nuclear state." But the coup leaders also recognize that there is "distrust and fear" both in the USSR and abroad, which they attribute to previous governments that had made the "hopes of the people [...] repeatedly frustrated." TASS quotes the coup plotters' criticism of Yeltsin's message, which was "conceived in a confrontational tone." In other words, on August 20 the justification of the coup plotters and the so-called Gang of Eight is given considerable space.

After that message from TASS, Prensa Latina reports that the "Constitutional Control Committee of the Soviet Union announced today that the legality of the State Committee on the State of Emergency [interim government] must be ratified by the Federal Parliament." Then an item appears saying that there is a state of emergency in Moscow, a decree of Yanayev is cited, and after this, other reactions are covered. First the National Veterans Council of the Soviet Union is cited supporting the coup plotters and their state of emergency, then a statement appears from the president of Kazakhstan, who calls for calm, also indicating that he accepts the coup plotters' line.

The second to last item is called "Reactions in the West." This item includes information from EFE and AFP along with those of Prensa Latina. This news is more pluralistic than the rest of the coverage, in the sense that it recognizes the existence of conflicting viewpoints on the situation that has arisen. One fragment reads: "In different parts of the Western world the news of the situation in the USSR has been received with caution, concern, and even surprise, according to reports from press agencies." *Granma* cites US president George Bush, who "stated that this event could have serious consequences for the relations of the USSR with many countries, including the United States." To include these comments from the US is almost obligatory due to the country's importance at the international level, but it can also be convenient because the reader is somehow informed that the new Soviet government cannot be so bad, if it is rejected by the enemy of Cuba. Then French President François Mitterrand appears, an actor with much better relations with the Cuban government. He, the text reads, "ruled out the use of sanctions against the new Soviet leaders" and described the situation as an "internal matter."[66]

Others are also cited. Japanese Prime Minister Toshiki Kaifu "expressed concern about the events in the Soviet Union and asked the new leaders to continue the political reform line established by Mikhail Gorbachev, EFE reported." Helmut Kohl "urged to comply with international treaties signed by the Soviet government in recent years" and asks to "avoid the spilling of blood in the Soviet Union." *Granma* then quotes the secretary general of the United Nations, who "expressed his satisfaction at the guarantees given by the new Soviet leadership to respect the commitments made by that country" (the information came through the AFP news agency).

At the end, the last, smaller item on the topic appears: "Declaration of the Chinese Foreign Ministry." China considers that what has happened is an internal affair of the Soviet Union, but they point out that the Chinese–Soviet relations "will continue their unstoppable growth [...]." Again, the positive tone here appear to indicate Chinese official approval of events.

The impression that Cuban authorities somehow approve of the coup plotters is very much confirmed later in the same newspaper as a lengthy pronouncement of the Soviet "Emergency Committee" is published, this time on page 5. In general, this appeal contains criticisms of Gorbachev's reforms. The new rulers promise to cleanse society of crime and disorder and rescue national pride. These are certainly important points in common with Cuba.

But also—although it does not receive more space in the statement—they also promise to diversify the economy and support "the private entrepreneurial spirit, giving it the necessary possibilities for the development of production and the service sector." Although this might be intended to calm Soviet reformists and radicals, these positions are a contrast with those that had prevailed in Cuba during the years of the Process of Rectification since the 1980s, which had the aim of removing what little there was of "capitalist methods" from the construction of (unreformed Cuban) socialism.

---

66   While perhaps surprising, it is correct that Mitterrand's immediate reaction was—or at least was widely interpreted as—a recognition of the new Soviet government. See, for example, Forbes et al., *Contemporary France: Essays and Texts on Politics, Economics and Society* (London; New York: Taylor & Francis, 2014), 41.

Therefore, this statement from the coup plotters really reveals that there was quite a bit of distance between Cuba and the Soviet coup plotters in ideological terms, although Gorbachev was even further away, and as we have seen, in the autumn of 1990 he accepted—under pressure—to gradually implement a full "market economy" in the USSR. But, without much doubt, the coup plotters were the closest ones to Cuba's position, and the important thing in that moment of crisis was probably not so much the exact ideological position of the coup plotters—as long as they were not radical pro-capitalists, and they were not—but the prospects of the USSR surviving as a functioning state, as a counterweight to the US and that it continued supporting Cuba.

Whatever Cuba might have known or not about the coup in advance, for a short time on the 19th or 20th of August 1991, it probably seemed a more real possibility to Cuban authorities that the coup plotters would continue in charge and achieve their promise of returning order to the USSR, than of the Gorbachev administration returning to power and returning order to the USSR—although they must have been skeptical about the viability of both options.

On August 21, the Spanish newspaper *El País* published an article called "Cuba keeps an obligatory silence," in which they quote a Cuban diplomat who says that "there has not been any official reaction yet" on the coup, and explains what must was quite clear to anyone familiar with the situation: "It is not easy to issue a Cuban statement on a *coup d'état* carried out by communist hawks, since, although the return to power of the ultraconservatives favors Fidel Castro, the Cuban leader has always insisted on his good relations with Gorbachev, despite the divergent course of his policies."[67]

It should be said that on August 21, a late pronouncement of the *Granma* newspaper on the coup was actually published: It said that Cuba remained neutral and that the USSR has to solve its internal problems. Interestingly, the copy of the newspaper of that day was not in the *Granma* newspaper archive. I discovered this absence when I no longer had the practical possibility of looking for it in the National Library of Cuba, where copies of *Granma* are also kept. Therefore, our information on *Granma's* statement is based on an AP story published in *El Tiempo* de Colombia.[68]

---

67 News agencies, "Golpe de Estado en la U.R.S.S.: Cuba guarda un obligado silencio," *El País*, Aug. 21, 1991. The Latin America Network Information Center, which has an index of the contents of the *Granma* newspaper of that day, does not mention any other material being published in the USSR on that day. However, the index does not include everything that has been published, so there might be some more information in *Granma* on August 21, 1991 that I have not been able to analyze.

68 AP, "Solución está en manos de los soviéticos: Cuba," *El Tiempo*, Aug. 21, 1991.

Considering the way in which *Granma* reproduced the coup plotters' statement on the 19th and the 20th of August, its own statement on the 21st is the first time it explicitly gives the coup a sort of explicit recognition, as it says that these events are internal matters of the USSR, but this statement could also be seen as distancing itself slightly from the coup plotters as they were coming under more pressure in the USSR, since that would also mean that the return of Gorbachov would also be considered an internal matter. As suggested earlier, *Granma* kept a small opening to Gorbachev should he return, perhaps considering that he might "feign ignorance" should he return to power. This said, the absence of an official statement by the Cuban side until August 21 is striking, especially as Cuba quite often pronounced itself on international issues, and actually, besides the statement of the coup government on August 20, *Granma* printed a statement from the Cuban Ministry of Foreign Affairs on North Korea, which was clearly of less immediate importance for Cuba. The delay before the statement arrived reflects how delicate the situation was.

On August 22, newspapers all over the world published the story that Gorbachev had returned to power. On the front page of *Granma*, one can read the headline, "Gorbachev reassumes presidential functions," with the extended headline, "He returned to Moscow from Crimea." This story has a visual presentation very similar to the main story two days before. The headline is superimposed on a red surface, but instead of Yanayev's photo, this time there is a picture of Gorbachev who is walking off a plane. It covers a third of the cover. The visual presentation of the news being almost identical to that of Yanayev two days before seems like a conscious move to signal that this type of news is published routinely, mechanically, without giving much thought to its content (see Figure 5). In other words, the news of the return of Gorbachev is presented as if nothing particularly important had happened, with a format similar to the news of the day before, thereby giving an impression of normality and signaling that *Granma* is just reporting on events and respecting the internal affairs of the USSR.

The first part of the USSR news on August 22, 1991 uses both Prensa Latina and the Soviet main evening newscast (Vremia) as sources, and they adhere to Gorbachev's version. "Soviet President Mikhail Gorbachev said today he has full control over the situation after reestablishing his ties to the country, cut off, he said, by the adventurous actions of a group of state leaders, whom he blamed as perpetrators of a coup that he described as right-wing, reported PL." Clearly, a right-wing coup is one of the most negative types that can exist in the vocabulary of *Granma*, but this characterization comes from Gorbachev and not from the newspaper, and therefore is not necessarily valued in the same way by Cuban authorities or the newspaper (see Figure 6).

ANALYZING THE NEWS ACCOUNTS

FIGURE 5   *Granma*, August 20, 1991; "Yanayev affirms that the most energetic measures will be taken to get the USSR out of the crisis"

At one point in the coverage of this day, the newspaper quotes Gorbachev, who says he has spoken with George Bush, who "said that the outcome of the events represents a victory of freedom and democracy." Again, it is logical to include a comment from Bush, the leader of the most powerful country in the world, but

FIGURE 6   *Granma*, August 22, 1991; "Gorbachev resumes presidential functions. Returned to Moscow from Crimea"

its inclusion on the front page of the *Granma* newspaper can also be a nod to the Cuban reader to point out that Gorbachev is no longer trusted, since he is the favorite of the United States. Again, without saying anything that Gorbachev (or others) could use against Cuba, the newspaper is giving the reader information that could underline Gorbachev's weakness (in perhaps implicitly, an "argument" or justification for the Cuban acceptance of the coup only a few days before).

After this, a review of the events of the last three days is presented: "Thus concluded three particularly dramatic days for the country and the world, especially this last day, when the confusion led many to wonder who really had the power in the USSR." Using the word *confusion* could be a way of distancing oneself from one's former position in the face of the coup, although it must also be recognized that there were doubts in the Soviet population, the international community, and in Cuba.

The censorship imposed by the coup government posed some challenges to the media of the world. There were not many alternative sources of information. When the coup failed and the political pluralism that existed in the USSR during Perestroika was reinstated, the *Granma* newspaper again referred to more Western sources than during the coup, although these were never totally absent. For example, on August 23, EFE and AFP, not TASS, are used to report on demonstrations and expressions of discontent in Moscow.

It is clear that a situation of such enormous potential implications for Cuba tends to imply an increased political control over news coverage. One of our informants in the oral history part of this study (Juan), who was a Cuban minister at one point, said that the Soviet coup of 1991 raised hopes among a part of the Cuban bureaucracy. But, as previously seen, there were also many reformists in the Party and perhaps especially in the press, whom the government would not like to alienate too much. Even so, in an event of such importance as the coup against Gorbachev, it is likely that the coverage was coordinated by the top echelons of the PCC. Taking into account the historically close relations between *Granma* and the top leadership of Cuba,[69] one could safely assume that the coverage of an event such as the Soviet coup of August 1991 would have been coordinated with senior government officials, including Fidel Castro. Although we have seen that government positions and orientations not the only factors influencing how international news is covered, in situations where Cuba's interests are strongly jeopardized, news tends to be more closely controlled.

To summarize, in the coverage of the coup in the USSR, the government seems to control in a particularly tight manner how news is given and present it carefully in a manner that suits its perceived interests. Although *Granma* does not say it directly, the coverage of the first day (August 19) shows that Cuba is willing to accept the coup, and the coverage given on the second day of the coup confirms and reinforces this impression. Still, to some extent, Cuba

---

69   García Luis, 82.

tried to disguise its posture as one of non-interference in internal affairs, first as it just continued to reproduce whatever came from the Soviet state press agency without saying explicitly that it supports the coup or the new government, and on the third day a bit more explicitly as it published a statement that said that these are internal matters of the USSR.

While the Cuban authorities in essence accepted and even somehow approved the coup, this was not done in the most explicit way possible, and as Bain has stated, its support was of a "noncommittal" nature. The view from the leading echelons of the PCC may have been characterized not only by enthusiasm, but by contrasting perceptions, "mixed feelings" and uncertainty.

The image given to the public through *Granma* was designed in such a manner that it avoided becoming too closely associated with support for a state coup and of keeping a (very small) opening toward Gorbachev and to his supporters in the USSR and in Cuba. When Gorbachev returned, it followed a similar script: printing whatever information came from TASS, now under Gorbachev's control.

The position of the Cuban government and how the news is covered are thus mainly motivated by pragmatism and necessity. Cuba considered the situation of the USSR to be extremely critical—something that put at risk Cuba's own stability—and it was so important to preserve that state and the binational links that it was willing to at least "play dumb" with regard to the disrespect for socialist legality implied by the coup. It was of course desirable to have close allies of Cuba at the helm of the Soviet Union, and this together with the coup plotters' promise to return stability to the Soviet Union might have made the coup somewhat attractive, but on the other hand, it also entailed political costs and, more importantly, a huge risk if it should fail or exacerbate internal problems.

In this sense, it must be taken into account that Gorbachev had defended Cuban–Soviet relations despite pressures. Ideologically, there was more affinity with the coup plotters, but most actors in the Soviet Union had at this point accepted market reforms, and Cuba probably had little faith of a "pure" socialism returning to the Soviet Union anytime soon. Given that its immediate goal was rather to safeguard the interests of Cuba and the international revolutionary movement, its interests were that what was left of the Soviet Union survived.

3   Early Post-Collapse Assessments (January–March 1992)

In this section, some examples have been given of the coverage of the crisis and fall of socialist governments in Eastern Europe and, finally, in the USSR.

However, what we have analyzed is mostly simultaneous coverage, that is, written and published as the events were taking place. Some materials that we have analyzed so far contain explicit or implicit assessments of what was going on. These became somewhat more explicit as time passed, but Cuba and *Granma* generally avoided giving too many opinions, possibly in part because the country had to avoid antagonizing allies or potential allies, even non-socialist governments in Eastern Europe that might be open to continuing some of the trade with Cuba, and also because it was difficult to reach conclusions as the final outcome was not yet known. It might also have been to avoid much public discussion about the problems of societies that had similarities to Cuba.

As we started this investigation, we supposed, a priori, that during the first months of 1992, there would have to be some analysis and opinion in *Granma*, as the Cuban public would ask for explanations. By this date, the Soviet Union and Comecon had formally disappeared, so there was little to win by opting for a diplomatic tone. But also these are of course also events that were basically "crying for explanations," more so even because the Cuban authorities had presented the Soviet Union as a solid, stable, and prosperous socialist country—during most of the preceding three decades.

At the beginning of 1992, *Granma* does not deny that there has just been a radical change in the international balance of power and that the international communist and revolutionary movement has suffered an enormous defeat. It is not surprising that the end of Soviet and East European socialism is evaluated as something extraordinarily negative, if we consider Cuba's affinity with this project and the brutal crisis that the Special Period implied. *Granma's* front page on January 1, 1992 reflects some general sentiments: There, it is recognized that the events of 1991 were bitter for the "international revolutionary movement" and that they imply "significant transformations in world geopolitics." The writers refer to events as a "capitalist restoration" (January 2, 1992) and a "disaster" (January 2, 1992) and use concepts such as "unipolar world" to describe the new world order. In an editorial—remember that *Granma* very seldom publishes editorials—events are considered to have increased the "arrogance" of the US and caused a more aggressive policy against Cuba (January 21, 1992).

The negative assessment of the Collapse, however, is seen above all, as Jorge Domínguez has suggested, in the news coverage, where news on crime and hunger in the former Soviet Union is what prevails. Of course, to some degree this also reflects the real crisis that took place, which would by any serious journalistic standards be worth covering.

Sometimes, still, the changes are presented as something that could be temporary and not definitive, for example when using phrases such as "hard setback/retreat [*retroceso*]" (February 21, 1992). *Granma* also published news that could give some hope for Cuban revolutionaries that the order of things is reversible. For example, "Walesa admits that the situation has become worse in Poland" (February 5, 1992), when the president of Poland warned that if the country's economic crisis deepened further, "the country will be shaken by a destabilizing wave that could reverse the current course of Poland." One could argue that the old system would be more or less impossible to resurrect for many reasons, but that statement could easily lead some readers to believe that it would be possible. Psychologically, the radicality and irreversibility of the changes had surely not yet been fully assumed by all Cubans, nor the difficulty it would entail to reverse them.

In these circumstances, *Granma* warns that there will be many sacrifices in Cuba, but that the solution is not to change political positions (which would also imply, in war-like metaphors that the newspaper often uses, surrendering to the enemy, metaphors that have some appeal in a country that has been in conflict with the US for so long).

During the first months of the Collapse, some causes were also presented. However, this analysis was sparse, considering the magnitude of the changes in the Soviet Union and the massive implications it had for Cuba. The Cuban government probably considered it to be better to have these discussions in more limited or closed arenas and not in the main newspaper. On January 4, *Granma* emphasizes the Cuban Revolutionary Party of José Martí and his idea that one has to work discreetly—an idea originated in the context of illegal resistance to the Spanish—which could be a subliminal message about the alleged impossibility of having a wider debate at that time, due to the vulnerability of the revolutionary project in this delicate situation.

At this point, a congress of the Young Communist Union is about to take place, and a series of articles on the preparations start appearing in *Granma*. When an interview is published with the second secretary of the Young Communist Union (February 28, 1992) about the preparations for the congress—just two months after the disappearance of the Soviet Union—the Collapse is not a topic; it is not even mentioned with a single word. This is somewhat surprising even given the context, as many young people will have questions and will have their own ideas about what has happened, and one would suppose that the topic will arise in some way at the congress. Finally, on March 25, 1992, the report on the congress is published; it is titled "The only option is victory." Neither are the events explicitly mentioned here, but it is discussed how to deal with the "current conditions" of crisis.

Overall, considering the implications of the Collapse for Cuba, relatively little space is devoted to it during the three first months of 1992. On the other hand, it would be an exaggeration to say that it is a complete taboo, as I will demonstrate with other examples. The editors of *Granma* (or the top echelons of the Party and the government) do still not seem to want a real debate on the subject on the events in Eastern Europe and the USSR. As in previous years (1989–1991), what could be called analysis or assessments often appear in a more or less disjointed way in different parts of the newspaper and within different types of journalistic articles; also, the assessments tend to come from a third party (someone not belonging to the editorial staff). There are still virtually no editorials. Short assessments instead appear in the middle of news on other topics (sometimes just a few sentences), but a bit more explicitly, profoundly, and frequently in speeches by Cuban leaders, in interviews with people from outside of Cuba, and so on.

Still, this is also a situation where there is a lack of paper and even *Granma* has become very brief, so this makes smaller, more subtle details (including comments) of importance to understand the position of the newspaper and the Communist Party of Cuba (a few years earlier they might have "drowned" amongst other texts). Some of these comments may have influenced Cubans' perception of the collapse, as at that time not many other sources of information were available to them, and the public was used to reading between the lines. I will cite, in chronological form, the most outstanding examples of materials that comment on the Collapse—directly or indirectly:

January 1. The following quote appears on the front page: "We are like fine roosters / and fine roosters / do not fly the fence, / do not abandon combat / they fight until the end; / we are not of the lineage of those who surrender / we are another class of people." This text that is presented almost like a poem is signed simply by "Fidel." A quote from José Martí also appears on the front page: "Weaklings: Show respect: Great people, march on! This is a job for the great." Although there is no explicit reference to the USSR in either case, both quotes refer to Cuba's strength or solidity and could suggest that the Cubans are steadier and stronger, not least ideologically, an appreciation that well matches a metaphorical description made by Fidel Castro of the Collapse as a *merengue* (sweet) melting down or falling apart, a *desmerengamiento*, a word apparently invented for the occasion[70] on November 1, 1991. As the sweet known as a meringue, the USSR seemed solid and hard from the outside but was soft on the inside; it

---

70 The earliest use of the word I have found appears in the following speech: "Discurso pronunciado por el Comandante en Jefe Fidel Castro Ruz, Primer Secretario del Comité Central del Partido Comunista de Cuba y Presidente de los Consejos de Estado y de Ministros, en la clausura del Primer Congreso de los Pioneros, efectuada en el Palacio de las Convenciones, el 1° de noviembre de 1991," Consejo de Estado, http://www.cuba.cu/gobierno/discursos/1991/esp/f011191e.html.

had the army and the institutions and so on but weaknesses on the subjective level, a lack of real *ideological consciousness and a combative attitude*.

January 1. A complete speech by Carlos Aldana, head of the Ideological Department of the PCC (defenestrated in October of the same year). This speech covers three pages, and it is about the need to defend Cuba. Aldana acknowledges that there are "counterrevolutionary groups" in Cuba that have obtained "a new impulse" thanks to the collapse of the Socialist Bloc. He considers that "they have always received instructions from the outside." He warns that some are presented as moderates and that this type of group "has as its main purpose to create a breach through employing confusion, utilizing to its favor the unsettlement that this defeat has provoked in some sectors of society." He also states that together with the most radical groups, they constitute "two alternatives that the United States manages simultaneously." Some materials that touch upon the same topics and use the same narrative do not necessarily say much about the Soviet Union; but, they talk of a Cuban opposition that it claims is artificially constructed by the CIA, with no will of its own, and this could create or strengthen a perception that the Collapse was a product of *external pressures and trickery*. Imperialism promises to bring democracy and so on, but its real aim is taking control and introducing "wild capitalism."

Aldana in his speech does touch upon the topic of the USSR reform process when he argues that many Cuban press workers had sympathized with Gorbachev's Perestroika. As previously mentioned, the Cuban population also identified Aldana himself with these ideas. The speech thus served in part to deny links to Perestroika, as he speaks of his former followers in Cuba in the third person and does not include himself in the category, but at the same time he tries to legitimize the position he had taken, as he recalls that Perestroika promised to solve certain problems in Soviet society. He distinguishes between two phases of Perestroika, saying that there was sympathy in some sectors of Cuban society with "that initial speech that spoke of ending benefits or privileges that did not derive from one's effort at work, of ending corruption, of creating order and social discipline, accelerating the economy, applying to the development of the economy advances that had already been achieved in the form of cutting-edge technology in the field of weapons; and all that generated sympathy." Aldana recognizes that *there were internal and structural problems in the Socialist Bloc, not only imperialist pressures, but he suggests that they are properly Soviet problems*, as if none of them existed in Cuba, and also that a tendency of blind admiration for the Soviets had been a mistake.[71]

---

71   Fragments have been cut out from the copy of the newspaper that I have available for analysis, therefore there may be further comments on the USSR that I have not been able to read.

ANALYZING THE NEWS ACCOUNTS

January 2. An article or short feature that has as its main topic a speech by Roberto Robaina, the leader of the Union of Young Communists (UJC). Robaina says "The magic kings will not arrive here, and they are not that much of magicians [...]," referring to the Spanish name for the three wise men, "the magical kings," that in Latin countries bring gifts to children on the Day of the Epiphany, January 6. Implicitly, *Granma* is saying that the people of Eastern Europe and the Soviet Union were fooled by Western propaganda's false promise that some miracle would happen if the old system just fell.

At the same time, he argues in favor of socialism and against capitalism, saying for example that in "other countries" there are no queues, because "you don't have the money to buy even a little bit of sugar," ruling out the possibility of Cuba following the path of the former Soviet Union. The text ends with the phrase, "Nothing and nobody will take away the Socialism that we are building," that is, it emphasizes the national character of the Cuban Revolution but also socialism as a process, underlining thereby that it could be improved. That is, Robaina *emphasizes external factors, especially trickery, as a factor for understanding the Collapse, while discreetly also underlining an important and real difference with Eastern Europe* (in Cuba, socialism was not imposed from outside).

January 4. News story: "Looking at the new map of the world." Here, the implications of the Collapse on the world of sport are discussed. It is stated that East Germany was assimilated by the western part (not reunited). *So, at least referring to the GDR, it suggests external pressure is an important factor.* Also, it warns that the Commonwealth of Independent States—an organization formed by 11 former Soviet republics after the Collapse of the USSR—"does not constitute a country, but an alliance," warning anyone who believes in a certain continuity.

January 15. Interview with Heiner Müller, referred to as "the most important German playwright today." Müller, from the former East Germany, is visiting Cuba. The news-interview appears at the bottom of page 4 and covers less than one-sixth of the page, but is notable as it talks quite openly about issues that have not been mentioned before in *Granma*. It is stated that the playwright had been critical of the GDR—among other things, he had criticized in his works the Soviet repression of the workers' strike in East Berlin in 1953. According to *Granma*, these works "were not presented on a stage until the 1980s (in the GDR)." This serves to underpin Müller's credibility as he is criticizing the new capitalist system; in particular, this might have given him more credibility to Cubans who want change or have a critical image of the old Socialist Bloc. Müller criticizes certain "errors" in the old system (as both Fidel Castro and more reform minded Cuban leaders had also suggested, they do not invalidate the system; they are aberrations that could be fixed). He even talks about the "schizophrenic effects of the [Berlin] wall"; this may be the first time the Wall has been so explicitly criticized in the Cuban press. Müller also considers, however, that the "Concrete Wall" has been replaced by a "Wall of Money," that the "Political Censorship" has been replaced by "commercial censorship," and that the cultural institutions of the GDR have been destroyed as a consequence of the dramatic changes in society.

Still, Müller clearly recognizes that *internal factors played an important role in bringing the GDR to an end,* and he touches upon some problems that were also familiar to Cubans—travel limitations and state censorship. Although he is a critic of capitalism, he was also considered a critical voice within the GDR. The publication of the interview—especially taking into account that he is currently visiting Cuba and has accepted to be interviewed by *Granma*—is a way of admitting that the GDR was not perfect and signaling that Cuba is open to these types of critical voices. *Granma* had never criticized the Berlin Wall or the official policies of the GDR. But as this is an interview with an "external voice," someone who is not from Cuba, and although the reader knows that *Granma* is at least open to the idea that his views might be right as they allowed them, by letting Müller talk about these issues, the newspaper avoids having to recognize these problems itself, which could have led to accusations of opportunism or lack of credibility, since it did not do so at an earlier point.

Comment on January 21, 1992. "*We will not allow the counterrevolution to rear its head [levantar cabeza,* meaning to start getting up or rebuilding itself]." This comment refers to a recent terrorist attack in the Cuban province of Cárdenas that is seen in the context of an "exacerbated imperial arrogance." The text repeats part of Aldana's argument on January 1 as it states that new dissident or opposition groups have appeared in Cuba that are presented as a third way between imperialism and the revolution and that they try to repeat a recipe used in the Socialist Bloc. It is also noted that some of their participants have studied in Soviet universities. However, *Granma* believes that the former Soviet opposition went from "pseudo radical demagogy to promoting the rise of wild capitalism and authoritarianism." It is argued that Cuba is in "a confrontation of life or death," and there can be no room for these as "pseudo-intellectual whims" (*veleidades intelectualoides*). They are, furthermore, put in connection with another type of counterrevolution, the "preachers of nonviolence" that the newspaper considers to be the ideologues of the disaster in Eastern Europe but really represent the "worst and most inhuman": that of the ruthless bourgeois system that creates unemployment, hunger, and exploitation. In this commentary, *Granma* attributes the Collapse to a mixture of external pressures and the inability of the Soviet system to resist these pressures:

"The disaster occurred in Eastern Europe [*el campo socialista*] and in the USSR, and was based on their *demonstrated inability to resist the ideological offensive and imperialist subversion.*"

January 24. "*Reclaim the existence of a Latin American line of thinking.*" Under this headline, the Italian researcher and critic Antonio Melis asserts that "They are wrong, those who mechanically link the perspectives of Cuba to what happened in other countries. The Cuban Revolution is something very different." That is, he *emphasizes the singular aspects and Latin American (not European) character of the Cuban revolution.*

February 7. An article with the heading "*Colin Powell: His political aspirations.*" Here, Powell is quoted as saying that "the USSR does not exist; we defeated it," and it refers to another interview where he has allegedly said that "[...] I am getting rid of the demons, I am getting rid of the villains, I only have Fidel Castro and Kim Il Sung left." If read in the context of the rest of the *Granma* coverage of the Collapse, this article basically serves to underline the notion that the US has forced the Soviets to change their system and that all Cubans should defend the sovereignty of Cuba; this is not a system failing by itself, we are talking about attacks from imperialism. So, again, reference *is to external pressure.*

February 15. Summary of a speech by Fidel Castro when meeting a Brazilian delegation (*Frei Betto, the famous liberation theologist priest, was among those present*). The following fragment is worth citing: "As you know, he [Fidel Castro] said, other [socialist] experiences collapsed there, other attempts [to build socialism], although one cannot say that this is the last word [...] because there can be no action without reaction, just as there cannot be revolution without counterrevolution." That is, Fidel Castro had presented the Collapse as a temporary setback, and he gives the hope that the international revolutionary movement can be resurrected, although he does not say how long this could take. "Today's setbacks for just causes or ideas, no matter how badly they have been interpreted or the mistakes made by men—today's setbacks will become a stimulus for tomorrow's successes." In other words, the Collapse is about errors, about human error, more than structural problems, or problems inherent in socialism. "They brought us [...] very sweetened words, like market economy, instead of saying capitalism, and wild capitalism, primitive capitalism." Furthermore, Fidel Castro sees the Collapse as part of a "neoliberal wave." *Fundamentally, the possible causes are human errors and the people having been fooled by propaganda.*

March 3. There is an unsigned comment titled "George Bush's anti-Cuban policy: Ultraconservatism, double morals, and astrology." In it, European and Soviet socialism is presented as merely a "concrete historical experience of building socialism" that "has failed in a specific geopolitical sphere, causing the hardest and deepest setback in the entire history of the revolutionary movement." But the comment also adds that capitalism is guilty of underdevelopment and hunger, and has therefore also failed.[72] These are arguments that might have more strength in a Third World country than in industrialized countries, although they might also generate sympathy in some sectors in the First World. "[George Bush does not understand that] we are not at a crossroads, like those who were left without a Revolution, without Socialism, and some even without a Homeland in Eastern Europe," apparently referring to the final fate of East Germany. Socialism and national independence or the presence of a homeland are thus linked together, in spite of the fact that for many people in Eastern Europe, socialism was linked to quite the opposite: Soviet presence and control over their own circumstances.

Granma questions Bush's discourse on "free elections," as it puts the term between quote marks, here referring to his proposals for Cuba. Cubans do not believe in this false discourse, it is indicated, which is promising a pacific transition while strengthening the embargo and supporting terrorism. The collapse of Soviet and East European socialism has made Cuba "the most independent country" on the planet, thus suggesting that there was some degree of independence. There is a strong suggestion that the *peoples of the former socialist countries were fooled by imperialism.*

March 17, 1992. The newspaper contains an inside two-page discourse by Carlos Aldana. One of the highlighted quotes says that "There is no room for frolicking with the enemy's alternatives." At the same time, Aldana emphasizes that people should not be labeled as dissidents or counterrevolutionaries "because they have a point of view or disagree on some issue." Although he is the politician who was most associated with a Gorbachevian position, Aldana was given a lot of visibility in the media at the beginning of 1992. He is portrayed as distancing himself from some of his former positions before he is finally removed from his positions. On March 17, he is also cited saying that "Any liberal formula, inserted in a socialist context, has only led to chaos." *That is, liberal reforms helped cause the Collapse* (says a former proponent of reforms in Cuba).

---

72   Fidel Castro, when giving a speech on December 7, 1989, said that "It is disgusting that many in the USSR are dedicating themselves to denying and destroying the historic feat and the extraordinary merits of that heroic people. This is not the way to rectify (*rectificar*) and overcome the unquestionable mistakes made in a revolution that was born in czarist authoritarianism, in a huge, backward, and poor country." In other words, historically, the Soviet leaders had made unquestionable mistakes, but the merits were much greater. The speech can be found online and was also published in the shape of a booklet in Cuba: José Eduardo Dos Santos and Fidel Castro, *Sabremos cumplir el papel que nos asigne la historia* (La Habana: Editorial Política, 1989).

Since *Granma* simultaneously also highlights discontent in the former Socialist Bloc in its news, this suggests that it was right in saying that they were deceived. One shorter heading reads, for instance, "Thousands of protesters in Moscow demand the USSR be reestablished" (March 18, 1992).

March 20. On the front page, *Granma* has included a cartoon-style drawing of what could be a caiman—a type of alligator that is also a symbol of the island of Cuba (see Figure 7). The animal says, while raising his fist: "For those alternatives there is no space!" In the background, a gray man is held up in the air by five inflated balloons on which the names of the following "institutions" appear: "Bourgeois Press," "pro-Yankee Party," "market economy," "private property," and "mafia Party." These could be associated with the current Soviet Union (and also Cuba's capitalist past). Imperialism, or *the enemy*, is trying to introduce into Cuba the reforms it had before promoted in the Socialist Bloc, and the attitude toward such proposals has to be combative.

March 24. A news story appears of small or medium size about singer-songwriters Luis Eduardo Aute (from Spain) and Pablo Milanés (from Cuba). In it, Aute criticizes "turncoats and quitters" with a clear reference to certain people that abandoned socialism, alleging they did it out of opportunism. He asserts that "there are too many teachers / professionals of freedom / who are making a flag / out of thin air." Aute speaks of people that were "at one time prophets of freedom, and today apostles of investment." The promises are empty, and the people who presented them are not to be trusted: *Opportunism, falseness, and a lack of principles—that is, not staying true to the revolutionary principles—helped bring down the system.*

March 31. A speech by Fidel Castro at the closing ceremony of the Constituent Congress of the Union of Scientists. "Today, imperialism has achieved what Hitler could not achieve, and it achieved this without firing a shot." That is, Fidel Castro emphasizes external pressure as a cause of the Collapse. He also says that "It is proven that steel does not collapse, steel does not crumble, and this is a people made out of steel!" This quote appears magnified at the end of the speech.

We can see from this and some other examples that Jorge Domínguez was right when he claimed that the main explanation offered by the Cuban official media about the Collapse was "A lack of leadership, not a system failure,"[73] and when he pointed out, furthermore, that according to this discourse, "Making concessions was especially wrong, because the enemies of socialism are never satisfied."[74] Still, it should be specified that in the assessments of the Collapse

---

73 Domínguez, *La política exterior de Cuba (1962–2009)*, 298.
74 Ibid.

FIGURE 7   *Granma*, March 20, 1992; drawing published on the front page

that *Granma* gave during January to March 1992, most references to the offensive of the enemies of socialism referred to a very specific type of pressure: the use of propaganda that implied false promises and thus deceived the population. There was an internal weakness that was not only due to the lack of leadership but also to a certain "softness": a lack of combative attitude, a lack of a real and profound ideological and political conscience, and so on. It should also be mentioned that *Granma* included references to problematic policies or characteristics of these societies, but mostly in a timid manner, and they were given little emphasis.

To summarize, the early post-Collapse assessments view what had happened as very negative. Cuban socialism was in a very dangerous situation, it was recognized, but the outcome would not be the same, because the Cuban revolution and society were different. Many of the explanations given at this stage focus on external pressure as the cause of the Collapse, although references to internal problems of different types are also frequent. It is suggested that people were fooled (by external and/or internal forces), sometimes also that the changes were not what the population requested or that they were introduced against their will. When problems of "real socialism" were mentioned, they were mostly problems that were alien to Cuban reality (or, in some cases, they were treated as if they were alien to Cuban reality).[75] There are certainly common characteristics and problems in the system that are not mentioned. Reference is often made to the strong human qualities and the level of consciousness of Cubans.

The coverage cited from January to March or 1992 indicates that the press was not used for thoroughly analyzing the Collapse. This could be a product to some extent of confusion, as these processes were complex and very recent, but was probably also part of a political strategy: Despite its particularities, Cuban socialism also had strong similarities with Soviet socialism, and because of this an analysis would be politically risky as it could have encouraged questioning Cuba's own model. The extremely tense circumstances in the early 1990s made the government even more cautious, and both those in power and society focused on "survival"—in several senses—more than opening up a discussion on the fundamental characteristics of Cuban society.

---

75   It is recognized openly, however, that the problems created by others will greatly affect Cuba. Cuban politician Carlos Lage, at the time a member of the Central Committee and secretary of the Executive Committee of the Council of Ministers—Cuba's government—was interviewed in 1992 by journalist Arleen Rodríguez Derivet: "In the last six months, the population has been explained a lot, in detail, the origin of our problems today that are not our mistakes, but those of others [...]" (*Juventud Rebelde*, January 26, 1992).

As seen in the review of the existing literature, in 1992, an analysis regarding the causes of the Collapse actually did circulate among cadres of the Party, and it seems that in that instance, more emphasis was placed on internal factors than external ones (I could not find any copy of the analysis, and rely on a summary published on Cubanet by Tania Díaz Castro).[76] If correct, this could mean that the Cuban authorities saw the need for Party cadres to be given a bit more explanation and that there were actually more comprehensive amounts of information and possibly debate amongst Party cadres, and another narrative that was a mostly critical towards certain leaders, especially Stalin, but that also may have come close to questioning certain systemic or structural problems of state socialism.

The explanations of the Collapse presented to the general public, that focus on problems or causes that were not present in the Cuban case, are a way of avoiding an in-depth debate about the weaknesses of a fallen model, by which Cuba had—though with some reservations—been inspired for years. The explanations that center on outside pressure from imperialism were also convenient as they appealed to nationalism and made calls for unanimity and sacrifice seem more logical. These explanations often suggest that people were fooled by propaganda or false and unrealistic promises, but also that there were internal weaknesses on a more subjective level, which made it possible for imperialism to defeat the system: bad leaders, a lack of a real revolutionary conscience and patriotism and so on. Socialism is something that one has to fight hard to win and that is under constant pressure from imperialist forces, so it demands social cohesion and a certain attitude that had become debilitated in the Soviet Union and Eastern Europe.

---

76   However, on one of the pages of July 1989 in *El Militante Comunista*, a magazine for members of the Communist Party, there is a reference to "the complacency that the process of Perestroika in the USSR has caused in the Western world […]." Until at least late 1991, *Granma* was quite indirect and not very explicit in its criticism of Gorbachev (and thus, his Perestroika), and although Cuba's official line was clearly that socialism in Cuba should not be reformed, it avoided explicit assessments of USSR internal policies. This commentary in *El Militante Comunista*, given in a publication that has a more limited but politically important readership within Cuba, states that the Gorbachev's policy of Perestroika was much liked in capitalist countries, and its wording clearly is clearly suggestive of it being a policy that favors Western interests and ideology. So, this might indicate the existence of a certain double approach where the Communist Party is being somewhat more explicit in its criticism of Perestroika in internal organs than in *Granma*, and where more criticism is directed at official USSR policies. Still, even in this type of space, Cuba is generally very careful not to offend its allies.

Still, within the PCC other explanations for the causes of the Collapse were circulating, visions that *Granma* did not refer to much, or referred to in a fragmented and implicit way, and this shows the need to complement *Granma's* vision with other sources, which we have done by interviewing people that were members of the PCC at the time. These are to be analyzed in the second part of the study.

CHAPTER 4

Reflections on the Written News

In Part 1, I have analyzed *Granma's* coverage of the Collapse of Soviet and East European socialism, focusing especially on the coverage of six major events or processes. In addition, I identified and analyzed materials published between January and March 1992 that contained some early assessments with regard to the Collapse and its causes. *Granma* did cover the crisis and the Collapse, so Cubans were informed about what was happening, but the ways of informing and the degree of detail varied considerably. There is often a lack of explanation and occasionally, the information seems to have been hidden away or presented in a manner that seems, even deliberately, confusing so it might not have been easily visible and accessible to all readers.

Some explicit and implicit assessments of the events appeared in the shape of "bits and pieces," that is, in a fragmented manner, but in general *Granma* offered few assessments, even when events were clearly of major importance to Cuba. A detailed and global analysis of the Collapse was never presented, not even in 1992.

The coverage of the six major events and processes highlighted that different countries were treated in very different manners.

For example, in the case of Poland (the elections of 1989) or the USSR (the economic debate in 1990), a seemingly neutral tone and style can be identified in much of the news. Although the coverage was in no way neutral—some actors and ideas were favored as they got more space, more attention was given to their arguments, and so on—the news essentially kept the readers informed.

During the coverage of the migration crisis in the GDR, however, the coverage is largely a repetition of the official version of that country's government. This is a narrative that is very politicized and often distant from social reality.

These differences in the coverage seem to depend on a series of factors related to the degree of political openness in a specific country at a specific moment (which influenced what type of news there was to cover as well as the variety and characteristics of the available sources), characteristics of the journalist (personal viewpoints, priorities, desire, and capacity to inform, even when events did not fit official ideology, and so on). Furthermore, the news is shaped by the exact historical moment and ongoing developments inside Cuba (the space permitted for reformist ideas narrows somewhat over time, though reformism in the USSR is still reported on *as news* throughout 1991, though at that point without room for any Cuban *endorsement* of these ideas).

The Cuban authorities' perception of the country also influenced the coverage (East Germany was seen as something close to a model country), as well as strategic interests (relations could be threatened if coverage became too critical, especially in the case of the major countries).

With regard to the last point, often there seems to be a tension between the desire to give complete information to the Cuban public and *Granma's* "responsibilities" as an official organ. Whenever a country permitted some political and media pluralism, this also tended to be reflected in *Granma*, as one had to report on, let us say, major anti-government protests, and this did not imply any risk of affecting bilateral relations (and perhaps the opposite, since these countries were accepting some pluralism in reporting on their social reality). This provoked a change in news coverage whenever a country became more permissive but did not affect the official opinions of *Granma*.

The coverage, still, did not always automatically favor the allied governments' version, except East Germany until at least late 1989. It tended to favor the Cuban government's anti-reformist stance, but there are also exceptions to this rule. At some decisive moments, the Prensa Latina (Cuban-based press agency) correspondent in Poland seemed to include veiled messages in favor of the reformists, and also in the case of Romania, the people who were rebelling or had rebelled against the Ceaușescu regime. In 1989, there was also news that seemed to reflect a considerable interest by the journalist in understanding the reform proposals in Hungary, though Fidel Castro was against such reforms. In the coverage of some countries, information from international agencies was often reproduced that conveyed news and did not very clearly sympathize with one side or another.

Although anti-reformist views were given more visibility, sometimes apparently convincing arguments by the reformists were presented, sometimes because the newspaper had no option but to publish these criteria, but at times also signaling a trust in the reader to decide for him- or herself. This happened in the case of Hungary in 1989 but also when debate broke out on economic reform in the USSR in the fall of 1990. Here, by this time there was even less doubt that Cuba preferred the "hardliners" who did not want reforms, but Cuba also needed to treat the reformist Gorbachev respectfully, as Cuba depended on Soviet trade and subsidies, and it certainly preferred his people to the radical pro-capitalist wing in the debate. Thus, all three wings of the debate were covered ("conservative communists," reformists, and radical pro-market forces), but the newspaper clearly favored the first two factions.

The coup in August 1991 is a particular case that has also been analyzed by other investigators. Here, *Granma* essentially reproduces the "hardline" coup plotters' statement but hidden behind a policy of non-interference. It continued to also reproduce news on events from international sources, including Western agencies. The accumulated texts (opinion, analysis, etc.) were often produced by ideologues of the Party who were close politically to Fidel Castro and sometimes foreigners that were also generally close to the Cuban government's ideological preferences.

On the other hand, the content of the news from foreign agencies or from Cuban correspondents was often influenced by the ideas and political circumstances (and conditions for doing journalism) that prevailed in whichever country they worked. They got a close and up-to-date perspective, reporting on what happened in their host country and depended less on Cuban ideological schemes. Sometimes the editors seem to have changed titles and presented news stories suggestively together with others that could exemplify the ills of capitalism and so on, favoring a certain political reading, even when the incoming news itself was basically reporting on events.

Whenever a given country transited to capitalism, *Granma* published a considerable amount of negative news about the situation in the country. In part, this reflects the serious crisis that these countries suffered, but any positive changes were given little publicity or relativized. This news served to confirm Fidel Castro's longtime warnings—in their time often made subtly so as not to annoy allies: Reforms or concessions to capitalism were dangerous.

Granma generally seems to have had as a policy that it would not directly criticize allies and former allies, and therefore it was mostly not very explicit in its criticisms. But at some points, news was published that mentions or alludes to errors and even abuse made by allied or former allied governments (most visibly, in the included examples, in the cases of Poland and Romania). These materials were often just news stories about (former) opposition actors, foreign powers, or even socialist leaders recognizing past faults, and as such not "signed" by *Granma* (but permitted). After the Collapse, the general tendency was to close ranks and talk about other topics, but occasionally some critics were admitted, such as with the publication of an essay by a well-known friend of Cuba (Eduardo Galeano) who accused the former Polish government of state terror, and in a short interview with respected German playwright Heiner Müller who after the Collapse of the GDR gave a frank view on the Berlin Wall and GDR censorship, though he was also criticizing the new capitalist society.

Still, the inclusion of such commentary happened very infrequently, and there was none or almost no focus on the possible *structural problems* of Soviet-style state socialism. One could find discreet references to *inherited* internal problems; that is, problems inherited from other historical periods and that their leaders at the time (1989–1991) could not be held responsible for. The tense relations between the Soviet Union and Eastern Europe were, for example, very subtly alluded to at some points, and there were some suggestions that there might be different ways of building socialism. The main tendency with regard to the *causes* of the Collapse was to emphasize errors and problems that had no equivalents or no obvious equivalents in the Cuban case and that excluded a critical view of the system itself (Cuba's system was similar).

A bit of attention was also given to (real or alleged) external pressures against those states through the entire period (1989–1992). But perhaps these explanations were especially present in 1992 (January–March), which fit very well the political necessities at the time: to promote close unity and avoid too many self-critical views on the Cuban reality. *Granma* did not avoid recognizing the Collapse, although the topic did receive less attention than what its implications for Cuba would suggest. There was still no completely uniform narrative about the causes of the Collapse, but two main explanations were emphasized: 1) There had been interference by the West (pressures, selling false dreams, etc.), and 2) there was an internal weakness in the former socialist countries, notably on the subjective level and the lack of real revolutionary consciousness (Fidel Castro's thesis of the *desmerengamiento*). At some moments, it was suggested that the international revolutionary movement would recover.

One could say that all along, at least since 1989, the particularities of the Cuban Revolution, and perceived particularities of the Cuban Revolution, were emphasized, but this tendency became even stronger by 1991 and early 1992.

The material as well as other sources suggest that there were other interpretations in the population, in the Party, and in the political elite. As previously written, Party cadres seem to have been given a slightly more critical analysis in the shape of a publication. According to a news article that I cited, it emphasized some problematic aspects of Soviet society that—although blamed on Stalin or Stalinism—could in several cases be said to be recurrent in countries with state socialist models including Cuba. These include the constant violations of socialist legality and bureaucratism, problems that might not have had the same character in Cuba but that were certainly not absent.

Although *Granma* as a major newspaper can tell us a lot with regard to what information people had, as well as official interpretations and official ways of presenting events to the public in such a manner that they did not provoke further negative repercussions on the Cuban political project—the existence of these texts reminds us that *Granma* does not reflect all that was thought, written, and said in the Party nor, much less, how events were perceived at some chronological distance from the events. As we shall now see, the oral sources are also important and they will help complement the larger picture.

PART 2

The Collapse as Viewed by Cuban Party Members

CHAPTER 5

Contextualizing the Testimonies

The following part of this study revolves around an exploration and analysis of the fall of the Soviet Union as seen from the perspectives of 17 individuals who were members of the Communist Party of Cuba in the period between 1989 and 1991.[1] The sources used for the analysis consist of the transcripts resulting from 17 semi-structured interviews carried out over the second half of 2013 in Cuba. These essentially provide the views and perceptions of the informants more than two decades after the Collapse, although they also give information about their perspective at the time of the Collapse.

As seen in the introduction of this book, existing work that analyzes how the Collapse was perceived from Cuba is largely based on written sources. The perspectives that these types of sources reflect are usually those of more or less influential people in society, who had the privilege of getting their words published and preserved even at a time when paper was scarce, and there was no independent media in the country.

There are, however, types of information that are usually not present in written, formal, and published texts. Oral sources may contain other types of information, such as doubts, representations, meanings, and personal assessments. In this regard, Alessandro Portelli argues that an oral source "tells us less about events than about their meaning."[2] They tell us "not just what people did, but what they wanted to do, what they believed they were doing, and what they now think they did."[3]

Oral sources do involve some specific challenges for the interpreter. According to Paul Thompson, the information that interviews could provide about *recent* or *current* events "can be assumed to lie somewhere between the actual social behavior and the social expectations or norms of the time,"[4] while if the interviews treat memories from the more distant past, there can also be distortions "influenced by subsequent changes in values or norms [...]."[5] In our case, the time elapsed between the Collapse and 2013 might have seen significant changes in values and norms in some respects, but even when this is not the

---

1 With only one exception, they were still militants at the time of the interview (2013).
2 Alessandro Portelli. *The Death of Luigi Trastulli and Other Stories. Form and Meaning in Oral History*. New York: State University Press, 1991, 50.
3 Ibid.
4 Thompson, 89–90.
5 Ibid.

case, we must take into account what is socially acceptable to say, which could influence the testimonies.

It is also necessary to take into account the effects of the passage of time.[6] An objection that sometimes arises with regard to oral history has to do with the fragility of human memory. Thompson, based on studies on memory in social psychology and gerontology, argues that we forget a lot of information during the first moments after having perceived something, and then we also forget during the first passing months. Afterwards, what we remember remains relatively stable for years and decades, although in general, the ability to remember depends on the person's interest in remembering something.[7] Thompson reminds us that most *written* sources are also retrospective and do not reflect reality but are an interpretation.[8]

I recognize the existence of studies that suggest that people more easily remember practical matters in their lives than their past attitudes.[9] With regard to this, it is necessary to analyze critically what they say about their past attitudes. In some cases, it may be possible to compare with other sources, but it is not always possible to know for sure if what the informants say reflects how they really thought. It is not possible to literally place oneself "in someone else's shoes," and it is not always possible to gain insight into their beliefs two decades ago. But I also reject the other extreme, the idea that these testimonies cannot tell us anything about what the subjects thought at a particular moment in their past. Such a position would reflect a radical distrust of the memory of the interview subjects and the historian's capacity for interpretation.

In this sense, Portelli reminds us that there are interview subjects whose positions have changed since the historical moment, which can lead them to conceal elements.[10] But he also states that "[o]ften, however, narrators are capable of reconstructing their past attitudes even when they no longer coincide with present ones."[11] It would be impossible to remove the distortions caused by the passage of time from the interviews, but I think it is important to take into account how people remember and, to the extent that it is possible, take into account important changes in society that can distort their testimonies. Therefore, I will provide some reflections on important and relevant changes that have taken place since 1991, that is, in the world, in Cuba, and in the PCC, which might be of help when interpreting the testimonies.

---

6   Ibid.
7   Ibid., 89–91.
8   Ibid., 89.
9   Ibid.
10 Portelli, 52–53.
11 Ibid., 53.

Oral history, while researchers need to be aware of its potential and limitations, seems to be a suited methodology to explore and analyze the views and perspectives of the Party members of the Communist Party that experienced and had a leading role in these historic events. Similarly, it will allow me as a researcher to respond to specific analytical problems related to the oral sources, asking the following questions: What were and are the perspectives of 17 PCC members on the collapse of the USSR? How can these perspectives help us understand the position of the PCC and its members when they were facing the Collapse of Soviet and East European socialism?

Before we proceed to the analysis, some information on the context in which the interviews were conducted will be presented. I will then go into detail about the methodology and the concrete steps that I have followed for the analysis, including some considerations on ethics in the following chapter. In Chapter 7, I will set forth the analysis of the interviews, which is divided into two parts: The first part focuses on Cuba and its relationship with Soviet and East European socialism. This includes some events in the history of Cuba that are important for the relation that arose with Soviet and East European socialism, as well as the way in which Cubans, and specifically Party members, perceived Soviet and East European socialism. The second part more extensively examines their views on the collapse of this model.

It will be important to present some contextual information, first about the historical moment at the time of interviews. Then, some notes will be given about what it means to be a member of the Communist Party of Cuba and changes in this situation in recent decades, which will complement the general background on the Party that was presented earlier. Furthermore, I will include some reflections on the challenges involved in oral history research in Cuba.

1   Context of the Interview Moment (2013)

The materials of the newspaper *Granma* that were analyzed in Part 1 of this study were contemporary with the Collapse. The interviews I analyze below, however, were conducted in 2013, and the testimonies can therefore be expected to be influenced by the time that has elapsed since the Collapse and by subsequent important events and changes in society.

In 1990, the Special Period in Time of Peace was declared in Cuba, a name that alludes to the crisis that emerged with the country's difficulties as a result of the crisis of the USSR. The name has also been associated with the policies that were employed to deal with the crisis. The crisis deeply affected the entire country, not only on the material level, on which several of its ravages are still felt, but it also brought profound changes to Cubans' lives and ways of thinking.

On the economic level, the worst year of the crisis was 1993, although in 1994 the tense political and economic situation became more evident to the world because of the street protests and riots that took place on August 5 (*El Maleconazo*), as well as emigration by sea ("Cuban Rafters Crisis"). During the summer of 1994 alone, 30,000 Cubans embarked on the sea in rafts.[12]

During the early years of the crisis, the Cuban authorities announced a series of political and economic changes. Among these were the opening for tourism (this started timidly toward the end of the 1980s, but the development of this sector accelerated from the 1990s); the admission of believers in religion to the Communist Party (since 1991); the decriminalization of being in possession of US currency (1993); and a greater opening to foreign capital (1995) and the national private sector (known in Cuba as self-employment [*cuentapropismo*], the growth of which was facilitated through several measures between 1993 and 1997).[13]

Another aspect of the Special Period is that the Cuban state lost a part of its capacity to regulate social life. According to Domínguez, the regime that emerged with the Revolution at one point even had totalitarian pretensions, especially during the late 1960s, although it was partially replaced by a "bureaucratic-socialist" regime in the 1970s. He asserts, however, that in the 1990s, an authoritarian regime began emerging in Cuba.[14] On the other hand, the Cuban sociologist Rafael Hernández stated in an interview in 2009 that Cuba was in the middle of a transition from a very centralized socialism to a less centralized model.[15] According to Velia Cecilia Bobes, during the Special Period there was a diversification of social life on the island, with new subcultures, identities, and actors emerging.[16] Although the name of the Communist Party and the one-party system were preserved, during those years, the country distanced

---

12   Cervantes-Rodríguez, 178.
13   A professor at the University of Havana told me informally that "if you had done your interviews in the 1990s, they would have answered you talking only about their economic difficulties."
14   Jorge I. Domínguez, "Comienza una transición hacia el autoritarismo en Cuba," *Encuentro* 6, No. 7 (1997): 9.
15   Rafael Hernández, "Norskstøttet tidsskrift på Cuba: Vil fornye sosialismen," interview by Even Sandvik Underlid in Verdensmagasinet X magazine, No. 4 (2009).
16   Velia Cecilia Bobes, "Complejidad y sociedad: cambios de identidad y surgimiento de nuevos actores en la sociedad cubana hacia el fin del milenio," *Sociological Studies* 18, No. 52 (2000).

itself from some of the Soviet thinking and policies. According to anthropologist María Gropas, Marxism–Leninism was relegated to a more modest role, and there was a "repatriotization" of the official ideology, with greater emphasis on the ideas of the philosopher and national hero José Martí than before.[17]

The Special Period began in 1990, and for some Cubans, the emergence of trade relations with Hugo Chavez's Venezuela around the year 2000 marked that the crisis was coming to an end. Two authors cite a speech by Fidel Castro in 2004 in which he states that Cuba is emerging from the crisis "with a thrust,"[18] a statement the authors themselves accept as true. Nevertheless, the crisis was never officially declared as over and the socioeconomic situation in Cuba remains complex. In 2013, when the interviews were conducted, the situation had improved considerably compared to 1993, though this process had not been without setbacks, changes of pace, and the surge of new problems (most notably, increased social inequality).

There was a reorganization of the national economy after the dissolution of Comecon, with economic reforms and the development of new economic sectors such as the export of services, remittances, tourism, nickel, biotechnology, and others. On the other hand, the country has managed to access new markets, such as China (in the 1990s) and Venezuela (since 2000), but other markets are also important, such as Canada, Spain, and in recent years, Russia and Brazil. The alliance with Venezuela and its supply of oil in exchange for Cuban medical services—considered a subsidy to Cuba by some authors, while an exchange of solidarity or complementarity by others—has been particularly important. Cuba maintains high indicators related to health and education compared to other Latin American countries and a high position in the Human Development Index, with a low homicide rate.

On the other hand, a number of social problems arose or became more serious during the years of crisis. According to a study published in 2014, 25% of the Cuban population was living in poverty, a higher figure than that of the 1980s.[19] Although I do not have any numbers to support the claim, my observations indicate that there is at least a widespread perception in the Cuban society that social discipline has been greatly weakened since the 1980s.

At the international level, in the years after the Collapse, there was a neoliberal wave on a global scale, accompanied by the predominance of US

---

17 Gropas.
18 Guerra and Maldonado, 151.
19 María del Carmen Zabala Argüelles, ed. *Algunas claves para pensar la pobreza en Cuba desde la mirada de jóvenes investigadores* (Havana: Editorial Felix Varela, 2014), cited in "Jóvenes investigadores analizan la pobreza en Cuba," Inter Press Service, September 20, 2014.

unilateralism. Both of these elements were clearly unfavorable to a socialist country in conflict with the mentioned superpower. Following the terrorist attacks of September 11, 2001, the so-called *war on terror* redirected US foreign policy efforts toward the Middle East. Latin America and Cuba specifically was not one of its major priorities at that time.

During the decade of the 2000s, a space opened up for leftist forces in Latin America, following democratization as well as growing criticism of neoliberalism. Two key milestones are the elections of Hugo Chávez in Venezuela in 1998 and Luis Inácio Lula da Silva in Brazil in 2002. Cuba was an influential country in a part of this process, both as a symbol of resistance against the United States and by providing various types of assistance to allies in the region (doctors and other types of personnel, advice, intelligence services, etc.). Cuba was a key player in the creation of the Bolivarian Alliance for the Americas or ALBA (2004) and the Community of Latin American and Caribbean States, also known as CELAC (2010).

Once more, as during the Cold War, Cuba could be considered in 2013 to be playing a modest—but very significant, role in the region considering its size. This may have contributed to changing to some extent the collective political self-esteem of Cubans sympathizing with the government, since the country was very isolated at the beginning of the 1990s. When the interviews were conducted in 2013, US unilateralism clearly had been weakened and was, according to some analysts, coming to an end. The United States has nevertheless continued strength in several areas (military, cultural, financial, etc.) and maintained (and maintains) its blockade against Cuba. This situation has been condemned for years by almost all the member states of the United Nations.

At the time of conducting interviews for this study, Cuba and the United States did not have normal diplomatic relations. During the first presidency of Barack Obama (January 2009 to January 2013), the US lifted several bans on the Cuban-American community's contacts with Cuba and authorized educational trips. In December 2014, Barack Obama and Raúl Castro announced the reestablishment of relations, and embassies were opened in 2015, and negotiations started in late 2013, though they were not publicly known at the time.[20]

In spite of the existence of the blockade in 2013, Cuba's geopolitical context at the time of conducting the interviews was less tense than in the 1990s or the

---

20   Neither was it known, of course, that Donald Trump would reach the presidency of the United States, and from 2017 onwards reverse some of the Obama administration's policies toward Cuba. This, together with the loss of power of leftist allies in Latin America and the deepening of the Venezuelan crisis—one that has been aggravated by US sanctions—has by 2020 created a considerably more difficult situation in Cuba.

2000s. Even before the historic announcements of Barack Obama and Raúl Castro in 2014, there were some areas of cooperation with regard to the fight against drug trafficking, environmental issues and the extraction of petroleum in the Gulf of Mexico. Negotiations related to postal services between the two countries were also underway, as one of several visible signs of a slight rapprochement between the two nations. Tensions were certainly lower than during the terms of Bill Clinton and George W. Bush. During Clinton's presidency, the relation saw serious crises provoked by the Cuban Rafters Crisis (1994) and when Cuba shot down two airplanes used by an opposition group based in the US that was violating Cuban airspace (1996). Right after the start of the US invasion of Iraq in 2003, during Bush's presidency, three men who had hijacked a passenger ferry were executed in Cuba and 75 opponents were arrested and imprisoned.[21] This also led to increased pressure on the Cuban authorities and negative publicity.

The interviews were conducted at a time when the international stage was considered dynamic and subject to change. This could be viewed as dangerous in many aspects but also promising for the members of the Communist Party of Cuba, as US unilateralism seemed to be coming to an end. At the same time, the effects of the global financial crisis affected Cuba to some degree. For the interview subjects, this global crisis certainly confirmed yet again Karl Marx's thesis on the periodic crises of capitalism. International preoccupations with regard to the degradation of ecosystems as well as new military tensions and wars were also very much discussed within Cuba. Especially relevant to this study is that during the fall of 2013, when the interviews were conducted, there was a favorable view of relations between Cuba and Russia in the Cuban media, and shortly thereafter, the two countries reached an agreement on the elimination of most of Cuba's debt with the former USSR.

The changes at the international level, together with Cuba's international relations and internal changes, seem to have created a more open political and cultural environment in Cuba. There were also a series of economic and political changes after Raúl Castro temporarily took the lead of the country in 2006, when his brother and the historical leader of the Revolution, Fidel Castro, became ill. This was even more evident after Raúl was elected president of the Council of State (this represents the Parliament between its sessions, which only takes place briefly twice a year) and the Council of Ministers (the

---

21 Of whom all have left prison and many have gone into exile following negotiations between the government of Raúl Castro, the Spanish government, and the Catholic Church, which opened in 2010.

government) in 2008. This stage of change is known internally as the *update of the model* and abroad as a process of reforms.

Although it is difficult to strictly separate politics from the economy, especially in a country with a state-dominated and largely centralized economy such as Cuba, it can be mentioned that the main changes until 2013 had been in the economic sphere, with a greater opening of the private sector than what had previously taken place in the late 1970s/early 1980s and then in 1990s (which were in both cases partially "pushed back" after some years). Politically, the opposition remains without official recognition, and according to several international human rights organizations, it suffers different types of harassment. However, during the government of Raul Castro, a range of measures were undertaken that were interpreted by many as the beginning of a democratization or modernization of Cuban society. Changes particularly worth mentioning, among others, include the establishment of a de facto halt to the death penalty, a limitation of public office to two electoral periods, various calls for criticism "without fear," decentralization of the decision-making in areas such as agriculture, a popular referendum on the Guidelines (the policy of the Communist Party for the period 2011–2016), and authorization to sell computers and cell phone subscriptions, as well as the removal of the requirement of an exit visa when travelling to another country.

By the 1980s, a considerable part of the "socialist puritanism" of the Revolutionary Offensive of 1968 (a few years of very radical or ultra-left politics) and the marginalization of artists that was at its strongest during the Gray Quinquennium (1971–1976) had already been left behind, but Cuban society was by 2013 in many senses more tolerant than during the Collapse. In addition to the aforementioned openness to religion, which has continued to deepen, the process of claiming rights related to sexual diversity on the island has gained more strength in recent decades, headed by the daughter of President Raul Castro, Mariela Castro. Through the Cenesex (National Center for Sex Education, an institution she is currently the director of, and which is working under the auspices of the Ministry of Public Health), she has achieved a notable presence and visibility in favor of these rights in Cuban society.

Cuba is sometimes understood as an isolated and very closed country, and these views need at least to be strongly nuanced. There were around three million foreign tourists to Cuba in 2013. In addition, since 1979, Cuban-Americans have been able to visit Cuba, and in 2013 alone, around 400,000 Cubans and Cuban-Americans residing in the US visited their home country. Currently, a considerable number of Cubans visit the US every year. There were always some Cubans that travelled abroad—a considerable part of them on official missions to other countries—but the flow of personal travel increased with the gradual relaxation and finally abolition (in January 2013) of the permit that was previously necessary to leave the country.

With the accelerated development of information and communication technologies (ICT) during recent decades, the penetration of capitalist culture has increased but also the possibilities of Cubans to communicate with the outside. Even though there are both internal and external factors that reduce the exchange with other countries, especially with one of the lowest internet connectivity rates in Latin America (due to internal and external factors); the prohibition of satellite antennas (by the Cuban authorities); and little access to mass tourism from the US (due to a ban by the US), there is a relatively fluid and very wide communication with the rest of the world. It must still be taken into account that much of the popular culture that is consumed comes from the US and other capitalist countries, and this is not new, as we have seen. Although permanent or regular access to the Internet was still by 2013 only for a privileged few, email was somewhat more common and reached about a fifth of the population. This figure was probably higher in the capital and certainly among some groups represented in the selection (intellectuals, journalists, and politicians).[22]

It should be mentioned that in Havana in 2013 there were numerous stores selling DVDs with the latest series, movies, and video clips from the US. It was furthermore quite common to use technologies such as memory sticks and Bluetooth to circulate entertainment content, and to a lesser extent political information, especially among the youth. In 2013, there were almost two million cell phones, some used to keep in touch with emigrated Cubans despite very high prices of service. From January 2013, it became possible to watch the Latin American channel TelesUR at least 12 hours per day, which might be said to imply a de facto abrogation of the state monopoly of information. Although this is a left-wing channel with a favorable view of Cuba and its allies, it had a style and content that more largely echoed foreign channels and often had perspectives and news that had little in common with Cuban media.

To measure Cubans' access to information not controlled by the state, the aforementioned must be taken into account, as well as difficulties in obtaining books and foreign printed press that are not imported by the State, and therefore not sold in book stores on the island. On the other hand, it must be taken

---

22 One of our informants, Mary, commented that most Cubans do not have access to the Internet. In the following statement she seems to attribute at least large part of this responsibility to official Cuban policies, and a lack of sufficient confidence in people: "I am one of those who defend the Internet for all (...) because Cubans are very well-mannered, educated, cultivated people, and if they have the real information they can interpret it without any problem."

into account that Cuba has very high rates of literacy and schooling compared to many Latin American countries and more people with higher education.

Finally, although the Cuban system seemed solid and had emerged from the most acute crisis, in 2013 it was also a country characterized by economic deficiencies, a certain fatigue in the system, and according to some people, some insecurity regarding its future. One day between my interviews I attended an open debate at Casa de Alba[23] in Havana, where a Cuban woman told the public in a personal intervention that she did not feel confident that the Revolution would reach its seventh decade (which would begin in 2019), although most Cubans did not seem to anticipate any drastic change in the near future. In general, my interview subjects also portrayed the socio-political system as something that would not go away easily, but some expressed concern about its future. The journalist Víctor, for example, portrayed the Revolution as at risk: "We went after things that we should not have persecuted; long hair, the knock-kneed (here he might refer to people perceived as irresolute; I was not able to verify this), homosexuality, womanizers, all of these were chased but were in the end of secondary importance; go instead after the lazy, the mischievous, the opportunists. I think we are at a key moment, now we might lose the Revolution, and is the first thing that people need to be told, we can lose it."

2 Some Notes on Party Membership and Its Implications

As stated in the "Historical and institutional context" in the introductory chapter of this book, the Communist Party of Cuba applies selective membership.

According to Raúl Castro, quoted by the official website *Cubadebate*, at the end of 2015, 671,344 Cubans were members of the Communist Party ("Raúl Castro inaugura en La Habana el VII Congreso del Partido Comunista de Cuba," April 16, 2016). That is approximately 7% of the adult population of Cuba.[24]

An old speech by Fidel Castro on what should characterize its members might help us better understand the "recruitment policy" of this organization.

---

23 A cultural institution whose objective is socio-cultural integration in Latin America and the Caribbean. It was inaugurated in 2009 in the presence of the presidents of Venezuela, Nicaragua, and Cuba.

24 The Party's policy for recruiting new members contrasts with that of the Cuban political and social organizations known as "Mass Organizations." Among the best known are the Workers' Central Union of Cuba (CTC), the Committees for the Defense of the Revolution (CDR), and the Federation of Cuban Women (FMC), all with a higher number of members. It has been almost mandatory to belong to one of these mass organizations, although in recent years this policy has been relaxed somewhat.

In 1962, referring to which people were desired as members of the United Party of the Cuban Socialist Revolution (PURSC)—predecessor to the PCC—the leader said:

> It is necessary to be an exemplary worker, but also, to accept the Socialist Revolution, to accept the ideology of the Revolution. It is also imperative to wish—of course—to belong to this revolutionary nucleus, to accept the responsibilities that being part of the revolutionary nucleus entails, but it is also necessary to lead a clean life [...].[25]

As can be seen here, Fidel Castro highlights several criteria to be a Party member: 1) be an exemplary worker, 2) accept the Revolution, 3) accept its ideology, 4) have a wish to be a part of the Party, 5) accept the conditions that being a member entails, and 6) lead a clean life.

It should be noted that Castro begins and ends by talking about the personal characteristics of the individual and seemingly speaks only of "accepting" the Revolution and its ideology. Another normative text, the Party rules from 1999, reiterate that "quality has been and is the guiding principle in determining entry."[26]

While these declared criteria do not necessarily reflect the real state of things more than half a century after the mentioned 1962 speech, it does suggest that strict allegiance to a very specific ideological position was perhaps not a priority (even if what was considered acceptable became very limited at some point). Party membership seems to require, more than anything else, that one assumes a higher level of compromise with the "Revolution." Aligning very strictly with some official ideological coordinates—or even having intimate knowledge of all the ideological fundaments—is not the only, and perhaps not the most important—criterion for acceptance. There is a whole identity surrounding Party membership ("la militancia"), and the informants sometimes use the word "militante" (militant, member, activist) when referring to other members of their party or when talking about themselves.

These words should not be confused with "revolutionary," as it is a broader category. In Cuba, it is very common to hear that a person considers him- or herself to be a "revolutionary." In a survey conducted by Gallup Costa Rica in Cuba in November 1994, cited by Marifeli Pérez-Stable, 21% of the interview

---

25   Communist Party of Cuba, "Historia del Partido Comunista de Cuba," http://www.PCC.cu/i_historia.php.
26   "Reglamento del Partido Comunista de Cuba," http://congresoPCC.cip.cu/wp-content/uploads/2011/01/reglamento.pdf.

subjects described themselves as "communists" or "socialists," while 48%, as "revolutionaries." The numbers would likely be different in 2013, as it was not that common to hear the words "communist" or "communism" uttered in Cuba.[27]

Being a Party member does not necessarily mean that one is part of any elite in economic terms. Though government members certainly live comfortably, not all the political elite live privileged lives in material terms, and certainly being a member of the Party in itself does not mean that one is necessarily privileged from a material or another point of view. Still, I have often encountered this perception, which might partly be due to the Soviet experience; there seems to be a consensus that the Party was the main "ladder" for ascending socially and materially.

In the Cuban case, there might have been some truth to this at some time, but the situation was not identical, and it has changed considerably over time.[28] First of all, it is important to take into account that when the current

---

[27] The noun "communist," if used to talk about current politics, could be referring to someone in the Party—a communist is supposed to be organized in a party—but *militante* or even "member of the Party" seems much more frequent. Neither is the official name "Communist Party of Cuba" used much outside of formal occasions and official documents; instead, it is more common to say "the Party" (el Partido), which *might* imply that the word has become somewhat of a taboo or even that the Party was not that much associated with what Cubans associate with communism. Sometimes "communism" refers to the ideology represented by the Soviet Union, or its local variants in Cuba, and sometimes it is opposed to *fidelismo* (despite Fidel Castro also clearly being inspired, at least since the early 1960s, by communist ideas). It might be used when referring to Che Guevara's radical variant of the ideology, and also when talking about the pre-revolutionary Partido Socialista Popular, the more pragmatically minded Communist Party that existed before the Revolution. As anywhere else, "communism" could be used to refer to the future class-less society described by Karl Marx, after the "transitory phase" known as socialism or the dictatorship of the proletariat. But since the 1990s, there is not much talk about communism in this sense as the political focus has been on building or defending "socialism"—most people do not think much about utopia—and some even suggest socialism has disappeared or that Cuba is still building socialism. There is a joke in the movie *Guantanamera* (by Tomás Gutiérrez Alea and Juan Carlos Tabio, 1995), where one of the main characters refers to a teacher who used to give classes on "Scientific Communism" before the crisis broke out. These classes allegedly consisted in talking about how the future society would be, according to the dialogue ("the land of milk and honey" or *el reino de la abundancia*). The person that mentions the teacher also suggests that "I think that today it is called scientific *socialism*," and the other one adds, jokingly, "and any day now, they will call it 'scientific capitalism.'" Occasionally I have also heard Cubans use "communism" as simply a word to describe their own system, a use perhaps imported from US discourse.

[28] Although our selection of informants is not intended to reflect the *miliancia* or party member base as a whole, informal observations during the interviews give the impression

Party emerged in the 1960s, for many years it could not be a major source of privileges because it was a small organization with relatively few resources at hand compared to the Soviet or East European ruling parties. The Cuban Party created after the Revolution had two major tasks at the time: on the one hand, to fight against bureaucracy, and on the other, to further economic development through the supervision of production. The Party became an institutional rival and a threat to government bureaucracy. According to William Leo-Grande, these features were important in order to "shape the development of the PCC's role in the political system."[29] Although in the 1970s it saw major changes, the particular origin of the Party could have marked the subsequent Party culture.[30]

Furthermore, there also seems to have been a conscious effort by the government to avoid the problem with political institutions and the PCC becoming sources of privilege or being readily accessible for those having this as their main motivation. In the case of the PCC, in order to enter, a person has to be referred by colleagues at their workplace, people that will normally have some idea of who the person is. Other colleagues can express their opinions. The Party then undertakes an investigation where the candidate's neighbors are asked questions (the people who should know them the best), in order to consider whether the candidate is respectable, leads a clean life, and so on.[31] The Party highlights that becoming a member is voluntary.[32]

---

that most of the informants were not especially privileged from the material point of view, compared to the average Cuban.

[29] LeoGrande, "El Partido Comunista de Cuba y la Política Electoral: Adaptación, Sucesión y Transición," 471.

[30] The young party that some of our informants got to know in the 1960s was a party where people from the military predominated; there was a much higher percentage of military personnel in the Central Committee than in the USSR; in 1965 they reached as many as 57%. Although this percentage dropped significantly during the next decade, it was still higher than in the USSR. Most grassroots members had a sixth grade of schooling or less. There was a very low percentage of women, partly because the PCC was (and is) organized in workplace branches, and at that time integration of women into working life had not come far.

[31] Several of the respondents cited problems entering the Party. A notable case is Víctor, who was first expelled for what he called "skirt problems" in the 1970s—he said that he was a womanizer. Then he returned to the Party in 1991 when the country fell into a crisis. Commenting on this, he said: "See, this is a moment when many people are fleeing the Party, who do not want to be in the Party because they say that it will sweep them along (as the Revolution falls), you tell me, the Soviet Union fell." On another side, Mery entered before she was of the age that is normally required to be a member, because "when you are a very good youth militant, they advance the process of becoming a Party member."

[32] The concept of *exemplary worker* (*trabajador ejemplar*), used in Cuba, could give the impression that candidates need to present an image of false perfection. The possibility of

Even so, it is true that the Party began to "attract the ambitious ones" around 1975,[33] as LeoGrande points out. However, the privileges one could obtain through being a member never reached the level of the socialist countries in Eastern Europe: "[w]ithout a doubt, tangible material benefits are subject to membership in the PCC (although the benefits are relatively few for the rank and file); but this was even more true in the East European parties [...]."[34]

At the time of the Collapse, the Party was a vehicle for social and material advancement for some and necessary for certain jobs and positions. Yet the crisis of the 1990s affected the general population and most if not all Party members (certain problems affected even people that could be considered privileged, such as the frequent power cuts and the deterioration of infrastructure).

Early on during the crisis years, possibilities of enrichment emerged and social divisions emerged with tourism, self-employment, foreign companies entering the country, and so on. These differences became especially visible as the depenalization of the US dollar in 1993 and the pricing of many goods and services in dollars implied that they were only available to those who could access this currency. However, the positions that could give such personal advantages were mostly open regardless of whether one was a member or not of the PCC. Therefore, in Cuba today, affluent or relatively affluent people are often those who receive remittances, work in companies with foreign capital, have a private business, engage to a large degree in activity on the black market, and so on. One can belong to any of these groups without belonging to the Party. Historically, leading positions in major state-owned enterprises are generally held by people that are Party members (if not always). Still, we have been made aware that there are cases where non-members hold leading positions in some smaller state companies, and as suggested, the state does not have a total monopoly on the economy today.

Party members may have less access to remittances, an important source of income for many Cubans; after all, emigration was considered a betrayal of the

---

some candidates or members living double lives might be unavoidable, but the statutes of the Party that were published in 1999 seem to reflect at least a desire to avoid an artificial and little sincere party culture where people pretend to be flawless for the sake of entering the Party. For instance, the statues explicitly state that it is possible to be readmitted to the Party after suffering a mental illness, after being jailed, or after being expelled from the Party. People who have resided abroad can also be allowed to re-enter, although it has to be "for justified family or personal reasons," and the candidate must have the support of the Party branch at the local diplomatic headquarters. See: Communist Party of Cuba, "Reglamento del Partido Comunista de Cuba," 19–20.

33   Kapcia, 75.
34   LeoGrande, "The Communist Party of Cuba and Electoral Policy: Adaptation, Succession and Transition," 42.

revolution during many years. Thus, Party members and their families might have been less likely to emigrate or to maintain close contact with relatives abroad. Additionally, being a Party member could in some cases make it less easy to benefit from the black market, as it could represent a problem if one openly engaged in such activities (although to engage in it on a smaller scale is difficult to avoid in Cuba, as some products can be very expensive or difficult to obtain in a strictly legal manner). A personal contact in Cuba used a rather explicit but commonly used word in Cuba to describe Party members (he said they were *comemierdas,* literally sh* eaters), the meaning of which could be a person that gets fooled, or "sacrificed people who take on tasks without receiving much in return." He gave the example of black market vendors in his neighborhood who avoid knocking on the door of people known as Party members to offer their products. Access to these goods can be an economic advantage.

With regard to the representative organs of politics in Cuba or "Organs of Popular Power"—being elected often implies so much sacrifice and so few benefits that a high percentage resign before they finish their term, according to Peter Roman.[35] This does not refer strictly to Party members, as one can be elected independently of being a Party member. Still, there is an overrepresentation of Party members in these organs, so this observation may still be relevant.

As Cuban journalist Yusnaby Pérez claimed on the website *Cubanet,* "Currently, being a Party member brings more problems than benefits [...]." Pérez mentions the monthly fee, the need to ask permission to go abroad, and the impossibility of having dual citizenship ("El Partido se está quedando sin militantes," May 29, 2014).[36]

---

35   Roman.
36   Just as there are myths about Party members outside of Cuba, many people in Cuba seem to believe that government opponents are generally privileged, because some of them receive material support from organizations abroad. This perception is stimulated by Cuban state propaganda that accuses members of the opposition of being unscrupulous, being in politics to get money from the US embassy, and so on. Members of the Cuban opposition suffer varying degrees of social marginalization, temporary detentions, and sometimes even threats, so in general it is not an attractive situation. But just like being "in the Party" does not necessarily mean that you are part of a privileged caste, being an open government opponent does not necessarily mean that you have problems paying your bills. Some lose state jobs, which can be very serious in the sense that it can ruin one's career, social life, and so on. That people can lose their jobs for political reasons is certainly highly problematic, but the material issue is not necessarily the main problem facing these people, as access to basic subsidized goods is generally the same independently of one's political beliefs and affiliations, and because there is now a private sector where jobs often pay much more than the state ones. For certain groups such as academics, however, there are few relevant work opportunities in the private sector. Cuba never made it any secret that the "universities are for revolutionaries." (The concept of a

The oral historian Elisabeth Dore quoted an interview subject in her recent project: "[T]he number of young people who want to join the Party is falling [...] Party membership does not give you a house, or a car, or money; quite the contrary."[37] This also coincides with my observations during my interviews. I visited the homes of many of the informants, and only one or two had what could be called an exclusive house within a Cuban context. Several of the houses had standards that would be above the Havana average but many were also of regular characteristics and some in a state of deterioration. The majority of houses that I visited during the interview process had a generally lower standard than the average rental homes for foreign tourists in Cuba, to give an example that some readers might be familiar with.

But again, there is an internal hierarchy. As we have seen, higher ranking members may have better access to certain material privileges. Cuban ex-diplomat Pedro Campos also suggests that there is a divisory line between the upper and the lower echelons of the Party with political implications, and claims that one could speak of *two communist parties*. He argues that this distinction already manifested itself in 1990–1991. According to Campos, the upper echelons are typically bureaucratic, dogmatic, and speakers of a discourse that is empty of any true revolutionary content. On the other hand, a significant part of the base level wants to remove obstacles to a participative and democratic socialism ("Los dos Partidos Comunistas de Cuba," *Diario de Cuba*, January 29, 2015).

In the interviews analyzed in this study, however, critical opinion could be found amongst elite members and also base members, as could opinions that mimicked official rhetoric. In general and to a varying degree, they all had critical remarks about their own social reality. Amongst the most critical remarks, there were dissenting interpretations and opinions even on delicate subjects such as Glasnost, the decision to continue with Fidel Castro in command of the country after the fall of the USSR, and even the future of the one-party system. These were often given by people with an academic background or a privileged access to information, but not necessarily of the political elite. In this sense, it is worth taking into account not just the hierarchic perspective but the possibility that identity and perceptions may have a lot to do with one's professional background; since the Party is also organized by workplace branches, there are also different "circles" of people that individuals belong to within the PCC. Belonging to a Party branch at a university is not the same as

---

revolutionary might today include some very critical voices, but not members of the pro-regime change opposition.)

37   Elizabeth Dore to NACLA, 2016, https://nacla.org/news/2016/12/01/cubans-remember-fidel.

belonging to a Party branch at a factory, and there are also geographic and other differences.

3   Undertaking Oral History in Cuba

Prior to embarking on this work, some colleagues and friends expressed serious doubts about the feasibility of conducting oral history in Cuba. People questioned whether it would be possible to obtain permission to conduct this kind of research "in a country like Cuba." Are there enough Cubans willing to speak freely with a foreign researcher? Will not all members of the Communist Party be replicating some official stance of the Party, "the Party line?"

As mentioned, few oral history studies have been conducted in Cuba. This may have different causes, and the following might interfere: A) It is not always easy to obtain an academic visa to perform this type of work, and the uncertainties can make the planning and financing of projects very difficult, especially since they are often given at the last minute; B) persisting restrictions by the United States, including the travel ban to the island,[38] that have made it difficult for researchers from that country to conduct studies in Cuba; and C) misleading and/or outdated ideas about Cuban society amongst non-Cuban researchers; notably, some have exaggerated ideas about the restrictions on freedom of expression or the possibility of interacting with people in present-day Cuba, and this might cause some researchers to avoid such projects.

However, I had some contacts and factors in my favor when I started out. I had the support of my tutor Dr. María Álvarez-Solar of the University of Bergen, who had previously been my supervisor while undertaking my master's thesis on Peruvian agrarian reform. In addition to supporting me in the preparatory phase, she prepared a letter for academic Cuban counterparts in the study and for access to the country's archives, in which she requested the provision of certain resources to me as a researcher (academic visa, access to files, etc.). I also could count on the support of the Latin American Faculty of Social Sciences (FLACSO, in Spanish), Cuba, several faculty members of which I met during one of my first trips to Cuba, in 2003. They helped assure me that I could obtain the necessary permits to conduct the fieldwork in Cuba and also that

---

[38]   There was a thaw in bilateral relations between Cuba and the US (with the first, historic announcements being made by Raúl Castro and Barack Obama in December 2014). The US then opened the door to greater academic exchanges between the two countries. However, not all restrictions were lifted, and under Donald Trump (2016–), new restrictions have been introduced. In any case, this happened after the interviews.

there were people who would be willing to be interviewed on the subject in case the project received institutional and financial support. This support materialized through a scholarship from the University of Bergen (Norway) in 2012. In July of the following year, the fieldwork began in Cuba. I did not encounter major obstacles in this process, only some minor issues.[39]

Regarding the interaction with people, there has sometimes existed a prejudice that people in Cuba are afraid to speak with foreigners, although they are also known for their openness and ease of interaction. The political situation has certainly prevented free interaction between Cubans and researchers from other countries. This is, in turn, influenced by factors such as the polarized climate resulting from the conflict with the US, as well as restrictive Cuban government policies. It is also affected by the tense relationship between the government and part of the international press, as well the impression of many Cubans that there is a media campaign against the country. This has resulted in distrust of foreign journalists and, as a secondary effect, sometimes also of foreign researchers.[40]

Without a doubt, it is possible to undertake oral history work in Cuba. Elisabeth Dore, who is working on a project with more than 100 interviews on the Cuban Revolution, affirms that "Cuba is the only socialist country where people have been willing to talk to interviewers with a certain frankness." She explains that according to her own experience, despite "initial apprehension [...]," her team's interviewees "told the story of their life with considerable candor, even, or especially, when it contradicted the official narrative of the Revolution."[41]

According to Dore, Cubans who were interviewed explained that "the economic crisis [of the 1990s] had freed them up—'liberated' is the word they

---

[39] Our academic visa did not arrive on time so I had to travel with a tourist visa to Cuba. I was not very much surprised by this as it has happened to me previously when I applied for a journalistic visa. After spending some time doing the necessary paperwork in Cuba—to change my tourist card to the necessary academic visa for this type of stay, the registration in FLACSO, in order to have an internet connection from my temporary residence and access at FLACSO's premises, etc.—I was able to work fulltime on the project.

[40] Although sometimes exaggerated, there is certainly some objective basis for the certain fear and suspicion that some Cubans have toward foreigner researchers and journalists. The US has used both students and journalists to obtain information in the country. Shortly after the conclusion of our interview work, the Associated Press was informed that the US had sent Latin American students to Cuba to participate in a regime change program, behind the facade of anti-HIV activities.

[41] Elizabeth Dore, "Cubans' life stories: the pains and pleasures of living in a communist society," *Oral History* 40, No. 1 (2012): 36.

used—to talk more openly."[42] One of my own informants, Lenin, said that "If it were 20 years ago you could not have interviewed me, and look, today you are interviewing me, and I tell you what I think because I am independent, I am a free, sovereign man, and as I told you, I am a Party member, and I have my opinions." The political atmosphere was also possibly slightly more "relaxed" in 2013 than during 2004–2010, when Dore conducted her project.

The author of this study already had the experience of working two years in Cuba as a teacher at a private academic institution for foreigners (between 2007 and 2009) and carrying out journalistic work in Cuba (in 2010). The latter activity was related to the preparation of a book of travelers' accounts. Therefore, I already knew that this kind of interaction with people was possible. Conducting interviews only with members of the Communist Party, however, was less familiar terrain, and I had for years heard comments from contacts in Cuba claiming that "the Party members have to take care of their image," "the Party members lose a part of their freedom upon joining the Party," and so on. In addition, the Party professes democratic centralism; everyone must adhere to the "Party's official stance" once a position is taken.

To a certain extent, it was a surprise to find the remarkable diversity that came to light in the interview subjects' answers. It is likely that the assistance from particular respected academicians had an influence in this regard. These academic contacts were pivotal in establishing the first contact with various individuals to be interviewed, and in other cases, authorized me to refer to them when communicating with other people. My previous work experience from Cuba as well as a personal background as an activist of the Norwegian left, may have been advantageous, in order to bridge gaps and achieve a fluid dialogue.

Regarding the issue of democratic centralism and the alleged obligation to follow "the Party's official stance" on each issue, I found that this was practiced in a flexible way in many cases. As to the particular topic of this study, as noted earlier, the Communist Party of Cuba never developed an official stance. Thus, people have had the need to make their own interpretations from their own individual position. As one of the interview subjects, Juan, a social science researcher, argues:

> There was an absence of an official position, an official interpretation, not even a declaration of the Party, even though it was promised in the 1990s. There was an editorial of the Granma newspaper, which said that the experience of what had happened in Europe would be studied and

---

42   Ibid., 40.

conclusions would be drawn. In that editorial it was even recognized that there were many similarities between Cuba and those countries, etc. That never happened, so [...] at a political level there is no proposed consensus, each politician makes his or her own interpretation, and at the academic level the same happens, here the academic world also expresses the [levels of] information, it depends on which literature [each researcher] has access to, how well or how badly they are informed.

The interviews themselves confirm this, as a diversity of foci and opinions were found. But even on important matters where a dominant, semiofficial or official position existed, there were informants who differed from these.

Nevertheless, while analyzing the data, it is imperative to bear in mind how the responses can be influenced by factors such as fidelity to the Party, the country, and its leaders, as well as neighbors and colleagues. Possible taboos and fears inside and outside the organization and the desire of the interview subjects to project a certain image also have an impact, among others. However, most of these elements are not exclusive to Cuba and even when some might be, it does not make the interviews worth less. There is no ideal situation in which to conduct an interview, and these elements are rather conditions that must be taken into account for interpretation. I believe, furthermore, that when interpreting the data, one has to try to strike a balance in a healthy manner between a "hermeneutic of suspicion" and a "hermeneutic of affirmation."

CHAPTER 6

Oral Source Methodologies

As a general guide, I have followed the seven steps for qualitative interviews described by Kvale and Brinkmann,[1] who rely on Pierre Bourdieu: 1) thematizing, 2) designing, 3) interviewing, 4) transcribing, 5) analyzing, 6) verifying, and 7) reporting.[2] It is pertinent to make some comments on the first six points on this list, before moving on to the analysis.

The *thematizing* phase determines and formulates the purpose of the research and the "conception of the theme to be investigated."[3] The authors argue that the researcher must first clarify *why* and *what* and then the question of *how*.[4] Kvale and Brinkmann emphasize the importance of presenting existing knowledge on the subject.[5] I have aspired to comply with these guidelines in my review of the existing literature as well as in the rest of the study.

The second phase, *designing*, requires slightly more extensive comments. According to Kvale and Brinkmann, "the better the preparation for an interview, the higher the quality of the knowledge produced in the interview interaction, and the more the post interview treatment of the interviews will be facilitated."[6] They also suggest that the researcher become familiar with the culture and context of the interview subjects.[7] On the other hand, oral historian Donald A. Ritchie warns against excessive preparations.[8] I have tried to find a balance between their two recommendations, as it would quite clearly not be a feasible option to wait years until starting interviews, nor do I believe that doing research interviews on these complex topics would produce the desired results with little or no preparation.

During this step, I reflected upon how the required knowledge could be obtained. In accordance with my objective of understanding the perceptions of a

---

1 Steinar Kvale and Svend Brinkmann, *Interviews: Learning the Craft of Qualitative Research Interviewing*, second edition (California: Sage Publications, 2009), 47, 102–103.
2 Ibid.
3 Ibid., 102.
4 Ibid., 102–105.
5 Ibid., 107.
6 Ibid., 99.
7 Ibid., 108.
8 Donald A. Ritchie, *Doing Oral History: A Practical Guide* (New York: Oxford University Press, 2003), 16.

group of people regarding specific historical events, I assumed an approach that could be described as phenomenological/hermeneutical, seeking to approach the informants' life world or horizon. I opted for a semi-structured interview to the extent that it, contrary to a structured interview, allows for "getting more knowledge on aspects that are not easily perceived, like the world of feelings, social values and beliefs."[9]

In order to define the subjects that would participate in the interview, I made a *strategic selection*.[10] In oral history, it is not common to select people for interviews according to abstract criteria or statistical standards, so the researcher rather tries to find individuals who typify historical processes.[11] For this study, the main criterion of inclusion and selection was membership in the PCC between 1989 and 1991. In general, I already had this information before starting each interview; however, when starting or ending the interview, the following question was asked as a verification question: "Were you a member of the Communist Party or the UJC between 1989 and 1991?"

The design of the study attempted to include representatives from different social sectors. My initial intention was to create three "quotas" with four or five people in each one, with "workers," "academics," and "people belonging to the cultural sector." Later, I decided to implement a fourth quota called "professionals." With the support of my Cuban co-supervisor, I developed a list of possible candidates, which I subsequently used to contact interview subjects by phone or email. In some cases, the people I interviewed suggested other potential candidates, which made it possible to complement the strategic selection by using the recruitment technique known as "snowball sampling."

I aspired to interview both Party members from the grassroots and the political elite. Donald A. Ritchie finds that the best projects have been "those that cast their nets wide, recording as many participants in events or members of a community as possible."[12] This has been advice I have tried to follow. However, I prioritized finding people that I knew or considered could have some degree of influence in the area where they work and live.

Most of the people contacted for the purpose of interviewing them indicated a positive attitude toward the project from the first contact. Out of a total of 23 people contacted, five refused to be interviewed. Of these five, none cited

---

9 Alía Miranda, 349.
10 Sigmund Grønmo, *Samfunnsvitenskapelige metoder* (Bergen: Fagbokforlaget, 2007), 98.
11 Ronald J. Grele, "Movement without aim: methodological and theoretical problems in oral history," in *The Oral History Reader*, ed. Robert Perks and Alistair Thomson (London: Routledge, 2005), 41.
12 Ritchie, 24.

political reasons for not participating, but practical motives: that they did not have time, did not have knowledge of the topic, or the like. In total, I conducted 18 interviews and decided to preserve and use 17 of these.[13] All resided in the province of Havana, in urban areas, and belonged to the Communist Party of Cuba (PCC) between 1989 and 1991, although not necessarily during the complete three-year span and not necessarily in 2013. A list of their information appears in Appendix 3 of this study.

Of those interviewed, 13 are men and four are women. I found it more difficult to identify women than men who met the inclusion criteria. This is probably due to the fact that there is a lower representation of women than men in the Party, although the percentage of female members has been growing since the 1970s.[14] I do not have exact figures of the percentage of women in the years between 1989 and 1991, but in 1975–1976 they constituted 13.2%; 19.1% in 1979–1980; and 21.5% in 1984–1986.[15] Thus, unless the trend did not radically change in the late 1980s, and I do not have any indication or data suggesting this, they must have constituted about a quarter of the members in 1989–1991. Therefore, the percentage of women in this project likely corresponds to the percentage of women in the Party at that time.

Following the ethical standards proposed by Alver and Øyen, all interview participants received written information about the goals of the project and plans for its publication. On the same information sheet they were also informed that they could leave the project at any time, if they thought it could have any negative impact or consequence for them, in accordance with the suggestions of Bente Gullveig Alver and Ørjar Øyen.[16] My initial intention was to anonymize the interviews permanently, but this was not practical because the participants wanted their names to appear in the final study. For many, it seems to have been a matter of honor, and to appear as anonymous or "not assume responsibility" was not an option. I try to respect the principles of confidentiality and professional secrecy, respecting privacy and always making an assessment of possible risks before proceeding.[17] I consider this necessary as

---

13 In one case, an informant gave a series of answers that apparently did not have to do with the topic and criticized the subject of the thesis, which he considered as uninteresting or anachronistic. From a reliable source, I have received that this is probably due to health problems and not a general unwillingness to cooperate. For ethical reasons, I decided not to include the interview.
14 Pérez-Stable, 112–115.
15 Ibid., 114.
16 Bente Gullveig Alver and Ørjar Øyen, *Forskningsetikk and forskerhverdag: vurderinger og praksis* ([Oslo]: Tano Aschehoug, 1997), 109–117.
17 Ibid., 102–108.

the informants are identified through political affiliation, and it was expected in advance that the interviews could touch upon political issues that were sensitive in the Cuban context. The interviews were anonymized during the data analysis process. The recordings, notes, and so on were at all times under my supervision or kept in a safe in my rented room in Havana.[18]

Interviewing was conducted either at the informants' place of residence or at their workplace, except for one that took place at the home of my co-supervisor of the study, and one at a bookstore that kindly agreed to provide an empty room at the request of the interview subject. For the recording, I used an interview guide, although both the interviewer and informant often departed from it. Dialogues were recorded with digital equipment, and I took notes in a few cases only, as I considered it unnecessary and a factor that could disturb spontaneous interaction. All interviews were conducted in Spanish.

In the vast majority of cases, the interview subjects seemed motivated, and my impression was that many saw it as an opportunity to tell their personal story or express their version of events. Several pointed out, both in interviews and informally, that there is a lack of general knowledge about Cuba abroad and that there is an informative bias against the country. The opportunity to present "a different view" probably served in part as a motivation to participate in the project. Several interview subjects complained that there were many things that Cuban media did not reflect or did not reflect at the time of the Collapse, which may have generated sympathy for this project, possibly because they felt there had been too little openness and/or a real and inclusive debate on the topic.

Two interview subjects asked to have preliminary meetings in order to familiarize themselves with the project (and possibly the intentions of the researcher) before starting the interview itself. In one case, several meetings were needed for the interview to materialize. Another interview was interrupted because a political meeting was to be held at the house of the interview subject, and the completion of the interview was postponed twice due to health reasons.

All interview subjects exhibited a cooperative attitude during the exchange. Prior to the interviews, I feared that some people, especially those from the

---

18 Before beginning the fieldwork, the project was also approved by the Norwegian institution Data Protection Official for Research of Norwegian Social Science Data Service (NSD), which is responsible for ensuring that investigations are made according to the established norms of privacy and ethics, and I have aspired to follow their suggestions during our work.

political elite accustomed to giving interviews to the press, would attempt to "take control" of the interview and impose their own agenda. Nevertheless, in general, I perceived instead a curiosity about what would be the next question. Yet, it is not possible to reduce the parties in an interview to an active researcher and a passive informant who just answers questions; rather, the two tend to interact and "negotiate," partly unintentionally, about what should be discussed and how to say it, according to each person's beliefs, interests, purpose, and so on.

The interview subjects often had a clear idea of what they wanted to communicate, but their attitude was respectful, and they were helpful with regards to practical obstacles. Due to the tropical climate, Cuban houses are open to the street, and noise from the street is frequent. This can result in some inaudible fragments, creating lacunae in the transcripts. It is also common for neighbors and family members to enter and leave the houses without notice, as there is often more than one generation living in a house. Often, the interview subject asks for a break to speak with a person who enters or answers a phone call. Because of these interruptions, the thread of the interview is sometimes lost. Some of these events may also be attributed to Latin American, Caribbean, and Cuban culture, or to the socioeconomic conditions of Cuba today, and I do not believe that they will affect the quality of the interviews but rather confirm their authenticity. No one has requested, after the interviews, to withdraw their testimony from the project.

With respect to *transcribing*, an external transcriptionist, Raynier Hernández Arencibia, a Cuban social scientist, did the transcriptions for this study. I already knew him as a serious and rigorous academic, and I furthermore considered having a Cuban transcriptionist an advantage. This is because he would be accustomed to the Spanish of his countrymen (although he argued that sometimes it was difficult to understand some regional accents), as well as familiar with the country and the topic of the study. Hernández Arencibia's work resulted in approximately 400 pages of text.

According to Paul Ricoeur, the transformation of a text from orality to writing implies more than the "fixation" that "shelters the event of discourse from destruction."[19] The text furthermore gains autonomy with regard to the intention of the author.[20] It "transcends its own psycho-sociological conditions of

---

19 Paul Ricoeur, *Hermeneutics and the Human Sciences: Essays on Language, Action and Interpretation* (Cambridge: Cambridge University Press, 1981), 139.
20 Ibid.

production and thereby opens itself to an unlimited series of readings, themselves situated in different socio-cultural conditions."[21] Ricoeur cautions that the discourse is affected by this transformation in several ways, especially as "the functioning of reference is profoundly altered when it is no longer possible to identify the thing spoken about as part of the common situation of the interlocutors."[22]

In regard to this specific study, one element to keep in mind is that Cuban and Caribbean cultures are high-context cultures, according to the theory of anthropologist Edward Hall. This implies that nonverbal cues are more important in these cultures than, let us say, those of Scandinavian countries. I sometimes found this to be a challenge when re-reading the transcribed interviews.

Analyzing and *verifying* are the next steps (5 and 6) mentioned by Kvale and Brinkmann. For these steps, I have found support in the methodological proposals of Miles, Huberman, and Saldaña.[23] They distinguish between three simultaneous and interconnected processes that largely overlap with steps 5 and 6 of the list presented by Kvale and Brinkmann, based on Bourdieu. These three processes are: 1) Data Condensation, 2) Data Display, and 3) Drawing and Verifying.

The first of these involves selecting, focusing, simplifying, abstracting, and/or transforming the data in the corpus.[24] There are of course different ways to achieve this. Miles et al. propose the use of *coding*, a heuristic (exploratory) technique that has a cyclic character. The technique consists of assigning labels or codes (code) to fragments of a text. A code is "most often a word or short phrase that symbolically assigns a summative, salient, essence-capturing, and/or evocative attribute for a portion of language-based or visual data."[25]

The coding produces an indexed text where the original text and the index (the code system) are analyzed. Codes do not contain the same information but reflect the existence of information in certain parts of the original corpus, unlike Qualitative Content Analysis. The coding makes it possible to extract and categorize similar data; thus the researcher can "quickly find, pull out, and cluster the segments relating to a particular research question, hypothesis, construct, or theme."[26] The technique gives the researcher "an intimate, interpretive

---

21 Ibid.
22 Ibid.
23 Matthew B. Miles, A. Michael Huberman, and Johnny Saldaña, *Qualitative Data Analysis. A Methods Sourcebook*, 3 edition. (Thousand Oakes: SAGE, 2014).
24 Miles et al., 12.
25 Johnny Saldaña, *The Coding Manual for Qualitative Researchers* (London: MPG Books Group, 2010), 3.
26 Miles, Huberman and Saldaña, 72.

familiarity with every datum in the corpus."[27] While I have found the proposals of Miles et al. to be useful, it is also important to be aware of their limitations. For Jochen Gläser and Grit Laudel, many qualitative methods "claim to lead to an answer to the research question but do not specify all steps between the text and the answer."[28] They attribute this to the strong emphasis on interpretation in qualitative research, arguing that "Interpretation is an ill-structured activity for which no algorithm can be provided." Miles et al. actually make a similar caveat: Research is, they acknowledge, "actually more a craft (and, sometimes, an art) than a slavish adherence to methodological rules."[29]

However, Miles et al. also criticize the "intuitive" position that some researchers assume and argue that it is necessary to use methods that are "credible, dependable, and replicable" in qualitative terms.[30] Even if investigations within our field depend largely on interpretation, their proposals describe some general steps to be taken and useful techniques that could make the researcher more open to the data and able to discover details and patterns that would otherwise have been missed. To some extent, their proposal also could facilitate the gaining of an overview of a large corpus.

After I decided to opt for coding as a technique, an important decision was to choose what type of codes to use. Saldaña treats 22 types of codes that he calls *first cycle codes*.[31] These have names such as *thematic codes, evaluation codes*, and so on, and he suggests combining different types according to the needs of the study and according to whether they give substantial results or not. For some studies, the use of one of these types of codes may be sufficient, while in other studies, it may be necessary to use two or more. My study is largely phenomenological, as it is interested in the subjective, which implies that I am looking for "the essences and essentials"[32] of the experiences of the interview subjects. I had to select a way to codify the text that corresponded to the needs of the study, and I opted for the use of thematic codes, which are common in this type of work. The use of descriptive codes implies assigning

---

27 Ibid., 73.
28 Jochen Gläser and Grit Laudel. "Life With and Without Coding: Two Methods for Early-Stage Data Analysis in Qualitative Research Aiming at Causal Explanations," *Forum Qualitative Sozialforschung* 14, n.° 2 (2013).
29 Miles et al., 7.
30 Ibid., 5.
31 Saldaña, 46.
32 Miles et al., 8.

"basic labels to data to provide an inventory of their topics."[33] For example, two of my codes were "Gorbachev" and "Fourth Congress [of the PCC]."

Subsequently, I distributed and subordinated all descriptive codes to the main thematic categories, called "Cuba" (25 subordinate codes), "USSR" (14 subordinate codes), and "Relations between the two countries" (6 subordinate codes) and "Communist Party of Cuba" (5 subordinate codes, a category I later merged with the Cuba category). That is, in total I had 50 codes, grouped into four, and later three, main categories. Next to the thematic codes, I also created some versus codes. "These 'versus codes' identify in binary terms the individuals, groups, social organizations, phenomena, processes, concepts, etc., in direct conflict with each other."[34] For example, I created the code "Fidelism versus Communism" to reflect a certain (perceived) political contradiction within the Cuban revolution, and I used this label to mark fragments of text where this contradiction was reflected.

The people interviewed have dedicated a considerable part of their lives to politics and were therefore emotionally affected by the fall of the USSR. I was therefore interested in identifying and categorizing the emotional reactions to the Collapse and experimentally created emotion codes. These types of codes label feelings that the participants have had. According to Miles et al., they can help to gain insight into "the participants' perspectives, worldviews, and life conditions."[35] However, not everyone, and especially not heterosexual men, is willing to talk about their emotions comfortably or name them with accuracy.[36] Noticing that the interview subjects spoke relatively little about their feelings, I abandoned the emotional codes and grouped the most outstanding expressions of emotions under a more comprehensive thematic code, "Feelings."

Once this process was concluded, I decided to re-read the transcribed interviews and tag them with another type of code—again experimentally—called *in vivo codes*. These codes are essentially words or short phrases of what participants say, and which, according to Miles et al., can serve to make the researcher aware of the language and way of thinking of the interview subjects. I did this in accordance with my ideal of taking the interview subject seriously, to "honor the participant's voice."[37] Two examples of in vivo codes that emerged were "we are very nationalistic" or "they would show to you the very best"

---

33 Ibid., 66.
34 Saldaña, 94.
35 Miles et al., 75.
36 Michael L. Schwalbe and Michelle Wolkomir, "Interviewing men," in *Handbook of Interview Research,* eds. F. Gubrium and A. Holstein (Thousand Oaks, CA: Sage, 2002).
37 Miles et al., 74.

[interview subject talks about visits to the USSR]. In total, I converted 745 words and phrases into in vivo codes, which served to gain awareness of the language and the thinking of the interview subjects.[38]

The next challenge was displaying the condensed data.[39] According to Miles et al., credible analysis and trustworthy analysis "requires, and is driven by, displays that are focused enough to permit a viewing of a full data set in the same location and are arranged systematically to answer the research questions at hand."[40] Miles et al. present a series of matrixes that can facilitate such a panoramic view, but suggest adapting and inventing formats that are useful for the researcher. They argue that the important thing is not whether a table is "correct" but whether it is helpful.[41]

Following these tips, I prepared a total of 50 tables, with each table visualizing the data corresponding to each thematic code. For example, one table has the name "Predictability of the Collapse" where I gathered commentary from the informants on whether they—or others in Cuba—foresaw the possibility of the Socialist Bloc falling apart (see Appendix 4). The tables have a horizontal axis with three columns: 1) the first with the interview subject's name, 2) another with direct quotes from the interview subjects, and 3) the third with a summary, paraphrase, or abstract of what they say. The vertical axis of each table has 17 rows, one for each interview subject. I placed all the workers together, then the professionals, and so on, in order to detect more easily if the data could suggest some difference in the approaches, opinions, and so on between members of different sectors.

I tried to follow Miles et al. in making sure that each table could fit onto a page. They recommend organizing the data in a way that allows the researcher to see it all at the same time.[42] In this way, I was able to quickly scan visually

---

38   Saldaña, 48.
39   Although coding has its virtues and did seem to condense the data somewhat, I quickly discovered that one should not have illusions about its effectiveness with regard to the latter. Gläser and Laudel point out that although codification implies an exclusion process, since there are fragments of the original text that are not encoded, the text segments that actually are coded and do receive labels or codes, are left unchanged (p. 20). Therefore, "they still contain irrelevant parts and are inefficiently worded," and the result can be "huge amounts of text" (ibid.). With a larger corpus, such as the written sources I have employed in this study, this would have been a problem. Still, regardless of the time I spent on the interview coding process—about four months—the data did not turn out to be unmanageable. I believe that this method has been of help, although it is certainly time demanding and not suitable for all projects.
40   Miles et al., 108.
41   Ibid., 113–114.
42   Ibid., 114.

what the interview subjects say about a particular topic and reach initial conclusions using suggested techniques by Miles et al. to identify patterns and themes: making contrasts, comparisons, groupings, and counting.

The third phase of the analysis serves to *obtain and verify conclusions*. In my case, this phase intermingled quite a bit with the previous phase. In addition to the techniques outlined above, I also tried to keep in mind the 26 tactics for the analysis described by Miles et al.,[43] 13 of which are tactics to generate meaning, and 13 are tactics to verify results. For example, I sometimes used *counting*, one of 13 tactics to generate meaning proposed by Miles et al., which can help the researcher see "what's there." These tactics will not be described here as I consider that they are, to a large extent, integral to the craft of a researcher rather than a methodology. They are techniques that many discover on their own and that are mostly used without being named. I had access to and used the NVivo program for coding and display. In its authors' words, it is software that helps the user in "[...] gaining richer insights from qualitative and mixed-methods data."[44]

I agree with Miles et al. in that the use of this program is, above all, a convenient way to save and maintain the data corpus.[45] However, I did not find it essential for this project. One advantage of a program of this type is that it facilitates simultaneous coding, which means that two or more codes can be applied to the same data. In addition, it has some functions not strictly related to coding, one very popular function being word count, which makes it possible to see which words are frequently used. Still, the program has capabilities beyond my needs, and I often felt over-equipped. For many tasks like taking notes and making visualizations, other tools such as Word or even traditional pen and paper seemed just as practical for my needs.

---

43   Ibid., 277–309.
44   QSR International, "What is NVivo?," https://www.qsrinternational.com/nvivo/what-is-nvivo.
45   Miles, Huberman, and Saldaña, 48.

CHAPTER 7

Analysis of the Interviews

In presenting the analysis of the 17 transcribed interviews, I have divided them into two sections. The first examines the relations between Cuba and the Soviet and East European socialism as well as previous events in Cuban history, which are relevant to understand the perceptions the interview subjects had of the USSR and its collapse. The second section focuses on the Collapse itself, but also analyzes some comments from the interview subjects on the Soviet and East European historical backdrop that are related to the way in which they view the end of that historical project. To facilitate the reading, I include here a brief list of the interview subjects and their main activities between 1989 and 1991.

A more complete list of interview subject data is included in Appendix 3.

Name	Main activities between 1989 and 1991
Víctor	Journalist
Aurelio	Researcher
Pedro	Diplomat
Hector	Deputy Minister
Idulberto	Civil aviation pilot
Mavis	National Association of Small Farmers official
Eliécer	Medical doctor
Jorge	Council of Ministers Advisor
José Luis	Research Institute Deputy Director; Minister
Juan	Researcher
José	Director of a Telecom Workshop
Esteban	Research Center Director
Lenin	Agricultural worker
Zenaida	Retired worker
Alberto	Music Director, national television
Norma	Hospital seamstress
Mery	Radio station employee

1 Cuba and the Soviet and East European Socialism: "History Weighs Tremendously"

The interview subjects dedicated a considerable part of the interviews to talking about Cuban history before 1959, as well as about themselves as historical actors in the history of the Cuban Revolution. This is despite the fact that I fundamentally insisted on their view of the USSR collapse. I became more aware that the way they perceive Cuban history, including the history that preceded the relationship with the USSR, could help understand how the members of the Party in Cuba viewed the Collapse, as well as their political reaction when the Collapse took place.

Despite Soviet influences, they consider the Revolution to be a particular Cuban project, whatever happens in other parts of the world. Journalist Víctor, one of my informants, referred to the importance of the past in present-day Cuban politics and in inspiring people, using the following words: "There is a tradition; history weighs tremendously." That there is a specific view of history and the strong importance that it has in Cuban society and politics has also been pointed out by investigators such as Lillian Guerra and Louis Pérez Jr.

I will therefore start by briefly analyzing some of the interview subjects' views of Cuba's history up until 1959, that is, what they would describe as the roots of the Cuban Revolution. This was a stage in which Cuba was located within the sphere of influence of the United States and where the Soviet influence in the country was next to zero. Without understanding Cuba's past, it is difficult, or perhaps almost impossible, to understand the Cuba that emerges after 1959. Gaining basic knowledge on how the interviewees experienced this past and how they interpret it, is also essential for our purposes. Next, I will examine some aspects of what the interview subjects expressed about the relations between Cuba and the Soviet and East European socialism, with an emphasis on their links with the USSR itself, as this was the main country of Comecon and the Warsaw Pact.

The reader will notice how the interview subjects' view of Cuban relations with the USSR and East Europe, as well as their perspectives on Cuban history and their own lived experiences, in part determine how they view the Collapse.

1.1 The National Legacy: "We Started This in 1868"

Seven of the 17 interview subjects spent considerable time talking about the existence of a long tradition of revolutionary thought and action in Cuba that precedes Cuba's relationship with the USSR. They believe that this tradition is characterized by virtues such as heroism and resistance, and consider the revolution led by Fidel Castro to be a result of, and at the same time a part of, this tradition. They view the Cuban Revolution as a process that began long before Fidel Castro and the relations that Cuba developed with the USSR from 1959, and that is still ongoing.

The historical relationship between Cuba and Spain and Cuba and the United States receives considerable attention. The interview subjects highlighted Cuban resistance to foreign domination and injustices, as well as their national heroes. They placed particular emphasis on the national roots of the Revolution, as compared to the alliance with the USSR, which, although they recognize that it was decisive at the time, appear in the testimonies as something almost circumstantial or secondary.

Alberto, singer and Music Director of the National Television in 1989, maintains that "You can draw a line from the Hatuey rebellion (indigenous Taino leader who fought the Spaniards), through the whims of the Cuban Creole bourgeoisie, in José Antonio Saco, Félix Varela [Cuban critical thinkers of the nineteenth century], all in all, note this, parallel to the rebellion movements and the *cimaronaje* [Cuban slave resistance]." Eliécer, a medical doctor, expressed something similar when he said that "We started this [the Revolution] in 1868 and there we are because this is how we are, and it is the distinctive characteristic of being Cuban," referring apparently to an attitude of resistance and heroism of the Cuban people. According to José Luis, who served as director of the Center for Research on the World Economy when the USSR collapsed, there is "a revolutionary process with a long history" that began long before 1959. Jorge, advisor of the government between 1989 and 1991, claims that "Fidel is the result of a trajectory of thought that starts from the nineteenth century [...]." According to Pedro, a diplomat in Nicaragua coinciding with the dissolution of the USSR, "There is [...] an enormous historical load of US policy toward Cuba and also a load of Cuban patriotism that comes from the war of independence and our heroes; it comes from Martí; it comes ... it is present in all stages of Cuban history." According to journalist Víctor, "The resistance is within the Cuban people."

Víctor, a retired pilot, compares the level of sacrifice made by the Cubans at two different historical moments, noting that there is a continuity in the resistance: "The *mambises* [Cuban guerilla independence soldiers who fought the Spanish during the independence wars of the late nineteenth century] even ate the sole of the shoes, and nowadays they are talking about the only mare brought by Camilo's people [Camilo Cienfuegos, one of the main leaders of the insurrection led by Fidel Castro, who died in October 1959], which carried all the things, and that had to be eaten the second day because they had nothing to eat."

Víctor—although agreeing with Idulberto that there is a continuity from the struggles of the nineteenth century to the present—criticizes a certain variant of the narrative of revolutionary continuity: "There is a leap in Cuba sometimes in history and they go from the mambises to Fidel, and that is a lie; there is the Generation of the 1930s [the generation that brought about the 1930s Revolution, also known as the Revolution of 1933] that solidified this Revolution politically, ideologically, culturally, and even within sports. Without these people, without Mella, without Pablo, without Martínez Villena, without Guiteras, without Barceló [names and surnames of leaders of the Revolution of the 30s], without these people there would not be a Fidel, nor would there be a Victor Joaquín [name of the interview subject]."

The strength of the Cuban intellectual tradition is another theme that is repeated, and some interview subjects alluded to a close relationship between the intellectual tradition and that of revolutionary action in the Cuban case. Three of the interview subjects mentioned Cuban thinkers who, according to them, preceded the Europeans Marx and Lenin in their analyses. Jorge maintained that Enrique José Varona "has an essay [on imperialism] in 1905, 12 years before Lenin's book *Imperialism, the Highest Stage of Capitalism*." According to Idulberto, "Martí spoke of Marx, spoke of Engels, spoke about the development of socialism[1] and set out what imperialism was long before him [Lenin] [...], this Martí did in the year [18]90, in the previous century, you know?" Alberto also noted that Cuban intellectuals Enrique José Varona and José Martí made analyses of the phenomenon of imperialism before Vladimir Lenin. According to Alberto, the Cubans have been "privileged" with a history that "has been generating a [way of] thought," and uses Martí as an example, whom he considers a superior figure to the great political leaders and great thinkers of the United States:

> I was asked by a boy, a North American, why do you venerate Martí so much? I said, "Well, because you do not have a figure of the same level in the United States, sorry," I said, "sorry that I am so arrogant, but you don't have that, you don't have ... that is, neither Jefferson, nor Franklin, not even the great thinkers, Washington even less, reach that level."

When referring to the implementation of a single-party system in Cuba after 1959, the interview subjects do not usually refer to the theory of the vanguard party of Vladimir Lenin or the Soviet one-party model. Instead, they refer to the calls by the Cuban José Martí to unite all the forces that were in favor of progress in a single party, the Cuban Revolutionary Party (PRC), which he

---

1   It is not entirely clear what it is referred to here, but Martí spoke of what he understood as socialism in critical terms.

founded in 1892 in order to defeat the foreign powers of their time and achieve true independence. Víctor, for example, asserted that "the Party is fundamental and [there should be] one just like the one created by Martí." The fact that the members of the Communist Party of Cuba defend their country's one-party system, citing José Martí as a source of inspiration, is not a novelty, but until the 1990s, it was common to refer to both Lenin and Martí. In 1990, at a time when the USSR still existed, Fidel Castro defended the single party by referring both to the party proposed by Lenin but also to José Martí: "[...] we will also maintain the principle of the single party, which did not come from Lenin alone, it also came from Martí when he founded the Revolutionary Party for Cuban independence, and he did not create three or ten, but one to lead the Revolution and the struggle for the country's independence."[2]

My interview subjects tend to present the Soviet influence as secondary. The medical doctor Eliécer, for example, immediately after talking about historical continuity from 1868 to the present, added: "But the USSR was admired." In this sense, one understands that he considers it as something secondary or additional that does not erase the national tradition. José Luis also maintains that a relationship is established between these traditions, where there is a historical revolutionary process "with a long history that would naturally connect with a socialist path that in Cuba's history was different [...]." He uses the verb *entroncar* in Spanish, "to become related" or "to connect," thereby suggesting that the Cuban project was in place before the encounter with the Soviets, and that it remained a distinct thing.

With only slight variations, everyone repeats a similar narrative when talking about the roots of the Cuban Revolution. This is not surprising, as researchers such as Louis Pérez Jr. and Lillian Guerra argue that there is a grand narrative of Cuban history.[3] Although counter-narratives are disseminated by the diaspora, these have limited influence in Cuba and are rejected by my interview subjects.

Any narrative is a construction, and the narrative of the interview subjects is selective and politicized and debatable. However, the interview subjects' narrative about the revolutionary struggles before Fidel Castro generally relies

---

2   Fidel Castro, "Discurso pronunciado por el Comandante en Jefe Fidel Castro Ruz [...] en la sesión extraordinaria de la Asamblea Nacional del Poder Popular, celebrada en el Palacio de las Convenciones, el 20 de febrero de 1990. 'Año 32 de la Revolución,'" http://www.cuba.cu/gobierno/discursos/1990/esp/f200290e.html. It has also been publicado en la forma de un folleto: *¡Atrás ni para coger impulso!* (Havana: Political Editor, 1990)—its title meaning roughly "We will never go backwards, not even to gain momentum."
3   Pérez Jr.; Lillian Guerra *Visions of Power in Cuba: Revolution, Redemption, and Resistance, 1959–1971* (Chapel Hill: University of North Carolina Press, 2012), 3.

on known and documented facts, which gives it a certain sense of credibility (except for certain details such as the mambises eating the soles of their shoes, perhaps!). This said, there are of course statements that could be discussed and possibly refuted, especially with regard to the treatment of José Martí. Notably, he did not propose a one-party system as a form of government in times of peace but a united party to resist and win in times of war. Some Cubans would consider the years after 1959 to be war-like because of the heavy US pressure, while others would not accept this narrative. Furthermore, although one could argue that there are points in common between Martí and socialism or even Cuban socialism more specifically, he was no socialist himself.[4]

Still, most of the narrative supports itself in easily documentable facts, such as with regard to the role of the United States; for example, it should be noted that with the declaration of the Monroe Doctrine in 1823, the United States has had as its policy to play a leading role in the region.[5] In the case of Cuba, President Thomas Jefferson declared in 1809 that Cuba would be taken naturally by the United States, or the island would surrender itself to the US,[6] and President James Monroe also wrote in a letter that Cuba and Puerto Rico are natural annexes of the United States.[7]

The United States occupied Cuba for almost four years between 1899 and 1902. When the country received its independence in 1902, the famous Platt Amendment was added to its constitution by orders of the United States. The amendment restricts the foreign relations of Cuba and leaves a part of the province of Guantanamo and the Isle of Pines (Spanish name: Isla de Pinos, now it is called Isla de la Juventud) in the hands of the United States, in addition to allowing for intervention when US interests were threatened, the right

---

4 Martí was not a socialist, but neither was he the vehement antisocialist that he is sometimes presented as, even among some Cubans living in Cuba. Often cited as "proof" of Martí's alleged antisocialist attitude is his essay "La futura esclavitud" ("The Coming Slavery," 1884), but these readings are not entirely unproblematic. Here, Martí comments on English liberal philosopher Herbert Spencer's (1820–1903) warnings of a future where some type of welfare state or state-centered "socialism" would repress people and make the masses lazy. Martí's essay borrows its title from Spencer, and agrees that such an assistencialist and bureaucratic regime would be a bad thing; some Cubans hold that the essay is prophetic as Cuba implemented a very much state-centered model at one point. But the essay also includes very critical comments toward Spencer's elitism, and suggests attacking poverty at its roots. Moreover, while it is true that Martí distanced himself from Marx's ideas on class struggle, he wrote very respectfully on the thinker and his followers at the time of Marx's death.
5 Ward, 33.
6 Quoted in James D. Cockcroft, *América Latina y Estados Unidos: Historia y política país por país* (Havana: Editorial de Ciencias Sociales, 2004), 341.
7 Ibid.

of which the United States made use of on several occasions. Cuba was in reality turned into a protectorate, a status that would continue until the disappearance of the Amendment in 1934. Kapcia argues that "the potential roots of revolution"[8] emerged as result of two historical experiences: a prolonged colonialism and a neocolonial period from 1902 that "was unusually explicit."[9][10]

While it is uncontroversial to say that the US has had imperialist policies against Cuba, the parallels drawn by the interview subjects between the mambises of the nineteenth century and the communists of Fidel Castro might seem, at first glance, little more than a propaganda trick. José Martí, in the end, was not a Marxist and neither were the other mentioned heroes of the nineteenth century. Besides the differences, there are nevertheless common points. For example, the Partido Revolucionario Cubano (Cuban Revolutionary Party, PRC) was not limited to fighting against Spanish colonialism but also warned against US expansionist plans; in this sense, there is certainly an element of continuity in Fidel Castro's project.

Louis Pérez Jr. also argues that the two movements share ideas of social justice. Although national sovereignty was the most articulated demand of

---

8   Kapcia, 8.
9   Ibid.
10   It is often argued that this neocolonial period lasted until 1934. That year, there was a rupture with the *Platt* policies, as a result of the 1933 Revolution, which caused the fall of dictator Gerardo Machado. When writing on the period between the end of the American occupation (1902) and the Fidel Castro Revolution (1959), there are different evaluations. For example, in the view of Cuban historian Oscar Pino Santos, "From 1902 to 1934 Cuba's dependence on the United States clearly assumed the form of a 'protectorate' and only between 1934 and 1958 it manifested itself as a 'neo-colony.'" See: Oscar Pino Santos, "Lo que fue aquella República: Protectorado y neocolonia," http://epoca2.lajiribilla.cu/2004/n142_01/142_07.html. Marifeli Pérez-Stable also divides the republican period (1902–1952) into two distinct parts, named the First Republic (1902–1940) and the Second Republic, which began with the promulgation of a new constitution in 1940, widely known as one of the most advanced and democratic in Latin America (which was repealed when the Fulgencio Batista military coup of 1952 took place). Kapcia has criticized this periodization and considers that the only thing that the so-called "Second Republic" achieved (the author puts "Second Republic" between quotes) was "a partial modernization of the state (through various interventionist reforms)" and a "partial 're-Cubanization' of those parts of the economy where US capital had been withdrawn." See: Kapcia, 18. I agree with Pino Santos in that the repeal of the Platt Amendment is the most significant moment of rupture during the republic, as it ended the direct intervention of the United States, although the US intervention continued "more subtly and covert" (Pino Santos). Even so, I also consider that historiography produced within Cuba has had the tendency to ignore or minimize significant changes that occurred between 1934 and 1952, even the 1940 Constitution, which was important, although it did not fundamentally alter the economic structure or relations with the US.

nineteenth-century Cuban fighters, as was the case in other Latin American countries,[11] there were also more modern impulses and an "egalitarian vision" within the Cuban nation-building project.[12] The black mambises in the First War for Independence (1868–1878) not only fought for the separation of their territory from Spain but also for social justice. After the end of the first war, there was a *radicalization* among Cubans who supported independence. Antoni Kapcia mentions that a movement of "black consciousness" emerged between the black and mestizo populations, while Spanish immigrants brought the ideas of socialism and anarchism to urban workers.[13] The middle class, opposed to the oppression and restrictions of Spanish colonialism, increased. According to Kapcia, "a nationalism began to emerge which had a much greater social dimension than any contemporary nationalism in Latin America."[14] Pérez Jr. reminds us that José Martí tried to unite the Cubans without distinguishing between class, gender, or color.[15]

Marifeli Pérez-Stable observes that after the 1959 Revolution, the USSR and Eastern Europe served as important inspirations for the one-party model as those countries showed that such a model was efficient with regard to "consolidating and retaining power."[16] However, the author also asserts that Cuba's national revolutionary tradition offered precedents for a political vanguard: Both José Martí and Antonio Guiteras [the leader of the radical wing of the 1933 Revolution] had asked for unity in order to change the country.[17] Lack of unity had been "undermining" revolutionaries' success at other moments, while Fidel Castro's armed struggle had demonstrated the importance of unity.[18]

Certainly, there has been a nationalist turn in Cuba in recent decades, which raises the question: Would the interview subjects have talked about Cuban history in the same way if—hypothetically—we had interviewed them back in the 1970s or during the first half of the 1980s, when Soviet influence in Cuba was at its strongest?

There was a change in the official historical narrative in the 1970s and the early years of the decade of the 1980s. In those years, the Cuban Ministry of Education began to present Cuban history in a Marxist–Leninist framework,

---

11 Pérez Jr., 4.
12 Ibid.
13 Kapcia, 12.
14 Ibid., 13.
15 Pérez Jr., 71.
16 Pérez-Stable, 87.
17 Ibid.
18 Ibid.

emphasizing the importance of the laws of history.[19] Pérez Jr. cites an interview he conducted with Cuban historian Jorge Ibarra in 2012, who said that in the historiography of the 1970s, the history of Cuba "appeared to have developed into an appendix to the history of the Soviet Union."[20]

Of course, we do not know how people would have responded in an interview back then, but it is also possible that, at that time, many would have put emphasis on the more Cuban narrative of a hundred years of struggle. One could think that this is a narrative introduced by Fidel Castro, but he built his narrative upon a previously existing nationalist account of Cuban history that talked of a revolutionary continuity since the nineteenth century. According to Louis Pérez Jr., the political opposition in the Cuban Republic used to derive its discursive framework mainly from pro-independence narratives.[21] Before the coup by Fulgencio Batista in 1952, the reformist political parties presented themselves as heirs of José Martí, with the main parties in the 1940s consisting of the Cuban Revolutionary Party (Auténtico) and the Cuban People's Party (Ortodoxo). The first name refers to the original PRC of José Martí and the word "ortodoxo" in the second name of the party referred to rescuing the values and aims of the Revolution of 1933, also inspired in part by Martí.

The resistance movements that emerged after the 1952 coup, such as the National Revolutionary Movement (MNR), the Revolutionary Student Directorate (DRE), and the 26 of July Movement (M-26), all said they were going to complete the work that the liberators of the nineteenth century had initiated.[22] In general, by the 1950s, Cubans looked to the past and to José Martí, who served "as an inexhaustible supply of truths, for all occasions, on all subjects."[23] Pérez Jr. claims that the "brilliance" of the leadership of the 26 of July Movement was "to inscribe itself into the past and to reemerge as its proponent, to represent itself as the bearer of nineteenth-century truths."[24] For example, on January 1, 1959, Castro said that "the history of [18]'95 will not be repeated; this time around, the Mambises will enter Santiago de Cuba today,"[25] a historical comparison that referred to how the United States had denied the liberators entry to Cuba's Eastern "second capital" in 1898.[26] Pérez Jr. argues that the *motif*

---

19 Pérez Jr., 258.
20 Ibid.
21 Pérez Jr., 16.
22 Ibid., 189–196.
23 Ibid., 189.
24 Ibid., 196.
25 Eugenio Suárez Pérez and Acela Caner Román, "Primero de enero de 1959: Esta vez sí que es una Revolución," *Granma*, Dec. 31, 2015.
26 Pérez Jr., 208.

of "the hundred years of struggle" had served as the dominant framework for the interpretation of a generation and "the master narrative" of the Revolution in its early years.[27] In this sense, the nationalist narrative predated USSR relations, and when it gained strength again in official propaganda around 1990, it might have seemed to many as a return to their roots and not just as the political elite just inventing a new ideology to suit their needs, as they could not rely on imported ideas.

1.2 The Lived Past: "My Brother Was Found Dead in the Barrio Caribe"

Most interview subjects were born before 1959, and many are old enough to have memories of the pre-revolutionary era, especially the last years of the Batistato.[28] Their experiences from that time and/or the information they have received from other sources about Cuba of that era have repercussions on their understanding of the Revolution, the United States, the USSR, and the Collapse.

It is not surprising that references to the evils of the pre-1959 era are recurrent in an interview with members of the Communist Party of Cuba. These people had all entered that Party at some point, which implies a rejection of the capitalist past and the US imperialist policy, as well as a commitment to the changes that took place in Cuba in 1959. At first glance, some testimonies could easily be perceived as a mechanical reproduction of the official Cuban propaganda, where there is a tendency to highlight the evils of the past and to contrast those with the achievements of the post-1959 stage. The informants tend to place an emphasis on issues with more visible improvements since 1959, such as health and education, rather than talking about areas where there has been no such progress or even issues where the country is in a worse state.

Nevertheless, their stories from before the Revolution seem credible and fit in with already existing documentation on such evils of the past. The testimonies in some cases contain experiences of poverty, exclusion, or political repression prior to 1959, and, on the other hand, to concrete improvements they themselves have experienced after 1959. These might have been motivations for assuming and later for retaining their political affiliation and positions. With regard to the details of their stories, it is not always possible to document these, as they can in some cases be very local or personal experiences. Still, the testimonies were consistent with what the literature says about the different historical periods and in general seemed credible.

---

27   Ibid., 260.
28   That is, the period that begins with the coup d'etat of Fulgencio Batista in 1952 and ends with him fleeing Cuba in the early hours of January 1, 1959.

With regard to poverty, José—who between 1989 and 1991 was the director of a communications workshop—refers to his experience of the pre-revolutionary era when he says that "I grew up on a dirt floor, where my mother threw the ashes, because in those days one cooked with coal ... the ashes in the kitchen, dirt floors, roofs of what is it called? Of zinc, an 'escusado,' do you know what an 'escusado' is? No, no, that does not exist today. They are latrines that they made, a hole in the ground that was covered with a cap on top and of wood." He claims that the revolution brought a radical change in his life: "The Revolution turned me into a person, the Revolution turned me into a person." Zenaida, a retired worker, also contrasts a gloomy past with a better present, saying that her grandson has "[...] all the work he wants [...]" and that "they have never stopped having lunch or eating as people say, and in my childhood I faced many difficulties [pasé mucho trabajo], and my mom together with us, oh please!" She tells her grandchildren that "you have to die for this [the Revolution] because you don't know what it is to suffer. It is not possible to calculate [compare] this era with the previous era."

Two of the interview subjects had experiences of exclusion or racism in the pre-revolutionary era, seemingly of an institutional nature. Idulberto explains that "even one day in the Cristino Naranjo, today it is called Cristino Naranjo,[29] when it was the club of, how is it called, rowing, I was denied entry because I was a mulatto [...]." Eliécer tells a similar story of his best friend, a black man, Pepín, who he says could not enter a specific beach.[30] Álvarez talks about another type of exclusion when recounting how the University of Havana was closed in 1953, when she was a student: "The political situation in Cuba became

---

[29] He refers to a former beach club in the Miramar suburb of Havana, known as the Casino Deportivo, it was actually given its current name after the Revolution, when it was expropriated and given to schoolchildren. The name refers to revolutionary *Comandante* Cristino Naranjo.

[30] Clearly racism is a serious problem even in present-day Cuba, but not at a comparable level. Another of our informants, Esteban, had one particularly strong experience of racism—although he did not mention it during our interview, but in a conversation with the online publication *Havana Times*. He told them of an episode when he was 11 years old: "Long before 1959, when I was about 11, I won first prize in an essay contest on José Martí; it was organized by the 'Caballeros Católicos' [Catholic Knights] in my town. When I got to the ceremony, you could hear the murmuring throughout the hall. I figured out what had happened: the form I had filled out didn't include my picture, and it wasn't imaginable for those middle-class whites that a poor black kid like me would win the competition. They made me leave. Luckily for me, there was a certain banker on the jury. He was as white and middle class as all the others, but he was the brother-in-law of the woman who employed my grandmother as a maid. It seems that he kicked up a fuss and made them grant me the award." See: "Change in Cuba: Less Costly Than Clinging to the Past," *Havana Times*, Dec. 8, 2012.

very agitated and the University in particular was a focal point for the rebellion [...] this is precisely the time when revolutionary movements emerged and that is where all those movements against the dictatorship are incited, to such an extreme that Batista the dictator closed the University."

Four people refer to forms of repression involving the use of physical violence and, in some cases, torture and death. Idulberto explains that he himself was on an assassination list: "I have had the privilege of being alive thanks to the Revolution because I was imprisoned in the year '58, kidnapped in front of my house [...] imprisoned in the tenth police station, and the Revolution saved my life, because I was on the [death] list." Víctor tells the story of when he was arrested by the police, being "almost a child," for having said on the street that Fulgencio Batista was going to run the same fate as the dictator Marcos Pérez Jiménez in Venezuela, who was deposed on January 23, 1958: "In January of '58 I was imprisoned because I commented when passing by a lieutenant of the dictatorship, at that time to be a lieutenant was a lot, and I told him we will drag this one [Batista] down as in Venezuela. This he hears and he takes me prisoner with a gun to my head, he takes me with him, luckily my dad had money, he had connections and he got me out of the station before they beat me and tortured me, but I saw the blows that they gave to others and I was about to be beaten and tortured [...]."

The medical doctor Héctor—who served as Deputy Minister of Health during the Collapse—had been detained three times before the Revolution. He told us that in prison there was a policeman who tortured people, who was later to participate in the invasion of exiled Cubans at the Bay of Pigs, where he was wounded. Héctor had to treat him as a medical doctor: "I did not fail to fulfill in the ethical principles of my work when one of the wounded from the mercenary invasion of the Bay of Pigs had been a torturer, a police torturer when I was detained, because I was detained three times [before the Revolution]. I suffered imprisonment, and it happened that I was the doctor who treated him when he was there."

The cruelest of all the testimonies is that of the hospital seamstress Norma. She tells me about the time when Batista's forces murdered her brother, in their native province of Guantanamo: "My brother was found dead in the Barrio Caribe, do you know what the Barrio Caribe is?" she asks; the name refers to one of the neighborhoods in that eastern city.

It is commonly known that many other Cubans, for example those that migrated to Florida after the Revolution, have very different memories of the time before the Revolution and, above all, more negative memories of the next stage. This may have to do with their social class, values, and political stance, coincidences, and other factors. But the existence of other experiences does not make the testimonies of the Cuban party members less credible, which coincides with ample documentation of the social problems, repression, and brutality of the pre-revolutionary era.

On the other hand, it could be argued that this kind of emphasis on the past serves to hide evils of the revolutionary past and present. During my stays in Cuba, I have met people still living in poverty, who experience discrimination problems and even political repression (for example, by not receiving a particular job as they have expressed opinions against the government or suffering detention for unauthorized political activism). Even so, today's situation is different from the one before 1959. Although there is poverty in Cuba, for example, there is no extreme poverty in present-day Cuba, and the country has seen development in important socio-economic spheres. Amnesty International's reports from the late-1980s mention the lack of an independent judiciary, repression, and cruel treatment of prisoners—but not torture. In some later reports allegations of torture do appear, but the most grave crimes of the past seem to be absent or very rare, as the early revolutionary government took steps to stop and abolish such crimes—still widespread in Latin America. There are no extrajudicial killings.

Although revolutionary Cuba did limit and still limits some important civil and political rights, the absence of the brutal crimes that were common before the Revolution and in many Latin American countries in the second half of the last century has given legitimacy to the Revolution and the Cuban Government. The bad experiences lived by several of the interview subjects before 1959 would have contributed to their political position, often in their young years, and must also have early determined their view of the US and the USSR since the former was an ally of Batista and the USSR was an ally of the revolutionary government.

That being said, several of the interview subjects believe that the average Cuban had an unfavorable view of the USSR and its ideology in the 1950s and early 1960s. Eliécer argues that "talking about communism here was talking about something bad." José exemplifies this hatred of communism with an anecdote from his own life, specifically when he was working as a carpenter before the Revolution: "The capitalist propaganda had put in our head that being a communist was the lowest you could be," and jokingly he called a colleague a "communist!" He argues that at the age of 16 or 17 he did not know what communism was. "I said it to piss him off"; it was a "teenager thing." However, the colleague responded by throwing a hammer at him:

> He held up the hammer and if I hadn't thrown myself... pay attention to what I'm telling you... I would have been, damn, if it's a lie I might as well

die right here now, pay attention to this... I threw myself off the rebars, the hammer passed and fell in the courtyard of the last house, because he was a pitcher, they called him DiMaggio, he held up the hammer up and if he got me, if he got me ... boy, imagine!

Finally, many interview subjects stress that the insurrectionary struggle in Cuba (1953–1958) not only arose because of Cuban problems, but that it was also led by Cubans, without Soviet support. That is, contrary to the post-Second World War revolutions in Eastern Europe, there was no Soviet interference in Cuba, or at least not at this stage. We can speak then, of a *non-relation* with Soviet "communism," more than anything else. For the interview subjects, this makes the Cuban Revolution more authentic, more independent, and more legitimate than many other experiences where there was such interference. Some even see the lack of authentic revolutions in Eastern Europe as one of the causes of the Collapse of Soviet and East European socialism.

1.3 The First Contact: "The Blockade Had a Severe Impact and the Soviets Gave Us a Hand"

In this subsection, I will discuss some aspects of Cuban–Soviet relations in the early stages (1959–1972) that are relevant in order to understand the relation that arose and the perceptions of the interview subjects of the Collapse. The Cuban Revolution triumphs on January 1, 1959, and in the fall of that year the first "serious contact" with the USSR develops.[31] Over the next few years, the contact becomes closer, but there are also a series of contradictions and setbacks throughout the 1960s. The account by Jorge Domínguez that appears in the introduction of this book should be noted: Between 1962 and 1968, relations "oscillated between collaboration and confrontation."[32] The interview subjects who remember that stage well, often emphasize the differences between the two countries, highlighting (intentionally or not) an image of Cuba as independent.

My interview subjects tend to present the young alliance between Cuba and the USSR as strategic more than ideological and political. Some, especially academics, argue that Cuba had no choice but to ally with the Soviet Union, given the strong pressures by the United States in collaboration with Cuban counter-revolutionaries—both within the country and from exile. It can be recalled in this regard that 250,000 Cubans emigrated during the first years of the

---

31   Domínguez, *La política exterior de Cuba (1962–2009)*, 243.
32   Ibid., 244.

Revolution,[33] that many lost or left behind property and privileges in Cuba, and that the community of exiles pushed for the United States to work against the Cuban government with all means.

Jorge says that "We were challenging the most powerful country in the world, as a tiny country, and we had no choice but to rely on the USSR, you know?" Mavis expresses something similar and mentions the invasion in Playa Girón [April 1961] to underline the seriousness of the situation: "We had no other option because you cannot separate the problem from the context, the context was very hard, very hard, we had already even suffered direct military aggression with the invasion of Playa Girón, we had no alternative, the defense of the country depended on the Soviet Union."[34]

José Luis mentions the case of the blockade imposed by the United States: "The US blockade practically prevented us from turning toward any other alternative, therefore it had great significance and Cuba continues to be thankful, that event [the USSR offering support] is not forgotten here." Pedro maintains that "the irrational and visceral policy of the United States toward Cuba, had as an effect that a close alliance between Cuba and the Soviet Union formed rapidly."[35]

Although the interview subjects do not mention it much, the reader must keep in mind that the situation in Cuba was very tense during the first six or seven years after the Revolution. Rafael Rojas has characterized the situation in the country until 1966 as a civil war.[36] In the historiography made in Cuba, the situation is largely referred to as "struggle against outlaws," referring to

---

33   Number taken from Pérez-Stable, 83. According to Antoni Kapcia, people emigrated for both political and economic motives. See: Kapcia, 155.

34   Our informant Lenin mentions that during the early moments of the Revolution, the Soviets did not want to commit themselves directly to defending Cuba, as this could lead to problems with the United States: "Czech weapons arrived in Cuba, because they did not want to enter in confrontation as Soviets, as Russia, because then the Americans could say—well, Russia is involved in this." In other words, he describes a phase of rapprochement before this took the shape of definitive commitment. The claim that both Cuba and the USSR tried to avoid direct arms transfers in 1959 is backed by Tad Szulc, biographer of Fidel Castro: See: Tad Szulc, *Fidel: A Critical Portrait* (New York: Perennial, 2002), 498. Although Szulc also writes that towards the end of 1960 both Czech and Soviet arms began to enter the country, citing Cuban revolutionary veteran José Ramón Fernández as a source.

35   This explanation has also been used by leading government figures. For example, Carlos Lage stated on November 6, 1992 on the television program *Hoy Mismo* that "historically, our high level of integration with the socialist countries has its origin in the (US) blockade."

36   Rafael Rojas, *Historia mínima de la Revolución Cubana* (El Colegio de México, 2015), 121–131.

rural resistance groups that were opposed to agrarian reform and the revolution and that received support from exiles and the CIA. According to Guerra and Maldonado, between February and August 1962 alone, there were a total of 5,780 terrorist attacks and 716 "large-scale" sabotages.[37] On the other hand, according to Pérez-Stable, in the mid-1960s there were between 20,000 and 50,000 political prisoners[38] (the most frequently cited figure is 20,000) and thousands of Cubans were executed during this decade.[39]

Different assessments can be found in the literature about the causes that led Cuba to approach the USSR. Pérez-Stable refers to a radicalization process in Cuba that "entailed the elimination of capitalism, the suppression of independent institutions to settle political differences, and a turn toward the Soviet Union" and attributes this radicalization and polarization primarily to internal factors, amongst them Fidel Castro's attitude, but considers that "the Cold War aggravated" the situation.[40]

Domínguez claims that "as the Cuban government approached (*al abordar*) a break with the United States, it began courting the Soviet Union,"[41] which could imply that Castro had sought to move away from the United States from the outset, but not necessarily. Bain also writes that in 1959 "it may not have been" Fidel Castro's intention to align with the USSR but puts emphasis on the possibility that he did want to change the relationship with Washington.[42] With "increased US hostility [...] culminating in the Bay of Pigs invasion [in April 1961],"[43] he declared himself a Marxist–Leninist to ensure greater economic and military assistance from the Soviets.[44]

Rojas places emphasis on Fidel Castro's tour of the United States in April 1959, where Castro tried to forge contacts, and on some apparently positive signs such as diplomatic exchanges between the countries during that same year.[45] Rojas thus seems to suggest that in the early days there might have been

---

37   Guerra and Maldonado, 156.
38   Ibid. Historian Jorge Castañeda, considered a critic of Fidel Castro and Ernesto "Che" Guevara, have said about the executions of the first year of the revolutionary government that "It was not a bloodbath, nor was a significant number of innocent people killed [...] rather, it is surprising that the number of deaths and abuses remained so small." See: Jorge G. Castañeda, *Compañero: vida y muerte del Che Guevara* (New York: Vintage Books, 1997), 187.
39   Pérez-Stable, 83.
40   Ibid., 67.
41   Domínguez, *La política exterior de Cuba (1962–2009)*, 243.
42   Bain, 20–21.
43   Ibid.
44   Ibid.
45   Rojas, loc. 1968.

a real desire to find some common ground with the US and that the US was considering this option.

It is far beyond this study's purpose to delve deeply into the complexities of the Revolution's radicalization and Cuba's geopolitical realignment. There are many important moments and events. One of the major moments was the launch of the Land Reform of May 1959, which provoked desertions within the moderate First Revolutionary government of 1959, as well as tensions with the US. This government was eventually replaced by what Rojas calls the Second Revolutionary government, which took some rapid and very radical first measures to build socialism in Cuba.

According to Rojas, during this second government, a first phase of building socialism in Cuba and a "dramatic adjustment" took place in the country's international relations. This realignment took place "between 1961 and 1962, that is between the failed Bay of Pigs invasion and the Cuban missile crisis (October 1962)." He highlights the expulsion of Cuba in late January 1962 from the Organization of American States (OAS), and basically, from the Western Hemisphere, as factors that provoked even closer relations with the USSR. According to Rojas, the Bay of Pigs invasion contributed to making communism the state policy, citing Castro's speech on April 15, 1961, as a tribute to the victims of the military incursion.[46]

Independent of the actors' intentions, the options available to the new Cuban leaders were limited, as Thomas Skidmore and Peter Smith have stated: "It was inevitable that any Cuban government attempting to reassert Cuban control over its economy would collide with the United States."[47] Furthermore, they seem correct to affirm that the realignment with the Soviets "was neither a cause nor an effect of the clash with the United States; it was part and parcel of the same process."[48]

When the first contacts between Cuba and the USSR emerged, they were mostly strategic and implied that Cuba received material and economic aid to address a difficult situation.[49] Although both countries were against US

---

46 Ibid., loc. 13–107.
47 Thomas E. Skidmore and Peter H. Smith, *Modern Latin America* (New York: Oxford University Press, 2005), 311.
48 Ibid., 312.
49 On February 5, 1960, Soviet First Deputy Premier Anastás Mikoyán visited the island, with the purpose of signing a commercial agreement. Lillian Guerra cites an informal and non-representative "poll" in the press, where 9 out of 10 people that were interviewed, answered that they supported a trade agreement with the Soviet Union. However, the visit also provoked protests by students, who were shouting slogans in favor of Fidel Castro,

interference, the contact came to imply considerable ideological identification, with an important step being the declaration of the Cuban Revolution as a Marxist–Leninist in December 1961, but the Cuban ideology did not become identical and its social model was still very different from the Soviet one. As Eliécer, one of the interview subjects pointed out, at the beginning of the Revolution, there was still a strong anti-communist sentiment in the country. He recalls that "When people [...] really started to see what socialism was, its characteristics, like, the way in which it was influencing the political work that was going on, people in the end began to appreciate the Soviet Union and love the Russians."[50]

The interview subjects express gratitude to the USSR. Idulberto, for example, says, "We have to thank the Soviet people forever for defending us against Yankee imperialism, with its deficiencies, its slips, its tribulations, and its mistakes. [...] we owe it our life." Alberto says that "I personally had many things to thank the USSR for; it helped us greatly in a very difficult time, in the 60s, it was, it was very important because even with our contradictions we could survive very, very tough circumstances." Lenin says that "Everyone broke relations with Cuba, and the blockade had a severe impact and the Soviets gave us a hand, not just the Soviets, the Socialist Camp." Víctor also points out that "We are not going to deny the good things of the Soviet Union, otherwise I would not be here. We will be honest: the weapons, the sugar," while José states that "These people helped us extraordinarily; when the capitalist enemy is pointing cannons at us and closes all doors to us, they open them, they give us that opportunity."

The Missile Crisis is highlighted by many interview subjects (7 out of 17) as an example of a time when there were tensions between Cuba and the USSR; that is, a substantial portion of the interview subjects. This is significant due to the fact that there is no question about the Missile Crisis in the interview guide, and it was a historic event that had some recurrence in the interviews. They report that the Soviets did not act in the most correct way, since they began to negotiate with the United States to solve the crisis without including the Cuban side.

José Luis describes the tensions that arose later between Cuba and the USSR as a "quarrel." Mavis speaks of a "disagreement" between the two countries, but she also points out that the USSR did not behave properly: "They had also

---

but against Mikoyán, and there were even violent clashes between groups of protesters and the police. See: Guerra, 109–118.

50   In everyday speech, it is not uncommon for Cubans to use the adjective "Russian" as a replacement for "Soviet." In Cuba, the word "Russian," therefore, can sometimes refer to something or someone from another Soviet republic. See: Loss, 2.

surprised him [Fidel Castro] and not only had they surprised him, but they had fooled him [...] it made one think that it was best not to be too trusting." Víctor admits that the behavior of the Soviets bothered him and adds that in his opinion, "The Soviets had messed up," they had made a mistake. Eliécer points out that "It happened behind our backs, this was not upfront," that is, implying incorrect, arrogant, and/or disloyal behavior. He adds that Cubans had a strong reaction due to their nationalism. Idulberto, who was in Kiev during the crisis, uses the strongest words when he argues that "They played us, ugh, they could have talked to us, they betrayed principles in their relation with us," although he also stresses that "[after this] Nikita Khrushchev communicated very well with Fidel Castro." He also mentions a meeting in Kiev where he was present, related to the annual celebration of the Cuban Revolution shortly afterwards, on January 2, 1963. He emphasizes that there was a very good tone and that the relations between the people of two countries did not appear to be damaged, despite what happened at the governmental level.

The interview subjects clearly see the Cold War as an unequal conflict, where the greatest power (the United States) put pressure on the second (USSR) and also other, smaller countries. Although no one explicitly says it, a common attitude seems to be that the placement of missiles in Cuba was a legitimate response by Cuba and the USSR, two allied countries that, while not having the same foreign policy, were under pressure from the United States. This power already had missiles in a European country that could be used against the USSR and had, on the other hand, given its support to Cuban exiles with the invasion of Playa Girón (April 1961). The interview subjects nevertheless mention the Missile Crisis primarily as an example of independence from the Soviets, as Fidel Castro protested the way they spoke with the United States without considering the Cuban participants.[51]

Some interview subjects also highlight how Cuba's support for liberation movements went against the Soviet position of *peaceful coexistence*. José Luis, Alonso, and Jorge—all academics—emphasize that there were substantive disagreements on this issue. Juan, a researcher at the Centre for American Studies at the time of the Collapse, also pointed to these tensions.

Many Cubans believed that the Revolution would have to reach other countries for Cuba to survive. Alonso claims that by 1960, "there is [...] the idea that

---

51   These positions are very similar to the official Cuban version of the Missile Crisis, as expressed by Fidel Castro and other leading figures at different moments. There is no concrete sign that any of the interviewees disagree with this version. On the other hand, if someone really supported Khrushchev's handling of the crisis, this would be a controversial position in Cuba, so I cannot rule out the possibility that some of the interviewees might have another idea without saying this.

the Cuban revolution could not survive without a change in Latin America." Juan mentions that "If you consider the level of our involvement in the Latin American guerrilla movement between [19]61 and [19]70 as very high, even in a direct way, Cuban fighters in almost all guerrilla groups, etc." This situation was to be different in the 1970s, he said. The strong Cuban involvement had threatened pro-USSR parties in Latin America, as the guerrillas allied with Cuba challenged their protagonism: "The Cuban involvement, although appearing as the Communist Party of Cuba, threw the pro-Soviet communist parties in the region into crisis."

According to Jorge, "The USSR did not support the guerrillas in Latin America and did not want us to support them, [but] we nevertheless supported them." José Luis says that "Cuba's help to the liberation movements (in the Third World), for example, was not the Soviet stance," when he talks about differences between the two countries. Víctor maintains that the Soviets "believed more in the old communists [The Popular Socialist Party] than in Fidel, than in Raul and all that [...] not in the armed struggle either, etc. They did not support *el Che* (Guevara), what happens to el Che in Bolivia." Idulberto mentions that his daughter studied in the USSR and had problems due to being an admirer of Che Guevara: "They wanted to kick her out [of the study center] because the Soviets did not accept Che Guevara or the guerrilla struggle, and my daughter grew up with the idea of wanting to be like el Che."[52]

This whole situation could be interpreted as a strategy in which the USSR used Cuba as an intermediary to support the guerrillas, to prevent the United States from blaming them for aggression in their area of influence. Aurelio, however, suggests that this was not the case, and that the USSR actively tried to sabotage Cuban politics: "It was not a mere theoretical discrepancy, that was shown by the practice of the Soviet Union [...] to provide assistance to the Latin American forces on the condition that they were not guerrillas."

The differences mentioned by Aurelio are documented by the literature, although I should add there were some ambiguities and changes in USSR policy throughout the 1960s. The position of the USSR in the early 1960s was that the Cuban revolution was an example for Latin America but in terms of policies and not with regard to the armed means of taking power, and it considered Fidel Castro's calls for guerilla struggle in Latin America unfortunate.[53]

---

52   *Seremos como el Che*, "We will be like Che Guevara" is also a chant repeated by Cuban schoolchildren.
53   See Jacques Lévesque, "La Unión Soviética y Cuba: Una relación especial," *Foro Internacional XVIII*, Number 2, October–December: 235–241.

According to Jacques Lévesque, there were internal tensions in the USSR government on the issue in 1963 and 1964, but during this phase, support for the pacific line was the dominant and official position. When Khrushchev fell in 1964, the Soviets tried to solve its internal tensions and also the tensions on the Latin American left by organizing a conference with the communist parties of the region. Here, a compromise was reached—that all the parties present should support the armed struggle in six specific countries (Venezuela, Colombia, Guatemala, Honduras, Paraguay, and Haiti) but also support the peaceful struggle of other parties in the rest of Latin America. From that moment, the USSR sent material support ("large sums") to the Communist Party of Venezuela, which had opted for a guerrilla struggle. In 1965, due to the US invasion of the Dominican Republic and defeats suffered by guerrillas in Latin America, the USSR leant again toward the actors that opted for peaceful methods, and it refrained from intervening in 1966 when the Communist Party of Venezuela lay down their arms. Fidel Castro, however, called the Venezuelan Party traitors and criticized the Soviet party. In 1967, Cuba organized a conference (OLAS) in Havana where a number of guerrillas were invited but no Communist Party from the region. This represented a "huge [...] challenge" to the USSR.[54] The USSR opted for silence because it had invested heavily in Cuba and feared that a breach in the alliance could provoke a US invasion in Cuba. In reality, it sympathized with the Latin American communist parties that opted for peaceful means,[55] parties that "are very likely" to have pressured the USSR to sanction Cuba.[56]

It is notable that there are far fewer mentions of the Sino–Soviet crisis in my interviews, and those that comment on the subject have different assessments of Cuba's position at that time. José Luis argues that "In the Sino–Soviet dispute, Cuba did not adopt either the position of the Chinese or the Soviets; we stayed out of that row despite pressure from both sides to adopt one or another position."

On the other hand, Mavis remembers things differently: "[...] we practically expelled the Chinese from here, the Chinese military advisers, well, they practically left, they left because Cuba did not want to be involved in that confrontation, because the Chinese and the Russians transferred those discrepancies to Cuba and to wherever they were [...] and they wanted others to pick sides." She argues that Cuba did not want to get involved in the conflict, because the country was dependent on Soviet aid; however, what she first said indicates

---

54   Ibid., 235–240.
55   Ibid., 240–241.
56   Ibid.

that Cuba did pick a side, if it is true that they "practically expelled" Chinese collaborators. According to former diplomat Pedro, "relations with China had hit rock bottom" by the late 1960s. We have not reviewed in detail the academic literature on the subject, and possibly there are different interpretations on the early years, still there is no doubt that at some point these relations reached a very bad state. According to Jacques Lévesque, Fidel Castro accused the Chinese of joining the US blockade after they cut supplies of rice to Cuba in 1966. Lévesque also maintains that after that moment, relations "deteriorated considerably."[57]

When touching upon the early years of the Cuban revolution and Cuban–Soviet relations, the informants also say very little of the failed radical experiments that took place in Cuban society toward the end of the 1960s,[58] known as the Revolutionary Offensive. At first glance, this might seem odd, since these are examples of policies that differed greatly from the Soviets and therefore could be used as an example of Cuba's uniqueness, a uniqueness that they often highlighted during the interviews. However, though independent-minded, these policies were a fiasco and eventually led to increased dependence on the Soviets.

The political scientist Jeanette Habel quotes a Cuban economist, Alexis Codina Jiménez, who recalls a series of unrealistic measures that were implemented beginning in 1967:[59] the elimination of bonuses and overtime pay, the decoupling of the wage from the difficulty of the labor and its results, and the total abolition of rent, as well as the free use of the telephone and other measures.[60] Planning basically disappeared, and the production of non-sugar products decreased due to the preparation for The Ten Million Ton Sugar Harvest (*La zafra de los diez millones*) of 1969–1970.[61]

Since public institutions were very weak, during these radical experiments the "citizens had no check on public officials."[62] The experiments ended in economic chaos, and there was serious demoralization amongst workers.[63] In this situation, Cuba actually became more dependent on outside aid, while Fidel

---

57 Ibid., 238–239.
58 Habel, 72.
59 Ibid., 50.
60 Ibid.
61 Fidel Castro announced that he was going to produce 10 million tons of sugar for exportation, as a manner of boosting the national economy. The desired results were not obtained, despite the government diverting enormous resources to the sector.
62 Pérez-Stable, 104.
63 Ibid.

Castro was weakened politically[64] and offered to give up his position. At the First Congress of the PCC in 1975, the moral policies of the 1960s were labeled as "idealism," "voluntarism" and "extremism," lumping together the Revolutionary Offensive and policies that had been defended by Che Guevara between 1963 and 1965.[65]

Various interview subjects, though again mostly academics, refer to internal conflicts among Cuban revolutionaries regarding both the relationship with the USSR and different conceptions of socialism and furthermore dissociate Fidel Castro from the USSR in stating that he tried to avoid excessive influence from the pro-Soviet factions. They emphasize that many former PSP members pushed for a closer relationship with Moscow. On the other hand, some mention the Department of Philosophy at the University of Havana and its journal *Pensamiento Crítico* as examples of a more independent-minded tendency. This magazine belonged to the radical anti-imperialist left but was ideologically independent of the USSR.[66]

Conflicts erupted at various moments in which former members of the PSP were involved. After 1959, there were attempts to unite the forces that had supported the Revolution in a single organization, and in a first phase, this new party under construction was called the Integrated Revolutionary Organizations. In 1961, in the midst of a struggle for internal control, the former PSP leader Aníbal Escalante was appointed as the coordinator of the ORI. As we recall, this was the first organization established to unite the revolutionary forces (M-26, PSP, and the smaller DRE), and Escalante gained high visibility in Cuban politics but was severely criticized by Fidel Castro in 1962 and accused of sectarianism.[67] A few years later, at the beginning of 1968, the authorities accused a group of people they labeled the "Micro-faction" of being counter-revolutionaries. According to Habel, who relies on Carlos Franqui,[68] this is a group covertly organized by the KGB, composed of former members of the

---

64 Habel, 50.
65 This despite the fact that Guevara was opposed to the immediate nationalization of small businesses and had defended a certain wage hierarchy. Ibid., 47–48.
66 According to informant Aurelio, Department of Philosophy at the University of Havana, which was publishing *Pensamiento Crítico* ("Critical thinking"), had theoretical differences with the USSR. These had to do mainly "with theoretical aspects, and less with whether the Soviet model was efficient or not efficient, sustainable or not sustainable."
67 Also, in 1964, Cuban authorities accused former PSP militant Marcos Rodríguez of having collaborated with Batista's police back in 1957, contributing to the killings of four activists from the Directorio Estudiantil. This created a less favorable political environment for former PSP members.
68 A former Fidel Castro collaborator who later broke ranks with the government and went into exile.

Popular Socialist Party, to "eliminate" Fidel Castro.[69] The main figures were subjected to summary trials and received long sentences of imprisonment.

It should be noted that the people who had belonged to the PSP enjoyed a certain goodwill from the USSR. Alvarez suggests that despite their contradictions with Fidel Castro's movement and his government policies, former members of the old Communist Party had a point in their favor in this context: "They were, we could say, the intellectuals of communism, because in Cuba we had no history of this kind [in the construction of socialism]." At the same time, they wanted Cuba to enter into an even greater commitment with the USSR. According to Mavis, "There was a lot of pressure" from those actors. Juan argues that the USSR used the PSP and maintains that the two events mentioned in 1962 and 1968 "are two examples of the USSR's aim for internal control of the country [...]."[70]

A few months after the case of the Micro-faction, Cuban–Soviet relations were in crisis, and Cuba was in a position of weakness. This was partly because the economy was in a bad state, and the Latin American guerrillas were failing. Fidel Castro publicly supported the Soviet invasion of Czechoslovakia in August 1968.[71] Esteban argues that "The process in Czechoslovakia was considered

---

69   Habel, 72.
70   In the Cuban historiography, the PSP has often been a sort of scapegoat for problems and the decision by the leadership to apply policies that were later deemed as negative (as they were typically the ones most strongly defending whatever came from the USSR). Although my informants did not attack the PSP but talked about them in a respectful manner, neither did any dedicate energy to defending aspects of the "old communists'" activities. Some informants gave the ex-PSP members some of the blame for Cuba's increasing dependence on the USSR and the adoption of policies similar to the USSR in the 1970s, and while it is certainly true that they had pro-Soviet ideas, the old PSP members had also questioned some of Fidel Castro's policies in the late 1960s, policies that eventually ended in economic crisis and isolation, thus constricting Cuba's space for movement and perhaps strengthening the need to move into a close compromise with the USSR. Some informants might subtly have tried to suggest this, but generally they present Fidel Castro as a guarantor of Cuba's independence, while some of his policies that were intentioned to distance Cuba from the Soviet Union might have brought the opposite result.
71   Cole Blasier has argued that the USSR cut off the oil supply in 1968 to coerce Cuba. See: Blasier, 60. However, according to Bain, such a decrease in oil supply never occurred, and the shortage of the product at that time was rather due to an increase in consumption that exceeded the annual increase in supply. For Bain, Cuba's security situation is a key to understanding the decision to support the invasion of Czechoslovakia. Fidel Castro used that opportunity to ask rhetorically if the USSR was also going to defend Vietnam, North Korea, and Cuba in case Socialism was threatened there. Bain also quotes Peter Shearman, who argues that Fidel Castro saw events such as the Prague Spring as dangerous for the Socialist Bloc. See: Peter Shearman, *The Soviet Union and Cuba* (Routledge & Kegan Paul, 1987). In Bain, 24–25.

[by the Cuban government] as a counterrevolutionary process led by imperialism with the aim to separate Czechoslovakia from the Socialist Camp." Despite this decision, as we have seen, there were very considerable disagreements with the USSR during the 1960s.

The magazine or journal *Pensamiento Crítico* is mentioned by some informants as another example of the high degree of independence that Cuba had in the 1960s, since the government allowed it to circulate widely even though it took a different stance than that of the Soviet Union. Of those interviewed, Jorge and Aurelio were part of the journal's editorial team. Jorge especially characterizes it as "a center of independent thought." According to Jorge, "that journal, the one behind that is Fidel," and argues that Fidel Castro allowed in this manner alternative socialist ideas to circulate, ideas that would be considered heretical in the Soviet Union. He also explains that through Fidel's initiative, books of French thinkers and "ecological thinkers" who had been active in the USSR in the 1920s and 1930s and with alternative ideas about socialism were published.[72]

Furthermore, people displaying critical ideas about the USSR were allowed to hold high positions. Jorge mentions as an example Raúl Roa García—a prominent member of the University Student Directorate (DEU).[73] He says that before the Cuban revolution, Raúl Roa had written critically on the Soviet model: "Roa had warned about the dangers of Russian socialism; those books were not published afterwards (after 1959), but I had them because I bought them before the Revolution in old bookstores." Yet, even if those books did not circulate through official channels after the Revolution, Raúl Roa was Minister of Foreign Affairs until 1976.[74]

---

[72] Jorge also gave us an anecdote of how Fidel Castro was careful to signal at all times that Cuba was an independent country: "Cuba had difficulties buying airplanes, so it had to rent airplanes from the USSR. But since we were not able to buy them, the Cubana (state civil airline company) planes said *Cubana de Aviación* on one side, and on the other they said *Aeroflot*. When he learned that (…) he got annoyed because it was a question of national identity."

[73] The DEU was founded in 1927 in opposition to Gerardo Machado and dissolved in 1933; not to be confused with the Revolutionary Student Directorate (DRE), which was founded in 1954.

[74] Seeing how some respondents spend considerable time highlighting differences between Cuba and the USSR during the 1960s, it is striking that no one mentions "The Great Debate" of 1962/3–1965. The two most prominent participants in that debate were Ernesto "Che" Guevara (who came from the M-26) and Carlos Rafael Rodríguez (who came from the PSP). They differed, among other topics, on the use of material incentives to stimulate production. Rodríguez opted for a position close to that of the USSR during Khrushchev; this has been named the "orthodox" position. This foresaw a slower transition toward

By the early 1970s, few if any public spaces remained for thought critical of Soviet ideology. Notably, the journal *Pensamiento Crítico* was closed—"for State reasons" according to Jorge—by the same authorities that had previously supported its creation, in 1972, with the closing of the Department of Philosophy at the University of Havana. From this moment, Cuba engaged in a stronger commitment to the policies of the USSR.[75]

Many interview subjects again argue that this was done largely out of necessity, implying that it was not seen as an ideal solution.

1.4   Cuba in the Socialist Community: "It Was Not David and Goliath"

It should be recalled that in 1972, Cuba entered the Council for Mutual Economic Assistance (Comecon), the international organization for economic cooperation led by the USSR. A very close relationship developed between the states, and the tensions that were present in the 1960s were greatly reduced or disappeared. The interview subjects with more interest and knowledge of the Cuban–Soviet relations mention this closer relationship. Some interview subjects emphasize everything that was copied from the USSR at this stage, especially in internal policies. The predominant narrative is nevertheless that despite narrower relations, Cuba preserved a certain or even large degree of political independence and even influenced Soviet policies.

Three interview subjects try to explain why such an approach occurred (Pedro, Aurelio, and Juan), and they all present it as a product of necessity, rather than of desire. Pedro says that in the late 1960s, "We didn't have relations with any country in Latin America and practically not with some countries in Europe. At that time, we had relations with the socialist countries but at a very low level." As an example, he mentions the flight connections from Cuba: "You had to go to Prague, to travel to Lima, or to travel to Panama, or to travel to Argentina or any country in Latin America." He believes that "this was creating a

---

socialism, where one could use material incentives in production as a means of achieving growth and development. Guevara had a more radical stance, emphasizing the creation of socialist values; employing what he saw as capitalist methods would impede such a development. Famously, he warned against using "the blunted weapons left to us by capitalism."

75   Several informants reminded us that Cuba found itself at that moment in a situation of weakness. By the late 1960s, the guerrilla struggle supported and promoted by Cuba had not yielded results. Mervyn Bain states that the failure of the armed struggle was underlined by the election of the socialist Salvador Allende in Chile (1970), which seemed to show that the line of peaceful coexistence promoted by the Soviets was a viable one; at least until Augusto Pinochet's coup in 1973 (p. 25).

situation in which Cuba had to make a decision [...]. The decision was to develop our relations with the Soviet Union."

This description contrasts with that of Aurelio, who places emphasis on the internal causes: "After the failure of the Ten Million Ton Sugar Harvest and failure in general of the Cuban economy to forge its way to become sustainable at a minimum [level], Cuba had to request entry to Comecon." But there were also some leaders of the country for whom such an approach has proven desirable: "The previous leaders of the old communist party, were, we could say, completely pro-Soviet, pro-Soviet in a way that they perceived the Soviet system as, although not necessarily the perfect expression, the only valid one for socialist organization."

Aurelio thus distinguishes between a part of the country's leadership that accepted to enter Comecon by necessity, although it was not the most desirable, and another part that similarly considered this decision as a necessity but also as something desirable.[76] Although the relationship between the two countries was strengthened, this does not mean that the Cuban–Soviet relationship became like that between a patron and a client, as per the account of the interview subjects. Some metaphors playing on family relations appear in the interviews that can give an idea of what the interview subjects think about the matter.

Héctor describes the relationship as like that between two brothers: "It never felt like we were a satellite of the Soviet Union, that is a very important aspect. Our relations were *de tú a tú,* as we say here in Cuba,[77] from equal to equal, you are very big, and we are small, but it was not David and Goliath, no, no, it was the big brother with the little brother, but each brother with his own opinion, his own ideas and each brother with his own girlfriend." On the other hand, Mery, who worked at a radio station when the USSR fell, says that "we had the Soviet Union there as the mother, the motherland." Norma surprises by saying that the USSR was like "a son of Cuba, a brother of Cuba," that is, she reverses the most common image of Cuba as a child of the USSR, although being a son in this context could simply mean that they had a loving relationship and not that Cuba was the part that would guide the relationship. Even so, perhaps the comment reflects an idea that Cuba, at various times, was the force that was pushing the USSR, despite its size.

---

76   Aurelio was clearly critical of developments in the 1970s. He stated that the 1960s were "'the freshest' years of the Revolution; they were bolder, more diverse. This does not mean that no arbitrary acts were committed; arbitrary acts were committed, but there was also greater diversity."
77   Roughly, frank and on an equal level.

For the most part, the interview subjects seem to recognize that there was a very large flow of economic and material resources from the USSR to Cuba. One of my interview subjects, the economist Esteban, even says that "[it] was a subsidy, really, like a subsidy." But not everyone has this perspective. According to Héctor, one can speak of mutual aid, as suggested by the name of Comecon (Council of *Mutual* Economic *Assistance* [emphasis in italics added]). He states that "[r]egardless of them helping us, we also to a large extent helped the Soviets in many ways." Then he gives examples of how Cuba helped the USSR after the Chernobyl accident, receiving thousands of children for treatment, and how the country sent blood after the earthquake in Armenia in 1988. Lenin explains that "[m]any people said that the Soviet Union helped us due to the sugar," but rejects that position, "not at all, not at all, not at all, we are grateful to the Soviet Union." Although he seems to view the USSR as a country in solidarity, his response also makes it clear that there were people in Cuba who saw the USSR as the part that benefited, despite the fact that the price it paid for Cuban sugar was far above the market price.

When the Cuban authorities discuss the relation, they usually recognize that there was some kind of economic dependence on the USSR but deny the existence of political dependence. As an example, Marcos Portal, who served as Minister of Basic Industry in Cuba in the years of the Special Period, received the following comment from the interviewer in an interview with Contrapunto:[78] "But there was dependency [talking about Cuba and the USSR]." He responds: "Not with regard to politics."[79] My interview subject Aurelio, however, finds that the accession to Comecon not only brought more "intensity" to the relations and an economic dependency, but also some degree of political dependency. He mentions commitments to vote with the USSR in international bodies.

Víctor, speaking of the Collapse, argues that "We couldn't be—to a large extent—a dependency of that country [...] to the extent that we were ideological[ly], we liberated ourselves from that tutelage."

During the interviews, information is mentioned that would indicate that Cuba took, at different times, initiatives that were then followed by the Soviets.

---

[78] This was a magazine published in Miami on Cuban topics. Unfortunately, I have no more data on the source as I have only a few photocopied pages of an edition of the magazine, dated 1993.

[79] In our view, this idea that one can completely separate the topics of economic dependence from political dependence is something like partial truth, since economic dependence tends to impose certain limits on what political decisions one can actually take.

José Luis comments that Cuba had different positions to those of the USSR from the early 1960s to Perestroika (1985–1991). He gives several examples, one of them from the 1970s: "Cuba's support for the liberation movements [...] was not the Soviet position, it was Cuba's own position, that of Angola, Namibia, South Africa, all those countries." The Cuban military operation in Angola is also mentioned by Juan, Esteban, and José in the interviews as an example of a Cuban initiative, although the Soviets joined later. Juan states that by involving itself in Angola, Cuba not only showed an independent foreign policy but possibly managed to pressure the Soviet Union to commit and take part in this African conflict. This would give some support to the image that Norma used with regard to the USSR as the "son" or at least "brother" of Cuba, despite its size and the fact that the Cuban Revolution emerged much later than the Russian.

Even so, the idea that Cuba is sometimes the part that takes the initiative can be located in academic literature. Jorge Domínguez speaks of a "Soviet hegemony with a degree of Cuban autonomy" in the 1970s and 1980s[80] and states that it is assumed "above all that Cuba accepts the limits imposed by the Soviet Union on its foreign policy."[81] But he also maintains that Cuba played a leading role, just as much as an intermediary role, between the USSR and progressive movements in the Third World.[82] He maintains that in the 1960s, Cuba sometimes depreciated, and publicly criticized, the Soviet position with regard to revolutionaries "in the Americas and beyond," and that this led to what he calls "the Cuban–Soviet crisis of 1967–68."[83] From the 1970s, "Cuba would no longer publicly criticize the Soviet Union or its allies, even if they did not follow Cuba's leadership,"[84] and more care was taken in order not to generate a crisis. However, Cuba continued to play a leading role in 1975 and 1976 in Angola, "and then in Central America and the Caribbean."[85]

With regard to Angola, researcher Piero Gleijeses has undertaken extensive research in archives and conducted interviews with key actors in Cuba and the USSR. These confirm the claims of the interview subjects that Cuba did take the initiative of sending troops to that African country in November 1975 after the South African invasion, without the consent of the USSR.[86]

---

80 Domínguez, *La política exterior de Cuba (1962–2009)*, 242.
81 Ibid.
82 Ibid., 253.
83 Ibid.
84 Ibid.
85 Ibid., 254.
86 Piero Gleijeses, *Conflicting Missions: Havana, Washington, and Africa, 1959–1976* (Chapel Hill: University of North Carolina Press, 2002).

Such an influence by a small country on a world power may seem strange and even unlikely. In this sense, it should be remembered that Cuba was very important for the Soviets, more than the country's size could indicate. When the USSR achieved close relations with Cuba from 1959, this represented a "spectacular propaganda success" for Moscow[87] at a time when the Cold War was "at its height."[88] According to Blasier, Moscow considered Cuba one of its "political triumphs" after World War II.[89] Similarly, after Stalin's death, the USSR started looking more outwards, and post-WWII decolonization made it look for opportunities to have a presence in the developing world.[90]

The geographical position of Cuba and its anti-imperialist attitude served as the main reasons for this interest.[91] As Aurelio put it, "Cuba meant [...] a spearhead in the backyard of the United States, the rest of Latin America." The symbolic value of the Cuban Revolution was furthermore of great importance. Eliécer believes that Cuba "was the first socialist country in America that brought socialism to all of America." According to Esteban, "We also represented the possibility that the USSR could show a face in America, right? [...] besides, Cuba was the only socialist country in this entire hemisphere, including Africa, so it means that it had a very important meaning; it also represented a concern for the North Americans [...], [and] that psychologically also had an impact from the Soviets' political point of view."

This, and other factors, implied that there was counter dependency, and several of the interviewees stress this point. Juan argues that when "the Latin American guerrilla movement fails" in the early 1970s, "the Soviets could take a breath of relief." But the operation that Cuba started in Angola later revived this conflict. He considers the operation in Angola not only an example of Cuba's independent foreign policy but also of a situation in which Cuba managed to impose its policy on the USSR, following a tactic of Che Guevara: "Cuba's international leadership, totally disproportionate as to size, population, medical power, had in my opinion the dual purpose of challenging the United States in several arenas, a bit like the Guevarista thesis of [creating] many Vietnams

---

87   Bain, 18.
88   Ibid.
89   Blasier, 59.
90   Bain, 18–19.
91   Ibid., 19; Blasier, 60.

and committing the Soviets, dragging the Soviets to revolutionary, radical, anti-colonialist commitments in the region, right? Something that Cuba achieves, both challenging the United States and committing the Soviets."[92]

That being said, my interview subjects tend to emphasize Cuban autonomy and the leading role that Cuba assumed at different times but not the limits or times when Cuba followed the position of the USSR. For example, it is correct that Cuba plays an important role in the Third World with its leadership in the Non-Aligned Movement (NAM), but by the 1980s, the country was also "an integral part of the socialist community" and voted with the Soviet Union in international bodies. According to Erisman, when the Soviet invasion took place in Afghanistan, Cuba was the only NAM country that opted for a supportive position.[93] Nevertheless, when characterizing the bilateral relations, the differences did not cease to be real and important, as seen in the examples of independence mentioned by the interview subjects.

Another issue is the internal impact of the closer relations with the Soviets in the 1970s. According to Cuban researcher Hiram Marquetti Nodarse, Cuba's accession to Comecon forced the country to "find formulas that aligned us with those used by the remaining members of this organization. This situation resulted in the adoption of the more general aspects of the economic model in force in those countries, first and foremost the Soviet one."[94]

Similarly, my interview subject Mery believes that "A model was being copied that had nothing to do with ours" and argues that "even the buildings were

---

92 Informant Mavis understands the Cuban presence in Angola as part of a joint Cuba–Soviet action, and claims that there was no political discrepancy. "No, it is not that there was a discrepancy, it was a joint action of Cuba and the Soviet Union, they put the weapons, they guaranteed all weapons for the liberation war of Angola, Namibia and (...) it was intended to continue for South Africa (...) but they did not intervene, they did not put a Soviet–Russian soldier in Africa, we put the people."

93 Erisman, in Bain, 30.

94 Hiram Marquetti Nodarse, "La crisis del socialismo en la URSS y Europa Oriental: Implicaciones para Cuba," in *El derrumbe del modelo eurosoviético: Una visión desde Cuba*, ed. Román García Báez (Havana: Felix Varela, 1994), 151. Actually, the process of adopting Soviet experiences began in the 1960s, although more timidly and not systematically. Our informant Mavis says that in the 1960s she had to "learn what the Soviet rural development model was about and then work in Cuba to apply it, to do it, to install it." She is critical of the tendency there was to copy policies and practices uncritically, and states that "A work regime was established (in Cuba) that had nothing to do with the country's agrarian culture." Víctor also expressed criticisms of the centralized agricultural model installed at the time, which was inspired by Soviet and Eastern European socialism: "People did want the land, there was *Realengo 18* [a prolonged peasant struggle in Cuba during the Protectorate years] [...], they wanted the land and you cannot impose collectivization [...]."

of the Russian model, schools, the design [...] everything, everything, was a carbon copy," although she asserts that this started to change with the Rectification Process. Héctor pointed out that the health system was different and uniquely Cuban. Aurelio argues that there was a strong Soviet influence in general and suggests that it was very negative, saying that the Cuban institutionality was placed "under [...] the shadow of Stalinism, neo-Stalinism." According to Pedro, "The socialist model that we introduced in Cuba was in a certain way [...] a model taken from the Soviet Union," although he later mentions some differences, to which I will return later.

My interview subject Mavis refers at one point to the country's development model as "the copy," but she does not seem to have the same opinion about the political system, as she denies that the one-party model of the USSR was copied. She maintains that in Cuba there are mass organizations that resemble political parties. As an example, she points to the National Association of Small Farmers (ANAP) and states that "It is a party, but it is not called a party, however, it is a party," and argues that "that social framework is the work of Fidel, that did not exist in the Soviet Union, it is not a copy of the CPSU, that is the work of the Revolution." Although there were also mass organizations in the USSR that seemed similar in many senses to those in Cuba, it is possible that their functioning and role were somewhat different.

Peter Roman, referring to the creation of the electoral system—one where people vote for individual candidates rather than parties—states that a team was created in Cuba to study local governmental institutions in both socialist and capitalist societies (including Detroit).[95] In the Popular Power system

---

[95] The word Stalinism, used by several of my informants, can have slightly different meanings. According to *Encyclopædia Britannica*, for instance, it refers to "the method of rule, or policies, of Joseph Stalin, Soviet Communist Party and state leader from 1929 until his death in 1953." The encyclopedia states that "Stalinism is associated with a regime of terror and totalitarian rule." Our informant Aurelio uses both the word "Stalinism" and "Neo-Stalinism" to refer to the Cuban political and economic institutions that were introduced in the 1970s and that are still in place, although these have undergone changes. He calls this "[...] the institutionalism that had been approved under (...) the shadow of Stalinism, of neo-Stalinism," seemingly using "neo-Stalinism" as a term to describe the renewed Soviet model after Joseph Stalin's death even after Nikita Khrushchev had reformed this, and it was not characterized by the mass terror of the Stalin years. Aurelio uses the word to describe the current state of affairs in Cuba, and says that the Cuban state "continues to tend toward Stalinism, distributive Stalinism I mean, the Stalinist regime as a way of ... (it tends) toward the style of Stalinism." Esteban uses the word "Stalinist" when he refers to Polish leader W. Jaruzelski, saying he was "overbearing, a militarist, a Stalinist." Here he seems to be referring to a certain authoritarian style of governing, and possibly the leader's ideology, more than the specific methods (although some might be similar to Stalin's). The word is clearly meant as derogatory.

established at the local, provincial, and national levels in 1976, however, much was taken from the political system of the USSR, such as, in the words of Roman, "the mandate system and delegate recall, representatives who are not professional politicians, the structure of the assemblies, and the Communist Party in both instances having the primary role in policymaking."[96] He also emphasizes the Cuban model was significantly different in other aspects but mainly at the local level, where the voters themselves (not the PCC) were put in charge of nominating delegates and a model of competitive elections was installed. According to the law, there must be more than one candidate (in the USSR there was only one candidate)[97]—although election campaigns are not allowed. Unlike in the USSR, the locally elected representatives have to reside in the municipality where they were elected, which has "served to increase the esteem in which local government is held by the people and to strengthen the bonds between Cuban delegates and constituents."[98] There was also some degree of separation between the local Party branches and the municipal parliaments.

Still, the nomination of delegates for provincial assemblies and for the National Assembly was more similar to the system in the USSR, with no direct participation by the voters in the nomination, while the distinction between representative bodies and the PCC is less clear.[99] Since the 1992 Constitution and Electoral Law, the Party no longer has any formal role in the nomination process for the National Assembly (and the Provincial Assemblies), unlike the USSR.[100] The National Assembly is composed mainly of people who are also members of the Communist Party, and the reforms did not change the general functioning or role of the National Assembly. There was and is no residency requirement and many do not know who their representatives are.[101]

Members of the National Assembly sometimes feared expressing their opinions because they are elected as individuals without an independent support base.[102] The national parliament, according to Roman, "is still more a responsive body rather than one that takes independent initiatives."[103] My informant

---

96   Ibid., 244–245.
97   Ibid.
98   Ibid.
99   Ibid.
100   Ibid., 244–245.
101   Ibid., 244–245.
102   Ibid.
103   Ibid. The reader interested in learning more on these topics might be interested in having a look at Peter Roman's book. Also, Larry Catá Backer has made valuable contributions. In his blog, he gives a detailed and analytical look at the development in Cuba of a "Socialist Democracy 1.0" (in the 1970s), and later a "Socialist Consultative Democracy 2.0" (from 2008 onwards). See, for example: "Communist Party and Asamblea Nacional–Popular

Víctor praised the Cuban electoral system: "[I]n the world there are no elections that are more democratic than here." But he also seemingly acknowledged that there has existed or exists some kind of external pressure or incentive to vote, as in the USSR: "[E]verybody votes, everybody votes but if you don't vote, what will happen to you? I will be honest with you, and I say it up front, because you don't know if someone votes because he wants to or doesn't want to, it's a bit of a social construction (the informant might here be suggesting social pressure and a sense of duty)."

Another difference mentioned by at least one interview subject is the existence of the Committees for the Defense of the Revolution (CDR), which are present in each neighborhood in Cuba. Esteban states that "As far as I know, an organization that fulfills the functions of the CDRs did not exist in any country in Europe," when talking about the organization that emerged in the early 1960s and that has remained in force since then. The historian Antoni Kapcia describes the CDRs and the rest of the revolutionary civil society as elements that have played a role of surveillance or coercion, which in its historical moment included the persecution of long-haired youth.[104] But at the same time, he emphasizes that the CDRs provided a platform for the population to express their demands,[105] and the government used to listen more to its bases (formally and informally) than what was common in Eastern Europe.[106]

Víctor claimed that "We did discuss the constitution," seemingly in reference to the constitution that was implemented in 1976, and that has since then been revised twice.[107] He refers, I believe, to a debate on a proposed constitution that began in February 1975 at the local branches of the Communist Party, as well as in neighborhoods, workplaces, and educational centers, and so on, and which lasted for two months.[108] Thus, he suggests that, according to his perception, there was an attempt to involve the population in the creation of an authentically Cuban system.

Several of the interview subjects talked about the particularities of the PCC compared to ruling parties in the Soviet Union and Eastern Europe. Pedro, for example, reminds us that "the very system of how the Party worked has also been different from that of the socialist countries." This was reflected on earlier

---

Representation in the Shadow of Democratic Centralism in Cuban Socialist Democracy 1.0," http://lcbackerblog.blogspot.com/2019/03/part-10-communist-party-and-asamblea.html.

104   Kapcia, 134.
105   Ibid.
106   Ibid.
107   It was, in 2019, replaced by a new Constitution after a popular consultation and referendum.
108   Roman, 70.

ANALYSIS OF THE INTERVIEWS

in Chapter 5 of the present work in a background discussion of the Party and its role in society.

Although we have seen that the Cuban media had its peculiarities, Víctor emphasizes its centralization as a negative feature and attributes this to the Soviet influence. When conducting the interview, we were in the *Granma* building at the Plaza de la Revolución, where the main newspapers of the country are located. There he stated: "[W]e copied [...] many Soviet things, look, this very building is a negative copy of that grandiose vision of the Soviet Union, because the newspapers in Cuba, the media, all were, had their own [separate] building."

Whether all the differences cited are substantive or secondary issues could be a matter of dispute. Both Cuba and the USSR had a one-party model with a centralized planned economy. That is, were the differences more significant than the similarities? The general tendency among my interview subjects lies in emphasizing the differences, but there are great similarities that receive little emphasis in the interviews, despite examples such as the one given by Víctor, on the media. Even so, the differences they cite are significant because they show that the Cuban process preserved a degree of autonomy and that there was some level of popular participation, regardless of everything that was *not* decided democratically and everything that was brought from outside.

When respondents mention the years after Cuba entered Comecon, they often do so in relation to Cuba's economic situation. That is, the USSR is associated with something positive, with the relative well-being that existed in Cuba in the late 1970s and especially in the 1980s.[109] This can also influence their perception of the Collapse. As Lenin asserts, the growth in trade and the Soviet aid did not have an immediate effect but rather started producing results toward the 1980s:

> Ten years in which Cuba was rich was from [19]80 to [19]90 when everything was available, everything ... and with a minimum salary of 81, of 95,

---

109   US pressure on Cuba also decreased somewhat during the 1970s. After the failure of the US wars in South-East Asia, the superpower started looking more toward itself; this was accentuated by the resignation of Richard Nixon as a product of the Watergate scandal in August 1974. Thus, the threat of a US invasion was reduced, although when Ronald Reagan came to power in January 1981, the Cold War again intensified and Cuban–American relations got worse again. For Ward, the Reagan administration prioritized a "world-wide struggle against Soviet communism" and showed a "renewed warmth" toward Latin American military dictatorships. One point of tension was Nicaragua after the Revolution of 1979. There, the Cubans actively supported the Sandinista movement that took power, while the US financed what John Ward describes as an "obsessive campaign" against the government. See: Ward, 37.

of 118 [pesos] we lived, rich, oh and on the contrary, so that you get the idea, from [19]70 to [19]80 we were experiencing a crisis [...] a box of cigars on the black market had a cost of ninety pesos, the bottle of rum was eighty, is it a lie? Let them tell me, in the years of 70, 71, and 72 [that is, the years of crisis before entering Comecon].

Zenaida argues that in the good years, "Cuba was the same [as the industrialized socialist countries], one went to the markets and there was everything, as it was supplied by the Soviet Union [...] it was later that we worsened, at the time of the fall of the Soviet Union." Eliécer says that "We got used to a very large pipeline compensated by Comecon [...] and really our country was wonderful, and it was wonderful [...] a stage in which you, with a little bit of money, went anywhere, could be anywhere, had a life ..." He states that of the various stages he has lived in Cuba, "from capitalism until now," that one was the "most beautiful" and mentions that there were few social differences and little racism.

Not much is mentioned about material problems in the 1980s, although Eliécer mentions housing: "[A]t that time the only problem I had was the problem of housing, because that has always been a problem that we have been dragging along."[110] Mery adds that "[t]hings were not developed with those gains and with those resources that we had available, because there was perhaps no vision of the future, 'well this is not going to be eternal, we are going to'... and I think [the support] was used for other things that didn't, that didn't, didn't work out."

There was also a Soviet cultural influence, but it did not have much impact on the lives of the interview subjects (and, evidently, little on Cubans in general; I am of course referring to cultural influence in a more restricted sense, and not to Soviet influence on politics and economy). It is important to remember that most Cubans could not easily interact with the Soviets. Not only because of the distance but also because of the language, which naturally

---

110   In the late 1970s and especially during the 1980–1985 period, Cuban–Soviet trade increased. Bain states that by the mid-1980s, relations were "very healthy" and also "extremely expansive and" of an "all-encompassing nature" (p. 31). Each year, 8,000 Cubans studied in the USSR and that country had helped open 140 education centers in Cuba. Trade was a central part of relations, and Cuba had achieved high growth by selling sugar to the USSR, which the USSR paid for at above world market prices. The average had been 11 and 2 times the price, states Bain, "but in 1985 it bought 61 percent of the Cuban sugar harvest at a price in excess of ten times that of the world price. This jump in prices being paid, explains the increase in Cuba–Soviet trade during the 1980s. Cuba sent nickel, citrus, and tobacco, and imported 50 different products from the Soviet Union." See: Bain, 31–32.

limited the exchange of ideas. Idulberto explains that at the beginning of the relations

> We didn't have the slightest idea of speaking Russian. We worked with an interpreter who was a white Russian, who had come from Russia during communism and had become an electrician on Zanja Street, who spoke Russian from that era, he knew nothing about aviation, he was called Constantin, to the point where the translations were horrifying, to understand them, it could only be understood from technician to technician, what he said was 'the red cap smeared with fat' [imitating way of talking], and things like that, back and forth as lightning.

Mery, who is younger, indicates Russian language education specifically as an example of Soviet influence in Cuba. But this influence comes later: "[W]hen I entered to do a degree, the language that had been studied before I entered the year 70 [then says she thinks it was in 1976] and that was English, when I entered they tell me: it's Russian." But although Russian was the second language in schools, this did not last for too many years, and there was no Russification of the culture as such. In Eastern Europe and in the Soviet republics (outside of Russia), people might have felt that their national culture was threatened by the Russians. Víctor mentioned that someone told him during a visit to Hungary, seemingly with reference to the policy of changing the names of streets, places, and so on: "[L]ook at that street, they did not take your Martí away, but from us they took away our national leaders."

Although there was no Russification policy as such, Alberto mentions a situation in which there were internal differences in Cuba about the teaching of Russian teachers who worked in the country: "Russian music teachers were introduced in Cuba and began to direct the music in a way that no longer was exactly the way in which I understood that it should be directed." According to Alberto, there was always a conflict in Cuba between people with "Eurocentric" ideas that preferred what came from the north, be it from Western Europe, the USSR, or the United States ("the largest branch of Europe in America," he argues). On the other hand, there were people with a more anti-hegemonic, Latin American, and/or nationalist perspective.

Rather than involving the introduction of a foreign culture, Alberto claims that the Cuban Revolution gave more space to a certain part of Cuban culture. In this sense, he argues that "the Cuban Revolution opened an enormous space for struggle based on the fundamental values in the culture of ordinary people, to call it that." Although limitations were placed on the exercise of Christianity and perhaps especially Catholicism during one stage of the Revolution, the situation for Afro-Cuban beliefs and traditions was reversed, Alberto states. These traditions had been looked down on by high society before 1959, and were, according to him, more accepted after the Revolution: "[P]eople enjoy it when they suddenly find themselves without prejudice at a rumba dance, when they don't hide anymore, they don't hide the *Santeria* necklaces, you know? Because people in Cuba hid those things before, the necklaces and people became a *santo* in silence, you know?"

According to Jorge, "Soviet influence raised our standard of living, but it impoverished our spiritual life." Nevertheless, he finds that there were spheres of cultural life that were not like that, "not in the theater, because the Soviet theater and formation of Soviet actors was very good [...] that is what explains why we have such a high level of theater, a level of excellent young actors." In his view, "Where the Soviet influence did the most damage was in social thinking, that there were restrictions and Soviet thought could not be criticized, nor could there be criticism of literature." He maintains that the Marxism that arrived in Cuba "was not the true Marxism, it was Soviet Marxism." He also offers some examples of how dogmatic and restrictive it was by mentioning that in 1977 "the school of Psychology, of Sociology" was eliminated from the university where he worked, an act inspired by the Soviets who had eliminated sociology a few decades earlier. "We believed at that time that scientific communism would solve everything," he explains.

Víctor says that the cultural policy was more permissive than the Soviet one, especially in comparison with that under Stalin but also compared to later periods. By this he refers to the controversial phrase of Fidel Castro in his meetings with Cuban intellectuals in June 1961 ("Within the Revolution, everything—against the Revolution, nothing").[111] Víctor seems to interpret the phrase as a way of allowing, rather than restricting, cultural expressions, although it implies that counterrevolutionary expressions will not be allowed.

Referring to the Soviets, he says that "They killed their intellectuals, because when they were not kicked out [of the country] like Kandinsky and Chagall, they were killed in concentration camps or led to suicide like Yesenin and Mayakovski because they did not understand, because also, the artist you have to deal with him differently." He contrasts this with the case of Cuba, where official policy suggested that an artist could not oppose the Revolution but could nevertheless choose style and themes within that framework: "Look at that

---

111   Fidel Castro, "Discurso pronunciado por el Comandante Fidel Castro Ruz [...] Como conclusión de las reuniones con los intelectuales cubanos, efectuadas en la Biblioteca Nacional el 16, 23 y 30 de Junio de 1961," http://www.cuba.cu/gobierno/discursos/1959/esp/c160259e.html.

difference with Fidel meeting with them saying that against the Revolution nothing, but the guy could paint what he wanted, not only paint militias, that is."

According to Esteban, "You do not see the Russian influence anywhere [in Cuba], because there was no cultural influence. North American, yes, the North American influence is very strong, historically it has been very strong." Esteban seems to consider the Russian cultural influence as having been brief. This seems to contradict what Jorge raises with regard to the influence in the theater, although it may be that the phrase "you do not see the Russian influence anywhere" is meant as an exaggeration, as there are traces, as in the example of the theater.

This type of position could be questioned. Jacqueline Loss mentions a series of examples of this cultural contact, as well as an influence in the areas of ballet, sport, language, and so on. She argues that when the Soviet Union fell, many Cubans claimed to have inherited "next to nothing" from the Soviet Union[112] and even blamed "the Revolution's most repressive measures" on that influence.[113] Loss questions this attitude, although Cubans "traditionally, socially and culturally identify with the West."[114] She argues that there were points of connection and that there are still remnants of Soviet influence, not only in the economy and politics but also in culture. A figure that can support her argument comes from Richard Gott, who argues that in 1997 there were 300,000 Cubans who spoke Russian fluently.[115]

There clearly was, as Loss argues, some Soviet influence on the cultural level. But it is no less true, as some interview subjects argue that these influences were limited by a number of factors: geographical distance, different languages, cultural identification with the West, and Cuban cultural policy. The fact that the period with the strongest Soviet influence in Cuba did not last that many years can also be added.

---

112 Loss, 2.
113 Ibid.
114 Ibid., 17. Loss refers to former Cuban Culture Minister Abel Prieto and asserts that Prieto wrote that Cubans saw themselves as at least "aesthetically and sentimentally" superior to the Russian. She also quotes Prieto, as he claims that there were no hard feelings toward Russians as they were not colonizers (p. 3–4). Prieto wrote a book on the crisis of "real socialism" that was published "the same year he became Minister of Culture in Cuba." See: Abel Prieto, *El humor de Misha: La crisis del "socialismo real" en el chiste político* (Buenos Aires: Ediciones Colihue, 1997). For Loss, this is a way of Prieto distancing himself from the Soviet Union: "It is as if Prieto were ensuring his readers that Cubans are onlookers, rather than direct victims—that they are far removed from the sort of oppressive experience that evoked such a humoristic response" (ibid., 3).
115 Gott, 319.

1.5 Allies Drifting Apart: "We Built an Alternative Discourse"

It is in the 1980s that the first signs of increasing distance between Cuba and the USSR can be noted. My interview subjects perceive the Rectification Process launched by Fidel Castro in 1986 as a sign of the independence of Cuba, as well as an attempt to move away from the path that the USSR decided to follow, without jeopardizing bilateral relations.[116] The first clear signal of one part distancing itself appeared in 1982—when Soviet leader Yuri Andropov informed Cuba that the USSR would not be able to defend it in case of a military attack. Yet this was not known publicly then.

This notification must, however, have created concern among the Cuban leaders. Despite the fact that Cuban–Soviet relations were doing well at this stage, Juan assumes that the information had an impact on Cuban policies: "[T]he Soviets tell Cubans that in a conflict with the United States they cannot count on the Soviets, but this is classified information that we will not know about until the 90s." He adds that "While the entire party is not aware of that information, the leaders of the Party were, so it is implicit in its actions."

In the following years there will be other signs of a distancing when the two countries launch two political projects that go, at least in part, in opposite directions: the Soviet Perestroika, a concept introduced by Gorbachev in a party meeting on December 10, 1984 and approved by the Communist Party of the Soviet Union the following year, and the Cuban Rectification Process. However, since late 1984, Fidel Castro began to take a series of measures against the economic policy that had been implemented in Cuba until then, similar to that of the Soviet Union, through dismissing Humberto Pérez, president of the Central Planning Board. Pérez was "the main supporter of using certain market mechanisms within the context of central planning."[117] According to Domínguez, certain economic tensions arose between the countries during the brief Soviet government of Konstantin Chernenko (1984–1985),[118] but Cuba did not lose its privileged relationship with the USSR.

A feature of Cuba in the 1980s is that Fidel Castro increased his leading role in Cuban politics, promoting the policy of Rectification that marks a departure from Soviet policies, both those of Khrushchev and Brezhnev, as well as those that Gorbachev was introducing. Although one of my interview subjects emphasizes that Castro had been in a weakened position as a leader since 1970,

---

116 Events taking place from 1990, the year when Cuba officially entered into crisis, will be dealt with in the second part of this chapter.
117 Domínguez, *La política exterior de Cuba (1962–2009)*, 275. The author does not specify whether Fidel Castro began taking these measures before or after Gorbachev's speech.
118 "The Political Impact on Cuba of the Reform and Collapse of Communist Regimes," 105.

partly to the multifaceted crisis that Cuba suffered at that time, Jorge Domínguez goes as far as to argue that the regime was "depersonalized between 1965 and 1980." Independently of the exact starting point of this process and the exact degree of depersonalization that took place, Domínguez is without a doubt right to say that beginning in 1980, Cuban politics "reverted to the pattern of domination by Fidel."[119] To give an idea of the centrality of Fidel Castro in the late 1980s, it can be mentioned that when the parliament met on July 18 and 19, 1988, of a total of 204 interventions, 71 were from him. He participated in 75 out of 78 dialogues between members of parliament.[120]

The comments made by the interview subjects give an idea of the leader's popularity within the Party (and in a considerable part of the population, although I do not have exact figures). Some personal qualities that they attribute to Fidel Castro are: strength, clarity (Zenaida), vision of the future (Zenaida, Mery), being exemplary (Norma), ability to prepare the population for difficult circumstances (Eliécer), capacity to educate the people (Idulberto), very high morality (Héctor), a person who inspires a lot of confidence (Mavis, Esteban), of high intellectual and cultural knowledge (Jorge), being unbureaucratic (Esteban, Juan), and being characterized by brilliance and a natural authority (Juan).

He is credited with several specific functions besides being the *Comandante* or highest leader of the nation, mainly related to the task of guiding and educating people and changing the country: teacher/mentor (Idulberto: "After the Triumph of the Revolution, Fidel taught us to think, taught us how to analyze, taught us how to reason"), a type of liberator and savior (Idulberto: "He gave us the right to life, he gave us the right to education, he gave us the right to the most important thing, which is the right to live"), a mobilizer (Esteban: "Fidel ensured leadership in the proximity to the people, attending to the masses directly, etc."), and also, theorist, creator, and so on.[121]

---

119 "Leadership Strategies and Mass Support: Cuban Politics before and after the 1991 Communist Party Congress," in *Cuba at a Crossroads*, ed. Jorge F. Pérez-López (Florida: University Press of Florida, 1994), 2.

120 Roman, 84.

121 Criticisms are usually soft or expressed in a diplomatic manner. Víctor said, talking about Fidel Castro, that "not all is perfect, we are human beings." Jorge said that "Marx made mistakes and so what, and Fidel has made mistakes and so what, you cannot work and try to do things without committing errors." In the latter comment, Jorge recognizes Fidel Castro's errors but also places him in the same category as Marx, the father of modern communism and one of the most recognized philosophers in the world. Some of our informants mention "errors" for which Fidel Castro is fully or partly responsible—such as the persecution of homosexuals and people with long hair, erroneous economic decisions, etc. One could consider the word "error" to be a euphemism. In any case, these criticisms

With the Rectification, this leader, so admired by the informants,[122] proclaimed that it was necessary to place political work before what we might call an economistic tendency that he claimed had proliferated in the country. Thus, Rectification involved the elimination of the use of "capitalist methods," although the so-called "economic calculation" was allowed, which would still give a minimum of autonomy to state enterprises. As we have seen, the process represented a break from the previous management model that was imported from the USSR (SPDE) and that had been influenced by a more permissive Soviet pragmatism toward precisely what Cuba considered to be capitalist methods. Rectification also placed an emphasis on the people's participation in and identification with the revolutionary process, something it aimed to achieve among other ways through mobilization.[123]

Juan reminds us that "from [19]66 *El Che* was not talked about in Cuba again." With the Rectification Process, the Cuban government also points out that it wants to return to Che Guevara's ideas, who had said that "[e]conomic socialism without communist morals does not interest me. We fight against misery but at the same time we fight against alienation" (*L'Express*, July 25, 1963).

According to Habel, the Rectification Process had the *Revolutionary Offensive* of 1968–1970 as its precedent.[124] But the proposal was not a return to the extreme idealism of those years, during which, shortly after the departure and later death of Ernesto "Che" Guevara, policies were implemented that could be seen as an exaggerated variant or a caricature of some radical proposals of "El

---

do not constitute a general rejection of Fidel Castro, but rather a criticism of certain problematic actions or tendencies of his. Even so, there are comments that *could* be interpreted as indirect criticisms of his whole way of governing, for example when Aurelio—when asked about whether there was debate about political reforms around 1990—replied not very specifically that "There is in general a rejection of change, there is a fear of political change [...]," apparently referring to the political apparatus in Cuba. Since Fidel Castro was the one who was leading the country, one could say that he was also the main person responsible for promoting such change.

122 Fidel Castro, "Discurso pronunciado por el Comandante en Jefe Fidel Castro Ruz [...] en la clausura de la sesión diferida del Tercer Congreso del Partido Comunista de Cuba, 2 de diciembre de 1986," http://www.cuba.cu/gobierno/discursos/1986/esp/f021286e.html.
123 Among those informants that comment on the subject, there seems to be almost a consensus that the Process of Rectification was mainly economic (Pedro, Aurelio, Esteban, and José Luis explicitly say this). Juan, however, says that although *Rectification* was presented as an attempt to change the economy, it had as a result that Cuba "supposedly (got) a model of its own," although the changes were "actually more ideological than economic and much less political."
124 Habel, 72.

Che" for creating a new society and a new man, implementing almost overnight an economy that was to have socialist values and conscience as its engine.

My informant Juan argued that Rectification tried to merge and put into practice the thoughts of the two most important leaders of the Revolution, Fidel Castro and Ernesto Guevara: "[W]e had to invent another thing, a new thing, and as always what is invented is a mix, as happened in the 1960s, [this time it is] a blend of Fidelism and Guevarism, in 1987 [...] the Council of State publishes [Cuban academic Carlos] Tablada's book, *El pensamiento económico de Ernesto Che Guevara*."[125]

It could be added that after the book launch, Fidel Castro spoke—at the 20th anniversary of the Argentinian's death in combat—of rescuing Che's ideas. Castro recognized that Che's ideas had "been badly interpreted, and even badly applied,"[126] and sometimes one had also opted for policies totally contrary to those ideas.[127] José Luis, an economist, asserted that Rectification was an intent "to balance the economic calculation on the one hand with mechanisms of political mobilization, that is, avoiding pragmatism or extreme idealism, but making a mix [...]."

Informants disagreed on whether the Rectification was actually a response to Gorbachev's Perestroika. According to José Luis, "one thing has nothing to do with the other." The Rectification, he claimed, "has national roots, it has nothing to do with Perestroika, it coincided with Perestroika at that time, but the problems of the management and planning system that was implemented in Cuba in 1975 already had begun to cause difficulties in 1981, 1983, 1985, even before Gorbachev took over." Esteban, however, stated that the Rectification served to mark a distance from the USSR: "In reality [...] it becomes the counter-discourse of Perestroika."

Juan lays out the dilemma of the Cuban leaders: "Now after the political leadership has reached such a strong commitment to the Soviet model, how [is Cuba] to get out of it, when at that time even the Soviets are getting out of their model?" He explains that the leadership invented a model that distanced itself from the Soviet model *without* it appearing to be a critique of the USSR: "[T]he political operation that is undertaken, which Fidel Castro undertakes, with the brilliance that characterizes him, is to invent the Rectification; he doesn't

---

125 Carlos Tablada Pérez, *El pensamiento económico de Ernesto Che Guevara* (Havana: Casa de las Américas, 1987). The title means *The Economic Thought of Ernesto Che Guevara*.
126 Fidel Castro Ruz, "Discurso pronunciado por el Comandante en Jefe Fidel Castro Ruz [...] en el acto central por el XX Aniversario de la caída en combate del comandante Ernesto Che Guevara, efectuado en la ciudad de Pinar del Río, el 8 de octubre de 1987," http://www.cuba.cu/gobierno/discursos/1987/esp/f081087e.html.
127 Ibid.

speak of Perestroika at all, does not position himself against Perestroika, he agrees with the [need for] reform, so look, we were also going to create our reforms, ours are called Rectification, and we are going to rectify the Soviet model that was implemented in the economy and which is now manifesting serious limitations; we will also modify that model."

Several respondents believed that the Rectification was promising but stated that it could not be fully implemented for reasons beyond Cuba's control. In the first place, the economic situation in the mid-1980s, both in Cuba and internationally, severely limited the country's maneuvering space. Although Rectification brought the promise of a more independent socialism, economic dependency on the USSR actually increased during the years of the Rectification.

Juan explains that contradiction: "[I]nstead of what would be considered logical, to decrease our relations with the European Socialist Camp, we focus our trade with the European Socialist Camp even more, because the currency crisis of the years 84–85 does not allow us to access the world market, we have declared a moratorium, all the banks of the Paris Club suspend us [...] so we are forced to concentrate trade even more with the Socialist Camp and especially with the USSR. That goes against the grain, and we therefore built an alternative discourse, but we didn't denounce the USSR."

There can be no doubt that, beginning in 1984 approximately, there was a significant slowdown of the Cuban economy. This was due to, among other causes, low sugar prices, and later on, debt problems. According to Janette Habel, the Cuban authorities introduced some "timid" austerity measures on January 11, 1987,[128] and the author is suggesting that they might relate to the recommendation of the Paris Club the summer before to introduce austerity measures ("It is difficult not to make the connection," Habel argues).[129]

On the other hand, the Cuban government also took some actions that may have been intended to reduce dependence on the USSR over the long term. As an example, Cuba opened a major center for biotechnological research in 1986, and as of 1987, the government decided to prioritize tourism to generate foreign exchange.[130]

But above all, Rectification was affected and interrupted by the crisis and the Collapse of the USSR. Alberto asserts that "It was a very interesting process, unfortunately, unfortunately stopped by the tremendous shock from the

---

128   Habel, 65.
129   Ibid., 67.
130   María del Carmen Lloret Feijóo, Niurka Pozas Morera, and Alioska Valhuerdiz Santana, *El turismo y su incidencia en el desarrollo local de Villa Clara, Cuba* (Cuba: Juan Carlos Martínez Coll, 2007), 22.

economic blow we received when everything fell, that's why I said to you it came straight from hell [*del c... de tu madre*], because [it was] a tough economic blow, and one that changed us, it changed ... it changed overnight." According to José Luis: "The [Rectification] experiment did not turn out to be bad, what happened is that the Special Period came and all that was ... it practically had to be dismantled." Esteban expressed something similar, lamenting that "There was a separation between the Process of Rectification of errors and negative tendencies, and the process that we are going through now [...] that process should have continued until today."

Mavis considers that a Rectification did indeed take place but wonders if a rectification process was really enough in the first place. She maintains that "There was rectification, not change, neither of the system nor the structure." She states that "We were now realizing that some things we had copied from them [the Soviet Union] did not work as well here as we had thought, but we were always looking for an explanation, was it management errors, conceptual errors, lack of discipline [...] we did not go much further than that, of questioning the system itself, you know?"

Mavis refers to the model that was followed after 1989 as simply "The copy," something that Valdes Paz also expresses, although in other words: "The economic model, even after the Rectification, continued to a large extent to be the Soviet model [...], right?" Aurelio also does not seem to believe that Rectification implied a dramatic break, since he argues that "The influence of the Soviets was greater between 1972 or 1971 and 1989, approximately," that is, that the influence did not diminish in a considerable way at least during the first three years of Rectification. While Rectification may not have radically altered the model, it might have been successful in the sense of making Cubans feel more independent from the USSR, especially those who were concerned about political and theoretical issues.

The ideas of Perestroika came to Cuba through two routes, according to Aurelio, both of which were later closed at least partially. The first was through the thousands of Cuban students who were in the USSR and other socialist countries where these ideas circulated. These students "identify with Glasnost because they live the reality of those countries, that reform has a positive character there and they tend to become Cuban reformists from the outside," in the words of Aurelio. Toward the end of the eighties and beginning of the 1990s, they began to return to Cuba. The second route was the literature sold in Cuba that promoted ideas of Perestroika and Glasnost from other socialist countries.

Mery, still in her youth at the time of the Collapse, at the time "saw the changes in the Soviet Union as something very good, I noticed that there was a Glasnost [...] that what was happening was good, that there was no reason to worry, that it was part of their own development." Aurelio talks about young people who had studied in the USSR who "also had the idea of a Perestroika for Cuba." There were also, according to Juan, "important people in the highest levels, in the Cuban leadership, who in '85 and '86 appear to be excited about Perestroika."

In the Cuban political elite, some were also fearful of these ideas, and this fear increased as the crisis in the USSR evolved further. As stated by Aurelio, these preoccupations in part had to do with economic issues and also because Perestroika put in question the Soviet policy of supporting revolutionary forces in Latin America. In that sense, it should be remembered that Gorbachev withdrew support from the Sandinistas and met with the Cuban-American community toward the end of his time in power. Aurelio maintains that

> in Cuba there was a reaction that also explains [...], that is justified by the fear that with the Cuban economy being so weak and so subordinated to the Russian economy, Perestroika would lead the Cuban economy to collapse because the relationship with Russia was no longer the same, so this had an impact, so this was a reason for adopting a policy that was critical of Perestroika, because the situation that the attempt generated—not Perestroika as such, because it wasn't implemented [more pro-capitalist policies took over in the USSR before Perestroika was fully implemented]—but the situation that was set in motion by the opening of a reform process from Moscow, implied for us a questioning of the idea of continuing to work toward a revolutionary change in Latin America and other countries, so the Perestroika was not good, it didn't end up being acceptable to us, a change in Latin America had to happen, which would allow us to move toward socialism.

According to Juan, Fidel Castro at the time tried to limit the impact of the Perestroika ideology by developing a policy that "has two faces":

> On the one hand, at the official level, Fidel Castro declares his sympathy with the reforms, through which socialism is reformed, he does not refer to anything concrete, other than that it is good, socialism is reformed and the support for Gorbachev, and all in all, and on the other [hand], he publishes Gorbachev, there is a Cuban edition of the book Perestroika, let's say this is one side of the problem and the other side of the problem is what I'm telling you, that there are many measures to limit the influence this process has on the internal public opinion, here it is the same for the citizen in the street and the Party members, it is not that the Party

members are receiving special information, there is nothing like that, everyone adheres to Fidel Castro's discourse, the speeches of Fidel Castro and that is the policy that is followed.

What Juan lays out is supported in the book by Yuri Pavlov, who headed the Latin American directorate of the USSR's Foreign Ministry, who alleges that Castro gave orders to the Central Committee of the PCC to prepare, confidentially, arguments against Perestroika, "emphasizing differences between Cuba and the Soviet Union in size, level of social and economic development, history, culture and traditions."[131] A document arrived at the Soviet Embassy in Havana that said, according to Pavlov, that economic decentralization might be necessary in a country as large as the USSR but was not needed in a smaller country like Cuba.[132]

Despite the circumstances that prevented Fidel Castro or the government from being 100% explicit in their criticism of Perestroika, there was clearly some pressure against Cubans who accepted these ideas. Aurelio says that the ideas of Perestroika that came with the Cubans who had studied in the USSR "were not understood, some even were, some were ..." He does not end the sentence, but he seems to refer to the sanctions they suffered of some kind. Esteban says that "Glasnost and Perestroika was at the beginning perceived in a very negative way, then we began to see what it was, what positive sides it had [...] but in global terms, if they told you here that you were a *Perestroikan*, that meant that you were a guy who was outside our ideology." He recalls a conflict at his workplace, which seems to indicate that it was considered acceptable to sanction Perestroikans, at least in some spheres of society:

> I remember that there was a friend of mine, the general secretary of my [local] Party branch who in the middle of Perestroika of Glasnost went to give a talk to a military unit [...] and the military complained that he had, he had given the issue of Glasnost and Perestroika a lot of importance, and they sent a letter to the center, accusing him of being Perestroikan, etc. The rector [apparently of the university] sent me the letter and sent for us to come, when I got to talk to the rector he said, "Well, we will have to penalize the teacher because..." I said, "Look, I'll tell you something, if he is going to penalize him you will penalize me too, because I believe in all that he said and I agree 100% with all that."

---

131 Pavlov, 113.
132 Ibid.

Juan says that the Perestroikan politicians he mentioned were "going to lose enthusiasm [during the last years of Cuban–Soviet relations], they will try to move on to critical positions, but they would have already committed the sin of looking toward the East, when they should look toward Revolution Square, and they will be dismissed later, right?"[133] Other informants do not even remember the tensions in bilateral relations or the internal tensions between "Fidelistas" and Perestroikans.

Norma recalls Gorbachev's visit in April 1989 as quite positive: "Great ... I was working here in the Party Committee, as I tell you, I spent seven years working in the Party Committee, that was in reality extraordinary, it was very, very good, Gorbachev's visit here in Cuba was very good." She had looked optimistically at the future: "[W]e thought it was going to be a, another socialist camp like we had before the fall of the socialist camp, that we were going to move forward, that we were moving toward a future of having such a close relationship, a very close one with the USSR, but well, I don't think that it has been like that, it has stayed more or less on *stand-by*, I don't know why." Lenin says that, "I never saw any disagreement ... not with the Soviets that were here either."[134]

These answers may seem odd considering the differences we have described, yet suggest that the government had some success in its strategy of distancing the country from the Soviet Union without making the conflict too apparent. As we saw in Part 1, conflicts between Cuba and other allied countries were seldom spoken about that openly in *Granma*, and it was often necessary to read closely and even between the lines to be able to see those tensions reflected in what was written, except at isolated moments when very explicit statements or official information were published, such as on the withdrawal of Soviet magazines from Cuban shelves.

---

133   Jorge Domínguez believes that "at the top of the regime, those most closely associated with the ideas of opening were Carlos Aldana, Armando Hart, and Carlos Rafael Rodríguez." See: Domínguez, "The Political Impact on Cuba of the Reform and Collapse of Communist Regimes," 127.

134   The fact that some informants do not remember any conflicts could be explained by the point made by Juan that the official Cuban policy against Perestroika had two faces. But this had been a constant during many years and long before the Soviet reforms. Writing on the 1970s, Jonathan Rosenberg asserted that "Conflict within the Cuban state tends to be attenuated and muted when compared with that occurring in pluralist societies. Yet the conflicts are real and decisive" (p. 85).

2 The Collapse: "It Still Has an Impact on Us"

The informants often spoke with some passion about the early years of the Revolution, as well as on the years of crisis in Cuba following the Collapse of the USSR. However, when approaching issues more directly related to the Soviet Union and Eastern Europe at the time of the Collapse, some people hardly seem to remember these matters, whereas others talk about it in detail.[135]

Even if the level of detail varies considerably, there is a considerable plurality of interpretations and opinions. Some informants gave quite explicit and detailed interpretations for why the Collapse happened, and while many of the narratives of *Granma*, especially by 1992, seemed to give priority to explanations that would not endanger political stability in Cuba, the informants seemed freer in their assessments and included a broader range of explanations.

The informants' assessments will be treated in the following subsections and especially in subsection 2.5 on the *causes* of the Collapse.

2.1 The USSR's Traumatic History: "Unfortunately, Lenin Dies Very Fast"

The interview subjects frequently turn to the history of the USSR, even its early phases, to explain the Collapse of Soviet and East European socialism. They describe a difficult and traumatic history that preceded the Cuban Revolution and that left the Soviet Union and Eastern Europe with lasting wounds. They often divide Soviet history into periods according to who was in power at all times ("the Stalin Period") and generally attach great importance to the country's leaders. There are mentions of all the leaders of the USSR, except Georgy Malenkov, who served briefly as president after the death of Joseph Stalin in 1953.[136]

Those of the informants who have knowledge about these topics and talk about them often assume a somewhat critical position toward Soviet leaders or their policies, especially Stalin. The exception is Vladimir Lenin (1917–1924). The interview subjects generally mention the leader of the Bolshevik Revolution and the first president of the USSR as an important revolutionary leader, theoretician, and an admirable person. Zenaida, for example, told us that she was impressed by a visit she made to Lenin's tomb in Moscow: "Very impressive

---

[135] Juan stated that "Society in general [...] does not remember these issues and does not discuss them," referring to the Collapse. But he also considers that "In the minds of the political leadership that experience weighs very heavily, even in the policies they promote, that is to say that in their strategies and current policies, they take into account their interpretation of what happened in Eastern Europe."

[136] The informants' vision of Mikhail Gorbachev, the last leader of the USSR, will be discussed at a later point.

the site where Lenin was and we saw him lying there, and everything, we went there." Héctor described himself as "a great admirer of the Soviet people" and stated that "It cannot be denied at any time, starting, well, from the Lenin period, the role that Lenin played in shaping Soviet society." Another interview subject, Lenin, even pointed out that he himself bears Lenin as his first name and relayed that his father gave him that name: "He named my brother Carlos and, me, Lenin. What a coincidence, right?"

Several interviewees expressed their identification with Marxist–Leninist ideology. Using this concept implies placing Lenin at the level of one of the great social thinkers throughout history and the founder of modern socialist thinking, Karl Marx. José, for example, states that "Lenin was to me… and Karl Marx and those who wrote the theory… as I see it, they defended the working class [...]." Mery says that "I am a Marxist–Leninist and will continue to be so." Víctor shows equal admiration, although he considers José Martí to be equally important to Cubans as Marx and Lenin: "We have to be Marxist–Leninists without forgetting about Martí."

Among my informants with an academic background, they sometimes highlighted Lenin as a democrat, both as a politician and as a theorist. This is a controversial position in many parts of the world and even on the radical left. Jorge says that "Lenin was writing a book, and Bukharin answered Lenin. That was not a problem. There was conceptual diversity, diversity of thought." Valdes Paz argues that Lenin imagined a society in which there was a counter-power in order to avoid the concentration of power in the government or in the Party. He also contends that Lenin advocated for a democratic party in the sense that there would be debate and in which various political currents could coexist. Esteban refers to the previous point, although he maintains that it would not be applicable in Cuba: "In Lenin's party there were internal [...] factions with different opinions on different things. That is not our history, that is not our idiosyncrasy." According to Aurelio, Lenin had a vision in which the Communist Party, over time, should cease to exercise power and facilitate popular participation and a self-governing society.[137]

Several people asserted that Lenin's death was premature and that he did not have time to complete his work. For example, in Esteban' words: "Unfortunately, Lenin dies very fast." Jorge also refers to "Lenin's premature death." Jorge, despite also praising Lenin's intellectual capacity and leadership,

---

137 This criteria fits with a typical Marxist–Leninist reading of Marx, according to which it would be impossible to jump directly to communism from a capitalist society, skipping over a transitory phase that may be referred to as the "dictatorship of the proletariat."

criticizes what he perceives as a "fear" in Cuba of criticizing Lenin. This is even though he points out that Ernesto Che Guevara did in fact criticize the leader: "Look, now there is a book by Che, published here, where Che criticizes Lenin, and he says that Lenin is to blame for everything that happened. I wanted to buy it, but what happens is that it was very expensive ... nobody wants to talk about it, people are afraid to criticize Lenin, but Che criticizes Lenin, because Lenin was wrong, well, and so what?"

Lenin is often contrasted with his successor Joseph Stalin (1924–1953). When talking about Lenin's ideas about the institutionalism of the socialist society, Juan distinguishes between "Bolshevism" and "Stalinism." Aurelio also emphasizes this discontinuity and says: "I think that the real spirit of the Bolsheviks was distorted by Stalin." Several of the interview subjects explicitly say that it was negative that power fell into Stalin's hands after Lenin's death.

According to Esteban, "Lenin himself criticizes him [Stalin] before he dies. Lenin says that Stalin is not a suitable person to lead the Party." Several of the academics who were interviewed in this study emphasize that Stalin did not have the level of culture that Lenin had. Jorge recognizes his "great merits," but considers that "he was a person without culture, [though he was also] a very intelligent person." He contrasts his cultural level with that of his predecessors, making an implicit comparison: "Lenin, Bukharin, and the others, Trotsky, were people of high culture who studied and read in several languages. Lenin handled four languages, Bukharin also." They were "people of high culture who knew what was happening in the world."

Héctor seems to consider the Stalin period as particularly negative: "Yes, mistakes were made. There is no denying that there were [difficult, problematic] periods—like the Stalin period [...]." Although most mentions of Stalin are negative, some of the people who criticize him most strongly also allude to certain positive aspects of his government. For example, Aurelio refers to the industrialization process that took place in the USSR. He refers to this process, however, without mentioning Stalin, though it was in large part implemented during the years of Stalin's government. He says that the USSR developed from "a pure peasant economy and turned into an industrial country and a world power." Esteban, commenting on the role of Stalin in World War II, states that "I also believe that Stalin managed the problem of war very intelligently." However, he considers the Molotov–Ribbentrop Pact [the non-aggression treaty between Germany and the USSR] to have been a mistake.

None of the interview subjects seem to have a very favorable view of Stalin, but there are those who criticize him less strongly. José is not uncritical toward the leader, but seems to partly apologize on his behalf, describing his negative actions as mere "mistakes": "Lenin was to me… and Karl Marx and those who wrote the theory… as I see it, they defended the working class, and Lenin in the beginning, Stalin later with his mistakes, because we humans are not perfect […]."

Víctor says that in his youth he had "a different vision of Stalin," referring apparently both to a different one from the negative or critical vision that prevailed in the Cuban Revolution and also different from his current vision of Stalin. Yet, he is also quick to point out that "I was not blind either, and I was not in favor of … I sympathized with Kandinsky and Chagall as painters, that is to say culturally, I sympathized with Mayakovski [referring to victims of Stalin's policies and actions in the cultural sphere]. […] I wasn't that dumb, either. But politically I believed that it was, well, I forgave him all those mistakes, well, things can't be perfect."

Three interview subjects comment on Trotsky, who was murdered by a Stalinist agent in Mexico in 1940. The three largely defend the revolutionary, theorist, politician and leader of The Red Army. Aurelio argues that Lenin "had no misgivings about Trotsky" and that Trotsky understood the value of the political system based on Soviets (workers' councils) that were developed before the Revolution and later during the Lenin period. Yet my informant also says that Trotsky "was a man who had a lot of resentment […], he aroused passions."

To Esteban, Trotsky was an intellectual and a very capable military leader: "Time would later prove him right, in so many things, in so many things […]. Trotsky was a very strong guy, because he led the Red Army well, and he was the one who saved the Soviet Union under his leadership, that was how the Soviet Union was saved from the 17 invasions [referring to the intervention wars started by foreign powers], with the Red Army. And besides that, he was a very intelligent guy, he was an intellectual, but a very critical guy, and it seems like, in those times, guys who were as critical as him did not find support within the Party."

These comments are surprising, given that traditionally in Cuba, Trotsky has been considered among "the bad guys in history," and generally the official Soviet version of history was adopted in this regard. In general, his writings were neither published nor sold. In the newspaper *Granma,* which I have analyzed in Part 1 of this study, in the period between 1989 and 1992, I could not find any reference to Trotsky, despite being such an important figure in Russian history, which suggests that this individual was more or less a non-person in Cuba even by 1989–1992.[138]

---

138 I have not searched systematically for such mentions, so I cannot guarantee that there are none.

However, at the Havana International Book Fair in 2005, several spaces were dedicated to the leader of the Red Army,[139] and a few years later, the Cuban novelist Leonardo Padura published *The Man Who Loved Dogs*, which explores the life of Trotsky's killer and how he hid in Cuba; a story that still had been (and probably still is) unfamiliar to most Cubans. Considering the circumstances, it is not surprising that the informants do not mention him much, except Aurelio, Esteban, and Juan, who are academics, know the history well and probably have greater access to foreign literature than most of the interview subjects. I am not sure, however, whether their views on Trotsky are commonplace amongst Cuban academics today.

It is during the Stalin period, after the victory over Nazi Germany in 1945, that the USSR expanded its influence in Eastern Europe. As mentioned earlier, some informants contrasted the autochthonous origins of the Cuban revolution with the revolutionary processes in Eastern Europe. José Luis, for example, relays that "Cuba had nothing to do with the Soviet Union when Fidel Castro's struggle in the 50s, when the revolution rose to power. The relations with the Soviets began to develop later." Idulberto states that "the Soviets had imposed it on Germany, as they did in Hungary, they imposed one thing. What the Cuban people have is due to their sweat, to their tears." Víctor refers to a Hungarian who, as he recalls, told him: "The problem is that you made your own revolution, and, in our case, it was imposed upon us."

One of the interview subjects, José, points out that the authenticity of the Revolution in this regard has been key to the interest and support that most Cubans have given it. He contrasts Cuba with the systemic transitions that took place in Eastern Europe after World War II with the support or interference of the USSR and states that "The USSR simply made the revolution to a bunch of people who did not want it, and you love what you fight for, what you do not fight for, you do not love. How often do you think about the air you breathe?"

Nikita Khrushchev (1953–1964) is often mentioned in the context of his relations with Cuba and the Cuban Missile Crisis, as someone who did wrong but who knew how to rectify. He is the leader at a stage when the USSR is approaching the height of its power and is in power at the moment when Cuban–Soviet relations emerge. Hence, the Soviet influence in Cuba is to a great extent linked to the Khrushchevite or post-Stalin period. While there were disagreements between Cuba and the USSR, the Khrushchev period was perceived in a more positive manner. The greatest symbol of the splendor of the USSR was its space program, which at that stage achieved success by sending the first human

---

139   Fundación Federico Engels, 2005, http://www.aporrea.org/actualidad/n56335.html.

being into space. At least three interview subjects refer to the cosmonaut Yuri Gagarin (Norma, Eliécer, and Lenin). Eliécer claims, for example, that in his youth the Soviet Union was seen as "a country, a power that could fight against the United States. When [...] Yuri Gagarin journeys into outer space, to us that was something tremendous."

Some allude to the "de-Stalinization" led by Khrushchev in the years after Stalin's death. Víctor believes that Khrushchev failed to end the evils of the past: "[...] there were attempts, with Khrushchev, Khrushchev tried first but couldn't, and besides, he had not discarded all the dogmas." Alberto, on the other hand, mentions an incident he witnessed in the USSR, which illustrates that even after Stalin's crimes were made public, there were people who missed him:

> I even saw the fall of the statue of Stalin in the park of, in the most important park of [inaudible] and I also had the opportunity to listen to a Russian there who with tears in his eyes told me he was very sad because Comrade Stalin had died. Notice how different things can be, right? I was there at the time when the whole process of de-Stalinization was initiated in the USSR, so that's why I tell you that these are two very contrasting things, right? On the one hand, the statue was toppled, and on the other hand, a Russian who starts crying [...] but hey, that's their story.

In the interviews, references to Leonid Brezhnev (1964–82) are scarce—a figure often described as less than charismatic and associated with stagnation. The informants, still, sometimes refer to decisions or events during his government.

Héctor refers to the invasion of Czechoslovakia. He declares that earlier he had agreed with that decision; this was also Fidel Castro's position. He considered it necessary to prevent imperialist expansion. Later, Héctor changed his mind: "In the end, I think it was a mistake." Esteban expressed himself critically about the war in Afghanistan, which began in 1979: "I believe that the last mistake the Soviet Union made was to get involved in Afghanistan [...]. It was the Vietnam of the Soviets."

As the reader familiar with Soviet history will remember, after the death of Brezhnev, there were a few short-lasting governments led by Yuri Andropov (November 1982 to February 1984) and Konstantin Chernenko (February 1984 to March 1985). Esteban emphasizes that this "intermezzo" was something very harmful for the USSR itself, because "there was a kind of power vacuum [...]." He believes that already in the Andropov period, at least in universities, "one could speak more freely, until the freedom of criticism finally came with

Gorbachev." But he also notes that the Party paid little attention to the criticisms that circulated in society. There was a significant deterioration in Soviet politics at that time, he argues:

> When you read the book, the one by Vitali Vorotnikov,[140] you are going to realize how the Political Bureau was left isolated, and went crumbling, and gradually lost its grip on power [...]. The first who suffered the problem of, of the deterioration process in the 80s were the bases of the Party, the bases of the Party began to crumble, due to problems with corruption, problems of distrust, and problems with the lack of power.

José Luis maintains that Andropov tried to revive the processes of change that Khrushchev had promoted: "There was a certain process, we could say, of rectification starting with Khrushchev when the 20th Congress takes place [in 1953], but then it's reversed again." It is notable here that José Luis uses the term rectification, suggesting some identification between Khrushchev's intentions to improve socialism with those of Fidel Castro, although they did not always go in the same direction (for instance, in the economy, Castro closed farmers markets based on supply and demand whereas Khrushchev had favored a certain limited opening to the market).

Esteban also believes that after Brezhnev died in 1982 and was succeeded by Andropov, the latter made an effort to improve the functioning of the system:

> Andropov did not shine from the point of view of foreign policy. It does not seem to me that he has given much attention to that [...]. Andropov's impact was an internal impact, in trying to regulate, discipline, and try to solve some internal issues, for example in Moscow, there were, jokes and sayings are very important, right? And those things. In Moscow there was a joke about Andropov's milk because the problem is that either there was no milk in Moscow, or it was so difficult to get hold of it. And, when Andropov came to power, he put pressure on this issue, and the internal situation from the material point of view improved a little.

Although not all informants seemed especially familiar with Soviet history or felt to be in a position to express opinions on the subject, those who spoke with some degree of detail on the topic generally expressed a critical vision. They

---

140 Vitali I. Vorotnikov, *Mi verdad. Notas y reflexiones del diario de trabajo de un miembro del Buró Político del PCUS* (Havana: Casa Editora Abril, 1995).

often touched upon issues such as the problems that the young state had to face, as well as erroneous decisions and leaders who were not up to their tasks.

Also, as they often emphasized the early years of the Soviet process—even though the topic of most of the questions that I put forward were about the years surrounding the Collapse—it is recalled that the Russian and later Soviet attempts to create a socialist society preceded the Cuban process and that each developed in different circumstances.

2.2　*European Socialism in the Media and in Real Life: "I Saw [...] Great Singers, Great Dancers, Selling Stuff on the Subway"*

Most of the interview subjects obtained information from the USSR in two main ways: via Cuban media, and in some cases, visits to the country made by themselves or by other people they knew well. Several pointed out that an idealized vision of the USSR predominated in Cuba. In the following, I illustrate that those who traveled to the USSR sometimes, but not always, developed another perspective of the country. I also demonstrate how they have a critical view of the Cuban media coverage.

The way in which travel affected or not the interview subjects' perception of the USSR, and later its Collapse, seems to vary according to the character of their travels and when they went there. The trips that were made before the crisis in the USSR became deep and very explicit (1960 until the early 1980s) do not seem to have affected the predominantly favorable view of the USSR, or it may even have reinforced such a favorable view. In this sense, Mavis reminded us that "logically, when you went there, they showed you the best they had."

Those who made short trips often seem to have experienced or remember the more pleasant side. Eliécer explains he went for a short stay, and during a short stay one does not see everything: "We went for 15 or 20 days. We traveled there for matters of science, and could therefore only see very little, very little." Zenaida spent 27 days in the USSR as a tourist together with her husband in 1982: "The first impression, of leaving here, and taking a trip there, everything was great, absolutely great, it was very nice."

The timing of the trip may certainly have been decisive for the visitor's impression. Some respondents remember prolonged stays in the midst of the crisis of the 1980s or early 1990s, which negatively affected their image of the country. But the 1960s were a decade of growth and progress, and, according to Idulberto, Soviet people were excited about the Cuban Revolution. There were, however, more restrictions on communication with Soviets.

Idulberto mentions a visit on January 2, 1963, when he was a pilot, shortly after the disagreement between Khrushchev and Castro regarding the Missile Crisis: "At that time there was a very big closure, right. The Soviets were not

ANALYSIS OF THE INTERVIEWS

allowed to have private communication, that was not work related [...] with foreigners, nor with the Cubans, that is, the communication we had, we had a very affectionate round of drinks, with many incidents, which I will not tell you about here, there was a very nice one ... but that demonstrated the friendship, the affection, and the ideological communality that existed at that time between the Cuban Revolution—they referred to us as the Island of Liberty—and the Soviet Union."

In Eastern Europe, this was not always the case, at least not after Fidel Castro's statements in favor of Soviet intervention in Czechoslovakia in 1968. Idulberto states that after the Soviet invasion, "in the Intercontinental Hotel we were practically denied things because the Cubans did not tip and preferred to give it to, to the people in charge of money. That is, they told you that Cubans don't give anything, the Cubans this, the Cubans are communists, even us, you couldn't even speak Russian ... you spoke English, if you spoke English you were well received, but if you spoke Russian they would rather spit on you [...], if you spoke Spanish you were Cuban and you were not very well received."[141]

Those who visited the USSR during its last decade of existence often witnessed more serious problems that impacted their vision of the so-called "Actually Existing Socialism." José relays that he spent a month in Moscow in 1985 or 1986 and witnessed an episode from the streets when some adolescents approached him to sell pants from the black market: "If there is culture, if there are young people, assuming they have certain levels of schooling, they should not fall into that, and even with foreigners. What kind of impression do you give? Just to tell you one story, there were lots of things happening."[142]

Idulberto also describes a society with a lot of corruption during a visit he had sometime between 1989 and 1991. He relays that when trying to buy a

---

141 Two informants describe what they saw as a rejection of anything Russian in Czechoslovakia, but both seem to attribute it to a blind admiration toward the West, rather than a product of USSR policies in Eastern Europe. Alberto argues that "In Czechoslovakia nobody wanted to answer you in Russian, for example. Since I had been in the Soviet Union, I spoke Russian, and I wanted to speak to them in Russian and they did not answer me. They answered me when I spoke to them in English, I said now that is absurd because the Russians—well it's fine, you do not like them—but that they liked Americans better ... damn, that's f*cked up, really f*cked up." Idulberto observes that the people of Czechoslovakia treated the Russians badly, but attributes this to a "servile" behavior toward certain groups: "The Czechs in Czechoslovakia preferred to attend a German, this was before the Collapse, than to attend to one who speaks in Russian ... to attend the one speaking English, to attend the one speaking Spanish, that is called servility."
142 It should be added here that it is quite common that this happens to tourists also in Cuba, for example foreigners are often offered cigars made of stolen raw material.

windshield for a Lada, someone from the agency sent them to a parking lot where such products were sold illegally. They were warned that if they did not come to pay at a certain time, they would be in trouble ("if not, you will be in trouble. It's mafia"). He also conveys, however, that a short time after, another Russian, who identified with the Cuban people, appeared and offered them food out of solidarity.

Esteban, during prolonged visits as a student and researcher, also became familiar with many problems. He conveys that in the USSR during the 1980s, "I had the opportunity to observe a number of things, first of all to realize the deterioration process that was taking place, in all aspects, and the corruption process, it was very strong, in all aspects, and the breakdown of Party authority, and the authority of political power." José Luis relays that "I was living there for a year and one would come to realize that it didn't work, it didn't work."

Víctor says that in his youth he did not want to see the problematic aspects of the USSR: "Like the man who doesn't want to realize that his wife is cheating on him, I didn't want to see it." However, "When I was in Moscow I saw the terrible part when I saw that everything they had told me was false. Because it was a society in which people did not smoke, and then people were smoking in the stores."

Jorge was in East Germany between 1973 and 1977 and then traveled to other countries of the socialist camp "every two or three years for 25 years." As an example of the gap he observed between theory and practice, he points out that prostitution was common, despite having officially been eradicated: "The great German hotels, when socialism was still strong, an efficient socialism, a high-level socialism … those hotels were full of whores, but very refined whores, whores of high culture, but they were whores, expensive ones, whores, whores who aspired to a better life."

It might have been a shock for many travelers to encounter these aspects that were so alien to the official propaganda. But some travelers also say that they had a good impression of these societies, even during long stays and after getting to know the people well. Mavis praises the agricultural model that she saw: "As professionals, we were learning about a development model [of agriculture] that we could see was productive, that it was effective, that worked, because it improved the life of that population, we saw it wherever we went, Bulgaria, Czechoslovakia, to Germany." She saw no signs of crisis in the first half of the 1980s: "No, I admit, even I who had experiences of the Russian family from the inside, as you can see, because my son had been married to a Russian woman and everything, and I used to visit the family's house. I didn't go to a hotel […] or a Party camp, or anything like that." During the Gorbachev period, however, "It had deteriorated, the situation was really bad. I saw people, artists, such as musicians, great singers, great dancers, selling stuff in the subway."

Mavis admits that the end of East Germany caught her by surprise: "Another trauma that I suffered, in Berlin, I studied in Berlin, where they had everything, the showcase of European socialism. And then I see it on television, because I did not see it personally, how they tear down the Berlin wall and those same people whom I frequented, whom I had seen living so well, according to my perspective on things." The informants believe that the information provided by the Cuban media was incomplete or insufficient.

Norma relays that "we did not receive, we did not receive ... we heard something, some things were reported in the newspaper, but, to say it like that, like to say that this is how it was, like that and like that, this paper is white and it has writing in black ink, no, we did not perceive it." Mery, a journalist, argues that "There was not much press, what we had was radio and television, and I believe that these media did not transmit such informa[tion] ..." To Alberto, "the information was never the important one, nor was there enough information." When asking herself if the signs of crisis during the last two years of the USSR were reflected in the media, Mavis provided the example of nationality conflicts during the last years of the USSR. The researcher replied as follows: "No, those problems did not reach us." Then she states, "I think there was very little information."

José Luis also considers that the population "did not receive it [the information that was necessary to understand the Collapse]," although he later mentions Fidel Castro's speeches as a source of information through which he himself was informed about the circumstances. Juan states that between 1985 and 1989, the population was not informed about the changes that were taking place in USSR–Cuba relations. Eliécer states that "Yes, we received information about what was going to happen, about what was happening and how it was happening, but no, no, it was not complete as we should have received it." Yet he also says that after a period of "secrecy," "everything started to come out."

Pedro, who was outside the country during at least parts of the period, is the only person who gives a relatively favorable review of the coverage in Cuban media. He relates that the media reported on the central aspects of the USSR crisis, although "maybe not with so many details." But he argues that the crisis in Cuba may have limited the population's ability to stay informed. People were in survival mode. Sometimes they did not even enjoy the material conditions to keep abreast: "They knew that what was over there, had ended, that there were a number of things, they saw it, maybe they might not even have had the opportunity to see it on television, because here there were 15, 18, and sometimes 20 hours of blackout."

The apparent discrepancy between what is revealed through systematic analysis and what the interview subjects say about the media coverage could indicate that there was no general censorship in the media, as some of the testimonies might imply. It may also rather suggest that the way in which the news was presented made important information go unnoticed, or it was not understood.

As we have seen, there *was* information in the *Granma* newspaper about these phenomena, but the quality of this information and whether it was presented in an easily comprehensible way to the readers varied considerably. So it is interesting that several informants state that information about the problems did not reach them, as it might suggest the practice of *Granma*, and possibly also other media, of "hiding away" events visually, through other means, actually worked—even in the case of highly qualified readers. Technically, in the media coverage that we analyzed in Part 1 of the book, there was information on the crisis and the changes, but there was little explanation and analysis, and sometimes the news itself was not given much visibility, and maybe not even meant to be noticed by the reader.

It should be taken into account that reading the press more than 20 years after some events took place is not the same as reading it as they take place, as one knows the outcome and might see more clearly the bits and pieces of information that were eventually important to the final outcome.

On the other hand, some of the most critical comments may be influenced by memory and by the extensive public criticism that the Cuban press has received over many years but perhaps in a more open and direct manner during the last few decades.

Although one can say that there was contemporary press coverage on the events as seen earlier in the present work, few books have been published on the subject of the Collapse in Cuba, and the Collapse is given minimal attention in Cuban official and public history. It is not a taboo amongst people, and it is sometimes mentioned in the public debate, but there has been a certain tendency to avoid going deeper into it. In this regard, I refer to the text book *Historia de Cuba. Nivel Medio Superior*, published in 1989, and the currently available fourth edition of 2004. The textbook presents Cuban history chronologically and is written for 15–17-year-old students. Only in one appendix is the Collapse mentioned and then extremely briefly: "From 1989 onwards, the process that would end with the Collapse of socialism in Europe and the dissolution of the Soviet Union escalated. Cuba instantly lost 85 percent of its purchasing power, and its Gross Domestic Product dropped drastically. In Washington they believed the time had come to reinforce the blockade in order to put an end to the Cuban Revolution, an end they predicted to be near."

This might be partly explained by the book being on Cuban history and not about world history, yet it is still striking that the authors dedicate only one single paragraph (!) to a world event that was of huge importance to all Cuban society. Even if it is a new edition based on a book originally published in 1989, the lack of more information and/or analysis on the topic could suggest that the topic was seen as politically very delicate.

Various testimonies indicated that rank and file Party members did not, at the time of the Collapse, receive much more information than the rest of the population. According to Alberto, the Party members had "a bit more [information]" than the rest of the population but "not substantially more." José Luis states that "I do not remember there being one explicitly addressed to the Party members like that [...] there may have been some things, but I do not remember it like that." Juan, on the other hand, states that indeed some additional information was given to the Party members. This "must have been at the very end of the period [of the crisis and the Collapse of the USSR], it may have happened, I do not remember, but there may have been some information." Then he says, "I think they did create documents and some document was read, one of those things, [but it was] insignificant."

Norma argues that as a Party member, she received *some* more information. She relates that "in the Party, things are spoken at meetings, which other workers [recall that the branches are formed at workplaces], no matter how much merit they have, they do not perceive it and cannot understand it, because we are given the meetings, and that is, secretly, we cannot disclose." Eliécer agrees that the Party members were better informed: "We always [had] more information than the population. That has always been a characteristic of our Party." However, Norma and Eliécer both claimed that at some point the information they had was insufficient, so that difference cannot have been particularly significant.

On the other hand, intellectuals, journalists, and high-level leaders (the latter usually being members of the Communist Party) are groups that had a bit more access to information. Mery states that she had access to more information. This was not because of her status as a Party member; however, instead, as a journalist, she had an electronic device through which she received the latest news headlines or bulletins from abroad. Pedro argues that he indeed had access to the information needed in order to analyze the situation, perhaps because he was a diplomat and worked in Nicaragua.

Juan says that "As intellectuals, we had more access to information about what had really happened and what was happening, and therefore all those Party meetings, with intellectuals, they were also Party members, it seemed like a rather poor thing." Esteban states that "We intellectuals had a clearer perspective," and were "a little more informed." Regarding high-ranking leaders, in Mavis's opinion, "even the country's leaders had little information." However, Juan argues that the higher up in the ranks of the Party one looked, "information could be greater, the Central Committee could be included [it might have been given important information, strategic analysis, and so on], etc. Although I believe that the 'hardest' information was always kept within a much narrower circle, which probably did not exceed the Political Bureau of the Party."

Jorge stated that in 1986, which he also refers to as "four years before [the Collapse]," Fidel Castro warned that the *campo socialista* or Socialist Bloc "has no future." This happened at a meeting with the Government (*Consejo de Ministros*) in which a group of 10 or 12 people "from philosophy" at the university had also been invited.[143] While the exact wording and date of the meeting cannot be confirmed, this could indicate that the inner circle of political leadership provided additional information and more critical analysis to high-ranking officials and selected intellectuals; in this case, it is especially interesting since the intellectuals in question had earlier been marginalized during the "Sovietization" period of the 1970s. As we saw, members who worked in certain professions seem to have had access to more information for "natural reasons" (because they traveled, because they had contact with foreigners, etc.), and this might have been the case for government officials, prominent intellectuals, and so on.

Jorge's statement, however, suggests that there may also have been a conscious policy by the authorities to give more information to certain groups. If that is the case, it confirms what was suggested in the first part of this study, that somewhat more explicit and critical information and analysis was given to high-level cadres and military and other trusted groups. However, there seems to have been a certain flow of information and analysis that was not written down—possibly in part since critical analysis of allied countries would be delicate but also in part because of a tradition of self-censorship in the press and amongst academics.

This could suggest that the political elite had a communication policy that followed two different lines: to let the media provide the most necessary information, although in a careful manner to not affect Cuba's foreign relations and maintain calm in the country, but spread some information, both

---

143   Apparently he is referring, at least in part, to people who had been associated with the Department of Philosophy, which was closed down together with *Pensamiento Crítico* in 1972.

written and unwritten, to an apparently selected audience. One purpose of this must have been to prepare these people so that they would be mentally prepared for problems but also so that they could direct, guide, and explain the events to lower-ranking members of the state apparatus as well as the general population.

This policy may partly be related to the PCC statute that, in line with Lenin's concept of the vanguard party, states that the Party must orient the masses. Furthermore, it can be a way to make leaders feel "included," to feel trusted and assigned responsibilities but also so that the leadership could hear qualified opinions on the matter from people with other perspectives and skills.

It is also believed in Cuba that, sometimes, the authorities spread gossip about certain problems, sometimes as a strategy to see how the population responds, or more relevantly in this case, to prepare the population for a story or to diminish the political impact it would have if it was to be known to all the population simultaneously through the media. Commonly, this action is called *tirar una bola*.[144] It may be a strategy to prevent certain news from reaching the entire population simultaneously, which would make it politically more dangerous. Thus, an additional objective of giving more information to certain groups could be to diminish the impact of changes.

Although this goes against modern ideals of transparency and freedom of information, it is important here to add that a significant part of the population in Cuba believes that there are certain things that cannot be broadcasted. Often, this position is justified by the external pressure that the country faces. Some of my informants also justified the style of the press coverage in 1989–1992 by referring to US pressures and the risk that events could be used to destabilize Cuba.

When speaking about the media coverage in Cuba regarding the Collapse, Alberto stated that each journalist's worldview could have influenced the coverage but also said that there are "historical responsibilities in terms of exercising the truth," thus justifying at least a "careful" approach (my word). Juan suggested that control was reinforced from above, and besides, recalled that the journalists did not have a panoramic view of what was happening nor did they have much control or possibilities to write whatever they pleased: "These journalists have no initiative. They follow the editorial line dictated by the newspaper, which in turn responds to the DOR [Department of Revolutionary

---

144 Literally "throwing a ball"; in other countries, "bola" can mean a false rumor; in Cuba it typically means a rumor in a more general sense. To be *arriba de la bola* or "on the ball" means to be updated, to have information on what is happening (it can be in a political context, but not necessarily so).

Orientation], to the Party leadership, and the Party has not communicated on that, so that the maneuvering room they have is to take a piece of news and the DOR says 'Hey, look at this, this is bad, we don't like that information, look at it, and comment on it, don't imagine anything like a [global] vision of the process or an understanding of the process.'"

According to Mery, the press was "as in boxing, on the defense [...]." The journalist argues that this was "because it is a process that is taking place, and there is that ... let's see what will happen, how it will end, what will be the consequences, and as such, like if we are not part of the process, we are rather on the ... as in boxing, on the defense, instead of taking part in the process and providing the information of the whole process, as if one waits to see ...." She believes that the press reported "very cautiously." I have earlier suggested that a more critical coverage might have jeopardized relations with other countries—though *Granma* did not always favor allies' views—and made more people question the model in Cuba. However, Mery stresses another aspect that might also have influenced the coverage and how leaders spoke about the changes. She said that one ought to be respectful because "The Soviet Union was perceived as a friend for life, and they had saved us from a lot of things, so they had the right [to change], and that right should be respected."

Furthermore, according to Mery, the Collapse may have been perceived as something uncomfortable, shameful: "I will compare it to a relative, a relative who is imprisoned. That is an embarrassment for the family. It is not spoken about in the family and even less spoken about with friends, and then maybe the person was incarcerated for a silly or small thing [*una bobería*], do you understand? But there is a syndrome of silence that is not doing us any good." At the same time, she does not think that the authorities were afraid that the Collapse would spread to Cuba. Many of Europe's experiences were, according to her, of little relevance and could not serve as an inspiring example for Cubans: "What Berlin Wall is going to fall? Here?"

However, other informants argued that Cuban leaders may have been concerned with ensuring that some transformation processes that were taking place in that other context would not be imitated in Cuba. Valdes Paz states that the withdrawal of Soviet publications in 1989–1990 were part of the "measures to limit the influence this process [Perestroika] has on the internal public opinion." Esteban believes that coverage in Cuban state media was also designed to "try to keep those things from moving," that is, to avoid similar processes in Cuba.[145]

---

145   Esteban also argues that this is something that still happens, "Just like the problem of the Arab Spring [...] (the Cuban authorities) try to keep those things from moving over here,

2.3 Predictability of the Collapse: "Fidel Had Already Warned Us"

Regarding whether the Collapse was foreseeable, some informants claimed it was a surprise and some say it was not. Many report that Fidel Castro had warned them that the USSR could disappear. Others said that they had expected a complicated scenario but not a complete collapse.

Cuban scholars Luis Aguilera García and Nelson Labrada Fernández wrote in a book published in 1994, however, that the Collapse "was an unexpected process for all."[146] Yet, some of our interview subjects claim that they indeed perceived the possibility that the USSR could collapse or that they saw it as a possibility certain years before it actually happened. Here, it is important to be skeptical and aware of the fact that memory can be misleading and that people's judgment of what they, at a certain point in the past, thought about the future, may have altered with the passing of time.

However, one cannot rule out that someone in Cuba might have foreseen or reflected about the possibility of the USSR and Eastern Europe experiencing a major crisis. In fact, there were people suggesting publicly the possibility of a major crisis in the Soviet Union, although this was not a common perception. For instance, Norwegian researchers Johan Galtung et al., wrote in 1980 that the socialist countries' problems were going to turn more "explosive" in that decade than in the previous one, and that due to the amount and magnitude of internal contradictions, "political dynamics of huge dimensions could occur."[147] Cuban leaders also had close links with the USSR and Eastern Europe and thus privileged access to information.

In all, twelve interview subjects commented on the issue of whether the Collapse was predictable or not, although not always with the same clarity. This is normal when trying to remember an event from the past. Their responses varied greatly:

1) Five people want us to understand that, to them, the fall of the USSR *was a big surprise:* Zenaida, Norma, Mavis, Aurelio, and Mery. It is salient here that four of these five people are women and that all the women who were interviewed expressed similar views on the topic.

    Norma states, "We had an idea that the USSR was always going to be a support to us." She states that "I never thought that the Socialist Camp

---

here, internally, because I think that in Cuba, there are things with which there might be discontents, quite strong ones."

146   Luis Aguilera García and Nelson Labrada Fernández, "Socialismo real: Del 'modelo clásico' al derrumbe," in *El derrumbe del modelo soviético*, ed. Román García Baez (Havana: Editorial Felix Varela, 1994), 100.

147   Johan Galtung, Dag Viljen Poleszynski, and Erik Rudeng, *Norge i 1980-årene* (Oslo: Gyldendal, 1980).

was going to fall, ever. Especially when we had Tamayo [Arnaldo Tamayo Méndez, Cuban cosmonaut] who went with Yuri to space [...], we didn't expect it [...], nor did it ever cross my mind that the Socialist Camp was going to fall. That is the truth, never." When asked if she suspected that there could be a collapse, Zenaida replies that "[...] I never suspected it, never, never, never, never."

Aurelio states that "Nobody in Cuba thought that the Soviet model was going to collapse," although he also says that he received a warning from the economist Raúl León Torres, in 1984 or 1985, about economic problems in the USSR. That was the first time he heard a pessimistic view, however. Mery argues that "We thought that this would be eternal, that it would never fall." However, she also states that her father warned her that the USSR had no future. He worked at the USSR Embassy in 1989, which is three years before it was dissolved as a nation.[148]

2) There are two people who argue that they *expected a more complicated situation in and with the Socialist Bloc but not a collapse*. These people are Héctor and Juan. Héctor had been in the USSR and knew that the system there had "generated many bad things." However, he recalls: "I will not say that we believed that the Collapse of the Soviet Union could happen." Juan states that "It was easy to foresee that from the evolution of the Socialist Camp and from the events in the USSR, a much more complicated scenario was to come, right? Although it could not be measured exactly (how it would be in the future), it was a scenario that would be less favorable in terms of the economy, in the military, and in diplomacy." Here, he seems to be referring to how things were allegedly perceived amongst the political elite and intellectuals.

3) There are six people who argue that they perceived the possibility of a USSR collapse as real or plausible, already several years before it happened; that is, *it was not a surprise that it deteriorated strongly*. Several argue, however, that the speed and/or the totality of the processes of change that followed was surprising: José Luis, Esteban, Jorge, Pedro, Eliécer, and Víctor.

All of these are academics or professionals. These six people have all experienced "direct" contact with the USSR through their own travels or trips made by close relatives. Eliécer argues that it was not a surprise because "Fidel had

---

148 Mavis, in addition to clarifying that she did not foresee the Collapse, expresses doubts that there were other militants who suspected that the Collapse was going to take place: "Let no one say that in those days—and I will argue with anyone on this, with the greatest scientist we have—that in those days we had the very clear vision (of what was going to happen). This does not suit us, it is a lie, we do not think about it… Well, perhaps some, a visionary with a lot of life experience [...]."

already warned us about this, Fidel in Camagüey, on July 26, I think it was July 26 in Camagüey."[149] That speech surprised everyone, he insists: "Fidel had a light that was very much directed toward there [...] and when he warned us about that, everyone did like this, and began to see, damn, that's strange! But with confidence." However, he also maintains that his children, who had been in the USSR, had warned him of that possibility: "No, I already saw it coming, because the boys had already warned me." Víctor points out that Fidel Castro's speech opened his mind to the possibility that this project could collapse: "So, Fidel when he, as the first in the whole world, talks about the Collapse, I start, I say, what the ... but it doesn't take me by surprise; Fidel already prepared me."

Esteban had a direct relationship with the USSR and argues that "It did not take me by surprise because the problems I saw there, and the difficulties I saw there [he was there in 1985–1986 finishing his PhD thesis, and on other occasions] were problems and difficulties that could put an end to socialism."

Pedro says that "the people" knew that the situation was serious already before the second half of the 1980s: "Already before the Gorbachev process, we were informed here, and people knew that in the Soviet Union there was a disaster. People knew that, and that also things were happening there that were going to lead to a catastrophe. Yes, people knew it."[150]

Jorge reports that in 1986, Fidel Castro informed him and a group of 10 or 12 intellectuals that the USSR had no future: "At that meeting in [19]86 he said, he told us, the European Socialist Camp has no future. He said that four years before [the Collapse was evident]." Then he added: "[...] I think that if Fidel in [19]86 told us that the Socialist Camp had no future and that there were issues to prepare for, he must have said the same thing to the Party and to the Central Committee, [he must] have told them the same thing as to us."

José Luis stated that from 1987 he had serious doubts that the USSR could remain as a "rational thing that could function." The experiences he had gathered from visits to the country had allowed him, according to his words, "to have certain presuppositions on the Collapse of the USSR." He adds that, "I was not totally surprised, but, of course, I never thought it would happen so soon. Already from 1987 on, when the Party conference took place in January 1987, where the Party's leading role within Soviet society is practically withdrawn, in my opinion, already then, that initiated a path without return. There wasn't,

---

149 See: Castro, "Discurso pronunciado por Fidel Castro Ruz [...] En el acto conmemorativo por el XXXVI Aniversario del asalto al Cuartel Moncada, celebrado en la Plaza Mayor General 'Ignacio Agramonte,' Camagüey, el día 26 de Julio de 1989, 'Año 31 de la Revolución.'"

150 Although people may have heard about certain problems, my findings suggest that little indicates that a significant number of Cubans, even in the political and academic elites, foresaw a serious crisis in the Soviet Union or Eastern Europe by the early 1980s.

that is, I didn't see then that there was a chance that it would remain a rational thing that could function."

I would like here to mention an article published by José Luis in *Cuba Socialista* in the first half of 1989, as Associate Director of the Center for Research on the World Economy (Centro de Investigaciones de la Economía Mundial, CIES). In the article, he describes the development of the Cuban economy since 1959, which he sees as successful, even with "enormous difficulties and inevitable mistakes."[151] The future prospects of the USSR are not the subject of the article. However, when talking about the Cuban economy, which at that time was highly dependent on the Soviet economy, José Luis states that "[t]hese growth rates reflect the necessary efforts made to create the indispensable infrastructure that makes it possible—later—to enter a phase of accelerated development of the country, supported by its industrialization."

Although his statement is open to interpretation and does not suggest that Cuba necessarily would experience industrialization in the near future, it may give the impression that there were still conditions for growth in the Cuban economy and that an industrialization process could have been possible in Cuba in the 1990s or 2000s. One might argue that if José Luis really anticipated a major crisis in the USSR, it would have made little sense to suggest that an industrialization process would be possible in any near future, since the USSR accounted for three quarters of all Cuba's foreign exchange and that its crisis would eventually be a strong blow. In fact, when the Collapse took place, a large part of the factories in Cuba had to be closed down.

However, beginning in 1987, profound changes indeed took place in the USSR, and it seems credible that these might have created doubts about the future of the country and Cuban–Soviet relations in the Cuban intellectual circles to which José Luis used to belong and still does. As we saw in the introduction, Rachel Walker argues that from 1987 on, there was a "revolution from above" in the USSR,[152] and the crisis developed very quickly after this, although it was not before the beginning of 1989 that the CPSU and Gorbachev "quickly" began losing control.[153] So, well-informed observers in Cuba may very well have gotten an impression that things could quickly go out of control by 1987—though it was not the only possible interpretation, nor the only one that existed amongst Cuban elites—even after Fidel Castro's warning in July 1989, this could appear to have been far from the only perception. It is possible that José

---

151   José Luis Rodríguez, "El desarrollo económico y social en Cuba: resultados de 30 años de la Revolución," *Socialist Cuba*, No. 39 (1989): 61.
152   Walker, 84–85.
153   Ibid.

Luis is exaggerating the degree of clarity in his analysis at the time, that what he says does not really reflect what he thought at the time, but it is also possible that the article in *Cuba Socialista*, for whatever reason, did not fully reflect José Luis's real vision at the time.

In the previous paragraphs, I have demonstrated the informants' views on the predictability of the Collapse. These do not necessarily coincide with what the Cuban authorities perceived, although the line may be blurred in some cases: As I have presented earlier, the academic Jorge claims to have been warned in 1986 by Fidel Castro that a crisis could be coming.[154] José Luis said that by 1987 there was little doubt that the USSR would have serious problems. He was close to the government—in 1993 he assumed the position as Minister of Economy—and what Jorge says about Fidel Castro suggests these possibilities were talked about behind closed doors.

Several measures were taken by the authorities throughout the 1980s that also could be seen in relation to the government's vision of the future of the Soviet Union and Eastern Europe, as well as their vision on the perspectives of Cuban–Soviet relations, although the policies are contradictory and some may also have been motivated by other issues, for example, a general desire to strengthen the economy. In February 1982, a decree-law was signed in the Cuban parliament to allow foreign investment and "the first strong foreign investments," according to José Luis, which he said arrived in 1987. He stated that this (very) limited opening to foreign capital was related to the troubles that Cuban authorities—not the public—perceived in the USSR, as well as in the Cuban–USSR bilateral relations. There are other decisions that might suggest that the Cuban authorities were foreseeing a more difficult scenario, such as the mentioned opening of a biotechnology center in 1986 and the opening to tourism from 1987 onwards.

The counterargument would be that Cuba also concentrated more of its trade with the USSR during these years and thus became more dependent. However, Cuba was under an embargo, which often made it difficult, and sometimes impossible, to trade with other countries. Cuba also suffered other problems related to international trade and financial debt at the time, which may have partly forced these decisions. Furthermore, contrasting perceptions might have existed amongst members of the political elite, and these may have contributed to contradictory policies.

In any case, the measures suggest there was some effort to build a more independent economy, but that these were limited and contradictory and of

---

154 Jorge also alleges that Ernesto Che Guevara was already becoming aware of the USSR model's problems during a visit in 1961–1962: "Che realized everything that was happening, 40 years before (the Collapse), Che saw it."

such a nature that they could have been expected to give results only over the mid to long term. In this sense, it is important to recall what José Luis said about how he perceived the crisis: It was not easily predictable that things were going to happen so fast, nor could a complete collapse have been foreseen. Pedro also stated similar views: "The country's leadership never imagined that the process would be as fast and as abrupt as it turned out." Juan also expressed something similar, when he talked about how, by 1984–85, the Cuban leadership became aware that Cuban–Soviet relations were going to get worse, though they did not inform the public well:

> The Cuban leadership maintained the confidence that the USSR would go through a much longer process and that nothing similar to the dissolution of the USSR as a state would happen. Their imagination did not go that far. One thought that the reform process could lead to a USSR with fewer revolutionary commitments, to modify its commitments with others, such as with us, to a policy of détente with the United States, blah, blah, blah, but final termination it was not, it was totally anticipated [...] But the Cuban leadership did not prepare the population for that, it was handled with discretion, even in '85 there was a Party Congress and it was not talked about.

In light of the various political measures adopted by the government, as I have discussed above, what these informants say seems plausible, although it must be emphasized yet again that different actors within the system had different perceptions.

By the beginning of April 1989, Fidel Castro publicly acknowledged that the situation in the USSR was very difficult. A small book published by the Cuban authorities about Gorbachev's visit to Cuba in April of the same year states that Fidel Castro "referred to serious problems that exist in the USSR," and three months later he even warned that the state as such might disappear, in his speech in Camagüey.[155] Based on what we know, Fidel Castro knew that the situation was serious long before this, but if he had talked about this publicly, it could have contributed to the weakening of the USSR as well as having caused further tension in Cuban–Soviet relations.

Still, it is true that the government's internal response to events was not that fast either. Saving measures could have been implemented earlier on. And although the declaration of the Special Period in January 1990 was an explicit way of explaining to the population that very hard times could be close, the

---

155   Castro and Gorbachev.

first austerity measures in 1989 and early 1990 were relatively marginal.[156] This might have been partly because it would have been politically difficult to enforce such measures earlier, if a part of the ruling elite, as well as the general population still had a perception of the Soviet Union as something more or less solid. Also, even by early 1990, not even Fidel Castro, who was amongst the "pessimists," predicted the speed with which events took place.

Even so, a proactive foreign policy had been underway to avoid international isolation since at least 1989. According to Juan, the government "made an outward reaching foreign policy [*una política exterior de articulación*]." He also argues that "If you look closely, Cuba never broke relations with any of the Eastern European countries that made the transition to capitalism, and it established relations with all the states that arose from the dissolution of the USSR. Cuba [...] did not withdraw itself, rather quite the opposite. It issued all the pseudopods it could... it became equipped with tentacles. And like Spiderman, using all the threads available, Cuba clung to the international system that most resembled its own [...]."

It is important to keep in mind that nobody could confirm or foresee with absolute certainty that the USSR was going to disappear: What happens in the world depends on the will of historical subjects, coincidences, and other factors. There were events in the USSR and Eastern Europe that might have been avoided or at least postponed if certain historical actors had made other decisions (for example, if the coup had not taken place in August 1991 in the USSR).

In relation to this, it may also be important to remember that at that time there were still relatively strong movements on the left in some Latin American countries. Using counterfactual history, one may say that the situation in Cuba in the 1990s could have been somewhat less unfavorable if Carlos Andrés Pérez had not betrayed his mandate in Venezuela (during his 1988 electoral campaign he promised to move away from the IMF but did the opposite as president); if Luis Inacio "Lula" Da Silva had won the elections in Brazil in 1989 (he was an ally of Fidel Castro and was very close to achieving his goal); if the FMLN guerrillas had achieved military victory (which still seemed a possibility in the early 1990s); or if Daniel Ortega had not lost the elections in Nicaragua in 1990. Even if such governments had emerged, they would not have been able to replace a power such as the USSR as a commercial and military ally of Cuba. However, such a different scenario could have led to

---

156 It is also true that the government decided, in those years, to concentrate its foreign trade with the USSR even more, but it is possible that it was meant as a way of solving problems in the short term more than a long-term solution, and—as Juan suggested—because the US blockade and a situation of tensions in the Cuban economy gave the country few other options.

other changes that could have been favorable to Cuba.[157] It was not easy to predict a scenario with such negative implications for Cuba as the one that finally occurred: On an international level, almost everything that could go wrong went wrong.

Some might still question the testimonies. In general, those who claim that they were aware that in the USSR and Eastern Europe a crisis and major changes were likely to come, were people of medium or high educational level who had visited or had contacts in the USSR and Eastern Europe and/or belong to the political elite. It could be said that these people are also the ones who would have had the most to lose if they recognize that they had not been able to predict what was about to happen, since that could affect their prestige as academics and analysts. On the other hand, they were also the ones with the most information and perhaps the most capability for analyzing the situation and more importantly, as we have shown, there are elements that suggest that a significant worsening of the situation may have been seen as probable by some, and they had real reasons to suspect this.

A part of the political leadership shared such perceptions, notably Fidel Castro. The majority of the interview subjects attribute to Fidel Castro some capacity to analyze the situation and to prepare Cuba for more difficult times. Although they are not satisfied with the information they received through the Cuban media, the informants remember Fidel Castro as a solid source of information. His early perceptions that things might become worse, especially after his Camagüey speech on July 26, 1989, and his decision to alert the population, contributed to strengthening the perception of him as a visionary and responsible leader, and this was another factor contributing to unity as the crisis broke out.

2.4 The Immediate Response: "Like When My Mom Stopped Breastfeeding Me"

The interviews suggest a certain variety of immediate reactions to the news about the Collapse, amongst Party members. Such personal reactions are given very little attention in the official press that I analyzed in Part 1, and as I have demonstrated, *Granma* did not give much room to doubts, critical analysis, or pessimism, and certainly not from the early 1990s when the media became more restrictive with alternative views.

Hence, I found it particularly interesting to ask the interviewees about their immediate emotional reactions, which may have been more diverse than what

---

157 In a similar manner to what eventually occurred after the election of Hugo Chavez in Venezuela in 1998, which gave a considerable relief to the Cuban economy.

the official discourse acknowledged at that time. Moreover, in this subsection, I also present additional analytical assessments that some who were interviewed claim to have made during or immediately after the Collapse. In general, the interview subjects acknowledge having suffered, materially and emotionally. Some say that they changed their opinions on certain issues, but they decided to stand with the Revolution and continue as members of the Party. Rather than criticize or discuss the validity of the system, they agreed to participate in activities in favor of the Revolution, which also included, at least in the case of some, taking action to combat opposition activity.

The interview subjects mention some first emotional reactions, such as surprise, sadness, anger, confusion, anxiety or worry, and fright. On the other hand, when referring to other people who distanced themselves from the revolutionary project, they highlight loss of faith, doubts, and fear. Lenin says that the Collapse was "like when my mom stopped breastfeeding me, when I was five or six years old, careful with that … we saw ourselves (…) we found ourselves in a squeeze …" Zenaida also describes the change as dramatic, fast, and something that had a very direct impact: "How was I supposed to feel, since we experienced the suffering firsthand? We all felt it. The fall was so abrupt, so quick." It came as a big surprise to Mavis that the USSR was destroyed as a system, "because [it concerns] something you think is so solid." Again, it is useful here to recall the image of Fidel Castro of the "desmerengamiento" of the USSR,[158] which could imply that the superpower was softer or weaker on the inside than how it was perceived to be.

To Mavis, the Collapse had a moral and ideological impact that still prevails: "Look, if I let myself be carried away by my patriotic sentiments, I would tell you: 'Here I am, homeland or death, we shall overcome, we die covered in red blood!' All those speeches that we give [laughs], we have done it, and it is true that we are willing to do it, but […] I will not answer you like that, I will tell you that it is still affecting us, that it is still affecting us." She states that the fall of the USSR indeed aroused serious fears about the future of Cuba: "There is a very logical, very natural, and explainable foundation that there is something that was not functioning well, there is something that is not working […] and well, who can guarantee us that it will not happen to us, and that we will return to capitalism?" She argues that "If the CPSU over there (fell), which was the strongest organization of the non-capitalist world, if that happened there, what will happen here?"

---

158 As previously explained, this metaphor seems to refer to a merengue (sweet) falling apart, a *desmerengamiento*, and was used by Fidel Castro to describe the Collapse.

Juan speaks of "the three fears," which, according to him, used to be stronger or more latent in the population, although he recognized that by 2013 they were "perhaps now diminishing." These three fears consist of 1) losing sovereignty ("for people in Poland, on the other hand, the socialist counterrevolution gave them independence, so there it is really the other way around"), 2) losing what the revolution had achieved (some of these achievements are presented in Chapter 7), and 3) that a Third-World capitalism would be introduced in Cuba—not a Nordic model—which is what the people of Eastern Europe and the USSR were promised.

These three fears resonate with something written by Jorge Domínguez,[159] who believes that US pressure against Cuba in the early 1990s allowed Cuba to gain internal and international support. One might add that other countries in Latin America suffered strong pressures from the IMF and multinational corporations to introduce neoliberal policies. In Latin America, recent decades have brought few benefits to the majority of the population,[160] a situation that Cuban media and politicians have also taken advantage of.

Several interview subjects allude to the first of these fears, losing independence. Jorge's opinion exemplifies this when he argues that "We could not reinstate capitalism because that would be the death of the nation." Relating the Revolution and socialism to national independence is very common in Cuba. Likewise, the words *patria* (homeland), revolution, and socialism are "frequently emphasized and repeated in the state discourse," to the extent that it seems that one depends on the other, as stated by the anthropologist María Gropas.[161]

When asked if she feared that the US would attack Cuba, Zenaida responds by saying, "I think this [the Revolution] is very strong here. Here they do not dare [...]. And look they have tried indeed, and wherever they throw themselves, they are caught." As she responds in the present tense, it is not clear whether she also thought that such a risk was remote or nonexistent between 1989 and 1991. Héctor, however, says that he was aware of the possibility of an attack: "We were in a position at the time when the Soviet Union disappeared that we could be attacked."

But there may have been a just as strong, or stronger, fear that Cuban-Americans would return to the island and try to influence politics and even recover their properties that had been confiscated when the Revolution took

---

159 Jorge I. Domínguez, "US Policy toward Cuba in the 1980s and 1990s," *Annals of the American Academy of Political and Social Science* 533 (1994): 380–389.
160 Ward, 62.
161 Gropas, 539.

power. In this sense, some of the interview subjects, as well as other Cubans, may have had a personal and collective interest in avoiding political change. Víctor told us that one day he decided to visit a building that his dad had left when he departed from Cuba after the Revolution. There had been a clinic in the building, but in the early 1990s about thirty people lived there:

> I went and talked to people about how they felt about the fact that they were given a house in what had been my dad's clinic. But one day when I go there, I meet, just so you can understand, a woman [...]. She saw me, and she tells me [...] "Joaquinito, come here, you will drink coffee at my house, you are Víctor's son [...]." And after having talked for a while, the woman told me: "Joaquinito, if this [the Cuban system] changes, don't take my house away." This was in the year of 94, when people in Miami put a "letra" [annual prediction made by babalaos or priests belonging to the Yoruba religion] [...] believing that this was about to change.

According to Lenin, "It is true what *el Comandante* said, at that time everyone had the suitcase ready to come here, because they thought we were going down. It's like you fall into a pond and the water reaches up here [...]. They had the suitcases and everything, they gave it a deadline, 'This year is the end of Cuba.'"

Some informants explicitly recognized that they had not expected the crisis to be so long and so profound. Héctor admitted that "[w]e knew that hard times were coming, but well, the hope that one always has as a human being, we did not expect times to be so hard." Hernández Rivera conveyed that "[w]e thought it was going to recover faster, and look all the time it has taken," suggesting that the crisis was still in place in 2013.

Did the authorities employ a deliberate strategy of pretending that the crisis was going to be shorter than what was really anticipated, in order to avoid increasing discontent? This is certainly possible, but it is beyond the scope of this study to answer such a question with certainty. It is also possible that the authorities simply thought that they were going to quickly get out of the crisis. Indeed, optimism has been a constant since the Revolution. For example, in a 1959 speech, Fidel Castro said, "If they don't throw a wrench into the works, I am sure that within a few years we will elevate the Cuban standard of living above that of the United States and of Russia."

Some of the most optimistic Party members may, by the early 1990s, have dreamed of a recovery of the USSR (or that the increasing ties with China were going to help, with a change in US relations, the discovery of oil in Cuba, which has long been talked about, or any other possibility). These kinds of beliefs may also have helped some to endure the sacrifices of the Special Period. It is also possible that having suffered very tense and difficult situations in the past were factors that helped prevent panic.

In this sense, two interview subjects mentioned previous events that had affected their country strongly. To Eliécer, the Special Period was "the second thing to hit us [...] at the triumph of the Revolution the United States [was] depriving us of the sugar quota and it began with the blockade, to us here the financial squeeze was ... there was nothing, everything was very difficult." Idulberto makes the same comparison by mentioning that "now people talk about the crisis of socialism, but from the years after Girón [the Bay of Pigs invasion], to the 70s and so, there was nothing to eat here, my friend [...] there has been a crisis, what happens is that there are generations that did not live it, and some who do not want to remember." Héctor, on the other hand, draws a parallel between the Special Period and the Missile Crisis in the 1960s when he expresses the following: "I saw a greater possibility of disappearing during the October Crisis."

The informants recall that there were Party members who lost faith, distanced themselves, or broke with the hegemonic political project in Cuba. José mentions former colleagues "who were revolutionary" and who "lost strength." He explains such changes in relation to their attitude. According to him, they "feared that this [the system, the revolutionary project] would collapse." When asked if he knew Party members who lost their faith, José responds as follows: "Hahaha ... sure, sure, of course, it is not what most abounded," and he attributes this to the high demands or requirements that existed in order to enter the Party at that time. About his opinion and attitude, he reveals the following: "I didn't stop being revolutionary, but honestly, I tell you that I saw things [the situation] as very difficult."

José's claim that there was no mass desertion from the Party is echoed in the academic literature. There were even many cases such as Víctor, who decided to enter the Party in a situation where the Party's and the Cuban system's future was doubted by many, perhaps especially outside of Cuba. According to William LeoGrande, while communist parties in Eastern Europe "constantly lost members" during the 1980s, in Cuba, "on the contrary, the Party has grown rapidly through all the Special Period, at almost double the rate of the previous decade."[162]

Even so, Zenaida suggests that many members had their doubts: "Even many Party members did not believe that this was going to be survivable, because I had colleagues who even suggested at the meeting to ask for a leave from the

---

162 LeoGrande, "El Partido Comunista de Cuba y la Política Electoral: Adaptación, Sucesión y Transición," 42.

Party with the purpose of then leaving the country. But we went and calmed them down, and we were telling them, 'Hey, look, it is not like that, this will continue.'"

Víctor entered the Party in 1991 and also believes that indeed "many people" left the Party during those years (which might be true, although, as we have seen, the general tendency was one of growth). He explained this by saying that in difficult times "there are people who even get scared." This resonates with Eliécer's explanation: "Whenever there is a period like this, always, as we say, the weak give way [laughter] and the weak leave, I mean, they leave in the sense that they leave the [Revolutionary] process. It may be that they go to the US, they may stay here, but they lose strength." Both felt that this has had a cleansing effect on the Party. Nevertheless, it raised my attention that some informants mixed the topics of leaving the Party and leaving the country, implying a politicized view on Cuba migration.

By the time I worked in Cuba in the late 2000s and even more so in 2013, migration was generally accepted by most Cubans as an individual decision, and it was also common that Cubans showed gratitude toward friends and family abroad who by their personal sacrifice sent back remittances to the island. Also, it was obvious that migrants had different reasons for migrating, many of which were not related to politics. Yet several interview subjects cited the case of the *balseros* (Cuban rafters) who left Cuba in 1994 as an example of people who lost their faith—apparently in the Revolutionary project, in the nation, or in its future possibilities under the current order.

For those not familiar with the *Cuban rafter crisis*, this refers to a massive and traumatic departure of people by sea on fragile vehicles, which not only split families but also cost many lives. Several informants seemed, thus, to view emigration as a means through which people distanced themselves from "the system," protested against it, or at least said in some way that they were not willing to sacrifice themselves for certain principles. This despite the fact that even Fidel Castro claimed, at least in his later years, that most migrants had left the country for economic reasons.

In the academic literature, it is sometimes argued that Cuba has been using migration to get critics to emigrate instead of protesting against the government. Albert O. Hirschman, known as the author of the theory of "exit" and "voice," claims that this has been done "on a large scale" under Fidel Castro.[163] While migration has certainly contributed to the easing of discontent within the country, it seems unlikely that most of the people who emigrated in the

---

163   Albert O. Hirschman, *Rival Views of Market Society and Other Recent Essays* (Cambridge: Harvard University Press, 1992), 91.

early 1990s did so *primarily* or even to a high degree as a political protest. While anti-Castro sentiments are strong in older generations amongst the exiles in Florida, only a small fraction of the migrants in the 1990s have organized against the Cuban government, even though the US and their social context allow them to. Most migrants at the time probably had strong discontents with the Cuban system, and they suffered restrictions implemented as part of the system, but most Cubans are also fully aware that the critical situation was caused by several factors. They knew about the Collapse of the Soviet Union, and they were aware of the US embargo/blockade.

Yet several of the informants in this study claimed those who had left the Party or emigrated were weak with regard to their principles. The informants' attitudes sometimes resembled those of official attitudes some decades ago. Clearly, a situation where tens of thousands leave the country on rafts with an elevated risk of losing their life suggests that circumstances were extremely difficult. Although the US could be said to have stimulated this kind of migration (through the embargo/blockade, the visa policy, the Cuban Adjustment Act, the so-called "Wet foot, dry foot" policy), it was certainly not a far-fetched idea to blame the Cuban government's policies over the years, or characteristics of the Cuban system, for some or even many of the difficulties.

This being said, most informants seem to have held the idea, that one should stay in Cuba even if the situation was threatening and difficult. The idea that one was part of a collective and that resisting in Cuba was a dignifying act that one did not give in to outside pressures could have been a source of motivation for many. When socialist ideas were questioned throughout the world and also in segments of Cuban society, most of the Cuban Party members continued defending the system.

The members we interviewed seemed to have felt sincerely their reasons for having joined the Party and thus retained their validity and they knew that these still had considerable support in their surroundings, that is, amongst a sizable part of the Cuban population. Some might have been more disillusioned than they were willing to admit; they might have had more doubts, done things because of routine or social pressure more than a personal impulse and so on. Yet, there were also social pressures in Eastern Europe and the Soviet Union, and there is little reason to doubt that most Cuban Party members still had Revolutionary beliefs and an identification with the government.

In this context, rather than demanding a profound debate on the Collapse and on socialism in general or by distancing themselves from socialist ideas altogether, the informants accepted the decision taken by their Party and by Fidel Castro to defend the system ("the Revolution") and closed ranks and participated actively when asked to do so. In this sense, the informants represent the dominant tendency in the Party, in which a considerable part of the general population also participated.

Informant Norma said to me that "There was a lot of mobilization." The scholarly literature supports such an affirmation. Richard Fagen concluded in 1969 that "the Cuban revolutionary culture was shaped by action and mobilization."[164] Pérez-Stable emphasizes how Fidel Castro used popular mobilization, especially until 1970[165] and again from the 1990s and onwards.[166] The mobilization during the Special Period seems to have had different purposes, such as solving problems of production and distribution, involving and motivating people and promoting culture but also disciplining undesired behavior in society, including attitudes and actions that challenged the system.

When the crisis of socialism occurred, according to José Luis, "The [Cuban] Party played a fundamental role because it was the force that brought people together socially, that is, it was the political force that guided society and the one that translated general orientations into specific and practical measures that were discussed with the people; it promoted mobilizations, gave impulse to resistance."

Eliécer attributes to the Party a unifying and a leading role, one that depended on an "organized society" to function: "Through mass organizations, guiding the population, we had to guide the public about the blackouts, this and that, when these kinds of problems occurred, immediately communicate it to the zonal nuclei, to the basic nuclei of the labor organization, to the Federation of Cuban Women, to the Committees for the Defense of the Revolution. The Party is a unity, the Party has its strength in an organized society." According to Pedro:

> The role of the Party at that time was to engage mainly in supporting the population and to ensure that the few supplies that existed reached out to the people. I'm going to mention, as an example, some things here in this neighborhood. My oldest son who at that time lived here with me—now he is married and lives somewhere else—he was the delegate of the People's Power of this constituency [a delegate to the local parliament], and then he helped to distribute a type of hamburger to the population, daily, bread with a hamburger was distributed in a café and then for each Committee for the Defense of the Revolution.

---

164 Richard Fagen, *The Transformation of Political Culture in Cuba* (Stanford University Press, 1969), in Baloyra and Morris, 10.
165 Pérez-Stable, 100–101.
166 Ibid., 132–134, 145–146.

The interview subjects describe a situation in which the majority of the population relied on and automatically accepted the role played by the Party.

Héctor states, "I must say that the Party played a very large role in all this." According to Mavis, "The Party is again the rope that is thrown to you from the shore. What is it that we hold on to? [...] I think it would have been very difficult to maintain the Revolution without, without the leadership of that Party, of this Party." Though not referring specifically to the years of the Collapse, Lenin contends that "Without that party, this would have fallen." According to Jorge, "Here all those years the Party maintained the confidence it enjoyed in the population, and preparations were made to face the crisis." Alberto told me during the interview that "People had confidence, man!"

Internally, in the Party, our informants were willing to follow the instructions given from above. In the words of Zenaida:

> I have followed all the Party's indications, that is apart from [in addition to] what just comes naturally, all their indications. The same in the CDR as in the workplace, when there was a marathon of that [inaudible word], during the problems with people leaving as well. We fought that a lot, those that were called the scum (*la escoria*), and all the things I have managed to fight for, I have done it for the Revolution and now the same.

Among the other organizations that participated, Héctor mentions the CDR, which he says "played a huge role at that time, and the unions led by the Party organization at the workplaces, so that workers were not demoralized."

During the critical years, new organizations were also created to support the work of the Party in defense of the system. Héctor tells us that the Association of Combatants of the Cuban Revolution emerged: "Here it is very difficult in our country, until now, because, well, we are disappearing, it is very difficult to find a house in which there is no combatant [veteran] of the Cuban revolution [...] because imagine, three hundred thousand Cubans in Angola, several thousands in Ethiopia, several in Guinea-Bissau, others around here, international and clandestine doctors, the Rebel Army, very difficult. So, this has a great and enormous moral weight in the local community." Alberto mentions another example from the cultural sector: "The municipal coordinators of the UNEAC [National Union of Writers and Artists of Cuba] were created. They were artists who engaged in their communities to try to rescue what from a community level was important for the cultural life of the country. This was an effort to solve a problem generated by an absence of financing."

Some refer to activities known as volunteer work. For example, Norma participated in the Food Plan in Nueva Paz [municipality near Havana] for two months, "picking yams, picking *malanga*, cleaning sugar cane, because I also cleaned sugar cane, I spent two months in Nueva Paz." Although most of the Party members remained loyal to the authorities, and strict unity was enforced, certain tensions emerged outside the organization. Unauthorized or illegal opposition became more visible.[167] The informants disagreed on whether the opposition grew in numerical terms or not. Pedro believes that there was an increase in their activity in the 1990s but that they were the same opponents as always and that they were supported by the US: "Immediately when their [US] policy toward the Socialist Camp succeeded, they began to do the same in Cuba [...] [but] nothing happened here." The presence of the opposition was, according to him, the same as always: "There is a small sector of the population that since the last century has maintained an annexationist mindset, which is a pro-North-American mindset, who want capitalism to come here again."

Eliécer believes that there was a numerical increase in active government opponents, which he attributes to the difficult situation: "Every time there is a process like this, of difficulties etc., etc., look, as if by law, opposition surfaces, as if by law, believers increase in numbers, there is an upsurge in religious beliefs."[168] He still claims it was a "marginal" phenomenon. There was never a strong opposition to the government as in some countries of Eastern Europe and in the USSR. This was also pointed out by Esteban: "In other socialist countries, such as Romania, such as Hungary, such as Poland itself, Czechoslovakia, the process of criticism toward the system became an attitude against the system itself [while in Cuba it did not reach that point]."

Some interview subjects gave their explanations as to why that did not happen. Pedro acknowledges that these years were "politically very bitter" and "a direct suffering for the people," but he maintains that "never [...] in a way that such sentiments turned into sentiments of pro-system change." Another

---

167 We have avoided the use of the term *dissidents* to refer to the organized opposition. Although it is clear that the organized opposition is made up of people who disagree with (dissent from) official policies, this term can be interpreted as all other Cubans agreeing with—or at least not expressing their discontent with—official policies. The interviewees of the study themselves shows that even in the PCC there are many people who disagree strongly about certain issues without being considered or considering themselves as "dissidents."

168 Also, the references to specific members of the opposition in the interviews are very unfavorable. Esteban characterized a well-known opposition member as "very discredited" and said that another one, whom he also mentioned by name, as a person who was "good for nothing." After I had turned off the microphone, Suárez commented very unfavorably on the intellectual capacity of two specific and well-known opponents with whom he has spoken personally, one of whom he seemed to know through his work as a medical doctor.

explanation is the alleged non-independent nature of the opposition ("This opposition seems like a puppet opposition," Esteban argues), which might have made it lack credibility in the eyes of many Cubans,[169] the absence of a bourgeoisie (Esteban: "[in Eastern Europe] you had a bourgeoisie that stayed there, with its money and many of its properties and that could support you, but here in Cuba there was nothing left of that [after the Revolution]"), the identification of the opposition with a system that people did not consider a good one ("We had fifty years of a multiparty system in Cuba, a multiparty system made in American style; these were the 50 years of a pseudo-republic, and people don't want to go back to that in any way," said Pedro. He refers to the fear of "the people of Miami return[ing] politically").

The informants' narratives suggest, explicitly or not, a situation in which socialism is beneficial for the majority and that if someone expresses themselves against the system, they do so for reasons that are not the result of poor government performance or problems with the system, but for "individual reasons" such as the lack of an ability to analyze, that they have been deceived by capitalist propaganda, or even due to opportunism and personal gain. For example, they would seek financial support from abroad through regime change programs for Cuba by the US and try to position themselves for a capitalist Cuba. According to Pedro, in Cuba since the Revolution, "Nobody has ever been persecuted for their political ideas." He believes that "the law has fallen on those who conspire with weapons in hand, who cause sabotage, who kill someone, who place a bomb, yes." Then he added that "Those who are allies with and receive money from US politics are persecuted, of course, as in any other country."

This narrative is problematic. Amnesty International's annual report of 1990 cited 60 cases of detained opponents, and contended that many opponents were arrested simply for expressing their political opinion. It also referred to cases of violence against opponents.[170] In the 1990s, there was also an increase in discontent in the general population, which provoked an event sometimes

---

169 Although Esteban also said that there is a *legitimate* opposition in Cuba, of which he considers that he is himself a part. He described this as a revolutionary opposition within the PCC. Curiously, he claimed that Elizardo Sánchez, a well-known member of what is normally called the opposition—the non-authorized organized opposition—tried to recruit him (Esteban) to form part of his organization.

170 The number of prisoners of conscience in Cuba oscillates. In the autumn of 2015, in Cuba there was "only" one prisoner of conscience, according to Amnesty International ("Amnesty International declares Cuba graffiti artist a prisoner of conscience," Reuters, September 29, 2015). Other sources accuse Cuba of having replaced a practice of prolonged arrests of people considered to be politically dangerous, with a more frequent use of short-term detentions. This could be a strategy to avoid international criticism.

referred to as the *Maleconazo*, a street demonstration in 1994. Perhaps because it was a spontaneous manifestation and not something organized by the traditional opposition, and/or because of the considerable number of participants, it received a different treatment than what is usual: Fidel Castro went out to speak with the protesters in person.

The Party members also tried to fight opposition in all its forms in many different ways. José mentions organizations such as the Defense and Production Brigades, the Territorial Troops Militia, and the Rapid Response Brigades, which were aimed at maintaining political stability. (The first two have existed since the 1980s.) Explaining the need to employ these, he argues that "It was necessary to stop the element that was 'agusanando' [the adjective in Spanish refers to the term *worm*, used by Fidel Castro in reference to exiles, or counter-revolutionary Cubans, so *agusanado* would be something like becoming "wormified"] that could support those people."

The scholar Jorge Domínguez maintains that these brigades used informal targeted violence[171] on the streets, a type of violence that became more frequent from the middle of 1991 and onwards. According to Domínguez, this had not been a common practice until that time.[172] "Though not unprecedented, this use of targeted informal violence to stifle dissent was in many ways new," Domínguez asserts.[173]

José believes that these groups that were organized to defend the system emerged from the very population, but people did not always participate massively: "Groups were also organized to go out if someone threw bottles. What did they call them? The Rapid Response Brigades. But not everyone responded, so I had to go out alone, and there were two or three people who did not go out who should have done so." Apparently, he considers it necessary for revolutionaries to go out and enforce order in a convulsive situation.

Perhaps more surprisingly, journalist Víctor stated that he had taken part in violence against what he considered to be "negative elements," without even having been asked about this in the interview. He did not clarify whether he was referring to the organized opposition, but it seemed like a reference to spontaneous protesters. Víctor presented this violence as a kind of self-defense. He claimed that "Here, a demonstration against the Revolution has never been broken up by the [police or military] force. We have hit them, but it is the people who have fought here against negative elements that came out with

---

171 Domínguez, "The Political Impact on Cuba of the Reform and Collapse of Communist Regimes," 124–125.
172 Ibid.
173 Ibid.

their pots asking for more food and we put the pots in the head, but it wasn't the police, it was us, it wasn't people with a shield and sticks, it was us, because we also have the right to defend this."

In the case of Víctor's statement, it is not specified whether when he says that "[w]e have hit them" he refers to events during the years 1989–1991 or at another moment after 1959. Clearly, he sees himself as a victim of acts of indiscipline, intents to overthrow a system with majority support, or whatever—despite describing a situation where he has apparently attacked peaceful protesters in a physical manner. Such practices certainly constitute a disrespect for the Human Right of Freedom to assembly and might have been an efficient way of discouraging certain activities that were considered to be against the system, although the experiences of Eastern Europe and the Soviet Union suggest these do not work in every situation.

There were also Party members who said they were instructed to use dialogue and try to convince people, which might suggest a two-track approach to opposition from the authorities, but it could also suggest that different leaders on a local level gave different orders according to their principles and ideas. Norma relays that "During the meeting with the Party branch, the secretary told us: 'Do not let people speak badly of the Revolution, if you are at a bus stop and any citizens come out against the Revolution, you call that person and make her or him understand what you know of, of, of Cuba, of the Party, of socialism, of everything, you give that person a speech, you talk with them in a good way not in a bad way, do you hear me.'" She told me that when "I was in a *guagua* [bus] queue [...] I heard a guy who was coming against our revolutionary principles, I told him 'Man, come here, you are wrong, because this is so, and so,' and like that we fight for some ideals.'"

2.5 The Causes of the Collapse: "The Defenses Had Completely Fallen to the Ground..."

Although there was no national debate about the causes of the Collapse, it is an issue that has been discussed among Cubans for more than two decades, and there is a proliferation of opinions. Some interview subjects do not refer to an explicit cause—or several causes—of the Collapse. Others express diverse opinions on the subject, and the interviews clearly show that there is no consensus on this issue within the Party, although some ideas and explanations are often repeated. Among our interviewees, there were six people who do not express a clear opinion about the causes of the fall.[174] This may be due to a lack

---

174 In some cases it may be because we didn't ask the informant the question, in other cases they told us that they did not know or that they did not remember. Some also mention a

of information and a broad media debate on the subject. They may also avoid giving opinions on the subject because they are aware that it is an extremely complex problem and therefore difficult to provide definitive answers. In the following, I will first describe the opinions issued by the interview subjects and then analyze them in greater depth.

I will begin with the *six interview subjects who do not give (or do not very explicitly give) an explanation for the causes of the Collapse:*

1) Zenaida states that "In regard to that, I did not ... I did not realize that, well, *how* socialism collapsed, I tell you that sincerely. I don't remember how things happened."

2) Norma says she can't find the words to explain how the system fell: "What did they do to the USSR in order for it to break like that? What happened? An idea like that, maybe I don't have such a clear idea to be able to explain to you, I can't explain it because the words just don't come to explain it to you. But something big must have happened there." She reiterated her doubts: "Something big must have happened when the Socialist Camp [*campo socialista*] fell so abruptly."

3) Mavis did not explicitly state the causes of the fall of the model, although on several occasions she referred to popular support for Gorbachev's reforms—which apparently tried to modify the old system—and how happy the people of Berlin were when the Wall fell. This could indicate that the model suffered a crisis of legitimacy, although the causes of such a crisis of legitimacy remain unexplained.

4) Mery did not provide an explanation of the Collapse either but mentioned that she has changed her position on Gorbachev, who was the main exponent of reforms: First she maintained a positive position, but over time she has come to think that he contributed to creating new problems, though she did not believe he had intentions of destroying the system. He was also affected by his political surroundings and the unfavorable international context, she suggested, and mentioned something that her father had told her before the fall, though it is not clear if this is also her opinion: Gorbachev's "flirting" with the West was going to end the USSR.

5) Idulberto mentioned a series of problems experienced by Soviet society: especially religious discrimination but also corruption, material problems, and lack of ideological awareness (there was a lot of materialism in the sense that people wanted to obtain material goods), strong resentment

---

series of problems that these societies had, without necessarily saying which weight each one had or which were the main causes of the fall.

or even hate toward Russians in Czechoslovakia, the way in which the Soviet Communist Party recruited its members, and so on. He does not present a single explanation as to why there was a collapse.

6) Juan mentions problems of a political nature (there was no counterbalance against the power of the state, although Lenin had tried to create a structure, the Soviets—workers' councils—which could assume this function) and of an economic nature (there was excessive centralization of the economy, although he recognizes that Cuba exaggerated even more in this regard). In addition, he mentions that he has heard, within the Party, different opinions on the subject, "four, five, six" different basic views. He mentions four of these:[175] 1) Gorbachev was an agent of British intelligence, 2) the fall was the product of competition with the West on the economic and military levels, a competition that the USSR was not able to win, 3) the Collapse was due to the lack of social conscience, and the model was something like an empty "shell" without social support, 4) and what he calls the interpretation of Fidel Castro, that Gorbachev was a man of good intentions who wanted to fix the system but who made tactical mistakes, which led to counterrevolutionary forces taking control of the Party.[176] However, Juan does not reveal explicitly *his own* interpretation.

On the other hand, there are 11 respondents who try to explain why the Collapse occurred, although in several cases they express "reservations" stating that these are complex issues:

1) Lenin believes that the system fell due to the conflict between different nationalities: "And do you know where the system falls? This has always existed, all the republics [...] were countries, weren't they countries?" He believes that it was a problem that had been "swept under the carpet," that is, it had been hidden or suppressed, but as time passed, it was inevitable that these would reemerge, as there was a will for independence. "That was coming from the past ...," he claims. Lenin mentions that

---

175 Although he points out that there may also be other views.
176 When we interviewed Juan, he claimed that Fidel Castro's vision of the collapse of the USSR echoed early criticisms of Soviet society made by Leo Trotsky. Our informant said that "It is not an external conquest, it is not a counterrevolutionary force that takes power [...] is the same ruling class that splits and changes the formula, isn't it? So ... without it being said explicitly [Fidel Castro's analysis] approaches Trotsky's positions, when he, in *The Betrayed Revolution*, describes Stalinism as the bureaucratic dictatorship of a workers' state." See: Leon Trotsky, *The Betrayed Revolution: What is the Soviet Union and where is it headed?* (New York: Pathfinder, 1992).

"[e]veryone says that the Socialist Camp fell because of Gorbachev."[177] He declared that he did not personally agree with this: "One man does not generate that, he accelerated the system, the fall, he accelerated it [...]."

2) Jorge emphasizes that the Collapse has several causes but believes that the main cause is the formation of the political elites: "In my opinion, the main cause of the fall of the USSR and the Socialist Camp lies in the formation of the leading elite, the people who govern the society, the leaders' intellectual, scientific, and ethical schooling is what determines the development of a country. You cannot have a developed country when it is led by people with an underdeveloped mind." This made it more difficult to solve the problems of agriculture and to manage diversity of thought in society.

According to him, the problem is that socialism is immature and still does not know how to use the knowledge in society to its benefit; for these reasons, some leaders resort to repression.[178] Jorge paraphrases Marx's thesis that "The philosophers have hitherto only interpreted the world; the point is to change it" and adds that "When you change socialism, this thesis is turned upside down. The world has been changed, right? Now it's about interpreting it." The world becomes more complex, but the political elite does not rise to the occasion. Lenin was an intelligent and cultivated leader. Stalin was intelligent but not cultivated.

3) José mentions several problems that the USSR suffered and theorizes that the country ran out of force or energy because it brought revolutions to other peoples. The people in those countries, on the other hand, grew tired because they had not created the Revolution themselves; they had not made sacrifices and therefore did not value what they had. He asked rhetorically, "How often do you think about the air you breathe?" He asserted that intervening in Eastern Europe at the end of World War II to end Nazi occupation was the right thing to do, but the Soviets should have retired instead of demanding the establishment of a particular system. That task should have been left to the country's residents. I asked him, thus, why had the system in the USSR also collapsed, since the people there had created their own revolution (at least in the case of Russia). He says, "In my opinion, the system falls because they simply stop doing

---

177 It is our impression that amongst Cubans in general, a considerable number of people hold Gorbachev responsible, although as can be seen in this study, it is far from the only explanation that exists.

178 Jorge mentioned the film *The Lives of Others* (Germany, 2006), which deals with the state's surveillance of intellectuals in East Germany, and the repression they suffered in general. Jorge argues that "Those things that are there (in the movie) are true."

or stop seeing issues they had to see and fall into weaknesses [...]." He believes that "they started relaxing, and the enemy is working, the enemy is working."

4) According to Eliécer as well, the main causes are internal, but imperialism exploits internal problems in order to accelerate a change of regime. The internal crisis is due to weaknesses (he mentions mainly weakness or ideological softness) but also financial problems and other problems, such as nationality conflicts, which, together, had created a distance between the population and the Communist Party of the Soviet Union. With regard to external infiltration, he believes that Gorbachev made bad decisions and that American intelligence institutions "worked on him." He also refers to the role of the Catholic Church in changing the regime in Poland. He believed that the fall of the Berlin Wall was orchestrated by imperialism and that external forces were working to influence public opinion and convince people about the benefits of Western life.

This type of foreign penetration works, he argues, if one gives in to imperialism, and that it works best when there is neither ideological solidity nor awareness of the enemy's aggressive character. He quotes Che Guevara: "I still believe, as our commander Ernesto Che Guevara once said, there can be no trust, neither in capitalism, nor in imperialism, not even a tiny bit" [*ni un tantico así*]. But at the same time, he specifies that the root causes of the Collapse emerged long before, because although imperialism achieved its objectives, it only "helped to precipitate something that was coming. I don't know if you understand me; it's not that he [Gorbachev] did it, no, it was something that was already on its way and he speeded it up, as simple as that." He argued that some problems had their roots back to the Second World War.

5) Héctor states that the main causes were that ideological work was not taken seriously (there was too much emphasis on material growth and personal well-being) and that the enemy had influenced people over an extended period, for example, creating a favorable impression of Western societies. Hence, people made no resistance to the coup of 1991: "It was a people who, I would say, was prepared, or they had prepared them or ripened them in order to give them such a blow." He warns that "You can't become naïve; the Soviet Union was heavily besieged by multiple people, a permanent work of intelligence, and so on, from the opposite field, that is, from the imperial power, radio stations, propaganda, life in Europe, everyone has a great life, everyone has a car, a good two-story house, everyone is without problems and it seems like not, but it [the propaganda] keeps on creating and permeating, as we say in Cuba, permeating

ideologically." He compares it to the weakening of the human defense system: "The defenses had completely fallen to the ground, and, as we often speak of in medical circles, in order for any virus like that, or bacteria like that to penetrate society and destroy what was the Soviet Union."

6) Alberto believes that the Collapse had two main causes. First, "The economic structure led to ways of thinking that were prone to rejection [of the system or established order]." Secondly, "the impossibility of the cultural sphere to offer an alternative [to the hegemonic culture of the West]." He alleged that these two were connected and that "economic structures" were created "that facilitated certain, even certain social differences. That's how I see it. It generated, generated insurmountable internal problems, which further generated a way of thinking. When you, from a concept of bringing material goods to people, material goods and material goods to people, develop a thought related to that, the only thing that is developing is an insatiable thought." Apparently, he said, there *was* an emphasis on ideological work, but it was something that was done mechanically. As a problem, he also highlights the fact that the Russians began to play the role that the West had, according to him, previously played in Eastern Europe. That is, influencing the region by force. This created a resistance to the Russians. There was a "Russian Eurocentrism" in which other cultures were belittled, also those that existed within the USSR. In Alberto's opinion, the Socialist Camp failed to let go of Eurocentrism, and there was no "profound" or real solidarity.

7) Esteban argues that "The causes of the Collapse are internal, they are of internal deterioration and a system that at the end of the day did not work." He thinks that the country "the Soviet Union was born with a set of problems" and that Lenin understood that these were problems that needed to be solved. However, he died too early. He believes that Trotsky "was a very strong guy" who saved the USSR during the Western powers' intervention wars against the young socialist republic. On the other hand, he mentions that Stalin was not the best person to lead the Party, although mostly praising his leadership during times of war. The economic model was moreover adapted to times of war but was not the best for times of peace, and for the difficult situation after World War II, which favored a US that had not been destroyed by the war. Referring to the Gorbachev period, he states that the Party was so weak that it could not be used to lead the country. The political situation was very bad, worse than the economy, because they had waited too long to renew the system. Adding to this, the Soviet leaders had lost valuable years that could have been used to improve the system because of the power vacuum that

existed between 1983 and 1984, during the brief mandates of Andropov and Chernenko. There was also a "very thick cloud of censorship [*un cerrazón muy grande*] for many years" in relation to debates, and things suddenly opened up, so that "Suddenly people have the possibility to talk about all the outrageous things that were happening."

He believes that imperialism and especially the US took advantage of the crisis, but that the causes of Collapse were mainly internal: "Those who tell you that the causes of the Collapse were external, are making a big mistake. There were external causes too, but those external causes were marginal."[179]

8) José Luis believes that the Collapse has many explanations but claimed that political errors are more decisive than economic errors. There was a long process of decomposition, "from the mistakes of the Stalin era [he mentioned forced collectivization in agriculture and the purges of the 1930s], and later the failed reforms of Khrushchev, the stagnation with Brézhnev, the impossibility of action during Andropov, the stand-still under Chernenko, until Gorbachev entered practically, then there was an attempt to fix this." He states that in the 1980s, society had become a "completely gray thing," and he suggested that popular mobilization (which implies some type of active participation) might have been something that could have counteracted such a problem. Khrushchev had opted for popular mobilization in the 1950s, and according to José Luis, Gorbachev tried to revitalize this in the 1980s. However, he also had some unrealistic or naive ideas: "His thesis of a common European home, for example, and this, in the era of Reagan and of Thatcher, had no chance, and that practically led to the USSR beginning to yield unilaterally in order to seek peaceful coexistence, and that was impossible."

Gorbachev had an unfavorable political circle surrounding him, José Luis claims, mentioning as names Alexander Yakovlev and Eduard Shevardnadze as elements that hindered what he was trying to achieve. Gorbachev failed to create a government that marched in one direction. José Luis believes that Gorbachev "wanted to do things in a very responsible way, and everything went wrong." Still, the problems had begun long before him.

---

179 According to Esteban, the foreign policy of Gorbachev was based on some truth ("tenia algo de veracidad") as Gorbachev needed "an international environment in which the Soviet Union could maneuver"; however, he considers that the former Soviet leader was naïve in thinking that Thatcher, Mitterrand, and Reagan would permit the USSR to strengthen again.

ANALYSIS OF THE INTERVIEWS 295

9) Pedro argues that a combination of external subversion and internal weaknesses caused the Collapse. He talks more about internal weaknesses and believes that Soviet socialism and the Soviet party (and in Eastern European countries) had moved away from the masses. The problems had accumulated for many years.[180] There were so many internal problems (political, social, economic, nationalist and separatist sentiments, different conflicts) that, relative to what the leaders wanted, the system was destined to collapse. Gorbachev's decisions were not good, but the Collapse "was not only Gorbachev's fault. It was on its way before, long before."

10) Víctor makes a long list of all the problems in the countries of the Socialist Camp and specifically in the USSR, at different times in history. He says that they murdered their intellectuality, that there was a lack of individual freedoms, there was cultural chauvinism, a restrictive cultural policy (which, he pointed out, had been criticized by "Che"), centralization and grandiloquence (the megaprojects, for example) and often little attention was paid to people's everyday problems: "It is contradictory that you reach the cosmos, but the women do not shave their legs."[181] He said, however, that Stalinism ended the USSR. He points out Khrushchev and Gorbachev as leaders who tried to change society after Stalin, but they did not succeed, Khrushchev by not targeting the essence of the problem and Gorbachev because "they did not only throw the water out of the bathtub, they threw the bathtub with the child and everything." Even so, he believes that the USSR had "too many wounds" to be saved. He

---

180 Pedro also stated that it is very difficult to talk about the history of the USSR and responsibilities, because "No event has its origin in something specific or very concrete, they are historical issues that date back to World War II at the time of Stalin, Khrushchev, etc., to a series of different events (...) It was not about one single ruler, they were an accumulation of problems over many years."

181 He suggested that the lack of attention to people's everyday problems had also been a problem in Cuba. Referring to a visit to a hospital in eastern Holguín Province, he reports that "There, you see the issue, this is a place where they separate Siamese twins, and the toilets are clogged, isn't it so? You have cosmonauts and the toilets are not working, the machines have problems, no, no, there are common things that you have to—I say this in my personal opinion, and this happened a lot to the Soviets, a lot, a lot—they went out in the cosmos but people were lagging behind, behind, behind." On the other hand, when commenting on the unequal living conditions he saw in the USSR and the poor state of the health system, he says that in Cuba the situation was very different: "In Moscow 80 (Summer Olympics), when you travelled a short distance, like from Havana to Güira [a small place near Havana], people lived in terrible conditions, and public health was so bad, compared to Cuba, we have not had that sort of problems here."

also said that the Soviet Union denied their own history [apparently referring to past struggles and victories] during Perestroika.

11) Aurelio also mentions a series of problems in the countries of the Socialist Camp (extractivism, emphasis on heavy industry, a primitive vision of the economy, an attempt to compete with the West but adopting the premises of the West to generate more profit, etc.). He believes that the debate about the Collapse is very complicated and that not all its aspects have been discussed yet. He states that he previously considered it to be "primarily an economic debate," but over time he has come to the conclusion that Stalinism was the problem, "but not with Stalinism as in just the one person Stalin." He thinks that "the worst thing with Stalin was that he perverted the possibility of popular participation," that is, the possibility of a socialist democracy. When the economy suffers a moment of crisis, the population is very divided, and there is also "a disconnection" between the elite and the population, due to the centralization of power. The "merit" of Gorbachev was that he tried to end this, but he failed. It is not known whether Perestroika was good or bad because in 1989, the original Perestroika was changed to a more pro-capitalist plan.[182]

To sum up, six of my informants did not give any clear opinion regarding the causes of the fall of the USSR. With respect to the 11 people who do endeavor to give some explanation, in some cases it is difficult to highlight a single cause as the primary one because they mention many causes without ordering them hierarchically, without specifying the importance of each one. The wide variety of responses makes it more difficult to make generalizations beyond the mentioned pluralism of opinion. However, some trends are identifiable:

They give more importance to internal factors than to external ones. In general, the interview subjects who give their opinions about the causes of the Collapse agree that the main causes are internal and not external. However, a surprising number of people emphasize to a considerable extent the subversive role of the West as a relevant factor in understanding the Collapse. Eliécer, Pedro, and Héctor are the ones who most emphasize external factors, but two of them (Eliécer and Pedro) explicitly say that *internal* factors are the root

---

[182] Curiously, none of our interviewees blame Boris Yeltsin, although some respondents mention him as someone that played a highly negative role. Fidel Castro, in one of his "reflections" (*reflexiones*) published by the Cuban press in 2012, apparently referred to Yeltsin as a traitor and compared his attitude with the one of Erich Honecker, leader of East Germany ("the most revolutionary German I had ever known"). In contrast, he seems to be referring to Yeltsin when he talks of "the one who had sold his soul to the devil for a few swigs of Vodka." See: Fidel Castro, "Conducts Hard to Forget," *Cubadebate*, June 11, 2012.

causes of the Collapse. Héctor also seems to agree with such an analysis. José too mentions the work done by the West to influence values and political ideas in the Socialist Camp, but he does not identify it as either the first or the second leading cause. On the other hand, there are those who spend little or no time talking about Western politics in relation to the Collapse (Víctor, Aurelio, José Luis, Alberto, and Jorge), and Esteban states that "those external causes were marginal."

These latter interpretations, which identify internal factors as determinants, might be said to be in tune with Marxism-Leninism and dialectical materialism, in the sense that external contradictions affect internal constraints, but these are given less relevance. Still, all interview subjects attach some importance (between marginal and very significant) to the efforts of the West to destroy the system. However, no one seems to view these as the main cause and absolutely not as the only cause.

The success of these alleged strategies of imperialism depended on the strength of internal ideological work. Hence, several people refer to Ernesto Che Guevara's position, according to which imperialism cannot be trusted, "not even a tiny bit." It is important, thus, to recognize the power of imperialism, its intentions and its ability to manipulate, divide, and so on. In some sense, the academic literature supports their claim in this regard: John Ishiyama highlights "moderation" by the former communist parties[183] as a key in transition processes, and argues that this is the opinion of "many observers" about the changes. In Cuba, there was a stronger attitude of confrontation.

On the other hand, emphasizing the external threat could be "convenient" from a Cuban political point of view, because when emphasizing imperialism, one simultaneously justifies restrictive or authoritarian Cuban policies, that is, policies and practices that are very often justified by the presence of the United States.

The informants emphasize accumulated problems more than particular mistakes. Víctor's metaphor that the USSR had "too many wounds" or Héctor's—"the defenses were totally down"—seems to reflect a way of thinking that is shared by many interview subjects. There was an accumulation of problems over a long period. Other interview subjects do mention specific decisions that contributed to weakening the USSR. Héctor, for example, mentions that the invasion of Czechoslovakia "left a deep mark in the framework of the socialist countries," and Esteban underscores the war in Afghanistan and the power

---

[183] John T. Ishiyama, "Communist parties in transition: structures, leaders, and processes of democratization in Eastern Europe," *Comparative Politics* (1995): 147.

vacuum in 1983–84. These events and circumstances contributed negatively, although they did not alone determine the Collapse.

References to political causes predominate, although they also mention economic causes. Although many referred to economic problems of the USSR or problems that could be seen as derived from the economic situation (for example, corruption or admiration toward the West), political explanations predominated in the interviews (erroneous decisions, lack of [real, profound and not just imposed] ideological work, lack of participation or democracy, abuses, etc.). In the case of corruption, for example, or admiration toward the West, this is, according to the majority of the interview subjects, attributed to a lack of conscience, rather than to failures of the economic model. Alberto apparently had a different view since he did mention aspects of the economic model (not political aspects) as the primary cause of the Collapse and cultural and ideological aspects as the secondary cause, but he discussed the two as closely related (and it is not clear if with "first" he means that one thing is more important than the other or simply that he mentions it first in the order of his explanation).

They mention both "objective" and subjective causes. Many emphasize the "mistakes" of Stalin, Gorbachev, and other leaders. However, references to systemic problems and to certain practices are also frequent. It is important to keep in mind that there was a debate in the communist movement about the role of men in history.[184] The informants seem to agree that influential leaders can play an important role in certain historical circumstances, but they do not attribute the Collapse of the USSR to one man, nor do they deny the importance of such. José Luis recognized that "personality sometimes plays a terrible role in history." But all informants seem to agree with what Lenin said, one man does not cause such a system to fall, though he can accelerate it.

With this type of comment, they distance themselves from a certain type of caricaturized "Marxism" that exclusively emphasizes material conditions as a social explanation. Notwithstanding, given the Cuban interview subjects' own experience with a charismatic leader and the high level of personalization of

---

184 A central actor in this debate was Georgi Plekhanov, who wrote *On the Role of the Individual in History* (1898), in which, among other things, he argues that the individual does not change the general trend of history but "influential individuals can change the individual features of events and some of their particular consequences." For example, if Maximilien Robespierre had died by accident in January 1793, the French Revolution would have followed the same course, but his death might have advanced or delayed the process. "Great men" can thus strongly influence a process, but for that, the person must have a "particular kind of talent" and "this talent must make him more conformable to the social needs of the given epoch than anyone else." Furthermore, the existing social order must not close the doors to this actor.

power within the political systems they had been living under, it may be important to question if they may still be putting too much emphasis on the role of the leader, which may not be equally constructive when analyzing a country like the USSR, particularly not in the late 1980s when different actors were gaining influence over events.

At this stage, then, multiple influential actors coexisted and the circumstances of deterioration itself as well as the international situation limited the possibilities of action for the leaders. Within social psychology, the theory of "Fundamental Attribution Error," by Lee Ross, describes peoples' tendency to overestimate the importance of personal characteristics as a vehicle when explaining others person's actions, as opposed to the objective situation in which they find themselves, which could also influence their course of action. This objective situation, however, may be more decisive.

There are some references to Stalin that suggest that the leader himself was responsible to a great degree for negative developments under his watch and later. But when talking about Gorbachev, the respondents often emphasize the political environment surrounding the leader (Mery, José Luis, Esteban, Eliécer, possibly others) and the socio-economic one (Esteban and others). I would not say that the informants individualize to a very exaggerated degree,[185] but they do attach some importance to individuals—mainly Stalin and Gorbachev. This reflects the fact that powerful individuals have the power to shape history at some moments, and there is, of course, no definitive answer to whether they exaggerate or not the factor in these cases.

The informants sometimes suggest that Gorbachev lacked the ability to govern. Víctor states that "I don't believe it was his intention [to end the system]." Then he says, "He uncorked the bottle, he threw away the child with everything, that is, he did not read Engels." Uncorking the bottle could suggest that he let the genie or the forces of capitalism out, while the phrase "throw away the child" could imply that the best of the system slipped away from him; that is, along with the mistakes, good things were also lost. "[H]e did not read Engels" could indicate, in this context, that his main problem is that he was not a leader who possessed the necessary qualifications from a political-ideological point of view. Esteban, on the other hand, thought that Gorbachev had advanced ideas, which, said by a Party member, should imply that these were

---

185 However, there might be other Cubans that do. Juan said that some Cubans hold a belief that Gorbachev worked as an agent of the British intelligence service. This is of course an interpretation that gives a lot of weight to the actions of one person. (One could ask, if this happened to be true, why did the Communist Party, with its millions of members, not take any action against him earlier on?)

more specifically advanced revolutionary or communist ideas. According to José Luis, Gorbachev "wanted to do things in a very responsible way, and everything went wrong." Not valuing the leader, he suggests that Gorbachev could not have destroyed the system on purpose as he "was not capable, capable enough [to do so]." José Luis claimed that "one thing was the image that was sold of Gorbachev on the outside [of the USSR], and another thing was what was really happening on the inside."

Jorge did not directly state whether it was Gorbachev's intention or not to destroy the system, but seemed to consider his efforts to be well-intentioned, yet impossible to implement the way that he did: "No, he could not have succeeded because he didn't prepare the Party." He questioned Gorbachev's ability to govern: "It doesn't seem to me like he had a solid theoretical background." Eliécer says that "I don't think he [Gorbachev] had wanted to create a distance in the relationship to Cuba." Such a statement could also indicate a perception that his foreign policy too got out of control. The informant believes that American and British intelligence worked in order to make Gorbachev act in a certain way, but he did not see him as a simple puppet for such actors, nor did he describe Gorbachev's actions as the main cause of the Collapse.

In summary, thus, the general opinion on Gorbachev among the interview subjects was not very favorable but not totally unfavorable either. The intellectuals, Aurelio and Esteban, highlighted what they perceive as his merits. Aurelio shared that "I think that Gorbachev will always be worthy of the merit that he was the first who wanted to attack [certain problems within the socialist system]." Esteban believes that he was brave: "He bravely confronted it [the old structures], because they could have killed him too, because there were people there who did not want, under any circumstance, as there are here [in Cuba], still, there are people who do not want to change, right?"[186]

What happened in 1989–1991 was a new historical situation, a unique one. Hence, there were no existing interpretation schemes that could guide the observer. Neither Marxism–Leninism nor the writings of José Martí could describe such processes. Furthermore, there was no national debate on the issue in Cuba. Juan mentions that when the Communist Party tries to create a consensus on any issue, they usually do so by preparing a document that serves as

---

186 That being said, Esteban's vision on the subject seems somewhat contradictory, because on the one hand he gives the impression that Gorbachev really wanted to create a new type of socialism, or at least resolve problems, but Esteban also says that he thinks that Gorbachev already knew in 1986 that "there was no cure against [...] that the Soviet Union was going to collapse."

a starting point for a collective debate (although, he argued, in many cases the result after such a debate is the same document with only minimal changes). In this case, however, a debate about the collapse of the USSR did not take place at all: "The policy has been not to build a consensus on the events of the Collapse, to leave everyone with their own imagination." The Party achieved their goal in this sense, as the interviews show.

As Juan said during our interview: "If you get to discuss why the socialist Collapse took place, then you open a discussion about the domestic socialism, well, and why would it not happen to us, right? Look, if it is the same here, here there is also a Party, a Political bureau, a Central Committee, I don't know what ... a model [that is similar]. I believe that in order not to generate an internal discussion, they did not care about building consensus [...]."

Our informants are observers who make their interpretations, based on the information they have, but are also political actors. However, they were more free in their assessments than *Granma*. It might have been convenient for them to highlight foreign pressure as a cause behind the Collapse, like the newspaper had done. Many also did so, but no one portrayed this factor as the main one, probably because they understood that it was not. *Granma* often highlighted differences with the Soviet model to suggest the outcome would not be the same. Yet amongst the informants, some did point out similarities that existed or still exist. This might have been convenient for the reform minded, as one could also say that Cuban socialism could have the same destiny as socialism in the USSR if one waited too long to take care of these problems. But in general, most seemed to have felt free, as they interpreted events, based on the information they had, based on their ideology, and not having a very detailed or elaborate political agenda.

There are, of course, some points in common between *Granma* and what is said in the interviews. There was still a certain tendency to not discuss problems that might be inherent to the state socialist model itself, though there were also some informants who did. There was a certain tendency of highlighting problems that do not exist in Cuba, and there is a lot of Marxism in their interpretations but also to some degree, Cuban nationalist viewpoints, and views that resembles the criticisms made by Che Guevara and Fidel Castro on the problems of Soviet socialism. This said, many of the interpretations of Soviet and Eastern European were not that different from those reflected in debates on the Marxist left in Europe and among certain academic debates. The main differences regarded more how they see Cuba and their own situation. Furthermore, although some topics were delicate ones for Cubans, more than two decades had passed, and all the informants were able to view and comment on these from a certain distance, emotionally and otherwise.

2.6 From Socialism to Capitalism: "A Whole Sad History"

Some interview subjects comment on the effects of the transition processes in Eastern Europe and particularly in the USSR, which they generally evaluate as very negative. In the interviews, Cuban Party members also reflect on the counterfactual possibility of whether Soviet and East European socialism, especially Soviet socialism, could have been saved. There are different evaluations on the subject, although the opinion of the majority is that it would have been possible to save the system, at least up to some point in history. There are even those who expected it to recover in the 1990s or later.

The interviews evolved mainly around the topic of the USSR, and when talking about this country, the informants usually distinguish between an initial phase of the crisis and the current situation in Russia (as of 2013), seen through more positive eyes. There is a consensus that the Collapse was negative for the people of the USSR—the interview was less about Eastern Europe in this regard—although some of the informants acknowledged that there had been improvements in some specific fields. Generally, though, such mentions very few, as in *Granma*. Though they might recognize problems of the old model, there was little emphasis on what is often highlighted as advances with the arrival of capitalism, such as political pluralism or free enterprise.

There are, on the other hand, several comments about internal social problems of the USSR and Eastern Europe, mainly poverty, although the issue of (organized) crime and political persecution of the Communist Party in Russia in the 1990s is also mentioned. Their strong emphasis on these problems may be both due to their political positions and the objectively cruel reality of the USSR in the early 1990s. However, it may also partly have to do with Cuban media coverage at the beginning of the Special Period. As detailed in Part 1 of this study, and as Jorge Domínguez has also observed, Cuban media started to publish a very large amount of news about all the new social problems of Eastern Europe and the former Soviet Union.

According to José Luis, there is "a whole sad history of gangsterism in those years from 90, 91 to 97, 98 that is pure ... pure struggle for power by mafia groups on the one hand and by groups of bureaucrats on the other." He mentions a particular case: "This same Mr. [Boris] Berezovsky, who died recently in London, in exile, it is said that when he took control over the car factory, the VAZ, one of the largest car factories, it is said that after that, more than 60 people died. That is, assassinations of lawyers, union leaders, they were eliminated along the way [...]." In addition to references to the murders that José Luis mentions, Héctor states that there was also political repression. He argues that the Communist Party of the Soviet Union "was practically eliminated, was practically persecuted at a certain moment."

On the other hand, the informants have a negative view of the United States as an international actor. Hence, it is not surprising that they see the emergence of a unipolar world in which the US predominates as something negative. They see the fall of the Soviet Union as very negative for all revolutionary forces in the world, not only because of the material support that they might have represented, but also for being a beacon for socialist ideas. In the words of Norma: "The Collapse of the Socialist Camp, I think it affected all revolutionaries. Why? Because we had an idea that the USSR was always going to be a support to us; since we didn't have that, nor do we have it, nor do I think we will have it from the United States. They helped us a lot. When the Socialist Camp fell, we thought that we too had fallen."

When asked: *Are there positive assessments of what happened after the Collapse in the USSR?*, some informants recognized that not everything was negative but only very timidly. There are few mentions of improvements, and they are less specific, but somehow, they accept that not everything was negative. For example, Mery says that "everything has not been bad, I cannot say that the change has been ...." But then she changes the subject and states, "But for example in Russia right now, there is talk of mafia groups that you could not even have imagined. There is talk of a high degree of alcoholism, very, very, very high, of drugs, those things."

José Luis, however, says that "still today there are people who think that more things were lost than gained after the Collapse in 1991," and thus he indirectly acknowledges that there is also a significant percentage of the population of the former USSR who believe that they gained more than they lost. Juan mentions how Eastern Europe obtained more independence: "For people in Poland [...] the socialist counterrevolution gave them independence."

There is a more favorable view of Russia's current strong leader, Vladimir Putin, than of his predecessor, Boris Yeltsin. José Luis believes that "after 1991 came a terrible period with Yeltsin and a, let's say, less bad period, with eh ... What is his name ... ? Putin." It should be noted that his description of the current stage as "less bad" cannot be characterized, at all, as a compliment to the current situation. However, notably, some informants seemed to perceive much continuity from the USSR in Putin's Russia. According to such a position, after a brief neoliberal, pro-Western and weakened Russia, some or many things have been recovered from the USSR.

However, with regard to Cuban relations with Russia, there were also some exceptions, some parts of the relations that were also maintained during Yeltsin's epoch, at least on a popular level. Mery explained that "There are many [Russians] who stayed in Cuba and chose Cuba to live, many technicians of these Russians that I am telling you about, they stayed [...] 'give me a room,' whatever."[187]

Héctor seems to believe that Putin's foreign policy represents, in part, a return to an independent position, critical of the United States: "Regardless of what happened in the Soviet Union, the Russians have realized that they have to balance the weight because, regardless of whether they proclaim that they are no longer communist, the empire is there and wants to eat them, and I think that in this sense the role Russia is playing is of the utmost importance."

Esteban goes much further and states, "I think the Soviet Union recovered under other conditions; it is recovering under what is now Russia. The fact is that it is recovering. Russia is better today than what the Soviet Union was 20 years ago, right?" It is striking that a Cuban Communist Party member believes that the current capitalist Russia works better than the USSR, which supposedly was a socialist nation, even in its last years, when it went through a very serious crisis. He believes that the country was freed from the contradictions related to the many nationalities that were incorporated into the USSR and that it is improving in many areas:

> No, it does not have that contradiction [that of the many nationalities of the USSR], the economy is improving, the country is organizing, the Party organization has more power, that is, the political organization has more power. The administrative system is gaining more power, that is to say that this is still not defined. It is not definable, from a political point of view, to say well there, capitalism has definitely triumphed, no. Because it is not a capitalism like that of the United States, it is not a capitalism like that of France, like that of England. Do you understand?

Here, the parallel between the partisan organization of Putin and the Communist Party of the Soviet Union is particularly striking, which could imply that Putin represents a kind of continuity or return to the project of the Soviet Union. Also striking is the comparison between the capitalisms of Russia and those of other countries, in which he seems to view Russian capitalism as better or closer to socialism. There are also references to how relations between Cuba and Russia have improved in recent years. For example, José Luis refers to the prolonged dispute between Cuba and Russia because the Russians tried to collect the debt Cuba had with the USSR under conditions that Cuba did not

---

187 At a more political level, it could be mentioned that the Russian spy base known as Lourdes, near Havana, was maintained until 2002.

accept. "Now, with Medvedev's visit this year to Cuba, this year in February, they agreed to forgive that debt to the Soviet Union, after 22 years of discussion."

When asked: *Could the Collapse have been avoided if other decisions had been taken?*, many of the interview subjects emphasized the adversities that the country faced (civil war, interventions, World War II, etc.). In addition, they pointed to how difficult it is to build a socialist country in general (because of the resistance of pro-capitalist forces, because there was and is no recipe for the construction of socialism, etc.). None of them, however, said that USSR and Eastern European socialism were destined to fail from the beginning. According to many of the interview subjects, the problems had been accumulating for a long time. In that case, it probably would not have been enough to change one or two specific decisions in the Political Bureau. However, several mention "mistakes" that were bigger than others. Esteban, for example, mentions the invasion of Afghanistan as a big mistake (he is the only one who mentions it).

But more important for the interview subjects is the big picture and not specific decisions. Many, for example, see Stalinism as a deviation from the Bolshevik project. Hence, they may think that if things had taken another course in the 1920s, the country could have improved its long-term possibilities. On the other hand, there are those who criticize the economic decisions and also the lack of a deeper de-Stalinization in the years after Stalin's death, under both Khrushchev and Brézhnev. Such a critical view could indicate that some believe that if the USSR had made better decisions at that stage, under Khrushchev and Brézhnev, perhaps the socialist power would have survived more years or even until today. Some mistakes that are highlighted refer to long-term policies. Our interviewee Lenin, for example, mentions Soviet policies vis-à-vis Eastern Europe, while Aurelio believes that the economic development policies carry some problematic aspects. Another question would be whether it was possible to change these or if the leaders found themselves forced to employ them, for example in the case of Eastern Europe, in order to prevent that region from getting out of control, or in the case of economic policy, because it was really necessary to compete with the West.

There are those who do not consider themselves in a position to answer whether the Socialist Bloc could have survived, like Alberto: "Look, it is difficult for me, because I would have to be Czech, or I would have to be Slovak, or I would have to be German to evaluate that." But most interview subjects provide answers close to a yes or no. Pedro argues that "Undoubtedly, this was going to happen regardless of the will of the leaders." Víctor says essentially the same thing, although he expresses himself with some reserve: "I don't know, because I'm not there, nor am I a great philosopher or anything like that. But I think there were too many wounds on the body."

Our informant Lenin suggests that the dissolution process could have slowed down if there had been another leader or if he had made other decisions, but there were more profound problems. This resonates with what Eliécer says, although he appears to be talking mainly about Poland, which had been a subject of our conversation: "The process that happened there, everything, who was behind it was the United States looking for ways of, and it was achieved. Of course, they just helped to precipitate something that was already coming." José Luis has a similar opinion. He states that the Soviet Union could not easily have been saved in the mid-1980s, but there could have been a different way out: "I do not say that Gorbachev could have saved the Soviet Union, but at least let's say it did not have to end the way it did; there could have been an intermediate path, not a transition to neoliberalism, which was what happened afterwards with Yeltsin."

Eliécer believes that it could have been "saved," although he does not enter into specifics. He believes that it would still have been possible in the 1980s: "It could have been saved, I do believe so, I do believe so, that's my opinion." Jorge replies that perhaps the process of change could have been more successful if he had prepared the Party officials better before initiating such changes, referring to the German economist Jürgen Kuczynski. Jorge argues that the author "says that Gorbachev and the Soviets unleashed the process of change without the cadres being prepared [...]" and continues by drawing a parallel between the Gorbachev process and ongoing changes in Cuba: "not here, we have been preparing the cadres and the processes of change have taken place little by little. The Soviets unleashed the process of change that was forwarded without the cadres being prepared and they could not take control."

Esteban, on the other hand, believes that by 1985 it was too late to save the USSR, but he indicates that perhaps Gorbachev could have succeeded if he had emerged a few years earlier: "Those advanced ideas would have needed more time, and it would have been necessary, let's say, that Gorbachev had emerged, [...] if Gorbachev had emerged immediately after Brezhnev, I think there would have been a better chance of doing something."

For the most part, the respondents see the Collapse as something that could have been avoided. In this sense, they hold the same criteria as scholars like Stephen Cohen, who has characterized the common idea that the system was destined to fail as teleological.[188] This can also be an important aspect of understanding the informants' commitment to the Cuban Revolution after 1991. They do not see the Collapse as something "destroying" socialism as a proposal for liberation. Rather, socialisms in the Soviet Union, Eastern Europe, and

---

188   Stephen F. Cohen, "Was the Soviet System Reformable?" *Slavic Review* 63, No. 3 (2004).

Cuba were often seen as specific intentions to build socialism that could also be modified and improved.

Did the informants hope, at some point, that Soviet and East European socialism could be resuscitated? A Cuban researcher with whom I had an informal conversation told me that to believe that the Soviet model and system was going to be recovered after the Collapse, "one had to be very naive." And surprisingly, upon receiving the similar question, "Could something like the Soviet Union emerge again?" Víctor replied: "There is always that danger, that is my opinion, if we do not see it we are lost."

However, it is striking that three informants did respond yes—all female—when asked whether they had hopes at some moment that the USSR would reemerge. Zenaida states that "Yes, we thought it was going to recover, because in the meetings we had, it was always said, 'No, this will recover again,' but hey, that did not happen." Norma responds that "Yes, why not? ... and it is not just me telling you, as you are asking me, but many Party members, many Cubans, we were hoping that there would be 'an appeal.'" Mery states that she had such hope at the beginning, but after a while she lost faith: "I, personally, maybe I am a dreamer, I indeed thought that could happen, that something could happen, until ... I thought that, until it came to a point in which I saw that no ..."

In contrast to these opinions, Aurelio believes that "after the failure of the *coup d'état* by the military [in August 1991], there was no hope for anything." According to José Luis, after 1991 "it was impossible" for the Communist Party to return to power, "impossible, and nevertheless they were about to win the elections in 1996 [...] there was a great fraud." Zenaida, on the other hand, still has hopes that something similar, a Socialist Camp, will arise again: "We thought that something similar would emerge. I hope there will be something now."

The position of the three informants that hoped that the USSR could recover might be seen as naïve by some. However, it is important to remember that there were attempts to create a union of allied states in the area. The Communist Party also achieved strong results in elections and was close to winning at one point. It would have been impossible to rebuild the USSR as it was, but again, it would be deterministic to say that neoliberalism is the only possible way forward. It is possible that naivety or the saying "hope is the last thing to be lost" could partly explain the position of the three informants who assumed such a position, but it may also be an expression of their sincerity. For many of the informants, especially the intellectuals, it would not be convenient to reveal if they had ever believed that the USSR was going to recover (although it is also possible that they never had that view).

Still, it should be kept in mind that most Cubans had an idealized image of the USSR. If they had the impression that everything was going well and the foot. We ate nothing but soup, and they removed the elevators, and we worked on the sixth floor, and sometimes I did not have lunch [*almuerzo*] because it was preferable not to have lunch. It wasn't only me doing it, no. A lot of people did it." José Luis states that "I came here to the center [Research Center of the World Economy] by bicycle from my house, because there was no public transport."

The problems are also mentioned by Eliécer, who was a doctor: "Transportation was very difficult [...] bicycles were even distributed so that one could ride the bicycle to work; you cannot imagine, difficult, difficult." Although a minority had a car, they did not receive the necessary gasoline, since it was not sold freely but was rationed. And if it had been sold freely, they would most likely not have had money to buy it. Esteban states: "Because at the University, let's say you had your car, and they assigned you a quota of gasoline, and that quota of gasoline could be 120 liters per month, right? [...] A moment came when they gave me 20 liters a month, nothing more, that is, they cut me completely off, and I was a Center Director."

Víctor says he made a trip to the USSR shortly before its disappearance, sent by Cuban state media, but they did not give him enough money for a decent stay: "I was going as a leader of the club of sports journalists, and I was wearing torn shoes and I had no money. I had to sleep more than a day at the airport because I didn't have money for the hotel."

Eliécer worked in the most important hospital in Cuba, *Hermanos Almeijeiras*. The situation made access to supplies very difficult: "With regard to supplies, a lot were coming from the Soviet Union, and that change was felt hard, because later we had to buy them in third countries, at three times the cost and with higher freight." He gave an example of the difficulties in getting supplies, saying that they ended up buying insulin for diabetes treatment from Switzerland: "You can imagine what I am saying; Bayer [pharmaceutical company] did not sell us, the Merck did not sell us [because of the US blockade] [...]. We were sending a person to look for a little bit through Switzerland, over there." They tried to relieve the crisis by introducing alternative medicine into the official health system.

Mavis tells how difficult it was to go back in time in agriculture, for example going back to using oxen as a means of traction. This was due to the lack of supplies: "Going back was not easy because the young farmers no longer knew how to tame oxen to work with them."

The crisis assumed very specific characteristics due to certain characteristics of the Cuban system and the state's policies. We can say that there was a state policy aimed at alleviating the worst impacts of the crisis. The state did close a significant number of the country's industries and radically reduced public transport, but despite the high budget deficit, it did not close schools or hospitals. There was an intention to maintain a safety net and initially to preserve economic equality.

In this sense, José Luis argues that "We all entered the Special Period under the same conditions, we all had the same deficiencies [...] and later when the double monetary circulation enters [legalization of the US dollar in 1993], remittances enter the country, that begins to produce a differentiation between those who have access to hard currency and those who don't." Jorge uses a concept created by Aurelio Alonso, "poverty with protection," to describe the phenomenon of poverty in Cuba.

Other testimonies indicate that some groups were more affected than others. Héctor says that "Women suffered most strongly all of the misfortunes during the Special Period: the kitchen, the house, the clothes, the blackouts, this and that, come from work, the lack of transportation, it was terrible," while Jorge mentions youth as among the most vulnerable groups: "The most negative impact of the Special Period was on youth, because they were left without a scheme of interpretation of reality [...]." Mery, who was young at the time, says that she was not as affected as much as other Cubans due to her father's work: "My father before 1989 worked with the American embassy [the US Interests Section, this was before he started working with the Soviet embassy] and somehow when it comes to the economic part ... that is, as his children it never affected us so much, because Daddy helped."

At a time when Cuba had lost its main allies in Eastern Europe but before the USSR was formally dissolved, the PCC convened its Fourth Congress, which took place between October 10 and 14, 1991, in Santiago de Cuba, Cuba's second biggest city and in the eastern part of the country, where the Revolution had started. The months before the congress became the occasion for an exercise of popular participation. At the beginning of the year, the Party published a document, the extensive "Call to the Fourth Congress" (*llamamiento*), as a starting point for a debate on the future of the country.

Valdes Paz pointed out that during the first months, all the population debated the proposal at their workplaces, in the military, social premises, at universities, and so on. This debate had an open character, but there was little or no debate in the media.[190] In April, however, the authorities decided to stop

---

[190] The debate preceding the Fourth Congress had another form than the one preceding the Sixth Congress (2011). In the most recent case, a list of possible measures to be taken in the country was sold all over the country at a symbolic price, and the general public could then express their opinion on each proposal. Later, the PCC generated a new document taking into account the feedback of the population that it considered feasible and

the national debate, until it reopened in the summer of the same year.[191] Before reopening the debate, the Party made it clear that there were three issues that were out of the debate. In the words of Marifeli Pérez-Stable, these consisted of: "the one-party system, the socialist economy, and, implicitly, the leadership of Fidel Castro."[192]

José Luis says that "the massive discussion that takes place between March and May 1990 [...] the future of socialism was well discussed, if we were going to capitalism, the type of reforms that could be made, the market economy, all that was discussed, and there were people who voted for that option, but the majority did not vote for that option, that is, they underwent a referendum practically many of the things that were adopted in the Special Period." Juan believes that the Call opened a debate with "an unusual democratic character." Remember that later "The Party is instructed that there are three issues that are out of the question," but stresses that "everything else is an open agenda for the population to express." Esteban says he opposed the limitations imposed on the debate: "I had a tremendous discussion about that in the Central Committee once, because people began to argue [...] that the debate was free and democratic is true, but that the market economy and multipartyism were removed from the list of topics that were to be discussed, is also true."[193]

---

desirable, for example a fragment of text was included that talked about the need to facilitate the trips of citizens abroad, something that was eventually fulfilled a few years later. Still, five years after the Congress, only 21% of the proposals had been implemented ("Cuba implementó el 21 por ciento de las reformas planteadas y el 77 por ciento está en proceso," EFE, January 15, 2016). My informant Aurelio suggested that the main difference between the 2011 debate and what happened in 1991 is that while "the Call for the Fourth Party congress [*el llamamiento*] was an integral document, the guidelines [*los lineamientos*] are a series of guidelines, simply that, and it is less organic than the 1991 *llamamiento*."

191　Pérez-Stable, 130.
192　Ibid.
193　How many Cubans expressed a desire for radical changes during the first and most open phase of the debate? Mavis told us that she could not remember hearing any proposal in her "sphere of action" (neighborhood, work, etc.) to introduce several parties or other radical changes, inspired by changes in Eastern Europe, or in other public debates that took place in those years. José Luis says that "It was one in ten thousand or one in twenty thousand that expressed support for the introduction of a market economy and multipartyism"—this phrase could be meant as an overstatement to underline his point. Esteban, on the other hand, believes that if the debate on these issues had not been explicitly excluded from the debate, it is likely that an "important mass" would have asked for more radical changes: "One will never know in Cuba how many people were in favor of the market economy and how many people were supporters of multi-partyism." Although he also said that he did not believe that it would have been a majority, "but it would have been an important mass of people, in favor of multipartyism and a market economy, especially a market economy."

At the beginning of the congress in October, one month after the failed coup in the USSR and with an increasingly strong crisis in Cuba, the Party leaders had in their hands a series of proposals from the population. Juan asserted that there were "a number of proposals that on the one hand the management is not willing to digest completely and on the other the crisis [...] does not allow digesting them." In part, the congress decides to go in the opposite direction from what these proposals would suggest, although with a "commitment of the future" to introduce later the changes that the population requested:

> I give you an example: one of the latent demands in the population since then was the decentralization of the state, decentralize public powers, decentralize administration, decentralize management, etc. That was very strong already in the 90s and yet the crisis is going to impose on the country to have to centralize even more, isn't it? So that the crisis will move in the opposite direction of public opinion and the Party, what it says is that it takes note, that that remains there as a commitment of the future, and that is another story.

However, there were some significant changes. Aurelio recalls that the Congress "opened the possibilities of Catholics to enter the Party, well, opened a number of things and changed the character of the property and decided that Cuba was not a republic of proletarians but of the Cuban people and the Party was the Party of the Cuban people, etc."

José Luis highlights the electoral reform, which gives the voter more power: "Fidel was running for a municipality and the population [in that municipality] had to vote for him if he was to be elected deputy; if he was not elected deputy he could not be president."[194]

---

194 Although what is said here is correct, there is another way of becoming elected that does not imply first being proposed by one's local constituents; approximately half of the delegates to the National Assembly and the provincial parliaments are nominated through another mechanism; they are proposed by mass organizations and not by the population in their neighborhoods. There are as many candidates as there are seats to be filled. In such cases, voters still have the opportunity to vote against a candidate—if more than 50% of the votes go against a candidate, this should at least in theory cause a new nomination process. But in the case of this electoral mechanism, voters cannot directly participate in the nomination process. In 1992 the PCC also stopped controlling (at least formally) the nomination processes, as it is no longer a part of the so-called candidate commissions. These commissions are now controlled by mass organizations. At a 2015 congress of Cuban researchers, the introduction of direct elections in 1992 were used as an example that Cuba had democratized its society more than China. See: Martin K. Dimitrov, "China-Cuba: Trajectories of Post-Revolutionary Governance," https://cubacounterpoints.com/archives/750.html.

Mavis tells how her organization, the National Association of Small Farmers (ANAP), proposed to reintroduce the possibility of agricultural markets based on supply and demand, which had been closed with the Rectification of the 1980s. At the congress, she says, the proposal to reopen the markets was rejected by Fidel Castro, but it was approved two years later: "I was there [...] one of the points that were discussed was the opening of the peasant market, the peasant free market that he [FC] did not like, that he did not agree with at that time."[195] Despite the limitations, the debate was broader than the previous ones and involved popular participation. Haroldo Dilla argues that "It was the best structured debate for the purpose of democratic exercise,"[196] comparing it with that of the Third Congress in 1986 and another national debate, the Workers Parliaments (in 1993–1994). He points out that the results were assessed under secrecy: "The results were maliciously screened by the then Center for studies of the people's opinion [*Centro de Estudios de la Opinión del Pueblo*] [...] and were never published."[197] But he also acknowledges that the discussions had some impact on the policies that were followed: "Some of the most advanced proposals appeared 'as weakened echoes' in the constitutional reform and in the electoral law."[198]

When I asked Alvarez if she agreed that it was the freest and most democratic election in the Revolution's history, she replied that "I would not exaggerate so much by saying [the] freest and most democratic; I never liked those superlatives." Alberto also assumed a critical stance: "In many places, the debate was mechanical."

However, the debate shows that Cuba opted for another way to solve its problems than the USSR. The crisis in Eastern Europe and the chaos that prevailed in the USSR at that time may have been seen as somewhat distant, although the economic and ideological impact was already felt very considerably by early 1991.[199] Kapcia considers that although the debates in Cuba in the 1960s and 1970s took place mainly in the political and academic elite, from the Rectification in 1986 there were more inclusive debates,[200] and they were

---

195   According to Samuel Farber, regulations for overseas travel were also relaxed about the same time by that Congress. By then, the authorities had begun to give permits to visit relatives abroad to people younger than before. See: Samuel Farber, "Castro under Siege," *World Policy Journal* 9, No. 2 (1992): 342.
196   Haroldo Dilla, "¿Debatiendo la gobernabilidad en debates gobernables?," *Nuevo Mundo Mundos Nuevos* 1, n.º Questions du temps présent (2008).
197   Ibid.
198   Ibid.
199   Aurelio argued that "The Party suffered a strong shock at that time."
200   Kapcia, 86.

better than the debates in Eastern Europe, as losers were not usually expelled from the Party or totally marginalized.[201]

It is likely that at least part of the population felt that being able to take part in these debates would be a reaffirmation that they were part of the Revolutionary process. Our interviewee Zenaida, who helped collect proposals from the population before the Party Congress, described this process: "All the opinions we gave [at the public meetings], all, all of them were collected, and we filled in papers, and these was sent to the superiors, upwards, because that goes upwards step by step, from the nucleus to the municipality, from the municipality to the province." She said that "Everyone gave their opinion and I wrote the reports [...] people enjoy that."

It was suggested earlier that the Collapse coincided with an ideological "repatriotization" in Cuba.[202] There was a return to the roots, to the narrative of the Hundred Years of Struggle, the dominant theme in the first years of the Revolution. Louis Pérez Jr. has argued that "The moral void and political lacuna that ensued with the Collapse of socialism in much of Eastern Europe did not occur in Cuba."[203] This is a statement only partly supported by the testimonies gathered in this study. There was indeed a certain confusion and demoralization, as well as a considerable moral void and a political lacuna, even amongst Party members that had a particularly strong commitment to the Revolution.

It is true that it is important that there was all the time an underlying nationalist narrative that offered a way of interpreting Cuban history. Yet even so, it was unavoidable that the mixture of the ideological impact of the Collapse and the economic crisis that it generated also created a crisis at an ideological and psychological level. There are interviewees who talked about confusion, disorientation, and loss of values. Víctor recalled something that Armando Hart [a veteran of the Revolution and former Minister of Culture] said at a meeting: "I don't care about the economic part, we will get out of those problems ... now, I'm worried about what type of men [or people] we will have when the Special Period is over."

Jorge says that at the beginning of the crisis, "I talked with my family and my children [...] to tell them that there was going to be a very hard period, one of famine, and also very hard in terms of disorientation."

Twenty-three years after the start of the Special Period, Mery argued that the Cuban family has been affected by divisions, referring, it seems, fundamentally to migration, and that there has been a deterioration in values, and:

---

201 Ibid., 86–87.
202 According to the terminology used by Gropas.
203 Pérez Jr., 264.

"People's values have deteriorated, things that shouldn't be this way, but like the family, the family also suffered many divisions, that affected, that affected the average citizen." Jorge says that there was a Social Pact that broke down with the crisis: "Thirty years telling me one thing and now it's something else and then that creates the lack of commitment and demotivation this is about the Social Pact." As an example, he mentions prostitution, which increased sharply: "[someone] has a sister who becomes a whore [*se mete a puta*] to survive and the sister that is a whore is the one who makes the family live [...], then the community no longer rejects the whore."

At the beginning of the Special Period, many interviewees had experienced improvements in their lives in a few decades and attributed these to the Revolution and the government of Fidel Castro. Although the euphoria of the early years of the Revolution, or the idea that the World Revolution was just around the corner did not prevail in the late 1980s, there was probably no widespread perception of a serious crisis until about 1990. José Luis comments that Cuba had just won a great victory in Angola, and the Cuban Revolution in this sense seemed anything but dying: "Cuba at that time [...] was enjoying the triumph of a war that had lasted since [19]76, that is, what was [a moment associated with] the failure of socialism in Europe, it had nothing to do with what Cuba was achieving at the time."

There are data indicating that even as people were starting to feel the effects of the Special Period, there was strong popular support for the government and most of its policies. Jorge Domínguez cites a survey conducted in the spring of 1990—before the economic crisis deepened—of 600 Cubans nationwide. There, three-quarters of the respondents had a favorable view of the public health system and four-fifths of the school system.[204] Domínguez suggests that the survey is credible because it contains critical responses on other topics. For example, only 10% had a favorable assessment of public transport and 20% of food supply. Pérez-Stable affirms that in the 1992–1993 elections, when the country's economy was about to hit bottom, "up to a third [of the population] cast a protest vote,"[205] although different figures circulate and what constitutes a protest vote in Cuba could be a matter of debate.

What the interviewees perceived as the achievements of the Revolution could partly explain the continued support: the health system, the education

---

[204] Jorge I. Domínguez, "The Secrets of Castro's Staying Power," *Foreign Affairs* 72, No. 2 (1993): 97.
[205] Pérez-Stable, 137–138.

system, citizen security, access to employment, electrification, these things. There are others that highlight more abstract achievements, such as "conscience" or "solidarity."

In this sense, Norma talks about the rights of work and retirement: "You have a guaranteed job and tomorrow you can say I'm going to retire if you have the age and years of work, you ask for a checkbook that the State gives you. Take it and you can just sit at home if you feel like it." For Víctor, in "other countries, things are sometimes not as easy as in Cuba, where a student finishes his career and has a job." Jorge also emphasizes citizen security: "Sit there on a large avenue, in this one, you will see hundreds and hundreds of children who walk 6 and 7 blocks, 300, 400 meters alone, without parents [...] you go to Mexico, to Colombia, to Peru, even in Venezuela and Brazil there are high levels of insecurity and children go with their parents, hand in hand. Not here, here you see children going to school on their own."

The health system is the "achievement" that is most mentioned. Eliécer mentions that the infant mortality rate was 60 per thousand live births before 1959 and today is 4.6 per thousand live births, and Jorge says that in Cuba there is one doctor for every 137 inhabitants. During the interview with Mavis, we were reminded of the comprehensive and preventive character of the health system when an inspector knocked on the door, as he was looking for mosquito vectors in the area:

> Man at the door: Good afternoon.
> A: Good afternoon.
> Man at the door: Public health.
> A: Oh my heaven, now I don't know where you can find any of that... I'm alone here.
> Man at the door: How do you not know where ...
> R: What do you ...?
> Man at the door: See the deposits of ...
> A: Ah, but now I can't help you, honey [*mi cielo*, literally "my heaven"].
> Man at the door: We need to see them because there is dengue in this block.

The health system, in addition, is an example of a very national achievement. One of the interviewees, the doctor and former Vice Minister of Health, Héctor, commented: "Our health system in general was modeled here, but we had a stage with Czechoslovakian advisory." In addition to the institutions, medicine is also different from that of the USSR, as Eliécer recalls, "In medicine there have always been differences, because our medicine was always Western."

Several of the interviewees said that the Cuban health system was better than that of the Soviet Union.

By pointing out in this way what was achieved in health and education during the first decades of the revolution, they actually present another argument in favor of preserving Cuban socialism, regardless of what happened in the USSR, and one of the reasons why the Cuban militancy and the general population did not instinctively follow the steps of Eastern Europe and the USSR. Although some achievements were obtained in part with Soviet aid, these achievements still exist, to a greater or lesser degree, many years after the Collapse.

Internationalism was another topic highlighted by several interviewees. José Luis believes that the practice of sending medical personnel to other countries, on a large scale, is something typical of Cuba: "We have [had] doctors today in 134 countries; that is a policy of the Revolution." His claim about Cuban internationalism is backed by the academic literature: In the late 1980s, Cuba had about 46,000 humanitarian aid workers in other countries, something unique in the world, according to John Kirk and Michael Erisman.[206] Cuba sent a civilian aid worker for every 625 of its inhabitants, while the US had one for every 34,700 inhabitants.[207] Cuba's percentage of humanitarian aid workers amongst the Comecon countries was totally disproportionate.[208] Although the programs have been controversial in parts of the population as it has cost the country much resources and drains resources from the national health system, it is difficult to dispute Norma when she says that "It is true that we give a hand to anyone," and these programs must have some ideological effects, as they imply that many Cubans get to know other, poor countries, and, possibly, feel part of a major mission associated with the Cuban revolution.

When we asked if the Collapse brought something positive, Lenin seemed like he did not know how to respond: "I don't understand, I don't know how ..." Apparently he found the question surprising. A minority of the informants, however, mention some positive consequences that the Collapse also had. Víctor argues that during the Special Period, Cuba was freed from a lot of dogmatism: "I saw the Collapse as positive because I grew as a person [*fui más persona*], and I became more revolutionary because I was dogmatized in many things, and I began to better understand the Cuban Revolution since then." To

---

206 John H. Kirk and Michael Erisman, *Cuban Medical Internationalism: Origins, Evolution, and Goals* (Palgrave Macmillan, 2009), 2.
207 Ibid., 9.
208 Ibid.

our surprise, he also said that the Collapse "is the best thing that could have happened, because that [the societies of the USSR and Eastern Europe] was largely a farce, because it was a lie that they had achieved such a level of building socialism." He used a familiar image again, and said that the Collapse felt "like when you have a family member and you think that person is magnificent and then you discover some serious mistakes."

Several interviewees (Zenaida, Víctor, Pedro, Eliécer, Héctor, Jorge, and Alberto) recognize that the Collapse gave Cuba greater independence.

The end of Cuban–Soviet relations represented the rupture with an "authoritarian system of planetary scale," said Jorge. He considers that for the academic community in Cuba there was a positive impact: "For a segment of us, amongst the thinkers, the sociologists, the researchers" it was positive, since "Now we do not have to ask permission if this is against the Soviets, against the Spaniards, against the Americans, it represented independence of us, for us to think for ourselves and make our own mistakes." The Collapse meant that "The spiritual inertia that was here was overcome because we had to start thinking about surviving."

Eliécer said something similar: "Do you know what was the first lesson the Collapse taught us? That we could not depend on anyone; we had to learn to depend on ourselves [...] to learn for ourselves." In Héctor's words, the Collapse "helped us realize the value of things, the need for work, the need for nondependence, that we had to start working on ourselves to foster our development on a very [...] the character and spirit of sacrifice forged us more." Alberto said, "Those events helped me greatly to think about our own possibilities [...] as a response we had to look for our essences, about what we are, and we had to strengthen, try to find mechanisms for coping or survival from the depths of our being Cuban." On the other hand, he also believes that it has meant a return to the national and Latin American ideology: "Many of us did not master Martí [...] and much less the Marxist–Leninist thought developed by people here in Latin America."

As Pedro put it, "We are freer than before [...] and we don't depend on anyone. If we do, our dependence is now greater toward the countries of Latin America, but not toward the United States, Russia, China, or anyone else."

CHAPTER 8

Insights from the Oral Testimonies

During the second half of 2013, I interviewed 17 people who were members of the Communist Party of Cuba at the time of the Collapse of Soviet and East European socialism. The objective was to inquire about their perceptions and views of events and the role of the Party and its members at the time of the Collapse.

One very visible tendency is that the interviewees constantly returned to Cuban history, to which their vision of the Collapse was closely related. They emphasized the native roots of the Cuban Revolution, as well as the injustices suffered before 1959 by many Cubans and even several of those interviewed. They emphasized that the clandestine struggle led by Fidel Castro developed independently and that the country has had its own development. They also gave many concrete examples of how they and other Cubans participated in the process. They mentioned errors and negative experiences after 1959 and hardships during the Special Period that followed the Collapse but highlighted the achievements of the Revolution and their reasons for defending it. Up to this point, the narratives were similar, although there were also informants who touched less upon these issues.

More contradictory were their views and assessments of Soviet and Eastern European socialism and its disappearance. Although most of those interviewed had an idealized idea of Soviet and East European socialism, a good number of them never visited Eastern Europe and the USSR nor did they know the languages. Some of those who made long stays in the 1980s, when the crisis was prominent, adopted a more critical vision, but these were clearly not the majority of Cubans or Party militants.

Except those with very close ties to the USSR or Eastern Europe or those who had a special interest in those countries, the strong and genuine emphasis that many put on their most immediate experiences as Cubans reminds us that Eastern Europe and the USSR were in fact a very distant world, despite the identification that existed and the strong political, economic, and other links, especially on a state-to-state level.

The informants remembered Soviet and East European socialism (primarily the USSR, since it was the main ally) as an element that provided material well-being, development, and security to Cuba, in a context of constant threat from the US. Overall, the relationship between Cuba and the USSR was considered to be very positive. For decades, the USSR was mostly seen as a model society in Cuba and all who commented on the issue recognize that Cuba was strongly inspired by that model. Some, still, mentioned certain tensions and negative aspects of the Soviet influence.

In the interviews, made more than two decades after the Collapse, there is a tendency to highlight the independent character of the Cuban model and Cuban foreign policy. Some informants point out that when policies were copied, it was made by sovereign decision, and if one made the error of copying uncritically, this was in the middle of a learning process and under pressure from the United States. Some, especially academics, highlighted the differences between Cuba and the Soviet and East European socialism. They point out that Cuba had its own development and that it has changed in recent decades. This narrative serves a very clear political purpose, and one could argue that in many senses—for instance, in regard to the political and economic system—that the similarities were more important than the differences, yet the differences mentioned are also documented and had some importance for how society worked.

On the Collapse itself, a consensus prevails that the Cuban media did not report well on it. The militancy as a whole did not receive much more information than the general population. Some militants had a bit more privileged access to information, due to their travels or their role as academics, journalists, political leaders, and so on. As I have suggested in the first chapter, there might have been a conscious policy to prepare certain people in confidence with a bit more frank analysis, and there was information that circulated orally but not in written sources.

Those who do try to explain the causes of the Collapse show a considerable plurality of criteria; however, we can highlight some trends:

1) *Multifactorial explanations predominated.* Although sometimes the informants highlight one or more causes, such as the main one or the main ones.
2) *Many alluded to inherited and accumulated problems in the Soviet and East European societies.* There was a process of deterioration over a long time.
3) *They gave both "objective" and "subjective" explanations.* Many criticize specific leaders, or several leaders, but especially Stalin and Gorbachev receive criticism. No one sees Gorbachev—the last leader of the USSR—as the *only* culprit of the Collapse, and they generally avoid attributing to him an intention to end the USSR.
4) *Almost all respondents mentioned the pressure from the West.* But even if they did attribute a role to the West, the consensus amongst the informants

still seemed to be that the Collapse was fundamentally a product of internal issues.
5) *There was a tendency to emphasize political causes more than economic ones.*
6) *The informants disagreed on whether a major crisis/a collapse in the USSR and Eastern Europe was foreseeable in the 1980s and if it was, from what exact moment.*
7) Just like *Granma* did during the years of the Collapse, *most of the interviewees tended to emphasize problems in the USSR and Eastern Europe and that have no parallel in Cuba.* Unlike *Granma*, however, many of the informants talked in a more open, more explicit manner about similarities that could reflect negatively on the Cuban model (for example, economic centralization and authoritarian structures and practices), and a minority of the informants expressed very critical opinions on the model implemented in Cuba, which was inspired partly by the USSR and Eastern Europe and which is to some degree still in place. Still, their narratives *mostly* put an emphasis on the differences between Cuba and Soviet/Eastern European socialism and highlighted the Cuban Revolution as a process that must be defended. They expressed a strong conviction that the Revolution is a process rooted in Cuban reality and that it never stopped being independent, despite economic dependency on the URSS during three decades and despite that, during a phase, the USSR and some countries in Eastern Europe were seen as models in important aspects.

The independent development of the Cuban Revolution and the presence of important differences as compared to the Soviet Union and Eastern Europe meant that the Collapse—despite putting Cuba in an enormously difficult situation—was not felt and interpreted as something that necessarily "invalidated" socialism in Cuba or something that necessarily had to mean the end of the Revolution, since there were—besides the many similarities—considerable differences between the countries and their situations (in terms of history and the link to national liberation, in terms of the geographical and geopolitical context, the system and its leadership, the political culture, the ideology, and so on).

Many Party members also must have had serious doubts and nonconformities in moments of severe crisis, and there are surely things that are not said in the interviews. Yet to most Cubans at the time, and certainly to most Party members, the system was seen as something that had been favorable, and defending the Revolution was seen as a necessity. The Collapse might have affected their perception at the time of the Cuban system and the revolutionary project's perspectives, perhaps more than many are willing to admit, and there were a minority of individuals in the Party that distanced themselves from their former ideas. Yet, to our informants, most of the reasons for which they had first adhered to the revolutionary project were not really "disproved" by the Collapse, as these had more to do with their own situation as Cubans than with whatever had occurred in the USSR and Eastern Europe.

CONCLUSION

Viewing the Collapse through PCC Lenses

The collapse of Soviet and East European socialism, in addition to arguably being one of the most important events of the last century, caused a very deep crisis in Cuba but not the regime change that many observers expected.

This study has looked at how these events were reflected in the *Granma* newspaper, the official organ of the Communist Party of Cuba (PCC), between 1989 and 1992. Furthermore, it has recollected and analyzed the views and perspectives of 17 individuals on the same events, all of them members of the Party at the time of the Collapse. This was done through the use of semi-structured interviews undertaken in 2013. In the introduction, it was suggested that the perceptions, interpretations, and reactions to these events by Cuba's only political party—and its members—might help us better understand the "survival" of Cuba's socio-economic and political order.

The reactions were largely characterized by a consistent defense of the system. The analysis has centered around the PCC, an organization that has often been treated superficially at the cost of Cuba's charismatic leader for almost five decades, Fidel Castro. Special attention has been given to how important events in the Soviet and East European socialist countries were seen and to the Party members' reactions, as well as the political-ideological repercussions of the Collapse for Cuba and the Party. Other studies have often emphasized the socio-economic crisis in Cuba that resulted from the loss of the country's main allies. This study is partly based on oral history, something that has been little encountered in the study of Cuban politics and society and which permitted access to information not commonly found in written sources.

At the outset, the introduction of the Cuban revolution as rooted in the academic literature was highlighting its national roots, and pointing out that beginning from the early 1960s, a close affinity and collaboration between Cuba and the USSR began to develop, though not without moments of considerable tension. The Cuban revolution put a strong emphasis on participation, mobilization, and building a revolutionary consciousness. In the 1970s, Cuba entered into a tighter integration with the USSR as it adhered to the Comecon trade agreement and created a Constitution and an institutional setup that were similar to those of the Soviet Union and Eastern European socialist states. The arrangement was based around a Party with a double monopoly over politics and the economy, although with particularities such as the role of Fidel Castro as a charismatic leader, the electoral system, differences in ideology and political culture, and others. Soviet style Marxist–Leninist ideology became very influential during that decade, yet never fully replaced the ideology of the Revolution from its early years, inspired largely by national hero José Martí and earlier struggles for national independence, but also Cuban socialist ideology. From the mid-1980s, Cuba marked some distance from Soviet reforms, and a gradual "repatriotization" of ideology began.

With regard to the Communist Party of Cuba, it was developed after the 1959 Revolution, and though from the 1970s it had characteristics similar to the Soviet and East European ruling parties, there were also particularities: It had been created *after* the Revolution, unlike the Soviet party; in its early days, it was very small and without real power, and thus developed a certain "opposition" culture; its members had less privilege, and sometimes it could even be a disadvantage to be a member; its monopoly role was legitimized not only by the Leninist theory of the vanguard party but with the continued presence of external pressure from the US against Cuba; there was a different mechanism for recruiting members that might have contributed somewhat to its strength, which was greater than similar parties in Eastern Europe in the late 1980s.

As part of the background for the analysis, some constants and some changes in Cuban society after the years of the Collapse (1989–1991) were described, such as the major crisis it provoked (known as the Special Period), which has had a profound impact on society; the continuous presence of the one-party system with a centralized economy (although the model has seen modifications in recent years); a somewhat less omnipresent state and a certain opening in society; and global and technological changes that influence among other things the access to information.

Furthermore, there was a discussion of the conditions for doing investigations in Cuba as a foreigner, on the conditions for doing oral history in Cuba, and some questions related to interviewing members of Cuba's only legal party.

In the sources one can find was a mix of unity and diversity in the world views and in the views on the Collapse (*Granma* from 1989–1992, and the interviews, from 2013). There are strong similarities in some respects, and in others, a revealing mismatch.

One difference is the broader variety of viewpoints in the oral sources. Present both in *Granma* and the interviews is a national narrative that presents the Cuban Revolution as the culmination of a long struggle for national liberation and social justice and of socialism as the logical culmination of a long struggle for national liberation and social justice. When asking the informants about Soviet and Eastern European developments, they often responded by talking extensively about their own country's history, and it became clear that their lived experiences in their own country, as well as their understanding of national history, were fundamental to how they interpreted the Collapse. Even if our sources from *Granma* all centered specifically on Soviet and Eastern European issues, it was difficult to ignore the newspaper's strong focus on Cuba's past, which often implicitly suggested that Cuba was different from other socialisms and would continue whatever happened in other places.

The narrative refers to a Cuban tradition of heroism and resistance and a strong Cuban tradition of political thought and action. The 1959 Revolution arose in response to Cuba's problems, and it was a product of the sacrifice of Cubans. Although this might resemble nationalist narratives of other peoples, it is inspired by some historic events that were indeed to some degree particular and that have influenced the country's development, and previous academic work suggests there was a particularly strong US interference and that the Cuban independence movements really had a particularly progressive character compared to South American countries. In the interviews, several of the older informants gave testimony of how they or people they knew suffered injustices before 1959; in some cases, brutal forms of repression. By all the sources, the Revolution was described as something that cost a lot of effort and that has to be protected, and, not surprisingly, its achievements were highlighted.

Both *Granma* and the interviewees tended—again, not surprisingly—to emphasize the achievements of the Revolution and ills of capitalism. Still, unlike *Granma*, some informants were very outspoken about certain negative characteristics of Revolutionary Cuba, such as economic woes or authoritarian features.

In the newspapers of 1989–1992, there seemed to be little emphasis on the shared history of Cuba and Soviet and East European socialism, although I did not specifically search out materials addressing this topic. However, the informants, even when asked about the Collapse, often returned to the early relations between Cuba and the USSR. They said that military assistance and material help were decisive for the young Revolution's survival and often expressed strong gratitude toward the Soviets. Some also talked about and gave opinions on relations in the 1970s and 1980s.

The informants often talked about tensions and differences that existed between Cuba and the Soviet Union, especially in the 1960s, and they were much more explicit than *Granma* in their assessments of the Soviet and East European systems. While the newspaper avoided giving much explicit opinion on most other countries and more so on allies or former allies, neither did it (except East Germany) always automatically favor allies' official views. It was often suggested that reforms were not necessary, thus implying that the old Soviet-style system was better than the alternatives (though news occasionally suggested significant differences amongst Cuban journalists on the demands that were raised in these countries). The informants expressed everything from great admiration for Soviet and East European socialism to a very negative assessment of the system itself (one of the academics even spoke of an "authoritarian system of planetary scale"). There were also differences in how the Cuban system was perceived vis a vis the Soviet and East European ones—one informant went as far as to claim that by the 1980s, "everything, everything, was a carbon copy."

Most respondents ultimately put the focus on Cuba's particularities. Amongst the informants, there were some who seemed to find it difficult to say much about Soviet and East European socialism. They had had no personal link with those countries and genuinely seemed to remember little or find the topic complex and difficult to comment on. They often returned to Cuban history and society.

Both *Granma* (at the time of the Collapse) and the informants (in 2013) recognized that Cuba's relations with the Soviet Union and Eastern Europe were very close, and in some way or another all the sources underscored that Cuba was independent in political terms while recognizing economic dependence. The informants recognized that Cuba had benefited greatly from Soviet economic support.

Some informants described Cuba's close relations with the USSR as not just a product of "desire" or ideological identification; rather, there were mentions of the US blockade that left Cuba with few other options as it limited trade with the world; some mentioned that Soviet and East European socialism were natural sources of inspiration as there were few other referents on how to build a socialist society; and there were mentions of the influence of pro-Soviet actors in Cuban politics. Emphasizing these elements could serve to release Fidel Castro, the Party, and Cuba from responsibility from not having further prepared the country for surviving on its own, especially when it comes to the economy, and for having implemented to a great degree a model that eventually failed.

Granma's coverage makes it possible to discern some tendencies in how the Party leadership saw the crisis and collapse of Soviet and East European socialism, but the coverage was also shaped by a number of factors, often including how the newspaper's journalists or editors wanted the public to view (or ignore) events. Since *Granma* was the main source of information for people in Cuba, its coverage also gives us some elements to better understand how many Party members interpreted events. Some observations are:

Although it varies much how and to which degree, Granma *covered the events leading to the Collapse of Eastern European and Soviet Union.* There are many contradictory styles depending on who is reporting on Cuba's relation to a country, the circumstances within the country, the historical moment, and so on. Often, there is a certain level of pluralism, although East Germany is covered throughout 1989 basically repeating its authorities' official versions. By mostly opting for a more distanced and relatively inclusive style, *Granma* signals that events are distant from Cuba. There is a notable lack of context and explanation, which must have made news more difficult to follow, except commentary critical of capitalism and reform socialism by Fidel Castro and a few external authors. This way, the Party signaled that it did not want to start a debate on what the news meant or implied. Yet in some way or another it did inform about the events.

The newspaper tended to use certain techniques to minimize the impact of actors and events that were not consistent with the Cuban political and ideological order. Rather than omitting information, they made less visible any "uncomfortable" news by not using photos or by hiding the story at the bottom of the page or the end of the newspaper, by locating a news story beside another that was apparently unrelated but undermined the message of reformist or pro-capitalist forces, and there were also suggestive headings, images, and occasionally commentary. With these techniques and others, they highlighted some news and explanations and hid others, while most of the time shielding itself against potential accusations of censorship.

Though ideas and proposals close to Cuba's positions were clearly favored, there was some information on more adverse ideas and proposals. Demands and actions even by openly pro-capitalist sectors in Eastern Europe and the USSR were reproduced but in a brief and distant manner, often in the form of short demands, proposals, and so on, without including much surrounding argumentation and often complemented by other news or commentary that suggested that they were wrong. With regard to proposals for reforming socialism that were not (explicitly) pro-capitalist, these were reported in a bit more depth, especially in 1989, and, in the case of Hungary, seemingly with a certain "emphatic interest." After 1989, information on reformist ideas was also reflected in the news, but with a certain distance.

At some moments, the coverage became more politicized than what was normal, because Cuba's primary interests were under some immediate threat. This was especially the case when the so-called "hardline" coup took place in the USSR in 1991. Cuba essentially accepted and perhaps endorsed the coup government as it reproduced its official statement on the front page, disguised behind a tradition of faithfully reproducing whatever came from the official TASS news agency (in the hands of the coup government) and behind a posture of non-interference.

In the same sense, Cuba became more isolated as there was also a transition from a relatively open journalism to a more politicized "war" journalism. The limited pluralism was reduced and the focus was increasingly on defending the country, with a strong sense of nationalism. This happened gradually, and the tendency was not completely uniform.

There was a tendency to emphasize problems in Eastern Europe and the USSR that would not easily lead the reader to question the Cuban model. The news included many criticisms that were made in Eastern Europe and the USSR on the social order there, an order that had important points in common with the Cuban one. However, *Granma* was more inclined to give space to problems that had no equivalent or no obvious equivalent in the case of Cuba.

There was never a comprehensive and detailed analysis of the Collapse and its causes, even immediately after the formal dissolution of the USSR in December 1991. Considering the importance of events, this absence must have been part of a conscious strategy to avoid a national debate that could backfire on Cuban socialism.

When the sources suggest in some way or another the *causes* of the crisis and collapse of East European socialism, these causes were mostly "nonsystemic." That is, these were not related to socialism as a system but to the reforms or sometimes to inherited problems, political "errors," outside pressures, and so on.

This is especially true in the written sources. Throughout the period of 1989–1992, there were many mentions in *Granma* of external pressures against the socialist countries from the capitalist world, but there seemed to be more in early 1992. Such external pressures included propaganda; it is suggested on different occasions that people were deceived, and there were some references to internal weaknesses (suggesting perhaps a lack of real consciousness). If these two elements are combined (some external pressure toward the system that has internal weaknesses), these considerations could be related to Fidel Castro's metaphor of Soviet and East European socialism as a meringue that collapsed—in other words, a sweet that is hard on the outside but soft inside—an apparently strong system that lacks subjective beliefs and consciousness or genuine popular participation to hold it up.

In the interviews, there was a larger diversity in explanations for the Collapse. For example, there were those who did not give any explanation because they do not remember or do not know, which perhaps underlines that there are more important issues for them in Cuba, although it can also reflect the complexity of the matter.

Some interviewees presented an explanation where there is a main cause, for example, unresolved conflicts between nations, or the bad quality of the formation of elites, but most mention two or more causes, and in some cases there is no clear hierarchy that suggests which cause(s) is/are the most important. Thus, there is a list of problems regarding the processes studied rather than providing an explanation of what happened, according to the experience of the interviewees.

However, some trends in the informants' responses can be distinguished. For example, everyone saw internal factors as decisive (they were more clear on this than *Granma* in 1992; still, they did perceive pressure from the West, and some saw this as a considerable factor). They tended to place more emphasis on political causes than economic ones. References to the difficult history (World War II, Stalinism) were quite recurrent, and several spoke of a long process of decay or deterioration. This was also sometimes suggested by the press and by Fidel Castro. As in the case of *Granma*, the majority of the interviewees had a certain tendency to emphasize causes that do not have equivalents (or very clear equivalents) in the Cuban case, but there were also voices (mainly academics) mentioned such issues and that were even very critical of the Soviet and Eastern European models and their influence on Cuba. The press had suggested that the Soviet influence had been too strong and that this had been an error, but otherwise, there was really no critical analysis of the system in other countries or of the Cuban one.

None of the informants held Gorbachev fully accountable for what happened, and some academics even spoke about him in a quite "understanding" way, but the judgement that he committed great mistakes and/or was naive was common. A minority of the informants recognized that there were some important positive consequences of the Collapse, despite its negative impact overall.

This higher level of diversity of explanations and the certain will to be more explicit and to present more overarching or "complete" explanations may be explained in part by the moment when the interviews were done, since there had been time to process events, and criticizing the Soviet Union is less controversial. The greater variety furthermore reflects the lack of a national debate on the Collapse, which had given members a certain freedom to make up their own interpretations, because there was no "Party line." But they could also suggest that *Granma* did not reflect the interpretations of the Collapse shared by Cuban Party members but prioritized immediate political interests.

In general, it is worth taking into account that:

The lack of a major conflict or discontent in Party ranks in Cuba, as well as the Party members' defense of the Cuban system, does not fundamentally have to do with a lack of available information. The information the Party members and the general population had access to at the time often left quite a bit to be desired and was at times even presented in a confusing manner, but Cubans including Party members were essentially able to access at least basic information about events regarding the crisis of state socialism in the USSR and Eastern Europe. In addition, many respondents had knowledge about the situation through other sources, such as the Soviet publications circulating in Cuba until 1990, visits to countries in the socialist community, and, of course, they had lived their lives within a system that in many ways resembled the Soviet one.

Eastern Europe and the USSR were really felt to be a distant world. Though the political identification was strong, the distance had always been great in other terms: cultural, linguistic, geographical, and so on. Cuba was and is not located in Eastern Europe. There had also been a gradual process of political distancing between the USSR and Cuba since the mid-1980s. All of this must have diminished the impact of the Collapse somewhat—particularly on an ideological and political level.

Some of the concrete problems or situations that contributed to the Collapse were simply not present in the Cuban case. Notably, while in Eastern Europe the hegemonic system was frequently seen as something imposed by the Soviets, in Cuba socialism was associated with national independence. The Cuban Revolution also had particularly traumatic periods, but it did not experience the Nazi occupation or Stalin's rule. Cuba was not a country divided in half (such as Germany), the rulers had not recently murdered opponents (as happened on a large scale in Poland), there was no sultanic regime (Romania), Cuba was not an immense territory (USSR), and so on.

The Party members interviewed were genuinely convinced that Cuba was living an authentic and legitimate revolution. They might have given a bit different answers if I had interviewed them in 1991, when Soviet ideology and policies still had a strong presence, but the literature confirms that the Revolution always had a Cuban foundation. There was a national tradition and thus something "to fall back on."

The informants stated that the revolution had brought them and their compatriots more improvements than setbacks. In this sense, they refer to the achievements in health, education, culture, sport, and public safety, in addition to recognition from international studies and organizations. They did express criticisms of the political process and the system, and some might have discontents, even strong ones, that they did not express. But at the start of the Special Period and even in 2013, they also had important and credible arguments in favor of the system, many related to their everyday lives.

As the crisis began to deepen in Eastern Europe and the USSR, the Cuban Revolutionary experience was in "a better moment." Cuba had left behind the violence of the 1960s and the most severe restrictions of the 1970s, yet the Revolution was relatively young, and it had not entered a process of decay. The 1980s were of relative well-being, despite growing economic tensions since the mid-decade. One interviewee highlighted that Cuba had just won the war in Angola. There was still a charismatic Fidel Castro, and there was a stronger and more respected Party than those in the socialist camp, and its calls were followed by most Cubans.

The interviewees, though they certainly tried to give a favorable picture of Cuba, gave examples that suggest they sincerely felt like participants of the Cuban Revolution. The respondents gave concrete examples of active participation in mobilizations, debates, internationalist missions, and so on, but also in one case on a clearly negative note: participating in violence against opponents of the government. Yet in all cases, this level of "participation," good and bad, probably implied identification and stakes in the project. At the time of the Collapse and then after, there was a lot of mobilization to defend the system and to strengthen production, so the Party militants (and probably other Cubans) felt they were doing things to overcome the crisis.

Because of the strong conflict with the USA, there was a high level of polarization. This might have made demands for national unity seem more justified. Furthermore, there was a much more visible and close external threat that made it easier for the Cuban authorities or people who supported the authorities to justify any economic problems, restrictions, authoritarian practices, or weaknesses of the institutions. Some of our informants had personal memories of situations in which the US played a negative role.

Most Party members, according to their testimony, had more or less justified hopes that the Cuban revolution could survive and perhaps even advance again over time. A minority of our interviewees actually acknowledged having thought that Eastern European and Soviet socialism was going to recover, while others thought that the recovery of the Cuban economy was going to be faster. Possibly, there were some people—perhaps particularly academics, religious people, and people who had been or became critical of the Euro-Soviet model—who felt some relief, amid the difficulties, as they saw the possibility of a demarcation of negative aspects of a certain type of socialism.

There was no clear or obvious alternative that seemed desirable to most Cubans and certainly not to people with the backgrounds of the informants. Based on the characteristics and situation of Cuba, its historical experiences and those of neighboring countries, the alternative was not necessarily a relatively prosperous liberal democracy, although a removal of the embargo or blockade would certainly have been favorable. It was not hard to imagine a scenario where Cuba would become a Third-World capitalist state with a lower degree of national independence, with some superficial variant of liberal democracy or perhaps even a pro-market authoritarianism (the Latin American dictatorships were not distant memories at the time). The return of Cuban-American elites was feared, as these could reclaim properties and political hegemony. Notably, there was little internal opposition in Cuba.

On the basis of a critical reading of the sources, we can conclude that in the Communist Party of Cuba there was a particular way of viewing the Collapse. The narratives have in common that they exalt differences from the Soviet and Eastern European socialist experiences and often share a supposed irrelevance or little relevance of those experiences. They tend to tone down the large similarities between the political and economic models, although some informants actually talk explicitly about these aspects. What the sources say can evidently be questioned from many angles (for instance, the ideology and beliefs of the Party members, whether the policies and practices they defend are morally right, the credibility of some details, what they leave out, and so on). Yet, key points of their narratives coincide with the historical truth in the sense that they can be found in prestigious academic works on Cuban history and society, often even in those that have a more critical view of Cuban politics.

Furthermore, events since the early 1990s suggest that despite Cuba's similarities with Eastern European and Soviet socialism, there were also sufficient differences for Cuba's experiment to have another outcome—even as the country lost almost all of its foreign trade and as socialist ideology was widely discredited. The Collapse was seen with a great deal of trepidation by those belonging to the Communist Party of Cuba, but it did not paralyze the organization nor were there significant splits or a large mass of people abandoning the organization at the time. A critical reading of the data suggests that the Collapse did not fundamentally affect most of the reasons and motivations that had made informants join the Party in the first place. Members saw the Cuban political process and model of society as sufficiently solid, independent, and different as to at least warrant a belief in the possibility that it could survive and that further effort might not be in vain.

Afterword

Before closing this study, we should explain that as we did our work, we discovered collaterally that several informants spoke with a certain preoccupation with regard to the state of the Party (in 2013). They considered it weaker than in the 1990s, and at least one person talked about a real possibility of the system collapsing.

One informant, who presented himself as a supervisor to the government, suggested that multipartyism could be an option for Cuba if left-wing movements consolidated their influence in countries such as Venezuela and Ecuador, and gained power in Mexico, Colombia and Chile. He suggested this would improve Cuba's security situation and thus make it less dependent on being united in a single Party against foreign interference—a viewpoint that surprised the author of this study. (At the current moment, this possibility seems to have become more remote as left-wing movements have actually lost power in many countries in Latin America. Still, this suggests that at least some Cuban militants consider that the concrete form of the political model is not really what constitutes the essence of the Revolution, and that it could be changed if Cuba's circumstances change.)

The study also suggests, as has been seen, a certain pluralism of opinion within the PCC, at least in 2013, and not only on the issue of the Collapse. This observation runs counter in some sense to a very common impression that the organization was and is more or less monolithic. The topic of this study could be examined from other angles and with other sources. For instance, there are media in Cuba whose coverage of the Collapse should be studied closer, including radio and television, if possible. Not all countries of Eastern Europe were included in this study, and the coverage of the transitions before and after the 1989–1992 period might be worthy of more study. As Antoni Kapcia has commented, there is also a need for further studies on the Communist Party of Cuba. For instance, we have not encountered recent studies that investigate deeply its internal life, which could be examined by sociologists, anthropologists, and other investigators.

APPENDIX 1

Information for the Interviewees

The following document was given to all potential informants (original edition in Spanish).

I am a PhD student from the Institute of Foreign Languages of the University of Bergen (Norway). By means of my thesis, I want to better understand how the members (*militantes*) of the Communist Party of Cuba (PCC) saw and interpreted the Collapse of the USSR. I am interested in the subject because I think that the way of perceiving, interpreting, and responding to these facts by the PCC and its members can help explain why the political system in Cuba did not change at a stage as critical as the 1990s.

As part of my research, I would like to interview 12–15 people who were members of the PCC during the period 1989 to 1991 or who were members of the Young Communist League (UJC) and who are now in the Party. The questions of the interviews could be, for example, about the view one had of the USSR before and after its disappearance, about the relations between Cuba and the USSR, about the situation in Cuba around 1990, about the role of the PCC in the political processes in Cuba before and just after the disappearance of the Socialist Bloc, and so on.

I will use a recorder during the exchange/conversation. The interview will last approximately one hour. We will agree on the time and place.

Participation is voluntary and you—of course—have the possibility to withdraw from the project at any time, without needing to explain your reasons. If you withdraw from the project, all the information you provide about yourself will be deleted.

Your name and profession will appear in the doctoral thesis. Until its publication, however, the recordings will be handled confidentially and these (together with the notes, etc.) will be deleted when the project ends in late 2016. The thesis will be published on paper and electronically, and the interview transcripts will be part of the thesis and will therefore be accessible to other researchers.

If something remains unclear at this point, you can call me at the [phone number of the author of the study] or send an email to [email address of the thesis author]. You can also contact my tutor/project tutor, María Álvarez-Solar at the Institute of Foreign Languages of the University of Bergen [María Álvarez-Solar's email] or the co-author of the project José at the number [José's phone number and email].

The research has been registered with the Norwegian institution of protection of data in the Social Sciences, the Data Protection Official for Research of the Norwegian Social Science Data Services, as required by my university.

If you have any uncertainty about this research, or want to receive the thesis when it is published, please contact me via email or by traditional mail.

Sincerely,

Even Sandvik Underlid

[addresses]

APPENDIX 2

Interview Guide

1. **General information about the interview**
See separate information sheet.

2 **Personal information**
   a. Place of birth.
   b. Municipality of residence.
   c. What was your main activity between 1989 and 1991?
   d. What is your current status?
      __ Work at _____
      __ Retired
   e. Briefly, can you say a few words about your political career or "revolutionary integration," that is, political organizations to which you belong or have belonged?
   f. Were you a member of the PCC or the UJC between 1989 and 1991?
   g. Are you still a member of the PCC?

3 **The collapse of the USSR**
   a. Did you have any relationship with the USSR? Did you study or work there, visit the country?
   b. How did you perceive or feel about the Collapse of the USSR?
   c. What, in your opinion, are the causes of that collapse?
   d. When did that process begin? When did the Soviet project begin to go astray?
   e. What was most important, the human factor (the subjective role) or structural conditions?
   f. Internal or external factors?
   g. If the subjective factor was important, who, or what groups, are primarily responsible for what happened?
   h. In case Gorbachev had a part of the responsibility, do you think he *wanted to* take the country toward the dissolution of its political system?
   i. Gorbachev announced a new foreign policy. He had meetings with a series of leaders of the Western world (Thatcher, Mitterrand, Reagan, etc.), advocated for disarmament, and so on. Do you have any criteria or analysis of those policies?

INTERVIEW GUIDE

    j. There are certain events that occurred in the countries of the Socialist Bloc in Eastern Europe that also influenced the situation of the USSR. In books of history in my own country, Norway, the emergence of an opposition in Poland (the Solidarity union) and the fall of the Berlin Wall are often emphasized. Do you have any criteria for or analysis of these events and their significance for what happened in the USSR?

    k. Could the USSR still have done something to maintain unity in the socialist world?

    l. "The State Committee on the state of emergency" took power in the USSR on August 18, 1991, in a coup that lasted only three days. Do you have any opinion or analysis of these events?

    m. How did you see the fall of the USSR: Was it something positive or something negative? How do you see it now?

4 **Relations between Cuba and the USSR**

    a. What did the USSR mean to Cuba?

    b. Do you have any idea what Cuba meant to the USSR?

    c. Do you think you received the necessary information to keep track of, and understand, the fall of the USSR?

    d. Did the PCC members have access to more information about the situation in the USSR than non-members?

    e. In 1987, some Soviet publications began publishing critical articles about Cuba. What is your opinion about that?

    f. Gorbachev visited Cuba in April 1989. How do you remember that visit?

    g. In April of 1990, the *Pravda* newspaper predicted that commerce between Cuba and the USSR was going to grow by 8%. In December of the same year, a bilateral trade agreement was signed, different from previous agreements in the sense that its duration was only one year. It was planned to use market prices in trade between the two countries. At this point, could the relationship still have been maintained? At what time did you see that the relations had gone through "a line of no return"?

    h. After 1991, did you maintain any hope that the Communist Party would regain power in Russia, or that relations with Cuba could resurface or recover?

5 **The situation in Cuba**

    a. The Process of Rectification has been seen as a "Cuban response" to Perestroika. Do you agree with this? In your opinion, what was the objective of the process?

b. The Third (PCC) Congress in 1986 decided to establish the Popular Councils (*Consejos Populares*), which were supposed to contribute to greater democratization and participation. In 1990, this type of people's councils was established throughout Havana. Do you have any opinion about their function?
c. In 1987, Cuba opened the doors to foreign investments in certain specific sectors and in a controlled manner. Was there much resistance to this measure?
d. If you remember: What did you think or feel when Fidel Castro first spoke of the *Special Period in Time of Peace*? Did you understand how serious the situation was going to be?
e. The crisis affected the entire Cuban population. When did you begin to feel the effects of the Special Period?
f. Fidel Castro also spoke of the possibility of the *Opción Zero*, a scenario under which there was barely enough food and a more or less total collapse of the economy. Did you see that scenario as a real possibility?
g. During the crisis in the Socialist Bloc and right after the fall of the USSR, the press in the Western world made constant references to a growing opposition in Cuba. Do you agree with that statement? Did you see it, in that case, as a danger to the Revolution, to the system?
h. There was change of attitude toward religious people with the Fourth Congress of the PCC. Did this have any relation to what happened in the USSR?
i. In a situation as demanding for socialism as the one of 1989–1991, were there many members of the PCC who doubted the thesis of the irreversibility of Cuban socialism?

6   **The role of the Party**
a. Do you know of any differences between the role of the Communist Party and how it works, in the USSR and in Cuba, respectively?
b. Is there anything that you remember especially about how the PCC managed the crises in Cuba, around the time of the fall of the USSR?
c. Two of the main roles of the Party are: To orient and to mobilize the masses. How was this done and to what extent were the actions of the Party decisive?
d. Did you participate in any activity specifically related to that situation?
e. To what extent was there room for a debate about the future of socialism in the PCC? In your local branch, for example, do you remember that there were discrepancies?
f. The *llamamiento* (call) for the Fourth Congress became the starting point of a public debate, in 1990. One researcher has described this as "the most

free and democratic debate in the history of Cuba." Did you participate? Do you agree with this description? Why/why not?
- g. Please, give me an assessment of the role of the Party at that juncture.
- h. There was a constitutional reform and a new Electoral Law in 1992. Was it ever considered to change the role of the Party as a vanguard party, or "the superior force of society and the State" as it is known in the Constitution?
- i. Were there proposals to introduce some kind of multipartyism? If not, why were they rejected?
- j. Were there people that left the Party at that critical moment?
- k. (If the answer is affirmative.) Why do you think they left the Party?

7 **In retrospect**
- a. Do you see the fall of the USSR in the same way as in 1991?
- b. Did what happened in the USSR change your vision about Marxism as an idea, or of socialism as a viable system?
- c. Could the leaders of the USSR have done something differently?
- d. What are the positive and negative legacies of the USSR in Cuba?
- e. Could something similar to the USSR arise again?
- f. Cuba is currently in the midst of a process of change; can the country learn something from Gorbachev's reforms?

APPENDIX 3

Core Sources

1   Official Documents

- *Constitution of Cuba* (1992) (http://www.cuba.cu/gobierno/cuba.htm);
- *Regulations of the Communist Party of Cuba* (1999) (http://congresoPCC.cip.cu/wp-content/uploads/2011/01/reglamento.pdf).

2   Newspapers and Magazines

- *Granma*;
- *El Militante Comunista*;
- *Juventud Rebelde*;
- *Cuba Socialista*.

3   Interviews

Sex	Male
Name	Victor
Place of birth	Centro Habana
Militance in the PCC	He does not specify when he entered but was a member until 1974, then he was excluded. He joined again in 1991 and still remains a member.
Relationship with the USSR	He traveled "three or four times" to the Soviet Union, also visited other socialist countries (Vietnam, China) and a former socialist country (Hungary).

Interviewed by the author: Havana, August 21, 2013.

Sex	Male
Name	Aurelio
Main activity 1989–1991	Researcher
Militance in the PCC	Member since 1969. Still a member.
Relationship with the USSR	He traveled to the Soviet Union in 1977, 1979, and 1981. The longest stay was 15 days. He had short stays "in some capitals of Eastern Europe."

Interviewed by the author: Havana, August 22, 2013 and September 10, 2013.

Sex	Male
Name	Pedro
Main activity 1989–1991	Diplomat, business manager.
Militance in the PCC	Member since 1968/1970. He is still a member.
Relationship with the USSR	He visited the Soviet Union as head of scholarships for the socialist countries of the Ministry of Education many times.

Interviewed by the author: Havana, August 23, 2013.

Sex	Male
Name	Hector
Main activity 1989–1991	Deputy Minister
Militance in the PCC	
Relationship with the USSR	He earned a graduate degree there between 1967 and 1968. His daughter visited in 1983 and informed him about the situation.

Interviewed by the author: Havana, August 28, 2013.

Sex	Male
Name	Idulberto
Main activity 1989–1991	Civil aviation pilot
Militance in the PCC	Since 1968.
Relationship with the USSR	He was in Kiev in 1962 (during the October Crisis), received courses in the Soviet Union in 1963, 1973, and 1977. He also had a stay shortly before its dissolution.

Interviewed by the author: Havana, August 28, 2013.

Sex	Female
Name	Mavis
Main activity 1989–1991	Official in the National Association of Small Farmers (ANAP).
Militance in the PCC	Member of the PCC "since forever." Stopped being a member when she retired.
Relationship with the USSR	Went several times to the Soviet Union for work reasons; her son married a Russian woman. She was also in the GDR, Bulgaria, and Czechoslovakia.

Interviewed by the author: Havana, August 29, 2013.

Sex	Male
Name	Eliécer
Main activity 1989–1991	Medical Physician
Militance in the PCC	We do not know what year he entered, but he was a member between 1989 and 1991.
Relationship with the USSR	He was in Russia and East Germany in the "eighties," also went to Bulgaria.

Interviewed by the author: Havana, September 9, 2013.

CORE SOURCES

Sex	Male
Name	Jorge
Main activity 1989–1991	State Advisor
Militance in the PCC	He was a member between 1989 and 1991 and is still a member.
Relationship with the USSR	He spent four years in East Germany between 1973 and 1977, then visited again before and after the fall of the Berlin Wall?

Interviewed by the author: Havana, September 12, 2013

Sex	Male
Name	José Luis
Main activity 1989–1991	Deputy Director of Research Center, Minister
Militance in the PCC	He was a member between 1989 and 1991 and remains a member.
Relationship with the USSR	He did his PhD in the Soviet Union in 1978 and then traveled frequently to the country between 1983 and 1991.

Interviewed by the author: Havana, September 24, 2013.

Sex	Male
Name	Juan
Main activity 1989–1991	Researcher
Militance in the PCC	"I have been a militant for 47 years."
Relationship with the USSR	

Interviewed by the author: Havana, September 25, 2013.

Sex	Male
Name	José
Main activity 1989–1991	Director of Communications Workshop
Militance in the PCC	Since 1962 (originally in PURSC, predecessor to the PCC).
Relationship with the USSR	He was once in Lithuania and Russia, "in 85–86, more or less."

Interviewed by the author: Havana, October 14, 2013.

Sex	Male
Name	Esteban
Main activity 1989–1991	Research Center Director
Militance in the PCC	He was a militant between 1989 and 1991. The militancy was taken away in 2010 "for writing about corruption," then returned in 2011 after he had made a complaint to Raúl Castro.
Relationship with the USSR	He visited several times. He finished his doctorate there between 1985 and 1986.

Interviewed by the author: Havana, October 19, 2013.

Sex	Male
Name	Lenin
Main activity 1989–1991	Agricultural worker, hydroponic service
Militance in the PCC	Since 1969.
Relationship with the USSR	Never visited.

Interviewed by the author: Havana, October 18, 2013.

CORE SOURCES

Sex	Female
Name	Zenaida
Main activity 1989–1991	Worker
Militance in the PCC	Since 1982.
Relationship with the USSR	In 1982, her husband won a trip to the Soviet Union. The couple spent 27 days in Leningrad, Kiev, and Moscow.

Interviewed by the author: Havana, October 18, 2013.

Sex	Male
Name	Alberto
Main activity 1989–1991	Music director at the national television, then music director at the Casa de las Americas institution. Also a musician.
Militance in the PCC	Entered in 1981.
Relationship with the USSR	He was in the Soviet Union in 1962, in Uzbekistan. In 1976, he was in the GDR and Czechoslovakia.

Interviewed by the author: Havana, October 21, 2013.

Sex	Female
Name	Norma
Main activity 1989–1991	Hospital seamstress
Militance in the PCC	Since the early 1980s.
Relationship with the USSR	Never visited.

Interviewed by the author: Havana, October 25, 2013.

Sex	Female
Name	Mery
Main activity 1989–1991	Worked at a radio station.
Militance in the PCC	She was a militant between 1989 and 1991. She was given a special process to enter the Party when she was 27 years old (normally you cannot enter before turning 30).
Relationship with the USSR	Was never there, but her father worked with the Russian Embassy in 1989 and told her about the Soviet Union.

Interviewed by the author: Havana, December 11, 2013.

APPENDIX 4

Example Table for Data Visualization

TOPIC: PREDICTABILITY OF THE COLLAPSE

Workers

Respondent	It was a surprise, I never suspected it, never, never, never, never.	Surprise.
Respondent	I never thought that the Socialist Camp was going to fall, ever. Especially when we had Tamayo [Arnaldo Tamayo Méndez, Cuban cosmonaut] who went with Yuri to space [...], we didn't expect it.	Surprise.

Professionals

Respondent	Then Fidel when he talks about the Collapse first of all in the world, I start, I say *concho* (darn it)... but he doesn't take me by surprise, since Fidel prepared me.	It was no surprise.
Respondent	That had an extraordinary impact on Cuba, it had a great impact on Cuba, I would tell you that politically too, because obviously many people loved the Soviet Union, had another image of the Soviet Union [...] Already before the Gorbachev process, we were informed here, and people knew that in the Soviet Union there was a disaster. People knew that, and that also things were happening there that were going to lead to a catastrophe. Yes, people knew it.	It was no surprise.

Workers

Respondant	A: Fidel had already warned us about this, Fidel in Camagüey, on July 26, I think it was July 26 in Camagüey. [...] Fidel had a light that was very much directed toward there [...] and when he warned us about that, everyone did like this, and began to see, damn, that's strange! But with confidence. Q: And that speech in '89 was the first time you thought about the possibility of that ...? A: No, I already saw it coming, because the boys had already warned me. (They had been in the USSR).	It was no surprise.
Respondant	I will not say that we believed that the Collapse of the Soviet Union could happen, etc., but we saw that the system had generated many bad things.	Aware that there were many problems, but did not foresee a Collapse.

Culture

Respondant	We thought that this was going to be eternal, that the Soviet Union was never going to fall [...] In the year '89, my father is with the Russians, with the Russian embassy [...] and when this happens, he is the first to tell us, Gorbachev has screwed up and the state is going to fall.	Surprise, although the person received a warning in 1989.

EXAMPLE TABLE FOR DATA VISUALIZATION

Workers

Academics

Respondant	in the year 84–85, I think that '85, I heard him [economist Raúl León Torres] give a pessimistic vision of economic growth and development that existed in the Soviet socialist system [...] Nobody in Cuba thought that the Soviet model was going to collapse.	Surprise, although the respondant had received a warning on the economy.
Respondant	Yes it was a big shock [...] that was tremendous [...] Let no one say that in those days—and I will argue with anyone on this, with the greatest scientist we have—that in those days we had the very clear vision (of what was going to happen). This does not suit us, it is a lie, we do not think about it... Well, perhaps some, a visionary with a lot of life experience [...].	Surprise. No one knew, except perhaps some visionary.
Respondant	At that meeting in [19]86 he said, he told us, the European Socialist Camp has no future. He said that four years before [the Collapse was evident]. [...] I think that if Fidel in [19]86 told us that the Socialist Camp had no future and that there were issues to prepare for, he must have said the same thing to the Party and to the Central Committee, [he must] have told them the same thing as to us.	Knew it since 1986.
Respondant	It did not take me by surprise because the problems I saw there, and the difficulties I saw there were problems and difficulties that could put an end to socialism.	It did not take the respondant by surprise.

Workers

Respondant	I believe that the leadership, at its highest level, had since 84–85 without a doubt accompanying Perestroika the sensation that Soviet and Socialist Camp politics moved in such a way that it would impose on us very complicated scenario and in no way as favorable as we have had. The Cuban leadership maintained the confidence that the USSR would go through a much longer process and that nothing similar to the dissolution of the USSR as a state would happen. Their imagination did not go that far. One thought that the reform process could lead to a USSR with fewer revolutionary commitments, to modify its commitments with others, such as with us, to a policy of détente with the United States, blah, blah, blah, but final termination it was not, it was totally anticipated [...] But the Cuban leadership did not prepare the population for that, it was handled with discretion, even in '85 there was a Party Congress and it was not talked about.	In 1984–85 the management expected a more difficult scenario, but not a total collapse.
Respondant	Already from 1987 on, when the Party conference took place in January 1987, where the Party's leading role within Soviet society is practically withdrawn, in my opinion, already then, that initiated a path without return. There wasn't, that is, I didn't see then that there was a chance that it would remain a rational thing that could function.	Indicates foreseeing since 1987 that the Soviet Union was not going to maintain itself as "a rational thing."

Bibliography

Albelo, Víctor Figueroa. "La transición al socialismo y el derrumbe del socialismo de estado." *El Derrumbe del Modelo Eurosoviético*, edited by Román García Báez. Havana: Editorial Felix Varela, 1994.

Alía Miranda, Francisco. *Técnicas de investigación para historiadores: las fuentes de la historia*. Colección Síntesis Historia. Madrid: Síntesis, 2008.

Alonso, Maria Margarita, and Hilda Saladrigas. *Teoría de la Comunicación: Una introducción a su estudio*. Havana: Pablo de la Torriente Editorial, 2006.

Alver, Bente Gullveig, and Ørjar Øyen. *Forskningsetikk i forskerhverdag: vurderinger og praksis*. Oslo: Tano Aschehoug, 1997.

Argüelles, María del Carmen Zabala, editor. *Algunas claves para pensar la pobreza en Cuba desde la mirada de jóvenes investigadores*. Havana: Editorial Félix Varela, 2014.

Azicri, Max. "The Rectification Process Revisited: Cuba's Defense of Traditional Marxism–Leninism." *Cuba in Transition*, edited by Sandor Halebsky, John M. Kirk, Carollee Bengelsdorf, Richard L. Harris, Jean Stubbs and Andrew Zimbalist. Colorado; Oxford: Westview Press, 1992.

Bain, Mervyn J. *Soviet-Cuban relations 1985 to 1991: Changing Perceptions in Moscow and Havana*. Lanham: Lexington Books, 2007.

Baloyra, Enrique A., and James A. Morris. *Conflict and Change in Cuba*. Albuquerque: University of New Mexico Press, 1993.

Barlinska, Izabela. *La sociedad civil en Polonia y Solidaridad*. Madrid: Centro de Investigaciones Sociológicas, 2006.

Barnet, Miguel, and Esteban Montejo. *Biografía de un cimarron*. Havana: Ediciones Huracán, 1968.

Barroso, Oscar Julián Villa. "El papel de la política en el hundimiento del socialismo soviético." *Temas*, n.º April–June (2014): 25–32.

BBC News. "Poland marks communist crackdown." *BBC News*, 13 de diciembre de 2006. Acceso el 27 de abril de 2016. http://news.bbc.co.uk/2/hi/europe/6175517.stm.

Bell Lara, José. *Globalization and the Cuban Revolution*. Havana: Editorial José Martí, 2002.

Bell Lara, José, et al. *Combatientes*. Havana: Ciencias Sociales, 2014.

Bideleux, Robert, and Ian Jeffries. *A History of Eastern Europe: Crisis and Change*. London: Routledge, 1998.

Blasier, Cole. "The End of the Soviet-Cuban Partnership." *Cuba After the Cold War*, edited by Carmelo Mesa-Lago. Pittsburgh: University of Pittsburgh Press, 1993.

Bobes, Velia Cecilia. "Complejidad y sociedad: cambios de identidad y surgimiento de nuevos actores en la sociedad cubana hacia el fin del milenio." *Estudios Sociológicos* 18, n.º 52 (2000): 25–52.

Bolender, Keith. *Voices From the Other Side: An Oral History of Terrorism Against Cuba.* London: Pluto Press, 2010.

Borzutzky, Silvia, and Aldo Vacs. "The Impact of the Collapse of Communism and the Cuban Crisis on the South American Left." *Cuba After the Cold War,* edited by Carmelo Mesa-Lago. Pittsburg: University of Pittsburg Press, 1993.

Brown, Francisco. *Europa del Este: El Colapso.* Havana: Editorial Ciencias Sociales, 2002.

Brucan, Silviu. *The Wasted Generation: Memoirs of the Romanian Journey from Capitalism to Socialism and Back.* Boulder: Westview Press, 1993.

Bunce, Valerie. *Subversive institutions: The Design and the Destruction of Socialism and the State.* Cambridge Studies in Comparative Politics. Cambridge: Cambridge University Press, 1999.

Capote, Orlando Cruz. "Unas notas y dos visiones sobre la Perestroika y sus consecuencias." *Revista Cubana de Ciencias Sociales,* n.° 36/37 (July 2005/May 2006).

Carty Jr., James W. "Mass media in Cuba." *Caribbean Studies* n.° 6. Mass Media and the Caribbean (1990).

Castañeda, Jorge G. *Compañero: vida y muerte del Che Guevara.* New York: Vintage Books, 1997.

Castro, Fidel. 1959. "Discurso pronunciado por el Comandante Fidel Castro Ruz, Primer Ministro del Gobierno Revolucionario, en el acto de su toma de posesión como Primer Ministro, efectuado en el Palacio Precidencial, el 16 de febrero de 1959." Accessed June 6, 2016, http://www.cuba.cu/gobierno/discursos/1959/esp/c160259e.html.

Castro, Fidel. 1961. "Discurso pronunciado por el Comandante Fidel Castro Ruz [...] Como conclusión de las reuniones con los intelectuales cubanos, efectuadas en la Biblioteca Nacional el 16, 23 y 30 de Junio de 1961." Accessed June 6, 2016, http://www.cuba.cu/gobierno/discursos/1959/esp/c160259e.html.

Castro, Fidel. 1986. "Discurso pronunciado por el Comandante en Jefe Fidel Castro Ruz [...] en la clausura de la sesion diferida del Tercer Congreso del Partido Comunista de Cuba, 2 de diciembre de 1986." Accessed Sept. 10, 2016, http://www.cuba.cu/gobierno/discursos/1986/esp/f021286e.html.

Castro, Fidel. 1987. "Discurso pronunciado por el Comandante en Jefe Fidel Castro Ruz [...] en el acto central por el XX Aniversario de la caída en combate del comandante Ernesto Che Guevara, efectuado en la ciudad de Pinar del Río, el 8 de octubre de 1987." Accessed Sept. 10, 2016, http://www.cuba.cu/gobierno/discursos/1987/esp/f081087e.html.

Castro, Fidel. 1989. "Discurso pronunciado por Fidel Castro Ruz [...] En el acto conmemorativo por el XXXVI Aniversario del asalto al Cuartel Moncada, celebrado en la Plaza Mayor General 'Ignacio Agramonte,' Camagüey, el dia 26 de Julio de 1989, 'Año 31 de la Revolución.'" Accessed June 6, 2016, http://www.cuba.cu/gobierno/discursos/1989/esp/f260789e.html.

Castro, Fidel. 1990. "Discurso pronunciado por Fidel Castro Ruz, presidente de la república de Cuba, en la clausura del XVI Congreso de la CTC, celebrado en el Teatro 'Carlos Marx,' el 28 de enero de 1990, 'Año 32 de la Revolución.'" Accessed November 28, 2016, http://www.cuba.cu/gobierno/discursos/1990/esp/f280190e.html.

Castro, Fidel. 1991. "Discurso pronunciado por el Comandante en Jefe Fidel Castro Ruz, Primer Secretario del Comité Central del Partido Comunista de Cuba y Presidente de los Consejos de Estado y de Ministros, en la clausura del Primer Congreso de los Pioneros, efectuada en el Palacio de las Convenciones, el 1º de noviembre de 1991." Consejo de Estado. Accessed May 30, 2016, http://www.cuba.cu/gobierno/discursos/1991/esp/f011191e.html.

Castro, Fidel. 1993. "Discurso pronunciado por el Comandante en Jefe Fidel Castro Ruz, Primer Secretario del Comité Central del Partido Comunista de Cuba y Presidente de los Consejos de Estado y de Ministros, en la clausura del acto central por el XL Aniversario del asalto a los cuarteles Moncada y 'Carlos Manuel de Céspedes,' efectuado en el teatro "Heredia," Santiago de Cuba, el 26 de julio de 1993, 'Año 35 de la Revolución.'" Accessed November 24, 2016, http://www.cuba.cu/gobierno/discursos/1993/esp/f260793e.html.

Castro, Fidel. "Discurso pronunciado por el Comandante en Jefe Fidel Castro Ruz, Primer Secretario del Comité Central del Partido Comunista de Cuba y Presidente de los Consejos de Estado y de Ministros, en la sesión extraordinaria de la Asamblea Nacional del Poder Popular. Ciudad de la Habana. 20 de febrero de 1990. Año 32 de la Revolución." En *¡Atrás ni para coger impulso!*. Havana: Editora Política, 1990.

Castro, Fidel, and Mijail S. Gorbachev. *Una amistad inquebrantable*. Havana: Editora Política, 1989.

Castro, Tania Díaz. "La culpa es de Stalin." *Cubanet*, May 27, 2013. Accessed April 4, 2016, https://www.cubanet.org/articulos/la-culpa-es-de-stalin/.

Cervantes-Rodríguez, Margarita. *International Migration in Cuba: Accumulation, Imperial Designs, and Transnational Social Fields*. USA: Pennsylvania State University Press, 2010.

Chehabi, Houchang E., and Juan J. Linz. *Sultanistic Regimes*. Baltimore: Johns Hopkins University Press, 1998.

Cockcroft, James D. *América Latina y Estados Unidos: Historia y política país por país*. Havana: Editorial Ciencias Sociales, 2004.

Cohen, Stephen F. "Was the Soviet System Reformable?" *Slavic Review* 63, n.º 3 (2004): 459–488.

Dacal, Ariel, and Francisco Brown. *Rusia del socialismo real al capitalismo real*. Havana: Editorial Ciencias Sociales, 2005.

Dilla, Haroldo. "¿Debatiendo la gobernabilidad en debates gobernables?" *Nuevo Mundo Mundos Nuevos* 1, n.º Questions du temps présent (2008).

Dimitrov, Martin K. "China-Cuba: Trajectories of Post-Revolutionary Governance." http://cubacounterpoints.com/china-cuba-trajectories-of-post-revolutionary-governance-by-martin-k-dimitrov/.

Dimitrov, Martin K. *Why Communism Did Not Collapse: Understanding Authoritarian Regime Resilience in Asia and Europe*. Cambridge: University Press, 2013.

Dolz, Angel Marqués. "Un hereje en el convento. Conversación con Aurelio Alonso." *OnCuba News*, July 17, 2015. Accessed May 13, 2015, http://oncubamagazine.com/sociedad/un-hereje-en-el-convento-conversacion-con-aurelio-alonso/.

Domber, Gregory F. "The AFL-CIO, The Reagan Administration and Solidarność." *The Polish Review* 52, n.° 3 (2007): 277–304.

Domínguez, Jorge I. "Comienza una transición hacia el autoritarismo en Cuba." *Encuentro* n.° 6/7 (1997).

Domínguez, Jorge I. *La política exterior de Cuba (1962–2009)*. Madrid: Editorial Colibrí, 2009.

Domínguez, Jorge I. "Leadership Strategies and Mass Support: Cuban Politics before and after the 1991 Communist Party Congress." *Cuba at a Crossroads*, edited by Jorge F. Pérez-López. Florida: University Press of Florida, 1994.

Domínguez, Jorge I. "The Political Impact on Cuba of the Reform and Collapse of Communist Regimes." In *Cuba: After the Cold War*, edited by Carmelo Mesa-Lago. Pittsburgh: University of Pittsburgh Press, 1993.

Domínguez, Jorge I. "The Secrets of Castro's Staying Power." *Foreign Affairs* 72, n.° 2 (1993): 97–107.

Domínguez, Jorge I. "U.S. Policy toward Cuba in the 1980s and 1990s." *Annals of the American Academy of Political and Social Science* 533 (1994): 165–176.

Dore, Elizabeth. *Cuban Lives: What Difference Did a Revolution Make?* London and New York: Verso, 2017.

Dore, Elizabeth. "Cubans' life stories: the pains and pleasures of living in a communist society." *Oral History* 40, n.° 1 (2012): 35–46.

Dore, Elizabeth. "Cubans Remember Fidel." *NACLA*, ed., 2016.

EL PAIS. "Golpe de Estado en la U.R.S.S.: Cuba guarda un obligado silencio." *El País*, Aug. 21, 1991. Accessed Sept. 20, 2016, http://elpais.com/diario/1991/08/21/internacional/682725618_850215.html.

EL TIEMPO. "Solución está en manos de los soviéticos: Cuba." *El Tiempo*, Aug. 21, 1991. Accessed Aug. 3, 2016, http://www.eltiempo.com/archivo/documento/MAM-141475.

Engels, Fundación Federico. "Se agotaron libros sobre Trotsky en la Feria del Libro de La Habana." *Aporrea.org*. Febr. 15, 2005. Accessed Jan. 9, 2019, https://www.aporrea.org/actualidad/n56335.html.

Enzensberger, Hans Magnus. "Portrait of a Party: Background, Structure and Ideology of the PCC." 1970. Accessed May 19, 2016, https://www.Marxists.org/history/etol/newspape/isj/1970/no044/enzensberger.htm.

Erisman, H. Michael. *Cuba's Foreign Relations in a Post-Soviet World*. Gainesville: University Press of Florida, 2000.
Fagen, Richard. *The Transformation of Political Culture in Cuba*. Stanford: University Press, 1969.
Farber, Samuel. "Castro under Siege." *World Policy Journal* 9, n.° 2 (1992): 329–348.
Feijóo, María del Carmen Lloret, et al. *El turismo y su incidencia en el desarrollo local de Villa Clara*. Cuba: Juan Carlos Martínez Coll, 2007.
Fogel, Jean-François, and Bertrand Rosenthal. *Fin de siècle à La Havane: Les secrets du pouvoir cubain*. Paris: Editions du Seuil, 1993.
Forbes, Jill, et al. *Contemporary France: Essays and Texts on Politics, Economics and Society*. London and New York: Taylor & Francis, 2014.
Fukuyama, Francis. *The End of History and the Last Man*. New York: Free Press, 1992.
Fukuyama, Francis. "The End of History?" *The National Interest*, n.° 16 (1989): 3–18.
Galtung, Johan, et al. *Norge i 1980-årene*. Oslo: Gyldendal, 1980.
García, José Luis Rodríguez. *El Derrumbe del Socialismo en Europa*. Cuba: Editorial Ciencias Sociales; Panama: Casa Editorial Ruth, 2014.
García, Luis Aguilera, and Nelson Labrada Fernández. "Socialismo real: Del 'modelo clásico' al derrumbe." *El derrumbe del modelo soviético*, edited by Román García Baez. Havana: Editorial Félix Varela, 1994.
García Luis, Julio. *Revolución, socialismo, periodismo: La prensa y los periodistas cubanos ante el siglo XXI*. Havana: Pablo de la Torriente, 2014.
Geoffray, Marie Laure, and Armando Chaguaceda. "Medios de comunicación y cambios en la política de información en Cuba desde el 1959." *Temas de Comunicación*, n.° 29.
Gleijeses, Piero. *Conflicting Missions: Havana, Washington, and Africa, 1959–1976*. Chapel Hill: University of North Carolina Press, 2002.
Gläser, Jochen, and Grit Laudel. "Life With and Without Coding: Two Methods for Early-Stage Data Analysis in Qualitative Research Aiming at Causal Explanations." *Qualitative Social Research* 14, n.° 2 (2013).
Gott, Richard. *Cuba: A New History*. New Haven: Yale University Press, 2005.
Grass, Günter. *Unterwegs Von Deutschland Nach Deutschland: Tagebuch 1990*. Göttingen: Steidl Gerhard Verlag, 2009.
Grele, Ronald J. "Movement without aim: Methodological and theoretical problems in oral history." *The Oral History Reader*, edited by Robert Perks and Alistair Thomson. London: Routledge, 2005.
Gropas, Maria. "The Repatriotization of Revolutionary Ideology and Mnemonic Landscape in Present-Day Havana." *Current Anthropology* 48, n.° 4 (2007): 531–549.
Grønmo, Sigmund. *Samfunnsvitenskapelige metoder*. Bergen: Fagbokforlaget, 2007.
Guerra, Lillian. *Visions of Power in Cuba: Revolution, Redemption, and Resistance, 1959–1971*. Chapel Hill: University of North Carolina Press, 2012.

Guerra, Sergio, and Alejo Maldonado. *Historia de la Revolución Cubana*. Navarra: Txalaparta, 2009.

Gulyás, Ágnes. "Communist media economics and the consumers: The case of the print media of East Central Europe." *International Journal on Media Management* 3, n.° 2 (2001): 74–81.

Guzmán, Isabel Molina. "Competing discourses of community: Ideological tensions between local general-market and Latino news media." *Journalism* 7, n.° 3 (2006): 281–298.

Habel, Janette. *Cuba: The Revolution in Peril*. London: Verso, 1991.

Hamilton, Carrie. *Sexual Revolutions in Cuba: Passion, Politics and Memory*. Chapel Hill: The University of North Carolina Press, 2012.

Harbron, John D. "Journalism and Propaganda in the New Cuba." *Cuban Communism*, edited by I.L. Horowitz and J. Suchlicki. New Brunswick: Transaction Publishers, 1998 [1970].

Heredia, Fernando Martínez. "Cuba de 1959 a 1999 desde una perspectiva historica." Interview by Eric Toussaint (2015).

Hernández, Carlos Díaz, and Mabel Machado López. "Palabras sobre la 'glásnot': la llamada transparencia y la narrativa periodística sobre la historia soviética." *Revista Universidad de la Habana*, n.° 274 (2012).

Hernandez, Rafael, et al. "Political culture and popular participation in Cuba." *Latin American Perspectives* (1991): 38–54.

Hewett, Edward A., and Victor H. Winston. *Milestones in Glasnost and Perestroyka: The Economy*. Washington, DC: Brookings Institution, 1991.

Hirschman, Albert O. *Rival Views of Market Society and Other Recent Essays*. Cambridge: Harvard University Press, 1992.

Hobsbawm, Eric. *Age of Extremes: The Short Twentieth Century 1914–1991*. London: Joseph, 1994.

Hoffmann, Bert. "Cuba's Dilemma of Simultaneity: The Link between the Political and the National Question." *Debating Cuban Exceptionalism*, edited by Laurence Whitehead and Bert Hoffmann. New York: Palgrave Macmillan, 2007.

Hoffmann, Bert. "Transformation and continuity in Cuba." *Review of Radical Pol. Economics* 33, n.° 1: 1–20.

Isham, Heyward, editor. *Remaking Russia*. Prague, New York: Institute for EastWest Studies, 1995.

Ishiyama, John T. "Communist parties in transition: structures, leaders, and processes of democratization in Eastern Europe." *Comparative Politics* (1995): 147–166.

Kahl, Joseph A. "The Moral Economy of a Revolutionary Society." *Trans-action*, n.° 6 (1969): 30–37.

Kapcia, Antoni. *Cuba in Revolution: A History since the Fifties*. London: Reaktion Books, 2010.

Kapcia, Antoni. "Does Cuba Fit Yet or Is It Still 'Exceptional'?" *Journal of Latin American Studies* 40, n.° 4 (2008): 627–650.

Kirk, John H., Michael Erisman. Cuban Medical Internationalism: Origins, Evolution, and Goals. Palgrave Macmillan, 2009.

Kramer, Mark. "The Dynamics of Diffusion in the Soviet Bloc." *Why Communism Did Not Collapse: Understanding Authoritarian Regime Resilience in Asia and Europe*, edited by Martin K. Dimitrov. New York: Cambridge University Press, 2013.

Kreegipuu, Tiiu. "The ambivalent role of Estonian press in implementation of the Soviet totalitarian project." PhD thesis. University of Tartu, 2011.

Kvale, Steinar, and Svend Brinkmann. *Interviews: Learning the Craft of Qualitative Research Interviewing*. 2ª edition. California: Sage Publications, 2009.

Lara, José Bell. "Nota sobre la crisis y hundimiento del modelo de socialismo implantado en la USSR." *Visión desde Cuba*, edited by José Bell Lara and Clara Pulido Escandell. Madrid: SODePAZ, 1997.

Lara, José Bell. "Nota sobre la crisis y hundimiento del modelo de socialismo real. A veinte años de la Perestroika." *Revista Cubana de Ciencias Sociales*, n.° 36/37 (July 2005/May 2006).

Lavigne, Marie. *Del socialismo al mercado: la dificil transición económica de la Europa del Este*. Madrid: Ediciones Encuentro, S.A., 1997.

LeoGrande, William M. "The Communist Party of Cuba since the First Congress." *Journal of Latin American Studies* 12, n.° 2 (1980): 397–419.

LeoGrande, William M. "El Partido Comunista de Cuba y la Política Electoral: Adaptación, Sucesión y Transición." (2002).

LeoGrande, William M. "Party Development in Revolutionary Cuba." *Journal of Interamerican Studies and World Affairs* 21, n.° 4 (1979): 457–480.

León, Iván Emilio. *Europa Oriental: del derrumbe al neoliberalismo*. Havana: Ruth Casa Editorial, 2011.

Lévesque, Jacques. "La Unión Soviética y Cuba: Una relación especial." *Foro Internacional* XVIII, n.° 2, October-December (1977): pp. 219–242.

Lewis, Oscar, et al. *Living the Revolution: An Oral History of Contemporary Cuba: 1: Four Men*. Urbana: University of Illinois Press, 1977.

Lewis, Oscar, et al. *Living the Revolution: An Oral History of Contemporary Cuba: 2: Four Women*. Urbana: University of Illinois Press, 1977.

Lewis, Oscar, et al. *Living the Revolution: An Oral History of Contemporary Cuba: 3: Neighbors*. Urbana: University of Illinois Press, 1978.

Loss, Jacqueline. *Dreaming in Russian: The Cuban Soviet Imaginary*. Texas: University of Texas Press, 2014.

Loss, Jacqueline, and José Manuel Prieto. *Caviar with Rum: Cuba-USSR and the Post-Soviet Experience*. New Directions in Latino American Cultures. New York: Palgrave Macmillan, 2012.

Lutjens, Sheryl L. "Democracy and socialist Cuba." *Cuba in Transition*, edited by Sandor Halebsky, et al. Boulder, CO: Westview Press, 1992.
Martin, L. John, and Anju Grover Chaudhary. *Comparative Mass Media Systems*. New York: Longman, 1983.
Mesa-Lago, Carmelo. *Cuba: After the Cold War*. Pitt Latin American series. Pittsburgh: University Press, 1993.
Mesa-Lago, Carmelo. "Cuba and the Downfall of Soviet and East European Socialism." *Cuba: After the Cold War*, edited by Carmelo Mesa-Lago. Pittsburgh: University Press, 1993.
Mesa-Lago, Carmelo. *Cuba en la era de Raúl Castro. Reformas económico-sociales y sus efectos*. Madrid: Colibrí, 2012.
Mesa-Lago, Carmelo. "Cuba's economic counter-reform (rectificación): Causes, policies and effects." *Journal of Communist Studies* 5, n.° 4 (1989): 98–139.
Michaleva, Galina. "The Communist Party of the Russian Federation (CPRF)." *Schriften des Hannah-Arendt-Instituts für Totalitarismusforschung*, n.° 36 (2008): 437.
Miles, Matthew B., et al. *Qualitative Data Analysis: A Methods Sourcebook*. Third edition. Thousand Oaks: SAGE, 2014.
Mora, Frank O. "A comparative study of civil-military relations in Cuba and China: The effects of bingshang." *Armed Forces & Society: An Interdisciplinary Journal* 28, n.° 2 (2002): 183.
Navarro, Desiderio. *El pensamiento cultural ruso en Criterios*. Havana: Centro Teórico-Cultural Criterios, 2009.
Niethammer, Lutz. "Elecciones y fuente oral en la RDA (III-1990)." *Historia y fuente oral: Revista Semestral del Seminario de Historia Oral del Departamento de Historia Contemporánea de la Universitat de Barcelona y del Institut Municipal d'Història*, n.° 4 (1996): 155.
Nodarse, Hiram Marquetti. "La crisis del socialismo en la USSR y Europa Oriental: Implicaciones para Cuba." *El derrumbe del modelo eurosoviético: Una visión desde Cuba*, edited by Román García Báez. La Habana: Felix Varela, 1994.
Offe, Claus. "Capitalism by democratic design? Democratic theory facing the triple transition in East Central Europe." *Social Research* 58, n.° 4 (1991): 865.
Oppenheimer, Andrés. *La hora final de Castro*. Buenos Aires: Javier Vergara, 1992.
Padula, Alfred. "Cuban Socialism: Thirty Years of Controversy." *Conflict and Change in Cuba*, edited by Enrique A. Baloyra and James A. Morris. Albuquerque: University of New Mexico Press, 1993.
Padura, Leonardo. "Leonardo Padura: 'La realidad cubana es demasiado peculiar para explicarla con prejuicios a favor o en contra.'" Entrevista por Astrid Pikielny (2014).
Partido Comunista de Cuba. 2017. "Historia del Partido Comunista de Cuba." Accessed May 31, 2016, http://www.PCC.cu/i_historia.php.

Partido Comunista de Cuba. *IV Congreso del Partido Comunista de Cuba, Santiago de Cuba, 10–14 de octubre de 1991: discursos y documentos*. Havana: Editorial Política, 1992.

Partido Comunista de Cuba. 1999. "Reglamento del Partido Comunista de Cuba." http://congresoPCC.cip.cu/wp-content/uploads/2011/01/reglamento.pdf.

Partido Comunista de Cuba: Evolución histórica (1959–1997). Havana: Editorial Historia, 2011.

Pavlov, Yuri. *Soviet-Cuban Alliance 1959–1991*. Miami: North-South Center Press, 1996.

Pedraza, Silvia. "Democratization and Migration: Cuba's Exodus and the Development of Civil Society-Hindrance or Help." *Association for the Study of the Cuban Economy (ed.): Cuba in Transition* 12 (2002): 247–261.

Pérez-Stable, Marifeli. *The Cuban Revolution: Origins, Course and Legacy*. Third edition. New York: Oxford University Press, 2012.

Pérez, Carlos Tablada. *El pensamiento económico de Ernesto Che Guevara*. Havana: Casa de las Américas, 1987.

Pérez, Carlos Tablada. *Ernesto "Che" Guevara: hombre y sociedad*. Buenos Aires: Editorial Antarca, 1987.

Pérez, Eugenio Suárez, and Acela Caner Román. "Primero de enero de 1959: Esta vez sí que es una Revolución." *Granma*, Dec. 31, 2015. Accessed May 13, 2016, http://www.granma.cu/cuba/2015-12-31/primero-de-enero-de-1959-esta-vez-si-que-es-una-revolucion-31-12-2015-21-12-02.

Pérez Jr., Louis. *Structure of Cuban History: Meanings and Purpose of the Past*. Chapel Hill: University of North Carolina Press, 2013.

Perfiles de la Cultura Cubana. 2008. "Cátedra de Oralidad." Accessed May 31, 2016, http://www.perfiles.cult.cu/catedras.php.

Pfaff, Steven, and Hyojoung Kim. "Exit & Voice Dynamics in Collective Action: An Analysis of Emigration and Protest in the East German Revolution." *American Journal of Sociology* 109, n.° 2 (2003): 401–444.

Portelli, Alessandro. *The Death of Luigi Trastulli and Other Stories: Form and Meaning in Oral History*. New York: State University Press, 1991.

Prieto, Abel. *El humor de Misha: la crisis del "socialismo real" en el chiste político*. Buenos Aires: Ediciones Colihue, 1997.

QSR International. 2016. "¿Qué es NVivo?" Accessed June 1, 2016, http://www.qsrinternational.com/other-languages_spanish.aspx.

Ravsberg, Fernando. "Haciendo camino al andar." *BBC Mundo*, July 25, 2013. Accessed May 26, 2016, http://www.bbc.com/mundo/blogs/2013/07/130725_blog_cartas_desde_cuba_haciendo_camino#orb-banner.

Ricoeur, Paul. *Hermeneutics and the Human Sciences: Essays on Language, Action and Interpretation*. Cambridge: Cambridge University Press, 1981.

Ritchie, Donald A. *Doing Oral History: A Practical Guide*. New York: Oxford University Press, 2003.

Rodríguez, José Luis. "El desarrollo económico y social en Cuba: resultados de 30 años de la Revolución." *Cuba Socialista*, n.° 39 (May–June 1989): 35–65.

Rojas, Rafael. *Historia mínima de la Revolución Cubana*. El Colegio de México, 2015.

Rojas, Rafael. "Souvenirs de un Caribe soviético." *Revista Encuentro* 48–49 (2008).

Román, García Báez, and Ramón Sánchez Noda, editors. *El derrumbe del modelo eurosoviético: Una visión desde Cuba*. Havana: Editorial Felix Varela, 1994.

Roman, Peter. *People's Power: Cuba's Experience with Representative Government, Updated Edition*. Boulder: Rowman & Littlefield, 2003.

Ronda, Denia García. "¿Por qué cayo el socialismo en Europa Oriental?" *Ultimo Jueves*. Havana: Instituto Cubano de Investigación Cultural Juan Marinello, 2008.

Rosenberg, Jonathan. "Cuba's Free-Market Experiment: Los Mercados Libres Campesinos, 1980–1986." *Latin American Research Review* 27, n.° 3 (1992): 51–89.

Ruíz, Julién Richard. "Kilómetro 0. La desintegración de la USSR, una visión desde Cuba. Tesis de licenciatura.," PhD thesis. Faculty of Communications, University of Havana, 2012.

Saldaña, Johnny. *The Coding Manual for Qualitative Researchers*. London: MPG Books Group, 2010.

Santos, José Eduardo Dos, and Fidel Castro. "Sabremos cumplir el papel que nos asigne la historia." Havana: Editorial Política, 1989.

Santos, Oscar Pino. 2004. "Lo que fue aquella República: Protectorado y neocolonia." http://epoca2.lajiribilla.cu/2004/n142_01/142_07.html.

Schulz, Donald E. "Can Castro Survive?" *Journal of Interamerican Studies and World Affairs* 35, n.° 1 (1993): 89–117.

Schwalbe, Michael L., and Michelle Wolkomir. "Interviewing men." *Handbook of Interview Research: Context and Method*, edited by F. Gubrium and A. Holstein. Thousand Oaks, CA: Sage, 2002.

Shearman, Peter. *The Soviet Union and Cuba*. London; New York: Routledge & Kegan Paul, 1987.

Siebert, Fred S., et al. *Four Theories of the Press: The Authoritarian, Libertarian, Social Responsibility, and Soviet Communist Concepts of What the Press Should Be and Do*. Urbana: University of Illinois Press, 1956.

Skidmore, Thomas E., and Peter H. Smith. *Modern Latin America*. New York: Oxford University Press, 2005.

Soruco, Gonzalo R. *Cubans and the Mass Media in South Florida*. Gainsville: University Press of Florida, 1996.

Sparks, Colin. "Media theory after the fall of European communism: Why the old models from East and West won't do any more." *De-Westernizing Media Studies*, edited by James Curran and Myung-Jin Park. London: Routledge, 2000.

Szulc, Tad. *Fidel: A Critical Portrait*. New York: Perennial, 2002.
Thompson, Paul. *Voice of the Past: Oral History*. Third edition. Oxford; New York: Oxford University Press, 2000.
Trotsky, León. *La revolucion traicionada: ¿Qué es y adónde se dirige la Unión Sovietica?* New York: Pathfinder, 1992.
Vorotnikov, Vitali I. *Mi verdad. Notas y reflexiones del diario de trabajo de un miembro del Buró Político del PCUS*. Havana: Casa Editora Abril, 1995.
Walker, Rachel. *Six Years that Shook the World: Perestroika—The Impossible Project*. Manchester: Manchester University Press, 1993.
Ward, John. *Latin America: Development and Conflict Since 1945*. London; New York: Routledge, 1997.
Whitehead, Laurence, and Bert Hoffmann, editors. *Debating Cuban Exceptionalism*. Studies of the Americas. New York: Palgrave Macmillan, 2007.

Index

26th of July Movement   25–27, 213, 227, 229

Abalkin   120, 123–24
academic debates   3, 38, 301
academic literature   5, 29–30, 34, 40, 44, 59, 226, 233, 280–81, 297, 318, 325, 327
academics   50, 142–43, 189, 196, 218, 223, 255, 257, 266, 270, 276, 321, 328, 331, 333
academic visa   191–92
achievements   21, 214, 278, 308, 316–18, 320, 327, 332
admiration   298
Afghanistan   23, 235, 258, 297, 305
Aganbeguian   124–25
agencies   73, 113, 262
aggression   63, 114, 224
agreements   76, 83–84, 96, 181, 339
agriculture   15, 83, 118, 182, 262, 291, 294, 310
Albania   12, 39
Alberto   205, 207–8, 222, 241, 248, 258, 261, 263, 265, 267, 284, 293, 297–98, 305, 314, 319
Aldana   51–52, 158, 162
Allgemeiner Deutscher Nachrichtendienst (ADN)   92, 101
allies   17, 68, 71–72, 76, 78, 106, 118, 129, 133, 166, 170, 180, 183, 217–18, 233, 268, 275, 327
Alonso   53
Alver   197
Americas   3, 22, 180, 234, 241
Amnesty International   217, 286
Andropov   244, 259, 294
Angola   23–24, 77, 233–35, 284, 316, 333
ANSA   113–14, 122
archives   3, 58, 117, 233
arguments   20, 69, 82, 86–87, 89, 93, 112, 128–31, 133, 141, 153, 162, 168–69, 243, 251, 318
artists   49, 182, 242, 263, 284
Asian socialist countries   39
assemblies, provincial   28, 237
attitude   65, 106, 142, 163, 166, 199, 207, 243, 280, 282, 285, 296–97, 340
 anti-Soviet   79, 81
 official Cuban   142

Aurelio   205, 224, 229–31, 234, 236, 246, 249–51, 254–57, 269–70, 296–97, 300, 305, 307, 313–14, 343
Austria   91, 95
Aute   163
authorities   10–11, 14–16, 19, 22, 33, 91, 93, 98, 100, 106–7, 227, 230, 262, 266–68, 273, 279, 285, 288, 311, 314, 329, 333
 new   115–16

Bain   7–9, 17, 26–28, 31–32, 56, 142, 145–46, 154, 220, 228, 230, 234–35, 240
balance of power   155, 304
Balea   70–71, 75, 77–78
Baloyra   19–20, 283
Baltic countries   11
Barrio Caribe   214, 216
Batista   7, 26–27, 47, 88, 211, 213–14, 216–17
battles   115, 128, 138–39
Bay of Pigs (invasion of)   14, 48, 216, 219–21, 223
Bell Lara   13, 30, 33, 35, 336
Berlin   90, 100, 160, 263, 289
Berlin Wall   1, 56, 90–91, 97–101, 103–5, 107, 118, 133, 160, 263, 268, 289, 292, 339
bicycle   103, 310
Bideleux   11–13, 108
Blasier   228, 234
Blas Roca   27
blockade   63, 104, 180, 218–19, 222, 264, 280, 309, 333
Bobes   178
border crossings, new   100
borders   60, 91, 97–103, 107, 111
 opening of   98
bourgeoisie   286
box   66, 73, 75–76, 98, 101, 111, 113–15, 121–23, 135, 137, 143, 146, 240
BRD, see West Germany
Brezhnev   244, 258–59, 305–6
Brinkmann   195, 200
Brown   36
Bucharest   112–14
Bukharin   254–55
Bulgaria   12, 39, 118, 262, 344
Bunce   5

INDEX

bureaucracy   35–36, 187
Bush   22, 125, 151, 161–62

cadres   166, 306
Camagüey   1, 271, 274
candidates   28, 71, 137, 187–88, 237, 313
capacity, intellectual   254–55, 285
capitalism   53, 57, 78–79, 86, 90, 95, 105, 108, 118, 125, 130, 138–41, 159–60, 162, 170, 275, 277, 299, 302, 304, 327, 329
capitalist countries   85, 90, 134, 166, 183
  industrialized   21
capitalist world   104, 110, 330
  western   38, 53
Carty Jr.   45, 47
Castro, Fidel   1–5, 7–8, 13–17, 19–22, 25–27, 29–30, 43, 47–48, 68–69, 87–88, 138–39, 161–63, 169–70, 185, 206–7, 209, 211–13, 219–21, 223–29, 242, 244–47, 250–51, 259–60, 271, 273–77, 281–83, 287, 290, 296, 325, 329–31, 340
Castro, Raúl   3, 22, 25, 51, 180–81, 184, 191
categories   29–30, 33, 158, 185, 202, 245
CDRs   109, 138, 184, 238, 284
Ceauşescu   107–9, 111–14, 116–19
  death of   109–10
Central America   17, 20, 23, 233
Central Committee   13, 19, 35, 43, 46, 51, 69, 84, 114, 137, 165, 187, 251, 266, 271, 301, 312
Chaguaceda   50, 54
Chernenko   294
children   96, 136, 159, 232, 271, 311, 315, 317
China–Cuba   313
Chinese   148, 225–26
citizens   54, 70, 86, 90, 94–96, 98, 101–2, 105, 107, 111–12, 137, 226, 250, 288, 312
clashes   114, 221
classes   40, 157, 186, 212
  working   4, 25–26, 133, 254, 256
codes   200–204
  descriptive   201–2
  subordinate   202
  vivo   202–3
coding   200–201, 203–4
collaboration   8, 218, 325
Comecon   2, 11, 22, 39, 155, 179, 206, 230–32, 235, 240
Comecon countries   45, 52, 68, 76, 318

commentary   68, 78–79, 104, 107, 116, 138, 140, 160, 166, 170, 329
communication   37, 183, 260–61
communism   1–2, 4, 12, 34–35, 40, 104, 106, 128, 186, 217–18, 221, 228, 241
communist parties   25, 190, 225, 280
  former   27, 297
Communist parties in transition   297
communist party   76, 237–38
Communist Party of Cuba (PCC)   3–6, 13–14, 16, 18–19, 24–25, 27–29, 31, 43–44, 46, 67, 69, 79, 82, 131, 141, 153–54, 166–67, 176–78, 181–82, 184–85, 187–88, 193, 196–97, 224–25, 237–38, 285–86, 311, 325–326, 334–36, 338–40, 342–44
Communist Party of the Russian Federation (CPRF)   307
Communist Party of the Russian Soviet Federative Socialist Republic (CP RSFSR)   131–32
Communist Party of the Soviet Union (CPSU)   9–11, 17, 25–26, 28, 55, 80–81, 120, 131, 136–37, 236, 272, 277, 299–300, 307, 326
Communist Party of Venezuela   225
communists   25–26, 28, 32, 40, 45, 56, 72, 80–81, 85, 138, 186, 211, 217, 261, 287, 304
  young   56–57, 159
conflicts   10, 19–20, 23, 64, 67, 69, 72, 82, 84, 113, 116–17, 119, 122, 225, 227, 234, 241, 244, 251–52, 290, 295
confusion   51, 146, 153, 158, 165, 277, 315
congress   14, 17, 22, 43, 51, 71, 84, 131–32, 156, 259, 311–14, 340
conscience, prisoner of   286
consensus   34, 128, 186, 194, 246, 288, 300–302, 321
constitution   24, 26, 49, 80, 83, 143, 210–11, 238, 325, 341
Constitution of Cuba   342
context   1, 5, 7, 13, 47, 49, 75, 77, 112, 121, 136, 139, 156, 160–61, 177, 219, 228, 231
  historical   7, 10
continuity   5, 7, 9, 16, 77, 159, 207, 211, 303–4
contradictions   8, 13, 103, 107, 202, 218, 222, 228, 248, 304
contributions   4, 36, 38, 45, 85, 237
control   10, 13, 19, 28, 45–46, 108, 114, 150, 153, 162, 221, 267, 272, 300, 302, 305–6

correspondents 50, 67, 69, 76, 78, 86, 111–12, 117, 122, 124, 169
corruption 26, 88, 118, 158, 259, 261, 289, 298
cosmos 295
Council 2, 28, 39, 123, 165, 181, 205, 230, 232, 247, 256, 290
counterrevolution 81, 160–61, 278, 303
counterrevolutionary expressions 242
countries
 allied 65, 76, 83, 88, 109, 122, 223, 252, 266
 closed 109, 182
 developed 291
 developing 23, 126
 host 170
 important 60
 industrial 255
 industrialized 92, 162
 main 38, 206
 major 169
 non-socialist 94
 third 310
coup 44, 47, 88, 142–46, 149–50, 153–54, 169, 211, 213–14, 275, 292, 307, 339
 coup government 145, 150, 153, 329
 coup leaders 143, 147
 coup plotters 142, 144–47, 149–50, 154
coverage 54–55, 57, 59–60, 62, 68–70, 73, 76–77, 83–84, 86–89, 91–94, 101, 103–4, 106–10, 112–13, 115–16, 121–23, 125, 127–28, 138, 141–43, 153–54, 168–69, 267–68, 328–29, 335
 broad 72–73
 general 78, 86, 121
 positive 93
CPC, see Communist Party of Cuba
CP RSFSR, see Communist Party of the Russian Soviet Federative Socialist Republic
CPRF, see Communist Party of the Russian Federation
CPSU, see Communist Party of the Soviet Union
creation 13, 15, 109, 114, 124, 180, 230, 236, 238
crisis 2, 21–24, 35, 68–69, 116, 118, 120, 122, 137, 139, 146, 177–79, 186–88, 222–24, 240, 243–44, 262–65, 271–74, 276, 279–80, 289, 308–10, 313–16, 330–33, 340

 major 135, 269, 272, 326
 multifaceted 143, 245
Cruz Capote 36
Cuba
 history of 30, 177, 213, 341
 and East Germany 92
Cuban
 Cuban Adjustment Act 96, 282
 Cuban-American community 180, 250
 authorities 17–18, 50–51, 54, 57, 78, 80, 118–20, 144–45, 149–50, 154–55, 166, 169, 178, 183, 227, 232, 268, 273–74
 autonomy 233, 235
 ballet 69
 -based press agency, see Prensa Latina
 Communist Party, see Communist Party of Cuba
 economy 21, 90, 231, 248, 250, 272
 fighters 224
 nineteenth-century 212
 government 17, 21, 23, 73, 76, 78, 84–85, 112, 118–19, 135, 141–42, 146, 148, 154, 156, 217, 219–21, 246, 248, 308–9
 historiography 228
 history 8–9, 16, 30, 87, 138, 205–7, 209, 212, 264–65, 320, 328, 334
 interpreting 315
 present 212
 independence movements 327
 Institute of Radio and Television 46
 intellectuals 50, 88, 208, 242
 journalism 46, 48, 50, 64, 83, 99, 129, 327
 leaders 22–23, 37, 56, 134, 149, 157, 244, 247, 268–69
 new 221
 leadership 22, 118, 250, 274
 lobby 146
 important 17
 media 18, 46, 50, 55–56, 83, 89, 96, 135, 181, 183, 198, 239, 260, 263, 276, 278, 302, 321
 media coverage 260, 302
 Medical Internationalism 318
 military operation in Angola 233
 Missile Crisis 221, 257
 model 237, 321–22, 330
 opposition 74, 158, 189
 Party 4, 27, 83, 116, 187, 282, 302, 331

Party Members 89, 173, 217
people 26, 207, 257, 262, 313
People's Party 213
perceptions 3–4, 17, 32, 34, 134
policies 244
  authoritarian 297
  official 183, 252
politics 24, 29, 206, 227, 244–45, 325, 328, 334
  contemporary 4
  official 116
population 126, 141, 158, 179, 282, 340
power structure 46
press 30, 32, 44, 47, 49–50, 52–55, 63, 74, 104, 108, 160, 264, 296
project 206, 209
province of Cárdenas 160
qualities 138
Rafters Crisis 178, 181, 281
readers 93, 129, 152
Rectification Process, see Rectification
reformists 249
relations 206, 303
Republic 213
researcher 307
response 339
Revolution 1, 13–14, 16, 30, 33, 112, 159, 161, 171, 206, 209, 218, 222–24, 233–34, 241, 253, 256–57, 260–61, 284, 316, 318, 320, 322, 325–26, 332–33
Cuban Revolutionary Party (PRC) 24, 156, 208–9, 211, 213
revolutionary press 47
socialism 20, 55, 141, 165, 185, 210, 301, 318, 326, 330, 340
Socialist Democracy 238
society 43, 118, 158, 165, 179, 182, 191, 206, 226, 265, 282, 326
state 20, 47, 49, 64, 107, 135, 146, 178, 236, 252
system 3, 6, 30, 122, 184, 238, 279–80, 282, 310, 322, 328, 331
tradition of heroism and resistance 327
Women 19, 24, 184, 283
Cubanet 166
Cubans 7–9, 15–18, 20, 28–34, 53–56, 72–73, 86–89, 117–18, 141–42, 155–57, 159–63, 165–66, 171, 177–79, 182–84, 190–92, 207–8, 210, 212–13, 218, 222–23, 235–36, 238–40, 243–44, 249–52, 257, 261, 272–74, 281–86, 307–9, 311–13, 318–23, 329–34
Cubans and East Germans 104
Cubans foresaw 271
Cubans' life stories 192
Cuba's Defense 18
Cuba's internationalism in Africa 15
Cuba's Rectification of Errors and Negative Trends, see Rectification
Cuba's security situation 228, 335
Cuba Trade Exchange Protocol 92
Czech and Soviet arms 219
Czechoslovakia 12, 39, 45, 91–96, 108, 111, 228–29, 261–62, 285, 290, 344

Debates in Hungary 59, 83
Debating Cuban Exceptionalism 3, 90
debt crisis 22–23
democratic centralism 11, 79, 81, 84–85, 193
democratic socialism, see Socialism, democratic
democratization 10, 90, 182, 297, 340
Department of Revolutionary Orientation (DOR) 46, 63
de-Stalinization 258, 305
difficulties 71, 139, 183, 215, 229, 271–72, 282, 285, 309–10, 333
Dimitrov 12, 35, 80
disorders 110–11, 148
dissolution 44, 59–60, 65, 179, 207, 264, 274–75, 338, 344
Domínguez 14, 18–19, 21–22, 29, 31–32, 56, 86, 163, 178, 218, 220, 233, 244–45, 252, 287, 316
DOR 46, 267–68
Dore 33, 192–93

East Berlin 91, 105–6, 159
Eastern Europe 2–3, 11–13, 21, 27–28, 35–36, 38–40, 43–44, 47, 57–58, 64–65, 67–68, 76–77, 79–80, 83, 107–8, 139–41, 154–55, 159–60, 162, 238, 253, 257, 269, 275–76, 285–86, 302–3, 305–6, 308, 311–12, 314–15, 318–20, 322–23, 328–32

East European and Soviet Socialism   21, 34, 206, 260, 263, 333–34
East European   3, 6, 10, 13, 34–35, 37–39, 44, 51, 54, 59, 64–65, 67–68, 162, 168, 177, 187–88, 205–6, 302, 307, 320–21, 325–28, 330
East Germany   12, 60, 70, 83, 88, 90–101, 104, 103–7, 109–10, 113, 118–19, 137, 140, 142, 159–60, 162, 168–70, 262–63, 291, 296, 327, 329, 344
  authorities   93, 100, 107
  citizens   91, 94–95
  coverage   101, 119
  government   98, 106–7
  migration crisis   44, 106
economic crisis   50, 118, 156, 192, 228, 315–16
economic debate   120–23, 127, 130–31, 134–35, 137–38, 141, 168
economic reforms   10, 60, 98, 121, 125, 129–30, 133, 137–39, 169, 179
  debate on   44, 135–36, 139, 141
economic situation   10, 74, 76, 178, 239, 248, 298
economic structures   211, 293
economic systems   11, 142, 321
economy   10, 13, 15, 20–21, 28, 128–29, 182, 188, 221, 228, 243, 246–48, 270, 273, 290, 293, 296, 304, 308
ECURED   39
Editorial Ciencias Sociales   36
Editorial Félix Varela   34, 179, 269
editorials   36, 62, 65, 138, 155, 157, 193–94, 210
editors   34, 46, 48, 55, 79, 98, 106, 108, 125, 133, 141, 144, 146, 170, 328
EFE   73, 76, 147–48, 153, 312
elections   11, 24, 26, 59, 67–68, 71, 73, 76, 79, 168, 180, 230, 238, 275–76, 307, 316
  parliamentary   71–73
Eliécer   205, 207, 215, 217, 222–23, 234, 240, 245, 258, 260, 263, 265, 270, 280, 285, 292, 296, 299–300, 306, 310, 317, 319
El Militante Comunista   3, 43, 166, 342
Engels   208, 299
enthusiasm   119, 133, 145, 154, 252
Enzensberger   25–26, 31
Erisman   23, 31, 235, 318
Ernesto Che Guevara   247, 254–55, 273

errors   13, 35, 51, 93, 159, 161, 170–71, 245, 249, 320–21, 330–31
Esteban   228, 233–34, 236, 238, 243, 245–47, 249, 251, 254–59, 262, 265, 268, 270–71, 285–86, 293, 297, 299–300, 304–6, 312
Estonian Soviet Socialist Republic   76
European parties   29
European Socialist Camp   248, 271
European state socialism   2, 5
Euro-Soviet model   333
evils   73, 78, 130, 214, 258
exchange   108, 179, 183, 198, 241, 309
exclusion   71, 214–15
exiles   27, 181, 218–20, 227, 282, 287, 302
explanations   7, 36, 50, 64–65, 79, 119, 155, 165–68, 171, 249, 253, 285–86, 288–89, 291, 294, 296, 298, 329–31
external pressures   107, 158–61, 163, 165, 171, 238, 267, 326, 330

factories   65, 191, 272, 302
factors   11, 17, 23, 48, 79, 153, 159, 168, 191–92, 194, 198, 216, 221, 275–76, 280, 282, 299, 301
  external   159, 183, 296, 338
  internal   5, 37, 160, 166, 220, 296–97, 331
failure   144, 230–31, 239, 298, 307
family   94, 188, 268, 281, 315–16
Farber   314
fascists   94, 138
Federal Republic of Germany (FRG), see West Germany
Fernández   219
Fidel   5, 25, 43, 157, 207–8, 219, 224, 226, 229, 236, 245, 270–71, 313
fieldwork   191–92, 198
First Congress   27–28, 31, 227
Florida   23, 31, 216, 245, 282
FMC   19, 184
forces   20, 23, 25, 35, 37, 78, 80, 130–31, 133, 227, 231, 235, 238, 283, 287, 291, 293, 299
  counterrevolutionary   290
  radical   123, 126, 131
foreigners   62, 170, 192–93, 261, 266, 326
Fourth Congress   311, 340
freedom   18, 78, 86, 97, 105, 112, 151, 163, 191, 193, 258, 267, 288, 295, 331
FRG, see West Germany

INDEX

front page   61, 97, 105, 116, 122, 138, 143–44, 146, 152, 157, 163–64, 329
   newspaper's   52, 97, 122

Galtung   269
García   48–51, 153
gasoline   310
GDR, see East Germany
German Democratic Republic (GDR), see East Germany
Geoffray   50, 54
Glasnost   10, 55, 120, 190, 249, 251
Gorbachev   10–12, 17–18, 37, 57, 80, 120, 123–28, 130, 133–34, 140–43, 145–48, 149–54, 169, 244, 247, 250, 252, 272, 274, 289–92, 294–96, 298–300, 306, 321, 338–39
   and Western leaders   125
   government   134
   period   262, 293
   position   162
   process   271, 306
Gorbachev's control   135, 154
Gorbachev's criteria   126
Gorbachev's model of reformism   18
Gorbachev's Perestroika   13, 18, 50, 158, 247
Gorbachev's policies   133, 166
Gorbachev's reforms   13, 55, 146, 148, 289, 341
Granma   3, 6, 41, 43–44, 46–48, 51–52, 56–59, 61–70, 72–89, 91–114, 116–23, 125–35, 137, 139–57, 159–60, 163–71, 252–53, 264, 301–2, 322, 326–28, 330–31
   access   58
   editors of   86, 126, 131, 157
   front page of   146, 150
   general   168
Granma newspaper archive   149
Green Party   85
guerrillas   27, 224–25
Guevara   16, 19, 25, 186, 220, 224, 227, 229–30, 234, 246, 292, 301
Gulyás   45

Habel   14, 19, 30, 226–28, 246, 248
Harbron   43, 46–47
Havana   4, 7, 32–34, 36–37, 53, 55, 57, 142, 178–79, 183–84, 197–98, 209–10, 215, 225, 227, 230, 233, 235, 247, 295, 340, 342–44

Havana Times   51, 215, 309
health   179, 214, 216, 317–18, 332
health system   236, 295, 316–17
Héctor   216, 231–32, 236, 245, 254–55, 258, 270, 278–80, 284, 292, 296–97, 302, 304, 309, 311, 317, 319
Hirschman   281
historiography   4, 27, 211, 213, 219
history   2, 7, 30–33, 44, 47, 55, 61, 63, 97, 104, 108, 140, 206, 208, 213, 251, 253–54, 256–57, 295–96, 298–99, 302
Hoffmann   9, 90
homeland   95, 162
   Patria   277–78
honor   137, 144, 197
hotels   262, 310
HSWP, see Hungarian Socialist Workers Party (HSWP)
Huberman   200, 204
Hungarian debate   81, 83
Hungarian Parliament   85
Hungarian Socialist Workers Party (HSWP)   80–85
Hungary   2, 6, 12, 39, 44–45, 59, 68, 80–89, 91–92, 95, 107–8, 119, 140, 169, 241, 257, 285, 329

Ibarra   213
ideas   4, 18, 52, 54–56, 81–82, 84, 87–89, 139–40, 156, 158, 160–61, 168, 170, 211–12, 223–24, 229, 231–33, 240–41, 245, 247, 249–52, 282, 288–89, 329, 339
ideological affinity   92–93
ideological position   123, 185
ideology   24–25, 29, 61, 64, 68, 82, 87, 89, 130, 135, 146, 166, 185–86, 217, 251, 322, 325–26, 334
Idulberto   205, 207–8, 215–16, 222–24, 241, 245, 257, 260–61, 280, 289, 344
imperialism   89, 138, 158, 160–63, 166, 208, 229, 292, 294, 297
impression   4, 35, 74–75, 89, 98, 109, 143, 145–46, 150, 153, 186–87, 192, 198, 261, 272, 291, 300, 307
independence   7–8, 11, 23, 124, 162, 207, 210, 212, 223, 229, 235, 244, 278, 290, 303, 319
individuals   3, 175, 190, 193, 196, 202, 237, 298–99, 323, 325

influence, cultural   53, 240, 243
informants   39–40, 175–76, 183, 185–87, 193–94, 196–98, 214–15, 226, 228–30, 236–38, 245–47, 252–54, 256–59, 261, 263–64, 267–69, 273–74, 276, 281–82, 284–86, 296–303, 306–7, 320–23, 326–28, 331–35
information   31–32, 43–44, 46, 53, 60–62, 64–66, 73–75, 83–84, 93–94, 96–98, 100–101, 109–11, 113–17, 121–23, 137, 143–44, 147–49, 153–54, 168–69, 175–77, 183, 196–97, 200, 244, 263–69, 276, 301, 321, 325–26, 328–29, 331, 336–37
  contextual   177
  critical   108, 266
  false   117
  general   119, 338
  official   69, 252
  sources of   153, 157
information source   63, 263
information texts   64
  outline   64
inhabitants   21, 105–6, 317–18
initiative   27, 29, 35, 122–23, 232–33, 267
institutionalization   8, 14, 28
institutions   4, 6, 11, 16, 19, 28, 30–31, 158, 163, 182, 317, 333
Integrated Revolutionary Organizations (ORI)   25, 227
intellectuals   18, 48, 51, 85, 114, 183, 228, 242, 265–66, 270–71, 291, 300, 307
Inter Press Service   113–14
Intercontinental Hotel   112, 261
interests   4, 30, 32–33, 35–36, 56, 58, 61, 64, 75, 80, 103, 133, 154, 199, 230, 234, 246, 257
internal crisis   68, 292
internal problems   95, 106, 109, 149, 154, 165, 292, 295
internet   46, 142, 183
interpretations   4, 25, 34, 37, 44, 171, 176, 193–94, 199, 201, 253, 290, 297, 299, 301, 311, 325, 331
interview coding process   203
interviewees   44, 223, 254, 276, 288, 315–20, 327, 330–31, 333, 336–37
interviewees questions   39
interviewers   192, 198, 232

interview guide   38, 198, 222, 338–39, 341
interviewing   193, 195–96, 198
interviewing individuals   6
interview interaction   195
interviews   3–4, 11, 38, 40, 47, 50, 64, 138, 140, 156–57, 159–61, 175–81, 184–86, 190–99, 205–319, 321–22, 326–27, 330–31, 336, 338, 342
  qualitative   195
  semi-structured   175, 196, 325
  short   105, 170
  structured   196
  transcribed   200, 202, 205
interview subjects   176, 181, 184, 193–95, 198–99, 201–9, 211–12, 214–15, 217–19, 222–23, 230–33, 235, 238–40, 243–45, 253–58, 260, 277, 279–81, 284–85, 288–89, 296–98, 300, 302, 305, 308
  contact   196
invasion   23, 216, 219, 223, 256, 305
inversion   55, 139–40
investigation   29, 31, 38, 52–53, 56–57, 85, 155, 187, 198, 201, 326
IPS, see Inter Press Service
island   33, 46, 50, 54, 57, 97, 163, 178, 182–83, 191, 210, 221, 261, 278, 281
items   70, 72–73, 101, 111, 115, 122, 124–26, 137, 141, 146–48

Jeffries   11–13, 108
jobs   140, 157, 188–89, 217, 317
jokes   186, 259
Jorge   205, 207–8, 219, 223–24, 229–30, 242–43, 245, 254–55, 262, 266, 270, 273, 284, 291, 297, 300, 306, 311, 315–17, 319
José   205, 215, 217, 222, 233, 254–55, 257, 280, 287, 291, 297, 308
José Luis   205, 207, 209, 219, 222–25, 246–47, 249, 257, 259, 262–63, 265, 270–74, 294, 297–300, 302–4, 306–12, 316, 318
José Martí National Library   3, 58, 149
journal   4, 14, 31, 56, 229
journalism   37, 43, 50, 52, 54, 107, 170, 329
  war-time   6
journalists   46–47, 50–52, 62, 65, 68, 76, 78, 82–83, 86, 88–89, 104, 106, 108, 127–29, 131–32, 139, 141, 143, 168–69, 192, 263, 265, 267–68

INDEX

Juan   223–24, 228, 230, 233–34, 244–48, 250–53, 255, 257, 263, 265–67, 270, 274–75, 278, 290, 299–301, 303, 309, 312–13
justice, social   7, 26, 211–12, 326
Juventud Rebelde   56–57, 165, 342

Kapcia   5, 7, 18–19, 22, 27–28, 30–31, 188, 211–12, 219, 238, 314
KGB   136, 227
Khrushchev   225, 229, 244, 258–60, 294–95, 305
Kiev   223, 344
knowledge   5–6, 20, 65, 195–97, 217, 230, 253, 291, 331
Krenz   98, 100–101
Kvale   195, 200

languages   30, 55, 80, 116, 127–28, 139, 199, 202–3, 240–41, 243, 255, 320
Latin America   7–8, 22–23, 53, 139, 180, 183–84, 211–12, 224–25, 230, 234, 250, 278, 319, 335
Latin America and Cuba   180
Latin American   4, 16, 23–24, 29, 112, 161, 179–80, 183–84, 199, 212, 217, 224–25, 228, 234, 239, 241, 251, 275
Latin America Network Information Center   149
Latin countries   159
Latino news media   54
laws   13, 28, 46, 93, 111, 137, 213, 237, 285–86
leaders   5, 26, 29, 50–51, 69–70, 97, 100, 125–26, 144, 231, 244, 246, 253, 255–57, 260, 267–68, 288, 291, 295–300, 305–6, 321, 338, 341
  high-level   19, 265
  historical   27, 181
  new   79, 84, 116, 143, 148
  socialist   170
leadership   6, 9, 20, 22, 26, 28, 127, 134, 138, 163, 165, 213, 228, 235, 247, 254–56, 284, 293
legitimacy   25, 55, 84, 289
Lenin   136, 139, 205, 208–9, 222, 232, 239, 252–56, 258, 277, 279, 284, 290–91, 293, 298, 305–6, 308–9, 318
Leninism   4, 9, 18, 26, 83, 179, 300

Leninist   4, 8, 82, 220, 222, 254
Lenin's death   254–55
LeoGrande   27–29, 31, 187–88, 280
León   36
letters   62, 77, 191, 210, 251
Lévesque   224–26
liberation, national   322, 326
liberation movements   17, 223–24, 233
Ligachev   131–32
links   7, 69, 75, 90, 94, 158, 161, 206, 320, 322
list   25, 37, 58, 61, 195–97, 200, 216, 311–12, 330
literature   6–7, 29–30, 32–34, 38, 45, 61, 86, 166, 194–95, 214, 220, 224, 242, 249, 332
London   302
Loss   32, 243

M-26, see 26th of July Movement
magazines   18, 56, 166, 178, 227, 229, 232, 342
  Novedades de Moscú   17, 65
  official Communist Party   56
Main activity   338, 343–44
Maldonado   179, 220
Mambises   207–8, 211, 213
market economy   120, 124–27, 133–34, 136–37, 140, 149, 161, 163, 312
markets, black   188–89, 240, 261
Martí, José   4, 8, 26, 54, 87, 138, 156–57, 207–13, 241, 254, 300
Marquetti Nodarse   235
Marx, Karl   4, 40, 186, 208, 245, 254, 256
Marxist   4, 8–9, 25, 37, 47, 82, 211–12, 220, 222, 254, 301, 319
Marxist Platform   132–33
material goods   289, 293
materials   3–4, 43–44, 58–59, 62, 67, 69, 92, 121, 123, 138–39, 142, 149, 155, 157–58, 168, 170, 177, 320, 327
  relevant   58–59
Mavis   205, 219, 222, 225, 228, 245, 249, 260, 262–63, 269–70, 277, 284, 289, 310, 312, 314, 344
Mazowiecki   73–76
media   6, 19, 43–48, 50–53, 56, 62, 83, 117, 130, 153, 162, 239, 260, 263–64, 266–67, 276, 311, 335
  coverage   263–64, 267
  policies   46, 49
  systems   45, 53

medicine   310, 317
members   3–6, 11, 13, 18–20, 25–28, 39, 91–92, 97–98, 103, 109, 165–67, 175, 177, 184–91, 193, 196–97, 235, 237, 265–66, 285–86, 320, 325–26, 336, 338, 342–44
   family   100, 199, 319
   former   18, 132, 227–28
   interviewing   326
membership   24, 85, 188, 196
member states   180
memories   3, 33, 175–76, 214, 216, 264, 269
meringue (metaphor)   157, 277, 330
Mery   205, 231, 240–41, 245, 249, 254, 263, 265, 268–70, 289, 299, 303, 307, 311, 315
Mesa-Lago   3, 7, 14, 18, 21, 23, 31
metaphors   156, 277
method, capitalist   14–15, 148, 230, 246
migrants   91, 93–96, 106–7, 281–82
migration   48, 90–91, 93–94, 103, 107, 281–82, 315
migration crisis   90, 113, 168
Mikoyán   221
Miles   200–204
minister   28, 33, 36, 75, 100, 115, 123, 165, 181, 205, 229, 232, 243, 273
minority   95, 310, 318, 322–23, 331, 333
Miranda   60–65, 196
Missile Crisis   8, 222–23, 260, 280
mistakes   52, 68, 71, 91, 158, 161–62, 165, 222–23, 245, 255–56, 258, 294, 297–99, 305, 319
mobilization   14, 246, 283, 325, 333
   popular   283, 294
model   13, 15, 21, 35, 49, 51, 118–19, 133, 165, 177, 182, 212, 235–37, 246–49, 289–90, 321–22, 326, 328
   economic   11, 235, 249, 293, 298, 334
   one-party   87, 212, 236, 239
   state socialist   171, 301
   unified party   80
moderates   122–23, 141, 158
Modrow   98
money   94, 159, 189–90, 216, 240, 261, 286, 310
morals   138
morning   112, 142
Morris   19–20, 283

Moscow   7, 12, 17, 55–56, 124, 126, 131, 135, 137, 142–43, 146–47, 150, 153, 227, 234, 241, 250, 253, 259, 261–62
movement, left-wing   335
Müller   159–60
multiparty elections   87
multipartyism   2, 80, 82, 85–88, 137, 312, 335, 341
multiparty system   81, 85, 87, 286
municipality   237, 284, 313, 315, 338

narratives   253, 286, 320, 322, 334
National Assembly of Popular Power in Cuba   28, 57, 237, 313
National Committee   113
national debate   22, 288, 300, 312, 314, 330–31
nationalities   290, 304
National Union of Writers and Artists of Cuba (UNEAC)   284
Natvig   53
negative elements   287
negotiations   180–81
neighborhoods   15, 82, 189, 216, 238, 283, 309, 312–13
neighboring countries   20, 53, 92, 333
neo-Stalinism   236
news agencies   113, 143, 149
   official Soviet (TASS), see TASS
news article   78–79, 84, 96, 171
news box   100, 137
news coverage   79, 89, 107, 109, 125, 141, 153, 155, 169
news-interview   159
news items   69, 72–73, 79, 83, 86, 92, 95, 126, 135–37, 139
   short   84, 92, 103, 135
news materials   121–22
newspaper   3, 46–49, 52, 58–59, 61–67, 69–70, 72–74, 77–79, 82–87, 89–90, 92–98, 101–3, 109–14, 116–17, 121–30, 135, 138–39, 141–43, 145–46, 148–50, 156–58, 160, 169, 327, 329
   daily   44, 57
   government-controlled   106
   main   49, 156, 239
   major   56, 58, 171
newspaper texts   60, 62, 64

INDEX

news stories   58, 61, 64–65, 68–69, 79–80, 82, 86, 94–95, 97, 104, 107, 116, 127, 129, 131, 133, 135, 159, 163, 170
   main   127
   short   89, 95
New York Times   72, 109
nomination   75, 237
nomination processes   237, 313
Norma   205, 233, 245, 252, 258, 265, 269, 284, 289, 303, 307, 317
norms   175, 198
Nueva Paz   284–85

Obama   180–81, 191
object   37
observers   72, 300–301, 325
October Crisis   280, 344
Ofensiva Revolucionaria, see Revolutionary Offensive
official Cuban publications   43
official Soviet history   36
official Soviet positions   108
one-party system   22, 81–82, 87, 178, 190, 209–10, 312, 326
opinion   62, 76, 78, 88, 116, 223, 231, 234, 236, 289, 291, 296–97, 302, 306–7, 311, 315, 335, 338–40
opinion columns   65
opinion texts   65
OPP, see Popular Power, Organs of Popular Power (OPP)
opponents   120, 181, 285–86, 333
opportunism   160, 163, 286
opposition   25, 28–29, 67–72, 76, 79, 131–32, 135, 182, 189, 229, 285–86, 288, 339
   former Soviet   160
   legal   75, 93
   radical   76, 125, 127–30, 134
opposition groups   160, 181
opposition member   285
oral history   6, 29, 32–33, 176–77, 191–92, 195–96, 325–26
Oral History of Contemporary Cuba   33
Oral History Society   6, 32
oral history studies   6, 191
oral sources   3, 171, 175, 177, 326
   use of   33

organization   19, 25–26, 28, 39, 51, 132, 137, 184, 187, 189, 194, 235, 238, 277, 284–87, 325, 332, 334–35
   mass   24, 29, 70, 184, 236, 283, 313
organized opposition   285, 287
ORI, see Integrated Revolutionary Organization (ORI)
Orthodox Party   26, 213
Øyen   197

Padura   50, 257
Panama   23, 230
Paris Club   248
parliament   10, 28, 71–72, 80, 127, 181, 245
participants   19, 37, 94, 126, 160, 196–97, 202, 229, 287, 333
particularities   5–6, 49, 89, 165, 171, 238, 325–26
Partido Comunista de Cuba, see Communist Party of Cuba
Partido Revolucionario Cubano, see Cuban Revolutionary Party (PRC)
Partido Socialista Popular, see Popular Socialist Party
parties   3–4, 18, 25–28, 44, 73, 79–81, 83–85, 89, 97–98, 101, 185–87, 199, 209, 213, 225, 236, 244, 326
   single (sole)   24, 81, 208–9, 335
   sister   63–64
Party   4–6, 10–11, 14–15, 19–20, 24–29, 31, 81–83, 107, 114, 163, 170–71, 185–88, 190–91, 193–94, 197, 237–39, 244–45, 254–56, 259, 265–68, 271, 280–84, 288, 290, 293, 300–301, 311–15, 325, 328–29, 334–36, 340–41
   authority   262
   branch   82, 188, 190–91, 237, 251, 288
   brass   47
   cadres   166, 171
   Committee   252
   conference   271
   Congress   21, 29, 84, 274, 315
   culture   187
   Development   31
   directives   56
   elite   87, 100
   leaders   69, 313
   leadership   51, 268, 328

Party (cont.)
  meetings 244, 265
  member base 186
  members 7, 11, 28, 177, 185–89, 193, 196, 265, 276, 280, 282, 285, 287–88, 307–8, 315, 320, 322, 325, 328, 331–34, 339
  militants, see members
  New Hungarian 84–86, 133
  new Russian communist 133–34
  officials 306
  old pro-Soviet Communist, see Popular Socialist Party (PSP)
  organization 284, 304
  perceptions 57
  rules 185
Party's power monopoly 80
past attitudes 176
Patria, see homeland, Patria
Pavlov 31–32, 120, 251
PCC, see Communist Party of Cuba;, see Party
Pedro 205, 207, 219, 230, 236, 238, 246, 263, 265, 270–71, 274, 283, 285–86, 295–96, 305, 308, 319, 343
penalize 251
Perestroika 2, 9, 13, 16–17, 35–36, 55, 98, 120, 126, 153, 158, 166, 233, 247–52, 268, 296, 339
Perestroikans 19, 251–52
Pérez Jr. 9, 24, 30, 209, 212–13, 315
Pérez-Stable 13, 15–16, 19, 22, 25–26, 29–30, 197, 212, 219–20, 226, 283, 312, 316
period
  historical 170, 214
  neocolonial 211
perspectives 34, 79, 130, 161, 170, 175, 177, 183, 202, 206, 232, 260, 263, 266–67, 273, 322, 325
pesos 240
photos 74–75, 77, 98, 101, 103, 105, 115, 121, 329
Pino Santos 211
Platt Amendment 210–11
Playa Girón, see Bay of Pigs
Plaza de la Revolución, see Revolution Square
Poder Popular, see Popular Power
Poland 2, 6, 12, 39, 44–45, 67–73, 75–79, 83–84, 101, 107, 156, 168–70, 278, 285, 292, 303, 306, 332, 339
police 77, 102, 216, 222, 287–88

policies 14, 50, 52, 95, 134, 139–40, 165–66, 169–70, 177, 179, 182, 184, 224, 226–28, 230, 234, 236, 244, 246–47, 250–51, 253, 273–74, 314, 316, 318
  economic 125, 244, 305
  official 160, 242, 285
Polish cinema 78
Polish crisis 70, 73
Polish government 70, 72
Polish United Workers Party (PUWP) 67, 69
Political Bureau 91–92, 98, 103, 116, 132, 259, 266, 301, 305
political debate 90, 135
political elite 171, 186, 190, 196, 199, 214, 250, 266, 270, 273, 276, 291
political lacuna 315
political parties 10, 24, 82, 85, 213, 236, 325
political situation 68, 101, 192, 215, 293
political system 9–11, 14–15, 28, 30–31, 70, 187, 236–37, 256, 299, 336, 338
politics 14, 28, 30, 33, 37, 56, 65, 80, 83, 96, 105, 108, 148, 182, 189, 202, 206, 243
Popular Power 14–15, 28, 57, 209
  Organs of Popular Power (OPP) 28
Popular Socialist Party (PSP) 18, 25–27, 186, 224, 227–29
Portelli 175
post interview treatment 195
Post-Soviet 32
Post-Soviet World 23, 31
poverty 179, 214–15, 217, 302, 311
power 4–5, 7, 10–11, 23–25, 27–29, 36, 77, 80–81, 86–87, 134, 136, 142–43, 146, 149–50, 153, 155, 239, 253–55, 257–59, 290, 296–97, 299, 302, 304–5, 307, 309
Pravda 81, 128, 135–36, 339
PRC, see Cuban Revolutionary Party
Prensa Latina 71–73, 75–77, 83, 85, 92, 110–17, 122, 124, 131, 146–47, 150, 169
presentation 66, 132, 134–35
  visual 119, 135, 138, 145, 150
president 51, 67, 69, 72, 84, 115–16, 123–26, 140, 143, 147, 156, 184, 244, 253, 313
pressures 12, 22, 52, 88, 107, 143, 149–50, 154, 160, 165–66, 171, 223, 225, 233, 251, 259, 321, 330–31
  social 238, 282

prices   124, 129, 232, 240
   market   124–25, 232
Prieto   243
prime minister   68, 73, 75–77, 120, 129
private press   48
private sector   48, 182, 189
privatization   129–30, 132, 139
privileges   65, 139, 158, 175, 187–88, 216, 219, 326
problems   35, 51–52, 55–56, 68, 78–79, 93–96, 106–7, 160–61, 165–66, 170–71, 187–89, 219, 240, 250, 254–55, 259–61, 263–64, 267–69, 271, 273–74, 283–84, 289–98, 300–302, 314–15, 321–22, 330
   accumulation of   295, 297
   economic   270, 298, 333
   financial   124, 292
   main   189, 299
   material   24, 240, 289
   new   179, 289
   people's everyday   295
   ruling   69, 86, 98, 108–9, 116
   solving   275, 283
   systemic   298
   USSR model's   273
processes   2, 8–9, 11–12, 14, 16, 44, 49–50, 58–59, 65, 67, 80, 168, 179–80, 182, 202, 245–46, 248–50, 258–59, 268, 274, 285, 294, 297–98, 306, 320–22, 331, 338–39
   counterrevolutionary   229
   deterioration   259, 262
   historical   196
   industrialization   255, 272
   political   332, 334, 336
Process of Rectification of errors and negative tendencies, see Rectification
pro-Gorbachev ideas, see Perestroikans
project   3, 24, 33–34, 38, 45, 95, 127, 129–30, 132, 136, 155, 190–94, 196–99, 203, 271, 280, 333, 336
   revolutionary   156, 277, 281, 323
propaganda   43, 45, 51, 57, 96, 117, 161, 165–66, 292
   official Cuban   214
properties, private   80, 128, 131, 135, 163
pro-Soviet   231
   communist parties in Latin America   224
   elements   27

factions   227
ideas   228
party   18
strands   108
protectorate   8, 211
protesters   74–75, 97–98, 101, 103, 105–7, 111, 114, 123, 163, 222, 287
protest vote   316
PSP, see Popular Socialist Party
Putin   303–4
PUWP, see Polish United Workers Party

Quinquenio Gris   49
quota   196, 310

racism   136, 215
radical changes   21, 72, 91, 155, 215, 312
radical opposition's ideas   130
radicals   123, 127–29, 131, 140–41, 145–46, 148
radio   46, 54, 109, 114, 263
Rapid Response Brigades   287
Raúl Roa   229
Reagan   126, 294, 338
Real Socialism, see Socialism, real
recover   171, 278–79, 302, 307, 333, 339
Rectification   13–16, 19, 29, 51, 93, 148, 236, 244, 246–49, 259, 314, 339
Red Army   256–57
referendum   130, 238, 312
reform communism   18, 56
reformism   18, 87, 139–40, 168
reformist ideas   18, 50, 82–83, 86, 89, 329
reformists   81–83, 87–89, 133, 140, 153, 169, 213, 329
reform process   10, 12, 80–81, 136, 182, 250, 274
reform proposals   134, 169
reform socialism, see Socialism, reform
reforms   10, 12, 55–57, 80–81, 86–87, 90, 93, 99, 101, 118–20, 122, 124–27, 131, 133–34, 136–37, 162–63, 169–70, 248–50, 252, 287, 289, 327, 330
refugees   96
regime   5, 32, 34, 45, 56, 90, 107, 110, 116, 118–19, 178, 236, 245, 252, 280, 287, 292
regime change   4, 12, 22, 30, 63, 86, 89, 109, 117, 325

region   7, 23, 86, 142, 180, 210, 224–25, 235, 293, 305
relations   8–9, 17, 32, 34, 38–39, 47, 49, 52, 108, 116, 119, 143, 146–47, 180–81, 205–7, 218, 221–23, 226, 230–32, 239–41, 257, 273, 275, 303–4, 339–40
relationship   8–9, 12, 24, 33–34, 108, 137, 146, 177, 206, 209, 220, 227, 230–31, 250, 300, 320, 338–39, 342–44
  historical   207
remittances   179, 188, 281, 311
reports   64–65, 74–75, 85, 88, 91, 95, 100–103, 111, 113–15, 147, 295, 315
repression   23, 87, 110, 216–17, 291, 327
republics   10–11, 38–39, 116, 127, 129, 131, 137, 211, 290, 313
  former USSR   39
research interviews   195
research questions   200–201, 203
resignation   100, 123, 126, 137, 239
resistance   52, 133, 180, 206–7, 209, 283, 292–93, 305, 327, 340
restrictions   52, 85, 91, 99, 191, 212, 242, 260, 282, 332–33
reunification   94, 104
Revolution   5, 7–9, 13–16, 20–22, 25–27, 33, 36, 47–49, 138–40, 160–62, 184–88, 206–9, 211–17, 219, 222–23, 238–39, 241–43, 256–57, 277–80, 282–84, 286–88, 291, 315–16, 318, 322, 326–27, 332–33
  authentic   140, 218
revolutionaries   138, 185–86, 189–90, 233, 235, 238, 256, 267, 280–81, 287, 296, 303, 308, 318
revolutionary continuity   208, 213
revolutionary forces   227, 250, 303
revolutionary government   27, 217, 220
  moderate First   221
revolutionary movements   155, 162, 216
  international   141, 154–55, 161, 171
Revolutionary Offensive   182, 226–27, 246
revolutionary opposition   286
Revolutionary Party for Cuban independence, see Cuban Revolutionary Party (PRC)
revolutionary principles   163, 288
revolutionary process   25, 207, 246, 257, 315
  historical   209

Revolutionary Student Directorate (DRE)   213
Revolution Square   3, 252
Ricoeur   199
Robaina   159
Rodríguez   27, 229, 252
Rojas   55, 142, 145, 219–21
role   5–6, 17, 20, 31, 37, 44, 80–81, 138, 144, 179–80, 236–39, 254–55, 283–84, 292–93, 298–99, 320–21, 325, 336, 340–41
  leading   3, 25, 28, 80, 116, 177, 210, 233, 235, 244, 271, 283
Roman   30, 189, 237–38, 245
Romania   12, 25, 39, 60, 107–14, 116–19, 169–70, 285, 332
Romanian Communist Party   109, 111, 114
Romanian events   115
Romanian governments   110–11
Romania's problems   116
roots   7, 9, 206, 209–10, 214, 292, 296, 315
Round Table, Poland   83–84
Ruíz   37
ruling parties   5, 10, 24, 27, 68, 80–81, 89, 91, 97, 238
rupture   24, 211, 319
Russia   9, 36, 39–40, 128, 131–32, 136, 179, 181, 219, 241, 250, 279, 291, 302–4, 319, 339
Russian Federation (during Soviet times)   124, 126–27, 131
Russian influence   243
Russian revolution   36
Russians   32, 40, 53, 129, 136, 222, 225, 233, 241, 243, 258, 260–62, 290, 293, 303–4
Ryzhkov   120, 123–24, 126, 134–35

sabotage   22, 26, 48, 104, 135
Saldaña   200–204
Scandinavian countries   200
scenario   111, 134, 270, 275–76, 333, 340
Schabowski   98
Scintela   111
Second Republic   211
SED, see Socialist Unity Party of Germany
self-criticism   55, 96–97
sentiments   285
separation   28–29, 212, 237, 249
setbacks   7, 23, 71, 138, 161, 179, 218, 332

sex 33, 182–84
Shatalin 120, 130
Shatalin Plan 60, 120, 122, 127, 129–30, 134, 136
shortage 44, 130, 228, 309
siege mentality 22, 50
Silayev 129–30
Sino-Soviet crisis 225
slaves 32, 137–38
slogans 69, 101, 141
social crisis 121, 135
socialism 4–5, 8, 17–18, 34–36, 39–40, 67–68, 80–83, 118–19, 137–40, 159, 161–62, 166, 186, 208, 210, 221–22, 227–30, 250, 278, 288–89, 300–302, 306–7, 326–27, 329–30, 340–41
    construction of 34, 138, 161, 171, 186, 221, 228, 305, 319
    crisis of 39, 68, 120, 280, 283
    democratic 81, 84, 190
    enemies of 163, 165
    failure of 118, 316
    real 13, 15, 36, 84, 165, 243
    reform 17, 56, 118, 141, 329
    revolutionary 24
    word 40, 120
socialist 8–9, 34–35, 40, 68, 74, 80, 83, 85, 111, 161, 186, 210, 236, 301
Socialist Bloc 39, 59–60, 68–69, 89, 91, 93, 110, 130, 140, 158, 160, 163, 203, 228, 266, 270, 336, 339–40
Socialist Camp 39, 73, 222, 229, 248, 252, 262, 269–71, 285, 289, 291, 293, 295–97, 303, 307, 333
socialist community 1, 38, 60, 64, 67, 75, 119, 138, 230, 235, 332
socialist consciousness 14–15
socialist countries 32, 39–40, 45, 64–65, 75, 82, 91–92, 104, 107, 118, 121, 130, 135, 139, 188, 192, 230, 234, 238, 249, 342–43
    former 140, 162, 171, 342
    industrialized 240
    prosperous 155
    reform-oriented 109
socialist democracy 111, 237, 296
socialist economy 22, 40, 312
socialist ideas 282, 303
    heretical 229

socialist legality 35, 144, 154, 171
socialist news agencies 117
Socialist Party of Hungary 85
Socialist Revolution 185
socialist system 76, 300
Socialist Unity Party of Germany 91–92, 97–98, 100–101, 103
socialist values 230, 247
Social Pact 316
social problems 63, 75, 85–86, 90, 92, 137, 141, 179, 217
    new 79, 133, 302
society 4, 6–7, 40, 44, 51–52, 80–84, 155, 158, 160, 165, 175–77, 239–40, 253–54, 259, 261–62, 289, 291, 294, 319, 321, 325–26, 328
    capitalist 53, 236
    model of 107, 334
    organized 283
    revolutionary 14
    socialist 93, 255, 260, 328
solidarity 63, 75, 77, 111–12, 179, 232, 262, 309, 317
Solidarity (Polish trade union) 70–72, 73–75, 77
Solzhenitsyn 136
South Korea 104
Soviet Union (USSR) 8–9, 11–12, 17–18, 24–26, 33–35, 37, 39–40, 49–50, 53, 64–65, 67–68, 110–11, 120–23, 125–29, 131–33, 135–38, 140–42, 145–48, 154–56, 218–22, 228–29, 231–33, 235–36, 238–40, 243–44, 249, 251–53, 256–58, 268–71, 292–94, 302–7, 327–28, 342–44
    aid 9, 218, 225, 239, 318
    allies 133
    anti-socialists 128
    arms 219
    authors 56
    Bloc 12, 50, 105
    communism 239
    communist leaders 142
    Communist Party 134, 236, 290
    communist theory 45
    coup 149, 153
    crisis 225, 233
    culture 55
    dispute 225

Soviet Union (USSR) (cont.)
  dominance   13
  economy   120, 272
  elite   37
  Embassy (in Havana)   251, 311
  experiences   186, 235
  Foreign Ministry   73, 76
  government   17, 123, 133, 137, 148
    brief   244
    de facto   145
    new   146, 148
  government resign   129
  hegemony   233
  history   253, 258–59
  ideology   9, 230, 332
  influence   16, 32, 49, 67, 206, 209, 212, 239, 241–43, 257, 321, 331
    increased   49
    strong   236
  invasion   23, 235, 261
  invasion of Czechoslovakia   92, 108, 228, 261
  leaders   148, 162, 253–54, 293–94
  leadership   36, 141, 143, 148
  legislators   128
  legislature, new   115
  magazines   252
  Marxism   9, 242
  media   262
  military forces   108
  model   2, 9, 49, 227, 229, 236, 247–49, 270, 301, 307
  news agency TASS, see TASS
  one-party model   208
  Party   131, 136, 225, 295, 326
  people   128, 135, 222, 254, 260
  Perestroika   244
  policies   17, 230, 244, 250, 305
  pro-capitalist opposition   141
  publications   18, 50, 135, 268, 332, 339
  referential field in Cuban culture   55
  reforms   10, 17, 19, 56, 138, 252, 326
  relations   9, 16, 29, 31–32, 34, 60, 146, 148, 154, 218, 226, 228, 230, 244, 252, 257, 272–74, 319
  relationship   7, 231
  repression   159
  republics   124, 222, 241
  former   2, 159
  socialism   37, 161, 165, 295, 301–2, 333–34
  Socialist Republics   1, 38, 40
  society   37, 158, 171, 271, 289–90
  specialists   129
  television   114
  theater and formation of Soviet actors   242
  thought   242
  totalitarian project   76
  trade   146, 169, 240
  troops   73, 146
  tutelage   11
  universities   160
Sovietization   8, 53, 266
Soviets (worker's councils)   256, 290
Spanish-language Soviet publications   57
Sparks   45, 53
Special Period   3, 6, 21, 32, 38, 43, 177–79, 274, 280, 283, 302, 308, 311–12, 315–16, 318, 320, 326, 332, 340
speeches   14, 17, 43, 51–52, 65, 88, 92, 111–12, 122, 126, 138–39, 157–59, 161–63, 179, 185, 271, 274, 277, 279
Stalin   55, 166, 171, 236, 242, 253, 255–56, 258, 291, 293, 295–96, 298–99, 321
Stalinism   35, 55, 140, 171, 236, 253–57, 290, 295–96, 305, 331
state   4–5, 28–29, 35–36, 39–40, 72, 90, 93–94, 120–21, 147, 149, 181, 183, 188–90, 229–30, 274, 289–90, 300, 303–4, 310, 313, 339, 341
  revolutionary   48
state leaders   150, 236
state media   46, 48
statement   5, 97, 109, 111, 121, 143–44, 146–50, 154, 156, 169, 179, 272, 300, 315, 340
state socialism   107, 166, 331
state socialist countries   39, 81, 119
state terror   72–73, 79, 170
statues   136, 188, 258
steel   163
stories   58, 61, 69–73, 77, 80–82, 85–86, 89, 96, 98, 101, 104, 109, 111, 113, 115–17, 119, 122–23, 125–26, 128, 136–37, 150, 213–16, 257–58, 261
strategic selection   196
structural problems   37, 158, 161, 166

INDEX

students   52–53, 112, 114, 134, 192, 215, 221, 249, 264, 336
subliminal message   112, 119, 156
subsidies   46, 169, 179, 232
supplies   15, 52, 121, 179, 226, 228, 283, 310, 314
   oil   228
support   70, 73, 76, 98, 101, 104–5, 107–8, 125–27, 129, 139–40, 154, 188, 191–92, 220, 223–25, 228, 240, 243, 250, 256–57, 284, 286–88
   economic   118, 328
   material   189, 225, 303
Supreme Soviet   120, 124, 126
surprise   6, 147, 193, 263, 269–71, 277, 319
sweet, see Meringue (metaphor) Switzerland, 310
symbol   16, 104–5, 163, 180
sympathies   27, 76, 88, 92, 126, 139, 158, 162, 250
system   13, 15, 40, 67, 69, 79, 139, 159, 161, 163, 165–66, 184, 186, 208, 237–38, 249, 277, 280, 282–86, 288–91, 293, 297–300, 306–8, 322, 330–33, 340–41
Szulc   219

tactics   94, 204, 234
TASS (official Soviet news agency)   73, 75, 115–16, 122, 134, 143–47, 153–54
teacher   14, 163, 186, 193, 251
technicians   241, 303
Telegraph Agency of the Soviet Union, see TASS
television   10, 43, 46, 109, 114, 263, 335
television channels   54
Temas Magazine   36
tensions   8, 10, 18, 20, 23, 25, 44, 52, 106–8, 221–22, 225, 230, 239, 252, 274–75, 285, 321, 327
   internal   134, 145, 225, 252
terrorism   33, 162
testimonies   6, 33, 175–93, 199, 214, 216–17, 264–65, 276, 311, 315, 327, 333
texts   31, 35, 48, 52, 59–62, 64–65, 67, 69, 71, 77, 110, 114, 131, 135, 137, 143, 148, 157, 159–60, 199–203
   informational   61
Thatcher   294, 338
theater   242–43

Third Congress of the PCC   13, 15, 314
Thompson   6, 32, 175–76
time schedule   125, 134
Timisoara   110–11, 115–17
   city of   109–10
tone, subjective   127–28
trade   2, 22, 24, 49, 134, 155, 239–40, 248, 273, 339
traditions   107, 206, 209, 242, 251, 266, 329
   Cuban intellectual   208
   strong Cuban political   327
transformation   9, 17, 155, 199–200, 283
transition   2, 12–13, 18, 29, 40, 75, 82, 86, 90, 108, 124–27, 133–34, 178, 188, 297, 306, 329, 335
   variants of   124
transition processes   297, 302
translation   241
travelers   193, 262
Trotsky   36, 255–57, 293

UJC, see Young Communist League (UJC)
UNEAC, see National Union of Writers and Artists of Cuba (UNEAC)
United States   7–8, 22, 73, 75, 77, 86, 88–89, 125–26, 147, 149, 152, 155–56, 158, 179–83, 191–92, 206–8, 210–11, 213–14, 217, 219–24, 234, 241, 244, 274, 278–82, 285–86, 293–94, 297, 303–4, 306, 318–21
unity   87, 112, 212, 276, 283, 326, 339
University of Bergen   191–92, 336
University of Havana   37, 178, 215, 227, 230
uprising   117–18, 138
US invasions   23, 181, 225, 239

vanguard, organized   4
vanguard party   81, 208, 267, 326, 341
Venezuela   179–80, 184, 216, 225, 275–76, 317, 335
Víctor   184, 205–207, 209, 222–24, 232, 235, 238–39, 241–42, 245, 254, 256–58, 262, 270–71, 279–81, 287, 295, 297, 299, 305, 307, 309–10, 315, 317–19
Villa Barroso   37
violating Cuban airspace   181
violence   108–11, 114–16, 119, 286–87, 332–33

vision   35, 55, 98, 167, 240, 245, 253–54, 261, 268, 273, 320, 341
voices, critical   160, 190
voters   237, 313
votes   88, 105, 109, 232, 238, 312–13

Walesa   70, 156
Walker   10–11, 272
war   8, 23–24, 72, 87, 138, 140, 181, 207, 210, 212, 255, 258, 293, 297, 316, 329, 333
Ward   210, 239, 278
Warsaw Pact   11, 39, 73, 206
weaknesses   16, 139, 158, 166, 228, 230, 292, 333
  internal   68, 165–66, 171, 295, 330
weapons   158, 222, 235, 286
West Berlin   90, 94, 97, 100–104
Western countries   53
Western media   98, 105, 110, 117
West Germany   77, 92, 94–96, 98, 102–3, 105, 107
whores   262, 316

winning   23–24, 71, 307
women   33, 136, 187, 197, 215, 269, 279, 295, 311
workers   28, 48, 64, 85–86, 114–15, 124, 140, 159, 196, 203, 226, 256, 265, 284, 290
  exemplary   185, 187
  humanitarian aid   318
work fulltime   192
workplaces   82, 85, 187, 198, 238, 251, 265, 284, 311
world power   234, 255
World Revolution   316

Yanayev   143, 146–47, 150
Yeltsin   126–27, 129, 131, 146, 296, 303, 306
Young Communist League (UJC)   18–19, 56, 156, 159, 196, 336, 338
youth   18, 97, 183, 249, 256, 258, 262, 311
Yugoslavia   12, 39, 110–11, 114

Zenaida   205, 215, 240, 245, 253, 260, 269, 277–78, 280, 284, 289, 307–9, 315, 319